Grand Canyon

NATIONAL PARK

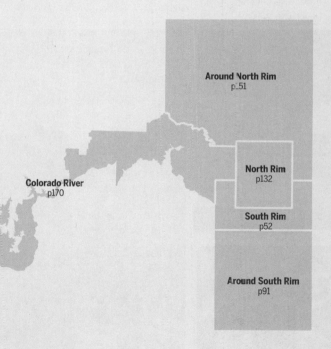

Around North Rim
p 51

Colorado River
p170

North Rim
p132

South Rim
p52

Around South Rim
p91

THIS EDITION WRITTEN AND RESEARCHED BY

Jennifer Rasin Denniston, Bridget Gleeson

PLAN YOUR TRIP

ON THE ROAD

NORTH CANYON P177

SQUIRREL P214

Contents

UNDERSTAND

SURVIVAL GUIDE

SPECIAL FEATURES

SOUTH RIM P52

Welcome to the Grand Canyon

The Grand Canyon embodies the scale and splendor of the iconic American West, captured in its dramatic vistas, dusty inner canyon trails, and stories of exploration, preservation and exploitation.

Sublime Vistas

We've all seen images of the canyon in print and on-screen, but there is nothing like arriving at the edge and taking it all in – the immensity, the depth, the light. Descend into the canyon depths, amble along the rim or simply relax at an outcrop – you'll find your own favorite Grand Canyon vista. Though views from both rims are equally stunning, the South boasts many more official and dramatic overlooks. One of the most beautiful in its simplicity, however, is the view that whispers from the Grand Canyon Lodge's patio on the canyon's quieter north side.

Hiking an Inverted Mountain

You don't have to be a hardcore hiking enthusiast to taste the park's inner-canyon splendor. Even a short dip below the rim gives a stunning appreciation for its magnificent scale and awesome silence; descend deeper and get a closer look at a mind-boggling record of geologic time. The park's raw desert climate and challenging terrain demand a slower, quieter, more reasoned pace, and that's just perfect. Because it's exactly that pace that is best for experiencing the Grand Canyon in all its multi-sensory glory.

Geology

One look at the reds, rusts and oranges of the canyon walls and the park's spires and buttes, and you can't help but wonder about the hows of whys of the canyon's formation. Luckily for laypeople with rock-related questions, the South Rim has answers, primarily at the Yavapai Geology Museum and the Trail of Time installation, and both rims offer geology talks and walks given by the park's knowledgeable rangers. For a more DIY experience, hike into the canyon with a careful eye for fossilized marine creatures, animal tracks and ferns.

Native American & Pioneer History

We all know about the canyon's distinct and unparalleled beauty, its awesome geologic canvas and its draw for outdoor types. Less recognized, perhaps, is the Grand Canyon's compelling human history, the drama that lies in its stories. Native Americans lived in and near the canyon for centuries, farming on its rim and in its depths. The region's national park history is also one of intrepid pioneer scientists and artists, prospectors, railroads and tourist entrepreneurs. Ranger talks are a great way to learn the park's stories, as are historic buildings and South Rim museums.

Why I Love the Grand Canyon

By Jennifer Rasin Denniston, Writer

I came to the Grand Canyon for the first time with my toddler and newborn in tow. Frazzled and exhausted, and always the skeptical traveler, I was prepared to be underwhelmed. But seconds after walking onto the veranda of the North Rim lodge, I understood. My canyon isn't about the view alone, which I knew from postcards and books, photographs and oil paintings. Its power lies in the grounding silence and dusty quiet, the smells of ponderosa and desert, the clarity that comes from feeling so very small. We return year after year.

For more about our writers, see p256.

For more about our writers, see p256.

Above: The Milky Way over the Grand Canyon

Grand Canyon National Park

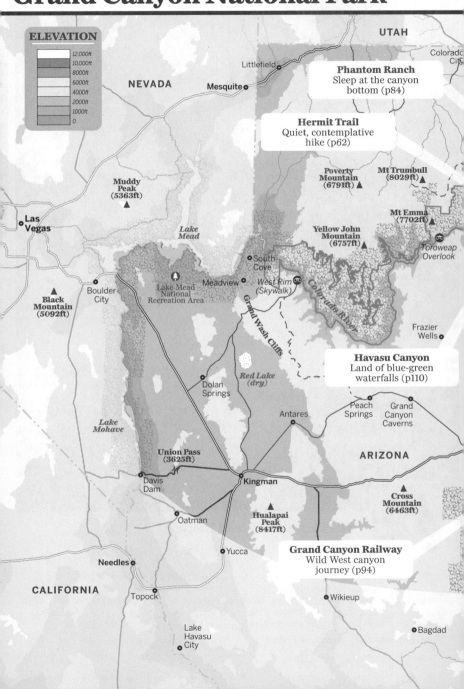

ELEVATION

12,000ft
10,000ft
8000ft
6000ft
4000ft
2000ft
1000ft
0

UTAH

Colorado City

Littlefield

NEVADA

Mesquite

Phantom Ranch
Sleep at the canyon bottom (p84)

Hermit Trail
Quiet, contemplative hike (p62)

Poverty Mountain (6791ft) ▲

Mt Trumbull (8029ft) ▲

Muddy Peak (5363ft) ▲

Mt Emma (7702ft) ▲

Las Vegas

Lake Mead

Yellow John Mountain (6757ft) ▲

Toroweap Overlook

South Cove

West Rim (Skywalk)

Colorado River

Black Mountain (5092ft) ▲

Boulder City

Lake Mead National Recreation Area

Meadview

Grand Wash Cliffs

Frazier Wells

Havasu Canyon
Land of blue-green waterfalls (p110)

Red Lake (dry)

Dolan Springs

Lake Mohave

Antares

Peach Springs

Grand Canyon Caverns

ARIZONA

Union Pass (3625ft)

Davis Dam

Kingman

Cross Mountain (6463ft) ▲

Oatman

Hualapai Peak (8417ft) ▲

Grand Canyon Railway
Wild West canyon journey (p94)

Yucca

Needles

CALIFORNIA

Topock

Wikieup

Bagdad

Lake Havasu City

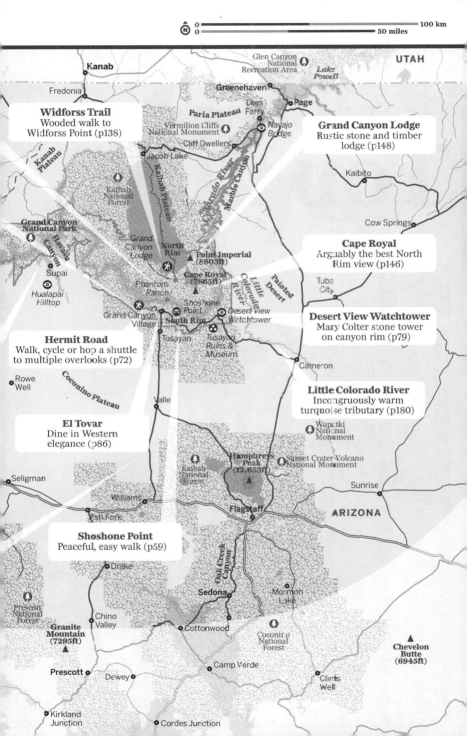

0 ·········· **100 km**
0 ━━━━━━ **50 miles**
Ⓝ

UTAH

Kanab

Fredonia

Glen Canyon
National ⓘ
Recreation Area

*Lake
Powell*

Greenehaven

Lees
Ferry

Page

Widforss Trail
Wooded walk to
Widforss Point (p138)

Paria Plateau

Vermilion Cliffs ⓘ
National Monument

Cliff Dwellers

Navajo
Bridge

Grand Canyon Lodge
Rustic stone and timber
lodge (p148)

Kaibito

Jacob Lake

Cow Springs

Kaibab
National
Forest

Kanab
Plateau

Kaibab Plateau

Colorado River

Marble Canyon

**Grand Canyon
National Park**

Havasu
Canyon

Supai

*Hualapai
Hilltop*

*Grand
Canyon
Lodge*

**North
Rim**

**Point Imperial
(8803ft)**

**Cape Royal
(7865ft)**

Little Colorado River

Painted
Desert

Tuba
City

Cape Royal
Arguably the best North
Rim view (p146)

*Phantom
Ranch*

*Shoshone
Point*

Desert View
Watchtower

Desert View Watchtower
Mary Colter stone tower
on canyon rim (p79)

Grand Canyon
Village

South Rim

Tusayan

Tusayan
Ruins &
Museum

Hermit Road
Walk, cycle or hop a shuttle
to multiple overlooks (p72)

Rowe
Well

Coconino Plateau

Valle

Cameron

Little Colorado River
Incongruously warm
turquoise tributary (p180)

Seligman

El Tovar
Dine in Western
elegance (p86)

Kaibab
National
Forest

Wupatki
National ⓘ
Monument

**Humphreys
Peak
(12,633ft)**

Sunset Crater Volcano
National Monument

Sunrise

Williams

Flagstaff

ARIZONA

Ash Fork

Shoshone Point
Peaceful, easy walk (p59)

Drake

Oak Creek Canyon

Prescott
National
Forest

Chino
Valley

Sedona

Mormon
Lake

**Granite
Mountain
(7295ft)**

Cottonwood

Coconino
National
Forest

▲
**Chevelon
Butte
(6945ft)**

Prescott

Dewey

Camp Verde

Clints
Well

Kirkland
Junction

Cordes Junction

Grand Canyon's
Top 20

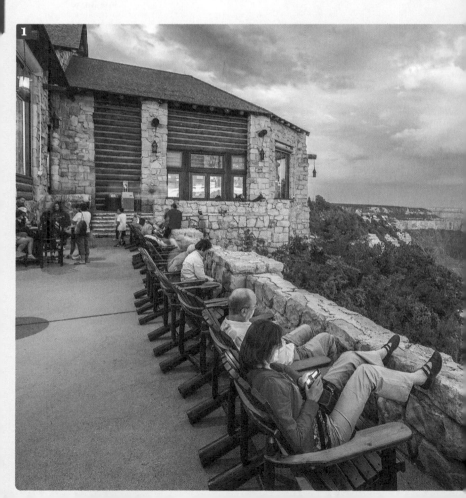

Grand Canyon Lodge

1 Perched on the canyon rim, this grand-daddy of national-park lodges (p148) promises a high-country retreat like nothing else in the Grand Canyon. Completed in 1928, the original structure burned to the ground in 1932. It was rebuilt in 1937, and in the early days staff greeted guests with a welcome song and sang farewell as they left. Today, you'll find that same sense of intimate camaraderie, and it's easy to while away the days at a North Rim pace.

South Rim Overlooks

2 The canyon doesn't have a photo-graphic bad side, but it has to be said that the views from the South Rim (p52) are stunners. Each has its individual beauty, with some unique angle that sets it apart from the rest – a dizzyingly sheer drop, a view of river rapids or a felicitous arrangement of jagged temples and buttes. Sunrises and sunsets are particularly sublime, with the changing light creating depth and painting the features in unbelievably rich hues of vermilion and purple.

CULTURA TRAVEL/WHIT RICHARDSON / GETTY IMAGES ©

TERUSHI SHO / GETTY IMAGES ©

CAROL POLICH PHOTO WORKSHOPS / GETTY IMAGES ©

Hiking Rim to Rim

3 There's no better way to fully appreciate the grand of Grand Canyon than hiking through it, rim to rim (p64). The classic corridor route descends the North Rim on the North Kaibab trail, includes a night at Phantom Ranch or Bright Angel Campground at the bottom of the canyon, crosses the Colorado River and ascends to the South Rim on Bright Angel trail. A popular alternative is to descend from the South Rim on the South Kaibab trail and ascend via the North Kaibab trail.

Above left: Hikers on the Kaibab Trail

Rafting the Colorado River

4 Considered the trip of a lifetime by many river enthusiasts, rafting the Colorado (p170) is a wild ride down a storied river, through burly rapids, past a stratified record of geologic time and up secretive side canyons. Though riding the river is the initial attraction, the profound appeals of the trip reveal themselves each day and night in the quiet stretches on smooth water, the musicality of ripples and birdsong, and the vast solitude of this awesome place.

Phantom Ranch

5 After descending to the canyon bottom, it's a delight to ramble along a flat trail, past a mule corral and a few scattered cabins to Phantom Ranch (p84), where you can relax with a cold lemonade, your feet up and your pack off. This lovely stone lodge, which was designed by Mary Colter and built in 1922, continues to be the only developed facility in the inner-canyon. Mule trips from the South Rim include one or two nights here, and hikers can reserve accommodations up to 13 months in advance.

Flagstaff

6 Flagstaff is (give or take) one part granola, one part wild game, one part craft brew, one part espresso, one part mountain man, one part medicine woman. But unscientific formulas aside, the sum of Flagstaff is fun stuff. It's a university town with a Route 66 flavor, where railway history, astronomy and culinary charms contribute as much to the town's zeitgeist as its haunted hotels and its New Year's pinecone drop. Come for the canyon and stay for Flag (p99).

Widforss Trail

7 This gentle North Rim hike (p138) rises and dips along the plateau, veering towards a side canyon and meandering 5 miles to Widforss Point. It's a mild, gentle amble, with canyon views whispering rather than screaming from the edges, plenty of shade, and room for children to run among wildflowers. A picnic table at the end makes a lovely lunch spot, and at the overlook you can sit on a stone jutting over the Grand Canyon dangling your feet above the rocky outcrop just below, listening to the silence.

Desert View Watchtower

8 At the eastern edge of the South Rim, Desert View Watchtower (p79) could almost pass as a Native American ruin, but it's an amalgamation of Mary Colter's imagination and myriad Native American elements. This circular tower encases a spiral stairway that winds five stories to the top floor, with walls featuring a Hopi mural and graphic symbols from various Native American tribes. From its many windows on all sides, you can see mile upon magnificent mile of rim, river and sky.

Cape Royal Point

9 A pleasant paved drive through woods with teasing canyon views leads to the trailhead for this most spectacular of North Rim overlooks (p141). It's an easy 0.5-mile walk to Cape Royal Point along a paved trail with signs pointing out facts about the flora and fauna of the area. The walk is suitable for folks of all ages and capabilities. Once at the point, the expansive view includes the Colorado River below, Flagstaff's San Francisco Peaks in the distance and stunning canyon landmarks in both directions.

Hermit Trail

10 The name seems apropos, even today, as you are unlikely to encounter many hikers and backpackers on the Hermit Trail (p62). Though easily accessible from South Rim shuttles and tourist hub, it feels marvelously remote. Day hikers connect with the Dripping Springs Trail to reach a little oasis where water seeps down from a small overhang festooned with maidenhair ferns. Take a moment to imagine the quiet life of Louis 'The Hermit' Boucher, the prospector who made this spot his home for many years.

Best Friends Animal Sanctuary

11 Angel Canyon, where dozens of old Westerns were shot, is now home to the US' biggest no-kill animal shelter (p155). Nestled in over 30,000 acres of spectacular red-rock landscape sit seven idyllic sanctuaries for lost, sick and abandoned animals rescued from natural and human disasters around the world. At any given time, about 1700 animals call this canyon home. Free tours are given daily, volunteers are always welcome and there are a handful of *casitas* (cabins) for overnight stays.

North Kaibab National Forest

12 Spreading miles across the Kaibab Plateau and towering over vast desert expanses of the Arizona Strip, the North Kaibab National Forest (p152) hugs Grand Canyon to the north and offers the traveler gentle respite from searing summer heat. Lush meadows are home to deer and buffalo, hiking trails wind through the aspen and ponderosa forests, and remote canyon overlooks lure adventurous travelers. You can camp anywhere for free, but after the first major snowfall the 44-mile road through the Kaibab to the North Rim closes.

RAINER GROSSKOPF / GETTY IMAGES ©

Mule Rides

13 There's something classically Grand Canyon about riding a mule into the canyon, a time-honored tradition that began with turn-of-the-century pioneering tourists. While less strenuous than hiking the canyon, mule rides (p38) are a physically active experience that require a sense of adventure. If you want to ride to the Colorado River, head to the South Rim for an overnight trip to Phantom Ranch. From the North Rim, you can descend into the canyon on a half-day ride down the North Kaibab, and both rims offer jaunts above the rim.

Shoshone Point

14 For a leisurely walk away from the South Rim circus, hiking through the ponderosa to Shoshone Point (p59) does the trick. The soundtrack to this mostly flat 1-mile walk is that of pine needles crunching underfoot and birdsong trilling overhead, and lacy shadows provide cover from the sun. Upon reaching the rim, you'll trace the edge for a short while to the stone point jutting out over the canyon depths. Shoshone Point, or the picnic area at the end of the trail, is perfect for a peaceful lunch.

Grand Canyon Railway

15 Things start out with a bang at the Wild West shootout in Williams, and then the 'sheriff' boards the train to make sure everything's in its place. Is it hokey? Maybe a little. Fun? Absolutely. Riding the historic rails (p238) to the South Rim takes a bit longer than if you were to drive, but you leave traffic and disembark relaxed and ready to explore the canyon.

Havasu Canyon

16 The people of the blue-green waters, as the Havasupai call themselves, take their name from the otherworldly turquoise-colored waterfalls and creek that run through the canyon (p110). Due to limestone deposits on the creekbed, the water appears sky-blue, a gorgeous contrast to the deep red of the canyon walls. The only ways into and out of Havasu Canyon are by foot, horse or helicopter, but those that make the 10-mile trek are richly rewarded by the magic of this place, epitomized by spectacular Havasu Falls.

16

Grandview Trail

17 Developed by prospector Pete Berry, whose crumbling stone cabin still sits on Horseshoe Mesa miles below the rim, this rugged and steep trail (p63) is a South Rim favorite of experienced hikers. The path descends quickly, with switchbacks of cobblestone. After crossing a couple of narrow saddles to Horseshoe Mesa, you'll find open mine shafts speaking silently of the canyon's past. Pace yourself on the hike out, allowing time to take in the grand views. Top: Horseshoe Mesa

Dinner at El Tovar

18 No one goes to the Grand Canyon for an epicurean adventure, but the finest dining on the South Rim is more than fine. Part of the dinner experience is sitting in this historic lodge (p86), absorbing a little of its bygone glamour and rustic architectural elegance. Relaxing over venison and a glass of wine in these environs feels especially decadent after a dusty afternoon walking miles from overlook to overlook along the canyon rim or days hiking the canyon interior.

Splashing in Oak Creek

19 Winding through Sedona's spectacular red-rock landscape and riparian Oak Creek Canyon, the cold and clear waters of gentle Oak Creek (p110) make a marvelous antidote to summer heat. Sedona offers several places to access its shallow tumbles, broad sandstone rocks and deep swimming holes, and it's an idyllic creek for little ones and adults alike. Favorite access points include East Fork Trail, Grasshopper Point, Midgley Bridge and Red Rock Crossing.

Lookout Studio

20 Perched on the South Rim, Lookout Studio (p78) has stone walls that harmonize so well with their environment that a squint could turn it into a rocky outcropping. Another of Mary Colter's masterful designs, this little structure was originally used by the railroads as a photo studio but is now a tiny gift shop. Browse the wares and have a peek through telescopes from the balcony, or wander down to the terraces below and admire the billion-dollar view.

Need to Know

For more information, see Survival Guide (p223)

Entrance Fees
$30 per car, $25 per motorcycle, $15 per person entering on foot, bicycle, train, shuttle or raft; valid at both rims for seven days

Number of Visitors
4.8 million (2014)

Year Founded
1908 as a national monument; in 1919 it became the country's 17th national park

Money
South Rim: ATMs at Market Plaza, Maswik Lodge and Desert View Market. North Rim: General Store and Roughrider Saloon. Credit/debit cards accepted everywhere

Cell Phones
Cell-phone coverage available on both rims, though spotty in some areas; unavailable elsewhere in the park.

Driving
Some South Rim roads closed to private vehicles. Fuel available at North Rim Campground and South Rim's Desert View.

When to Go

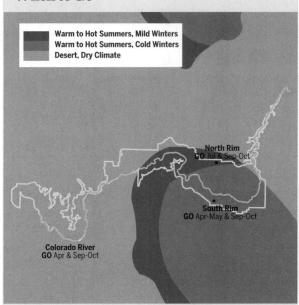

Warm to Hot Summers, Mild Winters
Warm to Hot Summers, Cold Winters
Desert, Dry Climate

North Rim
GO Jul & Sep-Oct

South Rim
GO Apr-May & Sep-Oct

Colorado River
GO Apr & Sep-Oct

High Season
(May–Oct)

➡ The peak of summer is the hottest and busiest season.

➡ Accommodations bookings in gateway towns increase significantly and sell out further in advance.

Shoulder
(Mar–Apr & Sep-Oct)

➡ Smaller crowds mean a more relaxed experience.

➡ Spring and fall bring cooler temperatures and wild colors.

➡ Note: the North Rim opens mid-May and closes mid-October.

Low Season
(Nov–Feb)

➡ The stream of South Rim visitors slows to a trickle.

➡ Fresh snowfalls promise dramatic, snow-frosted buttes and temples.

➡ The North Rim closes October 15 but is open for day-use or camping until the first snow closes Hwy 67.

Important Numbers

For long-distance and toll-free calls, dial 1 followed by three-digit area code and seven-digit local number.

Grand Canyon National Park	☎928-638-7888
Grand Canyon Lodge (North Rim)	☎928-638-2611
Grand Canyon South Rim Switchboard	☎928-638-2631
Xanterra (South Rim)	☎888-297-2757
Emergency Search and Rescue	☎928-638-2477

Exchange Rates

Australia	A$1	$0.76
Canada	C$1	$0.80
China	Y10	$1.61
Euro zone	€1	$1.09
Japan	¥100	$0.80
Mexico	MXN10	$0.64
New Zealand	NZ$1	$0.71
UK	£1	$1.52

For current exchange rates see www.xe.com.

Opening Dates

South Rim

Open year-round, 24 hours a day.

North Rim

All lodging, facilities and visitor services are closed between mid-October and mid-May.

The 44-mile road from Jacob Lake to rim is not plowed; visitors may enter park on foot, skis, snowmobile or snowshoes.

Backcountry permits must be obtained for winter camping.

Daily Costs

Budget: $40–$100

➡ Camping inside and outside the park: free to $25

➡ Self-caterers can get groceries and cheap eats in the park, but gateway cities have better selection and prices

➡ Tusayan to Grand Canyon Village Shuttle (May through October): free

➡ Guided ranger walks: free

Midrange: $100–$250

➡ Double room in a chain hotel or B&B: $100–$250

➡ Lunch and dinner in local restaurants: $15–$25

➡ South Rim bicycle rental: $40

➡ Car rental: $35

Top End: More than $250

➡ Double room in B&Bs and three-star hotels: $250–$350

➡ Sample the best of local culinary hot spots: $50–$200

➡ Mule ride from South Rim to/from Colorado River with meals and night at Phantom Ranch: $532

Useful Websites

National Park Service (www.nps.gov/grca) Weather alerts, events, planning.

Lonely Planet (www.lonelyplanet.com) Destination information, hotel bookings, traveler forums and more.

Xanterra (www.grandcanyonlodges.com) South Rim and Phantom Ranch accommodations and mule trips; activity links.

Grand Canyon Association (www.grandcanyon.org) Best online bookstore for the park; includes other useful links.

Grand Canyon Lodge (www.grandcanyonlodgenorth) North Rim accommodations.

Park Policies & Regulations

➡ Bicycles are allowed on paved trails and the South Rim's Greenway Trail.

➡ Open fires are prohibited except at established campgrounds on the rim.

➡ Leashed dogs are permitted in the South Rim's developed areas above-the-rim trails and pet-friendly rooms at Yavapai Lodge; the North Rim's Bridle and Arizona Trails; and at developed campgrounds on both rims.

➡ Weapons of any kind are prohibited on park grounds.

➡ It's illegal to feed wildlife.

Getting There & Around

If you're headed to the South Rim, the easiest way to arrive is to fly to Phoenix (228 miles). For the North Rim, fly into Las Vegas (265 miles). From these points, travelers can rent cars or make connections by bus or shuttle. Greyhound buses stop in Flagstaff, and regular shuttle services serve the South Rim from Sedona, Williams, Flagstaff and the airports in Phoenix and Las Vegas. A daily shuttle (with two daily departures mid-May to mid-October) runs from rim to rim (four to five hours). Apart from this shuttle, the only way to reach the North Rim is by car.

Flights, cars and tours can be booked online at lonelyplanet.com/bookings.

For much more on **getting around**, see p235

If You Like...

Hiking

South Rim Multiple trails offer the park's best selection of inner-canyon day hikes and overnight expeditions. (p56)

North Rim Those in the know come to this side of the canyon for peaceful high-country ambles among the pines and the North Kaibab descent. (p136)

Sedona A mecca for day-hikers, with spectacular red rock surrounds and alluring Oak Creek. (p113)

Flagstaff Excellent variety of easily accessible trails and multiple outdoor shops with experienced advice. (p101)

Dramatic Views

You can't go wrong anywhere, but early-morning and late-afternoon light add depth, color, dimension and drama.

Grand Canyon Lodge Settle into a rimside Adirondack chair for a sunset glass of wine. (p148)

Moran Point Named for the painter whose depiction helped secure national-park status. (p81)

Mohave Point Sublime South Rim viewpoint for sunrise or sunset – listen for Hermit Rapid. (p80)

Bright Angel Point Walk along a North Rim fin to a point surrounded by vast views. (p137)

Cape Royal Point Easy paved trail to one of the North Rim's best views. (p146)

Toroweap Long and rough road leads to sheer cliff that's hours from tourist hubs. (p143)

Native American Culture

Both the largest Native American reservation and the most remote (the Navajo and Havasupai, respectively) exist within and around the Grand Canyon, and the region is rich in Puebloan history.

Hopi Reservation One of the oldest continuously occupied villages on the continent sits on the Hopi Reservation. (p166)

Museum of Northern Arizona Craftsman-style Flagstaff museum with excellent exhibits on Native American art. (p99)

Walnut Canyon Moderate trails to Native American cliff dwellings inhabited from AD 1100 to 1250. (p109)

Wupatki National Monument Remains of one of the region's largest Puebloan cultures and home to the Wupatki less than 850 years ago. (p109)

Tusayan Ruins Explore Native American Grand Canyon history at the small ruins and museum on the South Rim. (p79)

Scenic Drives

The ever-changing landscape goes from bizarre red-rock formations to ponderosa forest to high desert flatlands – and the grandest canyon.

North Kaibab National Forest Driving through alpine meadows, ponderosa forest and aspen groves to the North Rim. (p152)

Desert View Drive Arriving through the South Rim's east entrance introduces the canyon gradually and elegantly. (p70)

Hermit Rd An 8-mile drive on the South Rim with multiple breathtaking canyon views. (p72)

Oak Creek Canyon Wind through riparian landscape from Flagstaff to Sedona. (p111)

Route 66 Back roads evoke nostalgia in spades and buckets of kitsch. (p96)

Kingman, AZ, to West Rim Expansive desert landscape populated with 900-year-old Joshua Tree forest and endless vistas. (p170)

STEPHEN SAKS / GETTY IMAGES ©

POE VALERA / GETTY IMAGES ©

Top: Seligman, Route 66 (p96)
Bottom: Wupatki National Monument (p109)

On the Water

Especially precious in the dry climate of the Southwest, the waterways of the Grand Canyon region offer some amazing experiences – rafting the Colorado River being the most obvious, but not the only one.

Rafting the Colorado The trip of a lifetime can occasionally happen last-minute if someone cancels their spot. (p174)

Smooth Water Floats Through Glen Canyon Motorized or rowing trips on the smooth water of the Colorado, from Glen Canyon Dam to Lees Ferry. (p161)

Oak Creek Cool, clear creek tumbles through red-rock landscape and wooded canyon around Sedona; several parks and trails offer access. (p111)

Kayak Lake Powell Explore the peaceful hidden side canyons of Lake Powell using your own paddle power. (p162)

Havasu Canyon Famous inner-canyon blue-green waterfalls and swimming holes on Havasupai Reservation. (p110)

Black Canyon A 30-mile smooth-water Colorado River float on a designated National Water Trail close to Las Vegas. (p120)

Lake Mead Massive lake formed by Hoover Dam, popular for water sports, fishing, houseboating and swimming. (p120)

Art

Kolb Studio Small museum dedicated to pioneering Grand Canyon photographic expeditions of the adventurous Kolb brothers. (p77)

Flagstaff First Friday ArtWalk Lively First Fridays throughout the year in Flagstaff's historic downtown. (p107)

Grand Canyon Music Festival
Live music of varying genres
livens up the cultural scene at
the South Rim. (p25)

**Grand Canyon Celebration of
Art** Includes a *plein-air* painting
festival with a timed 'quick draw'
event. (p25)

**Sedona International Film
Festival** Celebrate the moving
picture in picture-perfect red-
rock country. (p115)

Architecture

'National Park Rustic' style
was born when Mary Col-
ter, hired by the railroad,
designed South Rim build-
ings to blend harmoniously
with the indigenous land-
scape, incorporating local
materials and elements of
Native American design.

Hermits Rest Cozy stone resthouse with its gigantic fireplace
is something of a tribute to its
hermit namesake. (p69)

Lookout Studio Sits on the
edge of the South Rim with a
terraced path below. (p78)

Hopi House Inspired by and
modeled after Hopi Puebloan
dwellings. (p75)

Desert View Watchtower Circular tower at South Rim's East
Entrance affords views from all
sides. (p79)

Phantom Ranch Down at the
bottom of the canyon, this stone
lodge and canteen is still the
center of inner-canyon civilization. (p84)

Grand Canyon Lodge Stone
and timber masterpiece perches
on North Rim, with plate-glass
windows for canyon-viewing
perfection. (p148)

El Tovar South Rim exception to
Colter, this elegant timber lodge
offered some of park's earliest
accommodations. (p85)

Top: Desert View Watchtower (p79)
Bottom: Cycling in Sedona (p113)

Cycling

Sorry, mountain bikers: bombing down Grand Canyon trails is strictly verboten.

Rainbow Rim Trail This 18-mile single track outside North Rim weaves through forest with side-canyon viewpoints along the way. (p152)

Sedona Slickrock and single track amid red-rock monuments, fins and spires. (p113)

Greenway Trail Multiuse paved trail is a fantastic, easy and relaxing way to enjoy South Rim overlooks. (p69)

Flagstaff There's great high-elevation mountain biking in Flagstaff; check out woodsy Mt Elden for a start. (p101)

Bootleg Canyon Single-track course in bone-dry surrounds, particularly popular for its black-diamond descents. (p120)

Hermit Road Some of the South Rim's most memorable overlooks dot this 8-mile road. (p69)

Arizona Trail Long stretches of this north–south trail, which spans the length of the state, allow mountain bikes. (p33)

Wildlife

South Kaibab Trailhead It's not unusual to see elk loping along the rim here, helping themselves to gulps from the water-bottle filling station. (p61)

Condor Viewing Site About 75 California condors reside in Vermilion Cliffs north of North Rim. (p166)

Bearizona Not exactly wildlife, but a chance to see native North American animals in a quasi free-range setting. (p94)

Best Friends Animal Sanctuary An animal rescue that focuses on cats and dogs but also nurtures birds, bunnies and other critters. (p155)

North Kaibab National Forest Deer and buffalo frequent the meadows between Jacob Lake and the North Rim. (p152)

Food

Though the park itself is not known for its food, the Grand Canyon is surrounded by go-to hot spots for creative dining with a commitment to organic and local produce.

Sedona Of the city's many foodie delights, Elote Cafe shines as a regional jewel for fresh and tasty Mexican. (p118)

Rocking V Cafe An oasis of low-key fine dining in tiny Kanab. (p158)

Flagstaff Offers a plethora of excellent coffee shops, markets, cafes and upscale eateries in historic downtown. (p104)

Indian Gardens Oak Creek Market Bo-ho gathering spot for outdoor types flocking to Oak Creek Canyon. (p118)

DW Bistro Airy cafe far from Vegas strip with excellent New Mexican–Jamaican fusion fare. (p127)

Las Vegas Buffet extravaganzas, elaborate high-end splurges and celebrity chefs. (p126)

Historic Hotels & Intimate Inns

Grand Canyon Lodge Historic North Rim lodge with magnificent public spaces and cabin accommodations. (p148)

El Tovar Grande Dame of national park lodges. (p85)

Bright Angel Lodge Stick to rim-side cabins if you're looking for historic charm. (p84)

El Portal Friendly, gracious and handsome, dog-friendly Sedona favorite. (p117)

Briar Patch Inn Acres of grass and shade in low-key compound on Oak Creek. (p116)

L'Auberge de Sedona Lovely upscale boutique resort oozes romance and relaxation. (p116)

Little America Hotel A highway classic from the early 1970s. (p104)

Hotel Monte Vista Quirky downtown Flagstaff landmark with iconic neon sign and eclectic rooms. (p104)

Lodge on Route 66 Beautifully restored Route 66 adobe-style drive-up motel in Williams. (p97)

Parry Lodge Founded in 1931, this roadside motel in Kanab hosted some of Hollywood's biggest stars. (p158)

Month by Month

February

According to some, this is the best time of year to visit – an empty South Rim (North Rim is still closed for winter), with snow often frosting the canyon.

✯ Flagstaff Winterfest

Held throughout February, this Flagstaff winter festival features alpine and Nordic skiing, sled-dog races, concerts, food, skiing, a parade through historic downtown, art exhibits, theater, lectures, live music – oh, and skiing.

✯ Sedona International Film Festival

Founded in 1994, this festival is hosted by silver-screen veteran Sedona, whose red-rock backdrop has starred in numerous films. Takes place from late February to early March.

June

Summer is in full swing, with temperatures rising and crowds descending on the South Rim.

✯ Star Party

Annual Star Parties illuminate the week following summer solstice. Organized by local astronomy clubs, the North Rim Star Party is hosted on the Grand Canyon Lodge veranda; on the South Rim, find the party at Grand Canyon Visitor Center.

✯ Hullabaloo

Billed as a 'celebration of all things Flagstaff,' this quirky, family-friendly festival includes a street fair with local vendors, regional microbrew booths, music, a crazy-costume contest and circus performers. Held early June.

July

One of the best months to visit the North Rim. Be cautious hiking slot canyons during this time and through August, as monsoons can bring flash floods. Searing inner-canyon temps and lightning storms demand extra caution when hiking below and along the rim.

✯ Fourth of July

Show up at the North Rim for the Fourth and enjoy some old-fashioned fun: water fights, a fire-engine parade and barbecue. Fire danger precludes fireworks, but you may get to see Mother Nature's version instead.

✯ Flagstaff Fourth

Marking both the Fourth of July and the founding of Flagstaff, festivities include a parade, concerts, rodeo and fireworks.

✯ Hopi Festival of Arts & Culture

At Flagstaff's Museum of Northern Arizona, this well-established celebration of Hopi art, dance and food has been running since the 1930s. Arts and cultural demonstrations include storytelling and basket weaving.

August

Summer temperatures are still at their peak, as are South Rim crowds, both of which are bearable if you have a game plan. Or head to the North Rim for less of both.

Navajo Festival of Arts & Culture

Another Native American festival at the Museum of Northern Arizona in Flagstaff, this early-August event features weaving demonstrations, dancing and a juried art show.

Native American Heritage Days

During the first week of August, this North Rim festival celebrates several local Native American tribes with cultural and historical ties to the Grand Canyon; events showcase their music, art and food.

Western Legends Roundup

Tiny Kanab hosts all things cowboy and silver-screen Westerns, with cowboy poetry and wagon trains. Reserve spots in advance to dine with stars and starlets who filmed in the red-rock movie heydays when Kanab was best known as Little Hollywood (www.western legendsroundup.com).

September

Autumn arrives, bringing a respite from oppressive heat and the crush of crowds. September softens the harshness of the desert, and it marks the beginning of the shift into brilliant fall colors in the park.

Grand Canyon Music Festival

Chamber music, Native American flutes and other tunes enhance the aural dimensions of the South Rim in late August and early September; for more see www.grandcanyon musicfest.org.

Grand Canyon Celebration of Art

Plein-air painters (who paint outside, on location) paint at the South Rim as they engage with visitors. Though the events organized by the Grand Canyon Association happen in September, the art exhibition extends through January.

Flagstaff Festival of Science

Showcasing and celebrating science research in and around Flagstaff, this 10-day festival features free hands-on activities. Options include guided hikes, star parties and archaeological field trips, with opportunities for children to join scientists in labs, observatories and in the field.

Fall Colors

From now through mid-October, brilliant yellows, reds and oranges transform the landscape, and it's a perfect time for hiking, cycling and scenic drives Best spots for autumn splendor are the North Rim, Flagstaff and Sedona's Oak Creek Canyon.

October

Though North Rim services close mid-month, the earlier half of October is a fantastic time to visit. The days remain warm and sunny, but in the higher elevations nights drop to fleece and mitten weather; by the end of the month it's not unusual to see snow.

Celebraciónes de la Gente

Held at the same time of year as Día de los Muertos (Day of the Dead) at the Museum of Northern Arizona in Flagstaff, this late-October festival celebrates the town's Latino and Hispanic heritage.

Sedona Plein Air Festival

Open-air painters from all over the world are invited to visit Sedona's spectacular natural setting in late October to paint and show off their works (www.se donapleinairfestival.com). There are also wine and food events.

Sedona Arts Festival

This arts fest (www.sedona artsfestival.org), held in the high school in early October, showcases fine arts and crafts, cuisine and entertainment.

December

The region's elevation makes it a winter wonderland. The South Rim and surrounds feel festive but relaxed.

Festival of Lights

Thousands of luminaria light up Tlaquepaque in Sedona in mid-December, accompanied by hot cider, a visit from Santa and other holiday festivities. Live music includes carolers and wandering mariachis.

Polar Express

In Williams, the Grand Canyon Railway (www. thetrain.com) makes its magical trips to the 'North Pole.' Kids sip hot cocoa, nibble cookies and meet Santa. Reserve very early; Polar Express trains begin running in November and into January.

Itineraries

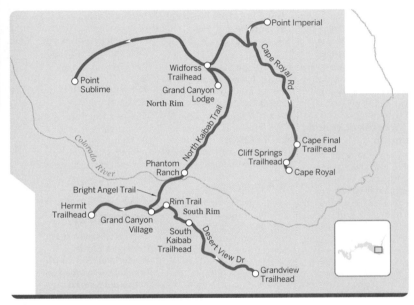

 Rim to Rim

Grand Canyon National Park, in essence, includes three distinct tourist regions, each with its own personality and perspective. This rim-to-rim expedition covers all three of them, offering travelers the breadth of the park's sights and activities. Begin with a few nights in a Western Cabin at **Grand Canyon Lodge**, on the bucolic and intimate **North Rim**. Drive to **Point Sublime**, **Point Imperial** and **Cape Royal**, hike the **Widforss Trail**, **Cape Final Trail** and **Cliff Springs Trail**, attend a ranger talk and stargaze on evening strolls. Relax with a glass of wine on the lodge's rim-side veranda, and eat dinner in its spectacular rim-side restaurant. Hike 14 miles down the **North Kaibab Trail**, spend a couple of nights by the river at **Phantom Ranch**, and start at dawn for the 10-mile haul up the **Bright Angel Trail** to the **South Rim**. Reward yourself with a hearty dinner at El Tovar, and spend four or five nights in **Grand Canyon Village**. Walk the **Rim Trail**, stopping at historic buildings, overlooks and museums along the way. Take an above-the-rim mule ride, and hike the **Hermit Trail**, **South Kaibab Trail** and **Grandview Trail** before catching a shuttle back to the North Rim.

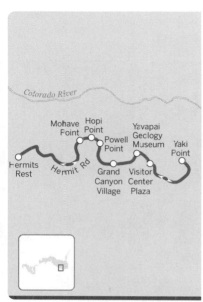

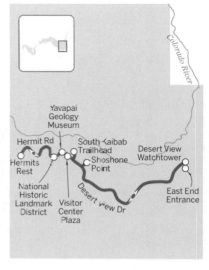

½ DAY South Rim in an Afternoon

Start with views and historic buildings in **Grand Canyon Village**. Admire the classic park architecture of El Tovar over lunch in the dining room, check out Native American art at Hopi House and stroll west along the Rim Trail. Stop at the History Room in Bright Angel Lodge, Lookout Studio and Kolb Studio before descending far enough down the Bright Angel Trail to look at the rock art in the first tunnel and to marvel at the canyon's scale from below the rim. Catch a shuttle to **Powell Point**, walk the rim to **Hopi Point** and **Mohave Point**, hop a shuttle to **Hermits Rest** and sit quietly in the picnic area with a snack before heading back to the village. Stroll east along the rim, pausing at the installations along the Trail of Time and the **Yavapai Geology Museum** on your way to Visitor Center Plaza. Grab a sandwich to go at Bright Angel Bicycle, hop on a shuttle to **Yaki Point**, wander away from the parking lot and find a spot from which to enjoy the evening light or sunset.

1 DAY South Rim in a Day

In one full day, you can take in the highlights of the South Rim, including hikes, museums, overlooks and a ranger talk. Arrive at park before breakfast – park at **Visitor Center Plaza**, grab a breakfast burrito at Bright Angel Bicycles and catch a shuttle to the **South Kaibab trailhead** for the 7am ranger-led hike into the canyon down the South Kaibab Trail. Remember to bring plenty of water. Shuttle to **Yavapai Geology Museum**, and walk west along the Rim Trail through the Trail of Time, stopping at sights and museums in Grand Canyon Village's **National Historic Landmark District**. Relax over lunch at El Tovar, fill up your water bottles, and take an afternoon stroll to overlooks along Hermit Rd, hopping on the shuttle whenever you get tired. At **Hermits Rest**, pause for a moment to sit in the silence at the Hermit Trail before taking a shuttle back to the village to connect with an express shuttle to your car. Drive **Desert View Dr** east to exit the park at the **East End Entrance**, stopping to stretch your legs at **Shoshone Point**, scenic overlooks and **Desert View Watchtower**.

Top: Mohave Point
(p80)

Bottom: Mather Point
(p81)

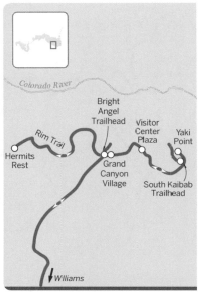

3 DAYS · South Rim in Three Days

Catch the Wild West shoot-out and board the Grand Canyon Railway train in Williams. Upon arrival at **Grand Canyon Village**, stretch your legs and check into a cozy Bright Angel cabin or a room at El Tovar, both just steps from the canyon edge. Meander along the rim through the village, stopping at historic buildings, museums and Trail of Time exhibits along the way. Hike overlook-to-overlook along the **Rim Trail**, picnic at **Hermits Rest**, descend into the canyon just a bit on the Hermit Trail and return to the village on a shuttle. Wake up early to head down **Bright Angel Trail** to One-and-a-Half or Three-Mile Resthouses. Sip a cocktail as you wait for a table at the Arizona Room, or bring a flashlight and attend an evening ranger talk at Shrine of the Ages. Take the ranger-led hike to Cedar Ridge on the **South Kaibab Trail**. Peruse the bookstore at **Visitor Center Plaza**, rent a bike and ride the Greenway Trail to **Yaki Point**. Make a point of enjoying dinner at El Tovar before catching your train back to Williams.

1 WEEK · South Rim in One Week

Take it slow on **Desert View Dr**, and bring a picnic for the amble to peaceful **Shoshone Point**. Learn about the canyon's human history at **Tusayan Ruins & Museum**, and climb the spiral staircase for spectacular views at **Desert View Watchtower**. Check out Mary Colter architecture, historic spots and museums in **Grand Canyon Village**. Attend a few ranger walks and evening talks, have a pizza dinner and see the Grand Canyon film at the **IMAX Theater** in Tusayan. Reserve a mule trip to the canyon bottom for a night at **Phantom Ranch**, or hike it down the South Kaibab to Phantom Ranch and up Bright Angel, with the second night camping at **Indian Garden**. Take a day hike on the Grandview Trail, walk the Rim Trail to **Hermits Rest** and get away from it all on the Hermit Trail. Rent a bike and cycle the Greenway Trail to **Yaki Point**, and enjoy a glass of wine on the patio at El Tovar and dinner at the El Tovar Dining Room.

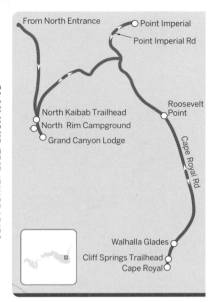

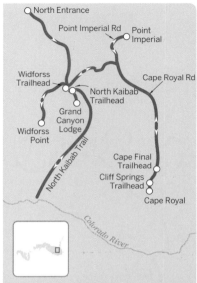

North Rim in a Day

1 DAY

For a day at the North Rim, you'll want to spend two nights at **Grand Canyon Lodge** or the **North Rim Campground**. Wake up with the sun and hike (or ride a mule) into the canyon on the **North Kaibab Trail**. Pause at Coconino Overlook and relax at Redwall Bridge, 2.6 miles below the rim, before tackling the haul back out of the canyon in time for lunch. Take your tray from Deli in the Pines to the lodge's sun porch and kick back in the Adirondack chairs, soaking in the view. Once you've refueled from the inner-canyon trek, head out to Cape Royal Rd. Pull over for a rim-side stroll at **Roosevelt Point** and a scramble to **Cliff Springs Trail**, check out ancient Puebloan ruins at **Walhalla Glades** and, at the road's end, walk out to Angel's Window and **Cape Royal**. On the drive back, detour a few miles to **Point Imperial** before returning to the lodge. Grab a beer from the Rough Rider Saloon, amble out to Bright Angel Point and watch the sun set over the canyon. After dinner at the lodge, take in an evening ranger talk and collapse into bed.

North Rim in Four Days

4 DAYS

Grand Canyon's North Rim transports even the most wearied spirits from harried lives of emails and deadlines into a slower time. Here, it's easy to find a quiet place to be alone with the canyon, and with four days you can settle into a groove that returns folks to the real world feeling just a little bit less weary and a little more inspired. Plan ahead for a Western Cabin at **Grand Canyon Lodge**. Enjoy one day taking in sights along Cape Royal Rd to **Cape Royal** and driving to **Point Imperial**; another hiking through meadow and woods along **Widforss Trail** to **Widforss Point**; a third day hiking or riding a mule down the **North Kaibab Trail**; and a fourth hiking **Cliff Springs** and **Cape Final** trails. Spend an evening walking the Transept Trail, perhaps catching the sunset over the side canyon, have a dinner or two in the lodge and take in a barbecue and cowboy singing at the Grand Canyon Cookout. Pepper in ranger talks on stargazing and condors, cocktails at the Rough Rider Saloon, long stretches reading on the lodge's rim-side sun porch and picnic lunches among the aspen, and you'll have experienced some of the best the Grand Canyon has to offer.

Hiking on the South Rim (p52)

Plan Your Trip
Activities

Stroll leisurely past overlooks on the South Rim, ride a mule into the canyon for a night at an historic lodge, hike from rim to rim, or simply relax under starry skies for a ranger talk. Whatever your inclination, Grand Canyon offers a breadth of activities for all ages.

Hike Classifications

The park service classifies canyon terrain into the following specific zones:

Corridor Zone

Grand Canyon's corridor trails refer to the South Rim's South Kaibab and Bright Angel Trails, and the North Rim's North Kaibab Trail. Heavily trafficked and well marked, sometimes with water available, these are the only inner-canyon trails that are regularly maintained and patrolled by National Park Service (NPS) personnel. Bright Angel's Indian Garden Campground, North Kaibab's Cottonwood Campground and Bright Angel Campground on the canyon bottom are the only three maintained NPS campgrounds below the canyon rim; all three require backcountry permits and are available by reservation only.

Threshold Zone

More rugged, less-traveled trails, with little or no water.

Primitive Zone

Little-used, unmaintained paths. For experienced canyon hikers who are comfortable with route-finding.

Wild Zone

Self-explanatory – don't expect to find trails in these zones.

Hiking and Camping

Hiking, both above and below the rim, is the most popular and accessible activity within the park; the beauty of it being that it's open to everyone, year-round. Hikes range from wheelchair-accessible paved trails to primitive, unmaintained treks that will challenge backcountry experts. Above-the-rim trails on the North Rim amble through meadows and Aspen forests to canyon peeks. On the South Rim, the Rim Trail hugs the canyon rim for much of its 13 miles, passing through tourist hubs of museums, restaurants and hotels, and multiple postcard-perfect canyon overlooks. From both rims, the descent into the canyon involves precipitous declines of switchback after switchback, rocky terrain and sharp drops from the trail edge.

Most hikes – both day excursions and backcountry overnight forays – follow established and well-marked trails. The majority lie within the corridor and threshold zones, though a section or two of the overnight treks may pass through a primitive zone.

Unique Environment

Hiking the Grand Canyon is markedly different from hiking elsewhere. The sheer terrain is uniquely challenging, made even more so by the environment and climate. Many inner-canyon trails begin with sharp descents, which translate into equally steep ascents at the end of a hike, when you're most exhausted. Add the effects of altitude, hefty elevation changes and the desert environment, and you've got a set of circumstances that demands careful preparation. Hike smart – take proper precautions, honestly assess and respect your limitations, and select hikes that best match your ability.

Promising snow-dusted buttes and crisp blue days, winter hiking is spectacular, though only the South Rim remains open. Trails are often icy in the early morning – to safeguard against glissading into the canyon, outfit yourself with a pair of crampons, available throughout the South Rim. You can still hike into the canyon from the North Rim after the first major snowfall, but you'll have to purchase a backcountry permit and then ski or snowshoe 44 miles to the rim first.

Difficulty Level

From first timers to veteran hikers, everyone will find suitable trails within the park. Most trails are also out-and-backs that cover the same stretch in both directions, making it easy to tailor a hike to your abilities. Rangers cite average hiking speed as 2mph going down and 1mph climbing up, an important consideration when selecting a trail and distance. On your first hike or two, observe how long each mile takes (both out and back).

Hikes can be organized into four difficulty levels. Remember that a single trail can have several difficulty ratings, depending on which segment you plan to hike.

Easy Less than 2 miles over fairly even, possibly paved terrain, with no significant elevation gain or loss.

Moderate Some elevation change (500ft to 1000ft) and longer or more exposed than those rated 'easy.' Generally fine for all ability levels.

Difficult Significant elevation change and longer mileage. Requires more hiking experience.

Very Difficult Tough hikes, involving the greatest exposure and mileage, as well as substantial elevation change (2500ft to 4000ft). Suitable for the fittest, most experienced hikers only.

Day Hikes

Generally speaking, the only truly easy hikes in the Grand Canyon are a handful of those above or close to the rims, including fairly flat trails like the Rim Trail on the South Rim. Another option is to hike short segments of more challenging trails. Anyone venturing below the rim should know that it's a place of extremes. Even on short hikes, preparation is key: whether you're hiking half a mile on the Rim Trail or six on the Bright Angel, always carry plenty of water.

Perennial favorites include the well-maintained corridor trails – Bright Angel, South Kaibab and North Kaibab. Though they may feel like superhighways in summer, plan on hiking at least one of these magnificent trails, if only for a short distance.

One lovely, rewarding, less trafficked interior canyon day hike on the South Rim is the Hermit to Dripping Springs Trail, and almost any trail on the North Rim will yield solitude. Unless you are hiking a corridor trail during the busy season when the trails are well traveled, or the well-populated Rim Trail, do not hike alone in the park.

Overnight Hikes

Provided you plan an appropriate route and itinerary that is within the capabilities of every member of your group, and you take your time, anyone with basic camping and hiking skills can experience the wonders of the inner gorge.

Before setting out on any overnight hikes check trail conditions, the weather forecast and water availability at the Back-country Information Center on the North or South Rim, or call park headquarters at ☑928-638-7888.

Backcountry Permit

Overnight backpacking at Grand Canyon National Park requires a backcountry permit for camping from the **Backcountry Information Center** (☑928-638-7875; www.nps.gov/grca/planyourvisit/backcountry-permit.htm; Grand Canyon National Park, PO Box 129, Grand Canyon, AZ 86023; ◷8-5pm daily, seasonal variation). The sole exceptions are hikers or mule riders with reservations at Phantom Ranch, the park's only non-camping accommodations below the rim.

Control of camper numbers is very tight, and demand for permits often far exceeds available slots. Due to overcrowding and environmental concerns, rangers limit the number of people per night at each of the park's backcountry campgrounds. If you're caught camping in the backcountry without a permit, expect a hefty fine and possible court appearance.

➡ Go to www.nps.gov/grca/ for the downloadable backcountry permit, and detailed instructions; allow three weeks for the permit to be mailed to you.

➡ Permits cost $10, plus an additional $8 per person per night; the nonrefundable fee is payable by check or credit card.

➡ Once a permit is granted, itinerary changes are not allowed, except for emergencies.

THE ARIZONA TRAIL

Established in 1988 and stretching the length of Arizona from Mexico to Utah, the Arizona Trail covers 800 continuous miles over Arizona's diverse landscapes, even passing through Grand Canyon National Park on its way. Many sections of the AZ Trail make excellent day hikes. On the North Rim, a particularly lovely section of the trail runs through Kaibab National Forest, roughly paralleling Hwy 67 north into the park, where, about 10 miles in, it then connects with the North Kaibab Trail.

Find more information, maps and current news on the trail at www.aztrail.org.

Camping at Havasupai Reservation (p110)

➡ Increase your chances of securing a permit by listing three alternative dates and routes in your application.

➡ Applications are accepted in person or by mail or fax beginning the first day of the month, four months prior to the planned trip; for instance, if you'd like to hike the Bright Angel in June, you can apply as early as February 1.

➡ If you're denied a permit or want to secure one last-minute, show up *in person* at the Backcountry Information Center on either rim. Add your name to the waiting list for a permit for the following day. Waits can take from a day to a week (with longer waits on the South Rim), and you must show up in person by 8am every morning to maintain your position on the waiting list.

Rim to River

The **Kaibab** and **Bright Angel** are the only two maintained trails in the park that lead from the rim to the Colorado River. The South Kaibab and Bright Angel descend from the South Rim, and the North Kaibab descends from the North Rim; regardless of how you get down, once there, all corridor trails essentially lead to Bright Angel Campground and the air-conditioned Phantom Ranch (p84), 0.3 miles apart on the north side of the canyon just up from the Colorado River.

Combine legs of these hikes to create multi-night inner-canyon backpacking itineraries, or head down by foot (or, from the South Rim only, by mule) in one day, spend a night or two at the ranch or campground, and hike back out from river to rim in one day. From March through September, you'll want to hit the trail back up by 6am to avoid hiking in dangerous heat.

> ### EMERGENCY CONTACT
> Before departing on an overnight hike into the canyon, be sure to leave your hiking itinerary, backcountry permit number, rim destination and date of your return with a contact person who will not be hiking. It's also important to take note of the **GCNP Search & Rescue number** (☎928-638-2477) as an emergency resource if you do not return as planned.

South Kaibab Trailhead to Phantom Ranch 7.2 miles; no campground en-route

Bright Angel Trailhead to Phantom Ranch 9.6 miles; Indian Garden Campground lies 4.6 miles below the rim

North Kaibab Trailhead to Phantom Ranch 13.6 miles; Cottonwood Campground lies 6.8 miles below the rim

Canyon newbies are often tempted to hike from the rim to the river and back in a single day, an outing that involves close to 9000ft of elevation change. But no matter how early you start, how many previous miles you've logged or how many energy bars you eat, it's just a bad idea, and it makes no difference if you're a fit 25-year-old or a 65-year-old trail veteran.

You'll need to plan in advance for a rim-to-river trek. Secure a backcountry permit to camp at Bright Angel, Indian Garden or Cottonwood Campgrounds (up to four months in advance) and/or a reservation for overnight accommodations at Phantom Ranch (up to 13 months in advance). If you want to hike rim-to-rim (down from one rim and back up to the opposite rim), arrange for shuttle transport back to your starting point (p64).

Responsible Backcountry Use

To help preserve the ecology and beauty of Grand Canyon National Park, strive to make as minimal a footprint as possible when enjoying the backcountry. For more information on low-impact backpacking, learn and live the seven principles of the Leave No Trace ethic at www.lnt.org.

Trash

➡ Pack out all waste, including food scraps and biodegradable items like orange peels.

➡ Don't bury trash; not only will it take years to decompose, but it's detrimental to the health of the animals that will likely dig it up.

Human Waste

➡ Where there are no toilets, bury solid human waste in a cathole (about 6in deep and at least 200ft from trails, campsites or water sources). Cover the waste with soil and a rock. In snow, dig down to the soil.

➡ To further minimize your impact, consider bringing along a 'poop tube' (Google it for online

PLAN YOUR TRIP ACTIVITIES

HOW MUCH WATER TO PACK?

Each hiker should carry and drink at least 1 gallon (4 liters) of water per day, and sip constantly, drinking 0.5 to 1 quart of water per hour. Replenish electrolytes every couple hours by snacking on salty foods, and/or by drinking a sports drink like Gatorade. Though there are a handful of places along the corridor trails that offer seasonal water, pipeline breaks regularly break off water supplies.

how-to) and dispose of your waste at a local sewage treatment plant or RV dump station after your trek.

➡ Urinate 200ft from water, preferably on sand or rock.

➡ When camping along the Colorado River, the sheer volume of water makes washing up and peeing in the river an acceptable option. However, this applies only to the Colorado and not to the creeks and rivers flowing into it.

Washing

➡ For personal washing, use biodegradable soap and toothpaste with a water container; disperse waste water at least 200ft away from any water source, scattering it widely to allow the soil to filter it fully.

➡ When washing dishes and utensils, use sand or snow rather than detergent.

Erosion

➡ Hillsides and mountain slopes, especially at high altitudes, are prone to erosion. Stick to existing trails and avoid shortcuts.

➡ Where a well-used trail passes through a mud patch, walk through the mud so as not to widen the trail.

➡ Avoid removing or trampling the plant life that keeps topsoils in place.

Fires & Low-Impact Cooking

➡ Open fires are prohibited in Grand Canyon National Park except at established campgrounds on the rim.

➡ Where fires are allowed, keep them in established fire rings or grills. Never leave fires unattended; extinguish them thoroughly with water.

Top: Hikers camping
next to the Colorado
River (p170)

Bottom: Mule ride
on Bright Angel Trail
(p60)

➡ Refrain from collecting wood; instead, purchase wood at Canyon Village Marketplace or the North Rim General Store.

➡ Cook on a lightweight kerosene, alcohol or white-gas stove, avoiding those powered by disposable butane canisters.

➡ Consider bringing food that doesn't require cooking, and reduce the weight in your pack by not bringing a stove at all.

Wildlife Conservation

➡ Discourage the presence of wildlife by wrapping up and packing out all food scraps (and watch those ravens – they're brave, clever and opportunistic!).

➡ Keep all food and fragrant items (soap, deodorant, toothpaste etc) in your pack and hang it from a tree overnight to keep critters at bay.

Hiking Outfitters & Groups

Group outings are a terrific way for first-time hikers to enjoy safe and social hiking. The highly respected Grand Canyon Field Institute (p229) offers many naturalist-led hikes and backpacking trips for all skill levels. These fairly priced, expertly guided expeditions generally last three to nine days. The national park service Canyon Field Schools (p229) offer multiday backpacking and rafting trips for middle-school and high-school students

Many local outfitters offer a range of guided hiking excursions in the park, sometimes combining hiking with cycling and rafting. Trips, prices, dates and styles vary widely, so definitely peruse a few before making your choice. In any case, you're best off reserving a spot at least five months in advance.

Pick up a full list of accredited backcountry guide services at the park's visitor centers or on the NPS website (www.nps. gov/grca/planyourvisit/guided-hikes.htm).

The following list is just a sampling of outfitters.

Discovery Treks (☏888-256-8731; www. discoverytreks.com; 2-person all-day hike from $195) Offers a wide selection of guided trips, from one-day hikes on the Grandview Trail to five-day backpacking excursions on the North Rim.

Backroads (☏800-462-2848; www.backroads. com; d per person 5 days/6 nights $2200) Cycling and hiking tours to both rims, including combination trips to Grand Canyon, Bryce and Zion national parks.

All-Star Grand Canyon Tours (☏800-940-0445; www.allstargrandcanyontours.com; 2420 N 3rd, Flagstaff, AZ; day-hike per person incl lunch beginner/advanced $200/300) Private and group day- and overnight-hikes with hotel pick-up in Flagstaff, Las Vegas, Sedona and a handful of towns near the South Rim.

Four Season Guides (☏928-525-1552, 877-272-5032; www.fsguides.com; 3-day hike South Kaibab to Bright Angel per person $1000) Straight outta Flagstaff, offering guided multiday backcountry trips, including the rim-to-rim and Havasu Canyon.

Just Roughin' It Adventure Co (☏480-857-2477, 877-399-2477; www.justroughinit. com; South Rim day hikes $185, 2-night/3-day Grandview Trail hike $850) Catering to hikers of all levels looking to challenge themselves.

Pygmy Guides (☏928-707-0215, 877-279-4697; www.pygmyguides.com; South Rim day hikes per person incl pick-up at Flagstaff, Williams or Tusayan $160) Excellent outfit guiding everything from day hikes to rim-to-rim. Attempts to accommodate special-needs travelers as much as possible.

Rubicon Outdoors (☏800-903-6987; www.rubiconoutdoors.com; 3-day/2-night South Kaibab to Bright Angel per person $1195) Consummate professionals and minimal-impact wilderness adventurers run trips from day hikes to the five-day Hermit Trail trip and teen adventures.

Wildland Trekking (☑970-903-3719, 800-715-4453; www.wildlandtrekking.com; all-day hikes $115-215, 3-days trips from $845) Regular hiking or backpacking tours are guided by experts, or you can design your own adventure.

Mule Rides

Mule trains have been making their way down Bright Angel and other trails into the canyon for over a century, taking delighted tourists below the rim and ferrying supplies in and out of the canyon. Perhaps the most iconic of all Grand Canyon experiences, traveling the trails on the backs of these mellow, sure-footed creatures is a time-honored park tradition that makes for a memorable trip for just about all ages.

Don't plan a mule trip assuming it's the easiest way to travel below the rim. It's a bumpy ride on a hard saddle, and unless you're used to riding a horse regularly you will be saddle-sore afterwards. Those scared of heights or big animals – gentle and cute though they may be – are best off exploring the canyon by other means.

Riders must be at least 4ft 7in tall, speak fluent English and weigh no more than 200lb fully clothed. Personal backpacks, waist packs, purses or bags of any kind are not allowed on the mules.

South Rim (☑303-297-2757; www.grandcanyon lodges.com) Trips depart daily for one-night stays

---

OVER THE EDGE: DEATH IN THE GRAND CANYON

Before heading to the park, it's worth reading some or all of Michel Ghiglieri and Thomas Myers gripping *Over the Edge: Death in Grand Canyon*. Each chapter is dedicated to various ways in which people have died in the canyon, offering detailed stories from the park's early history to today. On average, 12 people die every year in the Grand Canyon. Even in the park's most developed areas a moment of foolhardiness born from the illusion of safety can lead to tragic consequences.

---

at Phantom Ranch year-round; two-night stays are available November through March. This is the only inner-canyon option from the South Rim, and the only option for riding a mule to the Colorado River. Half-day above-the-rim rides are also offered daily. Reservations are accepted up to 13 months in advance.

North Rim (☑435-679-8665; www.canyonrides. com/grand-canyon-mule-ride) There are daily half-day trips along the North Kaibab into the canyon. Above the rim options are a half-day or one-hour ride along a wooded trail. Rides can often be booked at the mule desk in the Grand Canyon Lodge the day before.

Havasu Falls (www.havasuwaterfalls.net) At the Havasupai Reservation, four hours from the South Rim, you can arrange in advance for either a personal or gear-only mule. It's also possible to arrange horseback transport from Hualapai Hilltop to Supai Village (8 miles) or to the Havasu Falls Campground, about 2 miles further.

River Rafting

Rafting the Colorado ranks among the top outdoor adventures for many, not only for its thrill factor, but also for its romance. It's a geological journey through time, an adrenaline rush, secluded wilderness getaway and riparian paradise all rolled into one phenomenal ride.

Rafting season begins in mid-April and runs into September for motorized boats and November for oared vessels. Though the park carefully regulates the number of rafts on the Colorado, visitors have several options. Most rafters join a commercial outing with one of many accredited outfitters for trips lasting from three to 21 days. Each year, a few hundred private rafting excursions are allowed on the river as well.

While there are no river-rafting daytrips through Grand Canyon National Park itself, there are two options outside the park for those who want to experience the river without committing to a multiday excursion that requires significant advance planning. The Hualapai Reservation (p174) offers a white-water day trip that includes bus pick-up in Williams, a drive to the canyon bottom, and a helicopter ride back out of the canyon. Several tour operators partner with **Colorado River Discovery** (p163) for a smooth water day-trip through Glen Canyon.

Rafting the Colorado River (p170)

Cycling

Bicycles are not allowed on any trails within the park, with the exception of the South Rim's Greenway Trail, and they are not allowed below the rim. They are, however, welcome on all roads. Bicycle and backpacker campsites, closed to vehicles, are available at both North Rim and Mather campgrounds, and South Rim shuttles are equipped with two- to three-capacity bicycle racks. You can rent bicycles on both rims.

Though not known as a cyclist's park, several scenic routes make lovely rides. Distances listed are for one-way travel.

➡ **Desert View Dr** (South Rim, 25 miles) You'll have to concentrate to keep your eyes from wandering off the road to the stunning canyon views. This hot ride is best tackled at sunrise or in the late afternoon.

➡ **Grand Canyon Lodge to Point Imperial** (North Rim, 8 miles) A winding, shady ride through pine forests and thickets of aspen and bright-orange Indian paintbrush. Ends at a picnic spot on the rim with a spectacular view.

➡ **Greenway Trail** (South Rim) A paved trail that includes the particularly scenic easternmost 1.9 miles and westernmost 2.8 miles of the 13-mile Rim Trail. You'll find several spectacular overlooks and picnic spots.

➡ **Hermit Rd** (South Rim, 8 miles) This relatively traffic-free ride offers a series of breathtaking overlooks. Cold drinks and ice-cream bars await at Hermits Rest. The road, closed to private vehicles March 1 through November 30, is open to cyclists year-round.

➡ **Point Imperial to Cape Royal** (North Rim, 18 miles) Long and winding with lots of small rolling hills, this delightful pedal along a forest-fringed road eventually opens up to sage-dusted terrain and big views.

Horseback Riding

Horseback riding is offered outside the park. At the North Rim, try Allen's Outfitters (p154). Just outside the South Rim, near Tusayan, Apache Stables (p92) offers group rides along the piney trails of the Kaibab and campfire rides (BYO hot dogs and s'mores).

Photographing the Grand Canyon

Rock Climbing

Rock climbing is allowed anywhere in the Grand Canyon, except above established trails (for obvious reasons). While Arizona is rife with climbing areas, climbing in the canyon is not extremely popular, nor very visible. Climbers who plan to hike into the canyon and camp will need a backcountry permit.

Stop by Flagstaff Climbing (p102) in Flagstaff to hit up the employees there for info on climbing throughout the region. It also offers guided climbing trips in the Grand Canyon region, and sells guidebooks and gear.

Stewart M Green's *Rock Climbing Arizona* (Falcon, 1999) is a comprehensive guide to prime Arizona climbing areas and includes topographical maps and detailed route information. An updated *Grand Canyon Summit Select II,* by Aaron and Pernell Tomas, features more than 100 remote backcountry ascent routes in the canyon and is available online as an ebook.

Guided Tours

Bus and jeep tours of the South Rim stop at overlooks and selected sights and often include time for a walk along the rim. Day tours to the North Rim are far more limited.

Several itineraries combine helicopter flights, rafting and bus tours. Check the itinerary very closely. The West Rim, on the Hualapai Reservation and not part of the national park, is closest to Las Vegas and is very busy with bus and helicopter tours. It does not offer any sights beyond the handful of overlooks and the glass skywalk, and because it sits several thousand feet lower than either rim, views are less grand.

Among the best organized tours are those offered as classes through Grand Canyon Field Institute (p229) and Museum of Northern Arizona (p229).

From Flagstaff & Williams

Grand Canyon Custom Tours (☑928-779-3163; www.grandcanyoncustomtours.com) One-day and multiday tours to the canyon depart from Flagstaff, Williams or Tusayan.

Climbing a slot canyon

Marvelous Marv's (☏928-707-0291; www.marvelousmarv.com; per person $100; ☉year-round) Personalized tours by a quirky Williams local. He'll pick you up from your hotel or campground in or around Williams or Tusayan for a full-day tour at the South Rim in his 12-passenger van.

Open Road Tours (☏602-997-6474; www. openroadtoursusa.com) Offers jeep, hiking, day-trip rafting and helicopter tours, departing from the Phoenix area, as well as from Flagstaff, Williams and Sedona.

From Las Vegas

Canyon Tours (☏702-260-0796; www. canyontours.com) Bus, plane and helicopter tours from Las Vegas, including a $79 day trip bus-only tour to the South Rim. All tours to the North Rim include a helicopter or airplane leg.

Grand Canyon Tour Company (p125) A massive variety of tours depart from Las Vegas, Sedona and Phoenix.

From Kanab

Dreamland Safari Tours (☏435-644-5506; www.dreamlandtours.net) Options include photography tours, day trips to the North Rim and overnight trips to Toroweap. Maximum capacity is 18-people, and many are far smaller.

National Park Tourz (☏866-433-8492; www.nationalparktourz.com) Day trips to North Rim, Zion, Bryce, Glen Canyon and the Wave. The five-day Animal Lovers Tour includes a day at Best Friends Animal Sanctuary.

Scenic Flights

While it's a less direct experience than hiking, flying over the Grand Canyon does offer an incredible perspective, and air tours are understandably popular. Close to 100,000 flights take almost a million passengers above the canyon each year.

Canyon flyovers are controversial. They involve high-altitude takeoffs, sudden wind shifts, unpredictable air currents and few level landing areas should an emergency arise; there have been some 60 crashes over the past half-century. Furthermore, many argue that despite the restrictions in altitude and route, the daily cap of 364 flights per day, and incentives for companies to incorporate quiet technology (QT), the noise pollution from the thousands of scenic flights fundamentally transforms the wilderness experience of the canyon and detrimentally affects the experience of other visitors and wildlife.

More than 75% of park airspace is seasonally off-limits to planes, and flying below the rim is prohibited in all but the West Rim. As a result, noise and hustle of scenic flights at the West Rim give the area a distinctly military base feel – if you're

RANGER TALKS

Rangers are fonts of information, which they happily share in free programs on both rims. Their talks cover everything from condors to fire ecology, Native American history to constellations, while their hikes deepen your understanding of the canyon's fossils, geology and history.

Check *The Guide*, given to every car at the park entrance, or check park visitor centers for subjects and times of the latest offerings.

interested in a scenic flight, you're better off avoiding this mayhem.

Contact recommended companies for routes and rates, as each offers several options, but note that their prices are fairly competitive; airplane tours tend to cost less than helicopter trips. and cover more distance. For a 45-minute scenic airplane tour departing from the South Rim, expect to pay about $150; for a similar helicopter tour, it's about $300. Flights from the less scenic West Rim cost a bit less. If you're concerned about flight noise, ask whether the company uses QT helicopters.

Most air tours operate out of airports in Tusayan, Las Vegas, Phoenix, Sedona, Page and the Hualapai Reservation (West Rim). On the South Rim, the National Geographic Visitor Center & IMAX Theater in Tusayan, a few minutes' from the park entrance, is the best place to pop in to arrange last-minute reservations.

Grand Canyon Airlines (p42)

Grand Canyon Helicopters (☑702-835-8477, 928-638-2764; www.grandcanyonhelicopter.com)

Papillon Grand Canyon Helicopters (p111)

Maverick Helicopters (☑888-261-4414, 702-261-0007; www.maverickhelicopter.com)

Scenic Airlines (☑800-634-6801, 702-638-3300; www.scenic.com)

Westwind Air Service (☑888-869-0866; www.westwindairservice.com)

Cross-Country Skiing & Snowshoeing

North Rim

The North Rim and environs receive an average of 150in of snow annually, offering miles of snow-covered forest roads and a patchwork of wide meadows for those willing to make the trek. There are no designated trails, so you can ski or snowshoe virtually anywhere, opening up limitless options for backcountry exploration.

The road from Jacob Lake to the park entrance and on to the canyon rim officially closes from mid-October, or at the first snowfall, and there are no snowplow services; visitors must ski or snowshoe the 44 miles to the rim.

South Rim

The South Rim boasts a few groomed cross-country loops within the Kaibab National Forest, 0.3 miles north of Grandview Lookout Tower.

You can rent skis in Flagstaff, where you'll find groomed cross-country trails at the popular Flagstaff Nordic Center (p102), plenty of ungroomed trails throughout the national forest, and downhill skiing at Arizona Snowbowl (p102).

Plan Your Trip
Travel with Children

From lazy days fossil-hunting along rocky trais to white-water adventures down the Colorado, the iconic family road trip to the Grand Caryon makes for memories that imprint not only into photos but into the spirit. All it takes is a little planning, and a lot of patience and flexibility.

Grand Canyon for Kids

Long drives, precarious canyon overlooks, crowded shuttles and stifling summer heat can be a challenge. The rewards, however, rest in the most mundane of activities – a sunset picnic at Cape Royal, a bicycle ride along the rimside Greenway Trail, hot-chocolate under the stars, snuggled into an Adirondack chair on the patio of the North Rim's Grand Canyon Lodge. And the canyon's geology, human history and wildlife, accessible in concrete ways at every turn, make the park the world's largest classroom – kids learn without even trying.

While the South Rim has more sights, museums and a broader variety of ranger-led interpretive programs designed for children, the chaos and crowds can be intimidating and exhausting. The intimacy of the North Rim attracts families looking for a quieter vacation.

Ranger Programs

In the **Junior Ranger Program**, geared towards children aged four to 14, children pick up an activity book from the visitor center on either rim, complete three pages and attend a ranger program. Upon completion, a ranger solemnly swears them in as junior rangers and the child receives a certificate and a badge. While the whole

Best Activities for Kids

Ranger Programs

Stargazing talks around the fire, activity books and kid-friendly lectures.

Rafting

White-water trips through the canyon, perfect for older kids and teens, and calm-water floats along the Colorado River from Glen Canyon Dam to Lees Ferry for all ages.

Hiking

Scrambles through desert scrub, rambles through aspen and meadows and overnight expeditions down to the Colorado River; Grand Canyon offers plenty of fantastic hiking opportunities for young children and teenagers alike.

Mule Rides

Treks to the canyon bottom are offered from the South Rim only; half-day rides from the North Rim give a taste of the canyon interior and follow a less precipitous trai. Children must be 10, but the North Rim offers a rimside option for kids as young as seven.

BEFORE YOU GO

• •

It's possible to cruise into the South Rim, check out the museums and hike the trails on a whim, but for the following canyon highlights you'll need to make some advanced reservations.

➡ White-water rafting trips on the Colorado River through the Grand Canyon

➡ Family trips with the Grand Canyon Field Institute (www.grandcanyon.org/fieldinstitute)

➡ Canyon Field Schools for elementary, junior-high and high-school students (www.nps.gov/grca/learn/kidsyouth/camp.htm)

➡ Overnight stays at Phantom Ranch, on the canyon bottom (www.grandcanyonlodges.com)

➡ Accommodations at North Rim's Grand Canyon Lodge (www.grandcanyonlodgenorth.com)

➡ Grand Canyon Railway (www.thetrain.com)

➡ South Rim lodges and mule treks into the canyon (www.grandcanyonlodges.com)

➡ Museum of Arizona discovery programs and tours (www.musnaz.org)

➡ Volunteering at Best Friends Animal Sanctuary outside Kanab, UT and spending a night with a a borrowed cat, dog or pot-bellied pig (www.bestfriends.org)

thing sounds rather hokey, a leisurely afternoon completing the project just might be the highlight of your six-year-old's visit.

The **Discovery Pack Program** (ages nine to 14) begins with a ranger talk, after which children check out binoculars, a magnifying lens, field guides and other naturalist tools. Rangers use hands-on activities to teach children about the park's ecology and wildlife at **Way Cool Stuff for Kids** and **Kids Rock**.

Download a seasonal schedule of ranger programs from the 'For Kids' link on the park's website (www.nps.gov/grca). National monuments surrounding the park offer Junior Ranger and kid-friendly ranger programs as well.

Hiking and Cycling

Both rims offer opportunities for kids to get dirty and dusty on the trails, but each offers a distinct experience.

With miles of rimside rambles and several opportunities to descend into the canyon, hiking on the South Rim is particularly suited for older kids. The constant danger of the rim and rocky interior precipices can be nerve-wracking for parents of little ones; the Greenway Trail makes a lovely bicycle ride. On the North Rim, the grassy meadows, shaded trails and eleva-

tion offer relief from the summer sun, and it's almost guaranteed that you'll see mule deer or wild turkeys.

The paved Rim Trail on the South Rim is suitable for strollers, but if you plan on more extensive hiking, consider a front carrier for infants or a backpack carrier for toddlers. You can rent a jogging stroller at the bike rental in the gas station on the North Rim; at the South Rim, Bright Angel Bicycles rents bicycles with pull-along trailers, children's bicycles and strollers.

Children's Highlights
Family Hikes

Rim Trail Popular path to sights and overlooks on South Rim. (p58)

Shoshone Point Easy, wide, wooded dirt road to a quiet overlook. (p59)

Bright Angel At the first tunnel, check out the pictographs. (p60)

Widforss Trail Gentle hike through woods to the canyon rim. (p138)

Cape Final Jutting canyon view rewards a mild hike. (p140)

Children Aged 11 & Under

IMAX Grand Canyon Amazing aerial canyon footage. (p92)

Junior Ranger Activity books and hands-on fun. (p43)

Grand Canyon Cookout Experience Cowboy tunes and barbecue on North Rim. (p149)

Trail of Time Geologic timeline with rocks excavated from the canyon. (p75)

Cape Royal Dr Picnic at Greenland Lake and stroll out to Cape Royal Point. (p146)

Desert View Watchtower Children love climbing the spiral staircase and taking in the view at this Mary Colter classic on the South Rim. (p79)

Tweens & Teens

Raft the Colorado Ride the rapids through the canyon. (p174)

Mule Trek Ride a mule from the South Rim to an overnight stay at Phantom Ranch. (p72)

Canyon Field Schools Overnight adventures with a park ranger. (p229)

Rim-to-Rim Huff it down one side and out the other. (p64)

Planning

While any trip should allow plenty of time for serendipitous discoveries, anything more than a day trip requires some advance planning. If possible, try to come to the park during the fall, after the summer crowds of school-aged children ebbs and the gripping desert heat softens, but before that teasing hint of winter becomes a full-fledged snowstorm. It's the best time to be here, but remember, the North Rim closes October 15.

Accommodations

Reservations for park lodges are accepted up to 13 months in advance and you can cancel without penalty up to 48 hours in advance. If you travel with lots of gear, you might prefer to stay at the Yavapai Lodge (p85) or Maswik Lodge (p85) on the South Rim, as you can park right outside your door. Bright Angel Lodge (p84) offers two-room cabins, and El Tovar (p85) has several suites. On the North Rim, Grand Canyon Lodge's **Pioneer Cabins** sport two rooms and sleep six. Children under 16 stay free at all Grand Canyon lodgings, but there is a $10-per-day charge for cribs and cots.

Most accommodations outside the park do not charge extra for children under 12,

---

WHAT TO PACK

You'll be able to find just about anything you could need on the South Rim, but options on the North Rim are limited to the general store and a gift shop.

Children's paracetemol and ibuprofen You'll be glad you packed these if your child wakes up with a fever of 102°F at 3am.

Fleece Even in the summer, desert nights can be chilly and the North Rim can be downright bitter.

Rain jacket Yes, it's the desert, but summer monsoons bring torrential rains and passing showers are common.

Water sandals You'll want to splash in creeks without worrying about sharp rocks and desert pricklies.

Hiking shoes Bring something sturdy that ties and covers the toes, and socks.

Sunscreen and bug repellent Even in the winter the sun sears, and mosquitoes and ticks pester from March through October.

Water bottles Altitude sickness and dehydration bring headaches, nausea and worse.

Sun hat A must in the summer.

Beach towels For exploring creeks and reservoirs surrounding the park, and perfect for picnics.

Hiking in Grand Canyon National Park

and many have suites and pools. Bed and breakfasts often do not welcome children. In Flagstaff, Little America Hotel (p104) borders acres of forest, has an outdoor pool surrounded by grass and offers spacious rooms.

Dining

Even the fanciest restaurants in and around the park welcome families, and both rims offer cafeterias and plenty of picnic spots. There's a full grocery store on the South Rim and a limited general store on the North Rim. Not all rooms in the park have refrigerators, but you can buy ice on both rims; coolers can be useful.

Safety

It's easy to forget, as you're waiting in line for a shuttle or walking a rim trail with hundreds of other folk, that this is a wilderness. In most areas, there are no guardrails along the rim, and even where there are, there is room for a small child to slide through. Children and adults alike have plummeted to their deaths engaging in the most mundane activities in the most populated parts of the park. Secure toddlers in child carriers, always clutch young children's hands, and absolutely do not allow anyone to run and scramble along the rim. Hikes into the canyon can be treacherous – consider carefully before bringing children under 10 years old.

Arizona law requires that children five years old and younger sit in a car seat except on public transportation. Most car-rental agencies rent rear-facing car seats (for infants under one year old), forward-facing seats and boosters for about $10 per day, but you must reserve these in advance.

IN THE CAR

You can't avoid long stretches in the car when you're traveling to the Grand Canyon, particularly if you're headed to the isolated North Rim. But with the right frame of mind and some smart packing, here's how you can minimize backseat whining.

➡ Try not to squeeze too much in. Endless hours in the car rushing from overlook to overlook, sight to sight, can result in grumpy, tired kids and frustrated parents. After a while, canyon views start to look alike.

➡ Stop often and stay flexible.

➡ Remember sunshades for the window, and a football, soccer ball or Frisbee – any grassy area or meadow is a potential playing field.

➡ Surprise the kids with a Grand Canyon trip bag filled with canyon books (www.grandcanyon.org), a special treat, a car-friendly toy and game.

➡ Bring a journal, an enlarged Xeroxed map and colored pencils (crayons melt!) for each child. Kids can follow along on their map as you drive, drawing pictures of what they see and do, and record the trip in their journal.

➡ Pack music and audiobooks.

PARK & POKE FROM THE SOUTH TO NORTH RIM

Sometimes the best times are had by simply parking the car and poking around – no charge, no destination, no agenda. Break up the four-hour drive around the canyon from the South to North Rim with a few park and pokes.

Little Colorado Gorge (Hwy 64, east of South Rim's East Entrance) Peruse Navajo crafts and take in the view.

Cameron Trading Post (p120) Shady green gardens and tourist trinkets in Cameron.

Balanced Rocks (Lees Ferry) Scramble and hike among giant boulders in Marble Canyon; just west of Navajo Bridge, head north a mile or so on Lees Ferry Rd.

Historic Lees Ferry (p162) Picnic in the apricot orchard at Lonely Dell Ranch.

Jacob Lake Inn (p154) Grab a milkshake for the last leg to the North Rim.

Note that the North Rim is isolated and the closest medical facilities are 1½ hours away in Kanab, but basics like children's tylenol and first-aid supplies are easily available at both rims. Common safety issues include dehydration and altitude sickness.

Beyond the Park

Families with children of all ages could spend several days, even weeks, exploring the mountains and desert surrounding Grand Canyon National Park. Remember, however, that distances are long, particularly in and around the North Rim.

Las Vegas, a convenient place to fly into for Grand Canyon visits, makes a great place to indulge in a fancy resort with luxurious pools – in the summer, rates plummet.

Around the South Rim

Flagstaff With excellent parks, outdoor family movies and a pedestrian-friendly downtown, this mountain college town is an exceptionally kid-friendly base for the region.

Slide Rock State Park Slide down natural slick-rock of Oak Creek just outside Sedona.

Walnut Canyon National Monument Explore ancient Puebloan cliff dwellings.

Red Rock Crossing Splash in the the creek, hike through red rock country and picnic.

Sunset Crater National Monument Hike through the striking black basalt of a lava flow.

Around the North Rim

North Kaibab National Forest Gentle trails and meadows.

Kanab Small and quiet red-rock Utah town with kitschy Western fun.

Coral Sand Dunes State Park Kids love sliding down the soft pink sand.

Best Friends Animal Sanctuary Visit critters in the nation's largest no-kill animal shelter.

Lake Powell Houseboat or kayak on the cold clear waters of this massive desert reservoir.

Glen Canyon Smooth water day-trip along the Colorado River.

Plan Your Trip
Travel with Pets

While it's certainly possible to enjoy a trip to Grand Canyon with your pet, summer heat and park restrictions can be challenging. A little advanced planning will go a long way to making the trip smoother and happier for both you and your four-legged friend.

Best Spots for Dogs

Kaibab National Forest (North)

With miles of trails and dirt roads, no leash laws and plenty of big meadows, the national forest that borders Grand Canyon National Park to the north is dog heaven. Even in summer, the high elevation and thick shade of the Kaibab Plateau keep them cool.

Kanab

Down the road from the nation's largest no-kill animal shelter, this tiny Utah town a 1½-hour drive from the North Rim is particularly dog-friendly. Just about every hotel takes dogs, and most restaurants and shops have water bowls and dog treats.

Flagstaff

A college town with a soft spot for four-legged friends; most side-walk cafes welcome dogs, and there are a handful of dog parks.

Rules & Regulations

Dogs and cats are allowed at rim campgrounds and throughout the park's developed areas, but cannot go below the rim, ride the shuttles or enter any hotels, stores or restaurants on either rim, and they must be leashed at all times.

It is illegal to leave a dog tied up alone at a campground, and you must clean up after your dog. Official service animals are welcome throughout the park, but you must register at the backcountry office before taking them below the rim.

Health & Safety

The environment can be harsh on pets, and mountain lions, rattlesnakes, scorpions and other critters are prevalent in the region. Prepare for weather extremes. In the summer, do not leave them in the car or RV unattended at any time. Think twice before taking pets on desert hikes in the summer, as it's excruciatingly hot and the sand burns tender paws, and always bring a portable water bowl. The only complete pet-supply shops in the region are Flagstaff's **Petsmart** (Map p100; ☑928-213-1737; 1121 S Plaza Way; ☺9am-9pm Mon-Sat, to 7pm Sun) and **Petco** (☑928-526-4934; 5047 East Marketplace Dr).

Remember that dogs, like humans, need to be in good shape before taking off on extended hikes, and are susceptible to altitude sickness and dehydration.

Dog-friendly Trails
In the Park

The only trails that allow dogs are the Rim Trail in the South Rim, and the North Rim's Bridle Trail.

Beyond the Park

See Renee Guillory's recommended *Best Hikes with Dogs: Arizona* for a full listing of dog-friendly trails. In general, trails in and around Flagstaff are excellent for dogs.

Kaibab National Forest (North) Just outside the park's North Rim gate; all trails and dirt roads allow dogs and they are not required to be leashed (p152).

Paria Canyon Dogs are welcomed on this five-day wilderness hike, but you must pay $5 per day and pick up special dog-doo bags at the Paria Contact Station.

Buffalo Park An open mesa outside Flagstaff with a lovely 2-mile gravel loop trail. Leashed dogs only. (p101)

Dog-friendly Accommodations
In the Park

The only lodge within Grand Canyon National Park that allows dogs is Yavapai West (p85). A handful of dog-friendly rooms provide a kennel, food and water dishes and a leash – there is a one-time $25 fee for up to two dogs per room, and dogs are not allowed to be left in rooms unattended. Dogs are, however, welcome at campgrounds on both rims.

Beyond the Park

Several motels just outside Grand Canyon National Park, including just about every hotel in Kanab, UT, and several chain hotels in Page, AZ, welcome dogs and cats in some or all rooms. You may be restricted to a smoking room or have to pay a small fee. Best options include the following.

Kaibab Lodge (p154) About a half-hour drive from Grand Canyon Lodge on the North Rim; pet-sitting services available and a $15 one-time fee.

Drury Inn & Suites (p104) Clean and modern chain motel within walking distance to restaurants and bars in Flagstaff's historic downtown; pets $10 per night.

El Portal (p117) Exquisitely handsome boutique inn nestled in Sedona that warmly welcomes pets into rooms and the dining area.

Four Seasons (p125) Elegant non-casino hotel on Vegas Strip near the airport.

Staybridge Suites (p126) Spacious suites in chain motel, located in a quiet spot close to Vegas airport.

Best Western Plus Inn (☑928-635-4400; www.bestwesternwilliams.com; 2600 Historic Rt 66; r $189; P✳🛜🐾) Just off I-40 in Williams, with renovated rooms.

Kennels

Proof of vaccination is required for all kennels. Note that there is a kennel on the South Rim, but none on or even within a couple of hours of the North Rim.

South Rim Kennel (p88) Convenient for one or two days but not recommended for extended stays. There are no large play areas for the dogs, and individual walks are limited to one five-minute walk per day. Rates include meals.

Cinder Hills Boarding Kennel (☑928-526-3812; www.newsite.cinderhillskennels.com; 11110 Townsend Winona Rd, Flagstaff; dogs per day $28-39, cats $16) Dog and cat boarding and day-camp sits on 5 acres and offers plenty of outdoor playtime; for an extra fee, you can arrange for Fun in the Forest Hikes and car transport for your pet.

Railway Pet Resort (www.thetrain.com; per night dog/cat $25/18; ⊙7am-8pm Mar-Oct, from 8am Nov-Feb) Conveniently located next to Grand

---

DOG-FRIENDLY BARS

While several Flagstaff restaurants, winebars and cafes welcome dogs at their sidewalk tables, only a handful of places welcome them inside. Our favorite is Hops on Birch (p107), one block north of the historic downtown's Heritage Square. Not only are there loads of quirky microbrews on tap, but this friendly neighborhood hangout has more than a few four-legged regulars.

VETERINARIANS

Canyon Pet Hospital (☑928-774-5197, after-hours ☑928-266-5762; www.canyonpet. com; 1054 E Old Canyon Ct, Flagstaff; overnight dog standard/luxury $19/36, cat per day $15; ☺8am-8pm Mon-Fri, 9am-6pm Sat, noon-4pm Sun) Offers after-hours emergencies.

Aspen Veterinary Clinic (☑928-526-2423; 7861 N US Hwy 89, Flagstaff; ☺8.15am-5.30pm Mon-Fri, 8am-noon Sat) Messages direct you to emergency contacts after hours.

Kanab Veterinary Hospital (☑435-644-2400; www.kanabvet.com; 6676 E Hwy 89, Kanab; ☺8am-5pm Mon-Fri) A 1½-hour drive from the North Rim.

Page Animal Hospital (☑928-645-2816; http://pageanimalhospital.com; 87 S 7th Ave, Page) Only service between the South and North Rims.

Canyon Railway in Williams and timed to coordinate with the trains, this is an excellent option for travelers heading to the South Rim by historic rail.

Canyon Pet Hospital (p50) Boarding and grooming. Rates include meals. VIP packages, with extra playtime, walks and treats, are an additional $10 per day.

Doggy Dude Ranch (☑435-772-3105; www. doggyduderanch.com; Hwy 9 btwn Rockville & Springdale, UT; overnight/day boarding $26/20; ☺8am-6pm Mon-Sat, 9am-5pm Sun) Five miles outside of Zion National Park and three hours from the North Rim, this dog ranch offers quality day care and specializes in extended stays.

Sleepover Rover (☑866-656-0577; www. sleepoverrover.com; per night $40-50) Host families in Phoenix and Las Vegas dog-sit cage-free in their home. All hosts have dog-safe yards, are home full-time, and have been personally approved by the company's founder and owner.

Horse Trails & Equestrian Facilities

In the Park

Horses and pack animals are allowed in the park, including corridor below-the-rim trails, and there are corrals on both rims as well as at Bright Angel and Cottonwood Campgrounds inside the canyon that offer limited numbers of private horses. Trails include both the South and North Kaibab Trails, Bright Angel Trail and the River Trail, which means experienced riders can ride into the canyon and spend the night at Bright Angel Campground.

Visit www.nps.gov/grca/planyourvisit/ private-stock.htm for updated details and regulations, and contact the backcountry office (p33) in advance for the required overnight permit.

Beyond the Park

The **Kaibab National Forest** that borders the North Rim offers excellent riding opportunities with all trails open to horses, and miles of dirt roads. Ranchers who run cattle in the Kaibab have a permit to use corrals within the forest, and while they welcome riders passing through, you need to call or stop by the Kaibab Plateau Visitor Center in Jacob Lake for locations and current information.

In the Coconino National Forest just outside of Flagstaff, **Little Elden Springs Horse Camp** (☑877-444-6777, condition updates 928-226-0493; www.recreation.gov; day/night $9/20; ☺May-Oct) is a campground designated only for people with horses. It offers 15 horse-friendly campsites with hitching posts but no corrals. From here, riders can access more than 100 miles of equestrian trails, ranging from easy to the challenging Heart Trail. To get to Little Elden, head 5 miles northeast of Flagstaff on Hwy 89. Turn west on FR 556 and drive 2 miles to FR 556A. Turn right to the campground.

In Flagstaff, board your horse at **MCS Stables** (☑928-774-5835; www.mcsstables. com; 8301 S Highway 89A, Flagstaff; per night $25-35). You're welcome to camp on-site at no extra charge. The closest facility to the North Rim is Paria Canyon Guest Ranch (p161), 30 miles west of Page, about a two-hour drive from the park.

On the Road

South Rim

Best Hikes

➡ Rim to Rim (p64)

➡ Hermit Trail to Santa Maria Spring (p62)

➡ South Kaibab Trail to Cedar Ridge (p61)

➡ Shoshone Point (p59)

➡ Rim Trail (p58)

Best Places to Stay

➡ El Tovar (p85)

➡ Bright Angel Lodge (p84)

➡ Desert View Campground (p83)

Why Go?

It's a busy place, with throngs of tourists of all ages and nationalities smiling for selfies, shuffling on and off shuttles, and wandering through gift shops. But simply turn the other way, and there it is: the Grand Canyon, a truly majestic natural sculpture. And the South Rim, with its 19 official overlooks, is the best place to see it.

It's not just the grandeur of Grand Canyon that draws visitors. The South Rim's museums are the best places to explore the area's human and geologic history, and Mary Colter–designed buildings are perhaps the country's most iconic national park architecture.

Despite the South Rim's popularity, it's easy to find a spot here to discover your own Grand Canyon, a place you won't find in photographs or books. Your connection to this place comes in its smells, the breeze on your face, a stolen moment sitting in the sun alone.

Road Distances (miles)

	South Rim	Williams	Flagstaff	Sedona	North Rim
Williams	60				
Flagstaff	80	35			
Sedona	115	60	30		
North Rim	210	240	205	235	
Las Vegas	275	215	250	275	265

Note: Distances are approximate

Entrances

The South Rim has two park entrances: the South Entrance, 74 miles north of Flagstaff on Hwy 180, and the East Entrance on Hwy 64, 32 miles west of Cameron and 82 miles north of Flagstaff. Most visitors enter from the South Entrance. After tackling summer queues (upwards of 45 minutes), visitors then head a few miles north to the mayhem of Grand Canyon Village – home to the park's tourist facilities, including hotels, restaurants and the visitor center.

If possible, enter the park through the East Entrance. As you drive the 25 miles to Grand Canyon Village, stopping at overlooks along the way, your first glimpses of the canyon will be more dramatic and much less hectic.

DON'T MISS

As in life, the best things at the South Rim are free. Watch a sunrise or sunset at an overlook along Desert View Dr, stroll along the **Rim Trail** (p58) from Powell Point to Mohave Point, enjoy a picnic in a quiet spot along the **canyon rim**, descend into its depths on the **South Kaibab** (p61), and climb the winding staircase of the **Desert View Watchtower** (p79). Learn about the park's geology at the **Trail of Time** (p75) and its tourist beginnings at the History Room inside **Bright Angel Lodge** (p76), and take in a **ranger program** (p72).

Only slightly more expensive is renting a bike at Bright **Angel Bicycles** (p69) for a spin along the rim followed by prickly-pear margaritas on the porch swing at **El Tovar** (p86).

When You Arrive

➜ The $30-per-vehicle park entrance fee permits unlimited visits to both rims within seven days of purchase. Motorcycles cost $25. Those entering by bicycle, train, shuttle or on foot pay $15.

➜ Upon entry, you'll receive a map and a copy of *The Guide*, a National Park Service (NPS) newspaper with details on ranger programs, hikes, maps and park services.

➜ The South Entrance (in Tusayan) offers a separate line during peak season for travelers who already have entrance permits. Minimize wait-time by purchasing a permit in advance (p92).

Tip: Use a Storage Service

If you plan to do some hiking and don't want to leave laptops, passports or other valuables in the car, Bright Angel Lodge (p76) offers a storage service. It's on a space-available basis, though, and it does sometimes fill up.

LAST MINUTE

Because you can cancel lodge accommodation up to 48 hours with no penalty, it's not unusual even in summer to secure last-minute rooms. Keep calling (see p82) and stay flexible.

Fast Facts

➜ Rim trail length: 13 miles

➜ Highest elevation: 7461ft

➜ Elevation change: 4420ft

Reservations

➜ Reserve lodge accommodation and mule rides as early as 13 months in advance; if traveling in high season, reserve rooms as early as possible.

➜ Plan ahead for dinner at historic El Tovar (p86), the only restaurant on the South Rim that takes dinner reservations, overnights at inner-canyon Phantom Ranch and mule rides.

Resources

➜ **Grand Canyon National Park** (www.nps.gov/grca)

➜ **Xanterra** (www. grandcanyonlodges.com) Lodging, mule rides and tours.

➜ **Official Grand Canyon Trail Guides** Water-resistant paperback guide ($3.95) that fits in a back pocket and offers human and natural histories of the trail and easy-to-read maps. Available at most South Rim shops.

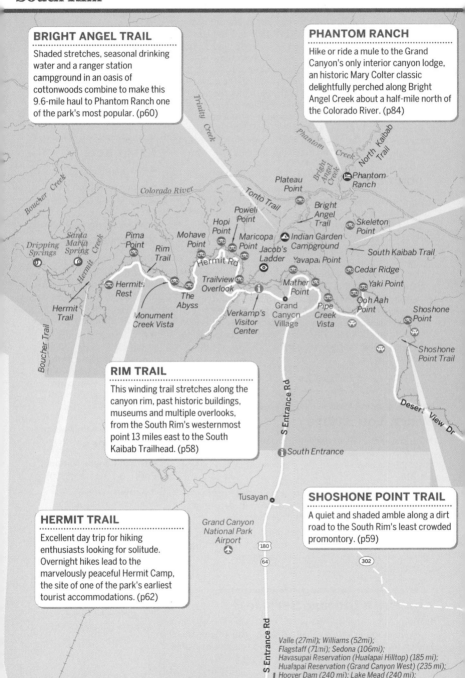

BRIGHT ANGEL TRAIL

Shaded stretches, seasonal drinking water and a ranger station campground in an oasis of cottonwoods combine to make this 9.6-mile haul to Phantom Ranch one of the park's most popular. (p60)

PHANTOM RANCH

Hike or ride a mule to the Grand Canyon's only interior canyon lodge, an historic Mary Colter classic delightfully perched along Bright Angel Creek about a half-mile north of the Colorado River. (p84)

RIM TRAIL

This winding trail stretches along the canyon rim, past historic buildings, museums and multiple overlooks, from the South Rim's westernmost point 13 miles east to the South Kaibab Trailhead. (p58)

HERMIT TRAIL

Excellent day trip for hiking enthusiasts looking for solitude. Overnight hikes lead to the marvelously peaceful Hermit Camp, the site of one of the park's earliest tourist accommodations. (p62)

SHOSHONE POINT TRAIL

A quiet and shaded amble along a dirt road to the South Rim's least crowded promontory. (p59)

Trinity Creek

Phantom Creek

North Kaibab Trail

Colorado River

Boucher Creek

Santa Maria Spring

Dripping Springs

Hermit Creek

Boucher Trail

Plateau Point

Tonto Trail

Powell Point

Hopi Point

Pima Point

Mohave Point

Rim Trail

Maricopa Point

Jacob's Ladder

Indian Garden Campground

Bright Angel Trail

Phantom Ranch

Skeleton Point

South Kaibab Trail

Hermit Rd

Yavapai Point

Cedar Ridge

Trailview Overlook

Hermits Rest

The Abyss

Monument Creek Vista

Verkamp's Visitor Center

Mather Point

Grand Canyon Village

Pipe Creek Vista

Yaki Point

Ooh Aah Point

Shoshone Point

Hermit Trail

Shoshone Point Trail

S Entrance Rd

Desert View Dr

South Entrance

Tusayan

Grand Canyon National Park Airport

180

64

302

S Entrance Rd

Valle (27mi); Williams (52mi); Flagstaff (71mi); Sedona (106mi); Havasupai Reservation (Hualapai Hilltop) (185 mi); Hualapai Reservation (Grand Canyon West) (235 mi); Hoover Dam (240 mi); Lake Mead (240 mi); Las Vegas (268 mi)

N

0 ———— 10 km
0 ———— 5 miles

Clear Creek

Cape Royal Rd

Basalt Creek

Unkar Creek

SOUTH KAIBAB TRAIL

Exposed crest line descends 7 miles to the Colorado River and Phantom Ranch, offering dramatic panoramic views. (p61)

Grand Canyon National Park

Vishnu Creek

Asbestos Canyon

Colorado River

Escalante Route

Tanner Trail

Tonto Trail

Horseshoe Mesa

Cottonwood Creek

New Hance Trail

Papago Creek

Watchtower

Navajo Point

Desert View

Lipan Point

East Entrance

Grapevine Creek

Grandview Trail

Hance Creek

Moran Point

Desert View Dr

TONTO TRAIL

While the entire 95-mile Tonto winds midway down the canyon's south face parallel to the Colorado River, shorter stretches of this wild and desolate ribbon can be accessed through South Rim Trails. (p63 & p68)

Grandview Point

64

Lee Canyon

Cameron (20mi)

Grandview Lookout Tower

302

Kaibab National Forest

GRANDVIEW TRAIL

Bone-dry trail plummets steeply into the canyon, a popular day hike and backcountry overnight expedition for experienced hikers. (p63)

HIKING IN SOUTH RIM

NAME	START LOCATION	DESCRIPTION
Bright Angel Trail		
To Mile-and-a-Half Resthouse (p60)	Bright Angel Trailhead	Short, rewarding hike along the Grand Canyon's most popular inner-canyon trail
To Three-Mile Resthouse (p60)	Bright Angel Trailhead	Following Bright Angel Fault, this trail zigzags to a shaded resthouse with panoramic views
To Indian Garden (p60)	Bright Angel Trailhead	The grueling switchbacks of Jacob's Ladder lead to the leafy bliss of Indian Garden
Plateau Point Trail (p60)	Bright Angel Trailhead	Not recommended for summer day hikes, this trail leads to the edge of Tonto Plateau
Grandview Trail		
To Coconino Saddle (p63)	Grandview Trailhead	This steep, rocky challenge winds up at a shady spot with phenomenal views
To Horseshoe Mesa (p63)	Grandview Trailhead	Stay on the steep and narrow on this, one of the park's most exposed hikes
Hermit Trail		
To Santa Maria Spring (p62)	Hermit Trailhead	Beautiful and serene day hike along a steep wilderness trail to small, lovely cliffside spring
Dripping Springs Trail (p63)	Hermit Trailhead	Peaceful and challenging hike to Louis 'The Hermit' Boucher's favorite hangout
To Hermit Camp (p65)	Hermit Trailhead	Hard but beautiful hike to a sublime, cliff-side camping spot
South Kaibab Trail		
To Ooh Ahh Point (p61)	South Kaibab Trailhead	Excellent choice for a taste of inner-canyon hiking
To Cedar Ridge (p61)	South Kaibab Trailhead	Steep descent along a ridge crest
To Skeleton Point (p61)	South Kaibab Trailhead	Panoramic views
To Phantom Ranch (p66)	South Kaibab Trailhead	Tough but rewarding hike to Colorado River
Rim to Rim (p64)	South Kaibab Trailhead	The park's classic rim-to-rim corridor hike; can also be started from the North Rim or from Bright Angel Trailhead
Rim Trail (p58)	multiple	Popular paved and dirt point-to-point trail connects South Rim overlooks
Shoshone Point (p59)	Shoshone Point Trailhead	Cool, shady walk to one of the South Rim's most spectacular viewpoints
Tonto Trail (p63)	South Kaibab Trailhead	Long, tough loop down the South Kaibab, across the mid-canyon Tonto and up Bright Angel

  Wildlife Watching

 View

 Great for Families

 Wheelchair Accessible

  Restrooms

DIFFICULTY	DURATION	ROUND-TRIP DISTANCE	ELEVATION CHANGE	FEATURES	FACILITIES
moderate	2-3hr	3 miles	1120ft		
moderate–difficult	5hr	6 miles	2120ft		
moderate–difficult	7hr	9.2 miles	3040ft		
difficult	8-10hr	12.2 miles	3040ft		
difficult	2-4hr	2.2 miles	1500ft		
difficult	4-8hr	6.2 miles	2699ft		
difficult	3hr	4 miles	1760ft		
difficult	5hr	6.2 miles	1040ft		
difficult–very difficult	2 days	15.4 miles	3660ft		
moderate	1-2hr	1.8 miles	760ft		
moderate–difficult	2-3hr	3 miles	1120ft		
difficult	6hr	6 miles	2040ft		
difficult–very difficult	2-3 days	18.6 miles	4714ft		
difficult–very difficult	3 days	20.9 miles	5770ft		
easy	5hr	13 miles (Hermits Rest to South Kaibab Trailhead)	200ft		
easy	40min	2 miles	50ft		
very difficult	7-9hr	13.1 miles (one-way)	3260ft		

 Public Transportation to Trailhead

 Drinking Water

 Ranger Station

 Backcountry Campsite

🏃 DAY HIKES

Hiking along the South Rim is among park visitors' favorite pastimes, with options for all levels. The popular river-bound corridor trails (Bright Angel and South Kaibab) follow paths etched thousands of years ago by geologic faults and water drainages. Several turnaround spots make these trails ideal for day hikes of varying lengths. Though the Bright Angel and South Kaibab trails can be packed during the summer with foot and mule traffic, more solitude can be found on less trodden trails like Hermit or Grandview.

Most of the trails start with a series of super-steep switchbacks that descend quickly to a dramatic ledge of Coconino sandstone about 2 miles beneath the rim. Hike another 3 miles and you'll hit the sun-baked Tonto Platform, which after another couple of miles opens up to inner-gorge vistas. Day hikers will want to stay above the Tonto Platform.

Day hiking requires no permit, just preparation and safety. Day-hike routes extend into overnight excursions, but overnight hiking requires either a reservation at Phantom Ranch (on the canyon bottom) or a permit for backcountry camping in advance of departure; do not set off for a day hike and then decide en route that you would like to stay below the rim overnight.

The Rim Trail and Shoshone Point hikes are excellent for families, as neither involves significant elevation change.

Above the Rim

🏃 Rim Trail

Duration 5 hours one-way

Distance Varies (up to 13 miles one-way)

Difficulty Easy

Start Hermits Rest

Finish South Kaibab Trailhead

Nearest Town Grand Canyon Village

Transportation Shuttle

Summary The Rim Trail can be walked in its entirety in a day with stops at overlooks, or explored in short segments.

Stretching from Hermits Rest on the rim's western edge through Grand Canyon Village to South Kaibab Trailhead, the Rim Trail connects a series of overlooks and is hands-down the easiest long walk in the park. By no means a nature trail, the central leg includes the tourist hub of Grand Canyon Village, and long swaths are accessible by wheelchairs. It's paved for the 6.2 miles between Powell Point east to South Kaibab Trailhead, and for the 2.8 miles between Monument Creek Vista and Hermits Rest.

Flexibility is a big draw, with the shuttles making it simple to jump on for a segment and hike for as long as you like. Each of the 11 overlooks along the way is accessed by one of three shuttle routes, which means you can walk to a vista and shuttle back, or shuttle to a point, walk to the next and shuttle from there. A helpful map inside *The Guide* (given upon arrival and available at visitors centers) shows the shuttle stops and hiking distances along each segment of the trail, and each leg is clearly marked along the trail.

The trail passes many of the park's historical sights, including **El Tovar, Hopi House, Kolb Studio, Lookout Studio** and **Verkamp's Visitor Center**. The 3 miles or so that wind through the village are usually crowded with people, but the further west you venture, the more you'll break free. Out there the trail runs between Hermit Rd and the rim, and though some segments bump up against the road, you're typically alone to amble along the rim.

One very pretty and quiet stretch is the 3.7-mile leg from Powell Point to Pima Point. Heading west from **Powell Point**, the trail turns rocky, not suited to strollers, hugging the rim and offering incredible views and peaceful spots along the 0.5 miles to **Hopi Point**. Here, the canyon opens majestically to the west and down to the Colorado River. Continuing the 0.9 miles to **Mohave Point**, the trail passes a wonderful rim-side picnic table with expansive views and relative isolation, and from Mohave Point to the **Abyss** (1.1 miles) and on to **Monument Creek Vista** (0.9 miles) there are a couple more picnic-perfect tables. From Monument Creek, it's 1.7 miles to **Pima Point** and another 1.1 miles through piñon-juniper woodlands to **Hermits Rest**.

Heading east from Hermits Rest, it's just a few minutes' walk to a wide, wooden, rim-side bench, but it feels miles away from the swirling activity of Hermits Rest. About halfway between Hermits Rest and Pima, another bench offers panoramic views west down the Colorado, a perfect spot for a quiet sunset.

Above The Rim – Day Hikes

The 2.8 miles between Hermits Rest and Monument Creek Vista and the 1.9 miles just west of the South Kaibab Trailhead are part of the park's designated Greenway Trail. These wide, paved stretches can be enjoyed on bicycle; rent one at Bright Angel Bicycles (p69). Leashed pets are allowed on the entire trail.

🏃 Shoshone Point

Duration 40 minutes round-trip

Distance 2 miles round-trip

Difficulty Easy

Start/Finish Shoshone Point Trailhead

Nearest Town Grand Canyon Village

Transportation Car

Summary With an elevation change of only 50ft and a sandy trail through ponderosa forest, Shoshone Point puts solitude within easy reach.

The gentle and cool amble out to Shoshone Point, accessible only by foot, can be a welcome pocket of peace during the summer heat and crowds. This little-known hike is also ideal for children. Chances are you won't see another person, which means you can have the spectacular views all to yourself.

The walk starts from a dirt pullout along Desert View Dr, 1.2 miles east of Yaki Point or 6.3 miles west of Grandview Point. There's no official trailhead or signpost, so look for the dirt road barred by a closed and locked gate. The park service deliberately downplays this trail, and makes it available from May to October for weddings and other private events. If the parking lot is full of cars, refrain from hiking there, out of respect for any private events taking place. When it hasn't been reserved for a special gathering, and during winter months, hikers are welcome on the trail.

It's a fast and mostly flat out-and-back walk along the wide forested trail, which weaves through fragrant ponderosa pines before reaching a clearing. This is a great spot for a family gathering, as you'll find picnic tables, barbecue grills and portable toilets. Nearby Shoshone Point juts out into the canyon, offering magnificent views of the North Rim's full sweep. Unlike the other scenic points, there are no safety railings here. You can walk to the tip of the slender plateau and its Easter Island *moai*-like formation, where it feels almost possible to reach out and touch Zoroaster Temple rock formation.

Below the Rim

In winter and early spring the upper reaches of the Bright Angel, South Kaibab, Grandview and Hermit trails can be icy and dangerous. In the summer, temperatures easily soar above 100°F. Between mid-May and mid-September, it's recommended that you stay off interior canyon trails between 10am and 4pm. Plan to start hiking at first light (4:30am in summer, and 6:30am in spring and fall).

Even if you're heading into the canyon for just for a short day-hike, check weather conditions, bring plenty of water and hike smart.

🎒 Bright Angel Trail

A wide, well-maintained and popular corridor trail, Bright Angel winds 7.8 miles and 4460ft down from the rim to the Colorado River. Long day hikes, safe for September through May only, descend 4.6 miles to Indian Garden (a popular campground) and from there 1.5 miles along a spur trail to spectacular views at Plateau Point. Overnight hikers continue into the canyon from Indian Garden 3.1 miles to the River Trail, another 1.6 miles to Bright Angel Campground and a final 0.3 miles to Phantom Ranch.

In contrast to the steeper and shorter South Kaibab descent, Bright Angel offers shady resthouses with seasonal drinking water and stretches along a delightful creek. Note, however, that water-line breaks are becoming an increasing problem and drinking water may not be available. Check the bulletin board at the trailhead for current water availability along the trail.

The trailhead is on the Rim Trail in Grand Canyon Village, directly west of Kolb Studio and a two-minute walk from Bright Angel Lodge. Restrooms and a water-bottle filling station sit by the shuttle stop and parking lot.

ⓘ DRINKING WATER

Bottled water is not available at the Grand Canyon, but water-bottle filling stations can be found year-round throughout the rim, including Bright Angel and South Kaibab trailheads, Hermits Rest, Yavapai Geology Museum, El Tovar (in the basement) and outside Verkamp's. There is no water anywhere on the 7.8 miles of Rim Trail between Bright Angel Lodge Trailhead and Hermits Rest. Fill up before hitting the trail.

BRIGHT ANGEL TRAIL – SHORT DAY HIKE

Duration Mile-and-a-Half Resthouse 2–3 hours round-trip; Three-Mile Resthouse 4–5 hours round-trip

Distance 3 miles round-trip; 6 miles round-trip

Difficulty Moderate–difficult

Start/Finish Bright Angel Trailhead

Nearest Town Grand Canyon Village

Transportation Shuttle, car or foot

Summary Test out your canyon legs with a hike to two historic stone resthouses, where you can relax in the shade before returning to the rim.

Bright Angel Trailhead (6860ft) is both exhilarating and intimidating. The canyon unfolds before you in all its glory, hikers bustle around adjusting their backpacks, and wranglers acquaint first-time mule riders with the curious beasts.

The piñon-fringed trail quickly drops into some serious switchbacks as it follows a natural break in the cliffs of Kaibab limestone, the Toroweap formation and Coconino sandstone. Start slowly. If you suffer vertigo, look to the left for a while – the first five minutes are the hardest. Before you know it, you'll grow accustomed and the trail gets interesting.

The trail soon passes through two tunnels; look for the Native American pictographs on the walls of the first. Just after passing through the second tunnel you'll reach **Mile-and-a-Half Resthouse** (5720ft), about an hour from the trailhead. Anyone starting late or hiking for the first time should turn around here. It has restrooms, an emergency phone and drinking water from May to September.

Continuing downward through different-colored rock layers, more switchbacks finally deposit you at **Three-Mile Resthouse**, which has seasonal water and an emergency phone but no restrooms. Down below, you'll see the iridescent green tufts of Indian Garden, a campground 1.6 miles further, as well as the broad expanse of Tonto Platform, a nice visual reward before beginning the ascent back to the rim.

BRIGHT ANGEL TRAIL – LONG DAY HIKE

Duration Indian Garden 5–7 hours round-trip; Plateau Point 8–10 hours round-trip

Below The Rim – Day Hikes

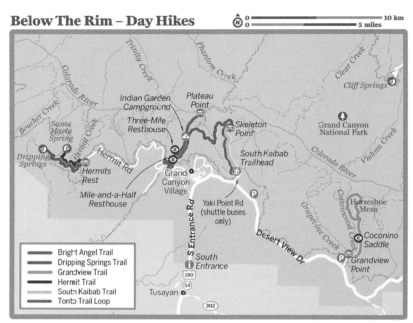

Distance 9.2 miles round-trip; 12.2 miles round-trip

Difficulty Difficult

Start/Finish Bright Angel Trailhead

Nearest Town Grand Canyon Village

Transportation Shuttle, car

Summary Continuing down the Bright Angel brings you to the shady oasis of Indian Garden; for a more challenging and very exposed hike to expansive views of the inner gorge, cross Tonto Platform along a spur trail to reach Plateau Point.

Follow the Short Day Hike and continue from Three-Mile Resthouse using the following hike description.

After Three-Mile Resthouse, you'll soon hit a grueling set of switchbacks known as **Jacob's Ladder**, which twist through Redwall limestone cliffs into the cool leafiness of **Indian Garden** (3760ft). Havasupai farmed here until a century ago, and these days it's a popular campground, with a ranger station, toilets, year-round drinking water, shaded picnic tables and a mule corral.

If this is your day-hike destination, linger in the soothing, albeit crowded, spot: eat lunch under a cottonwood, nap on the grass

and splash your feet in the creek. With an elevation gain of 3040ft, it's a hard and hot 4.6-mile climb back up to the rim – particularly the thigh-burning Jacob's Ladder. The round-trip takes about seven hours with a rest here.

From the campground, if you turn left and head west across Garden Creek, you'll soon reach the **Plateau Point Trail** junction, a spur off the Tonto Trail (a 95 mile inner-canyon trail that parallels the Colorado River). This ribbon of a trail unfurls north for just under a mile over the barren and yucca-studded **Tonto Plateau**, which is not as flat as it looks from above. The trail dead-ends at **Plateau Point** (3140ft below the rim) for a stunning view of the inner gorge.

Though Plateau Point is a popular destination for strong day hikers, do not make the round-trip trek from May through September. The long, exposed stretch can be searingly hot, with the 12.2-mile round-trip from the rim taking up to 12 hours.

South Kaibab Trail

Duration Ooh Aah Point 1–2 hours round-trip; Cedar Ridge 2–3 hours round-trip; Skeleton Point 6 hours round-trip

Distance 1.8 miles round-trip; 3 miles round-trip; 6 miles round-trip

Difficulty Moderate; moderate–difficult

Start/Finish South Kaibab Trailhead

Nearest Town Grand Canyon Village

Transportation Shuttle

Summary Unlike other interior-canyon trails, the South Kaibab follows a ridgeline rather than a side canyon, offering the park's most expansive views.

Blasted out of the rock by rangers in the mid 1920s, the steep, stark and sun-drenched South Kaibab offers unparalleled panoramic views and is one of the park's prettiest trails. The lack of shade and water, however, combined with the sheer grade and exposure to steep drop-offs make ascending the South Kaibab particularly dangerous in summer, and the trail sees a fair number of rescues. Take advantage of the Hikers' Express Shuttle to hit the trail at dawn.

From the South Kaibab Trailhead the trail starts out at a gentle decline, before spiraling steeply down to **Ooh Aah Point** (0.9 miles below the rim) and **Cedar Ridge** (1.5 miles and 1120ft below the rim). A dazzling spot, particularly at sunrise, Cedar Ridge is the turn-around point for summer day hikers. The ascent back up from here takes one to two hours. During the rest of the year, the continued trek to **Skeleton Point** (5200ft), 1.5 miles beyond Cedar Ridge, makes for a fine day hike, though the climb back up is a beast in any season.

For details on the 3 miles from the trailhead to Skeleton Point, as well as overnight hikes to Bright Angel Campground and Phantom Ranch, refer to the South Kaibab to Phantom Ranch walking tour (p66).

The trailhead, at the easternmost point of the Rim Trail, cannot be reached by private vehicle. You must ride either the Kaibab/Rim Route Shuttle or the early-morning Hikers' Express Bus. Alternatively, cycle along Desert View Dr and Yaki Rd or walk along the Rim Trail; it's about a 2-mile walk from the Visitor Center Plaza to the trailhead.

There are toilets and a water-bottle filling station at the trailhead.

🥾 Hermit Trail (to Santa Maria Spring)

Duration 3–4 hours round-trip

Distance 4 miles round-trip

Difficulty Moderate–difficult

Start/Finish Hermit Trailhead

Nearest Town Grand Canyon Village

Transportation Shuttle

Summary Unmaintained Hermit Trail (map p61) winds down into the often shady and usually unpopulated Hermit Canyon, connecting with several other trails to secluded canyon treks.

This wilderness trail descends into lovely Hermit Canyon. It's a rocky trip down, with some knee-wrenching switchbacks and long traverses that wend through the Supai cliffs. But if you set out early in the morning and take it slow, the Hermit offers a wonderfully serene day hike and glimpses into hidden corners.

In 1912 the Atchison, Topeka & Santa Fe Railway developed the trail for tourists to avoid tolls on the then privately controlled Bright Angel Trail. Mule trains ferried travelers to cushy Hermit Camp, which boasted a fancy stone cabin outfitted with a stove, glass windows, beds and wood floors adorned with Navajo rugs. Supplies arrived via tram from Pima Point.

The trail was eventually renamed in honor of Louis 'The Hermit' Boucher. When the NPS gained control of Bright Angel in 1928, luring away the mule tourism business, the Hermit was abandoned. Though officially untended since then, the trail is in remarkably good condition.

The best destination for day hikers is Santa Maria Spring. For a shorter but still worthwhile hike, turn around at the **Waldron Trail junction**, a round-trip of 2.6 miles with 1240ft of elevation change. The upper section of the Hermit is well shaded in the morning, making it a cool option in summer.

The rocky trail weaves down Hermit Basin toward Hermit Creek along a cobblestone route indented with steps and fraught with washouts. You'll reach the rarely used Waldron Trail (jutting off to the south) after about 1.3 miles, followed some 30 minutes later by the spur trail headed for Dripping Springs. The trail then traces over some flat rocks (a perfect picnic spot) before descending steeply to **Santa Maria Spring**, a cool, shady haven, marked by a pretty stone shelter adorned with green foliage and a wooden bench. The lush scene belies the spring, however, which is actually more of a trickle. You can drink the water provided you treat it.

The Hermit Trailhead is at Hermits Rest, 8 miles west of Grand Canyon Village. From March through September, private cars are not allowed on the road here and you must take the Hermits Rest Route Shuttle, walk the Rim Trail or cycle to the trailhead.

🕍 Dripping Springs Trail

Duration 5–7 hours round-trip

Distance 6.2 miles round-trip

Difficulty Moderate–difficult

Start/Finish Hermit Trailhead

Nearest Town Grand Canyon Village

Transportation Shuttle

Summary A great hike with an elevation change of 1040ft, Dripping Springs (map p61) is an isolated spur trail of Hermit Trail.

For the first 2 miles you are on the Hermit Trail. At the junction with the Dripping Springs Trail, turn left and head west along the narrow path as it climbs and meanders along the slope's contours. After 1 mile you'll hit the junction with the Boucher Trail; turn left here to continue following the Dripping Springs Trail as it winds up toward the water source, which sprouts from an overhang not far beneath the rim. Droplets shower down from the sandstone ceiling, misting myriad maidenhair ferns.

🕍 Grandview Trail

Duration Coconino Saddle 2–4 hours round-trip; Horseshoe Mesa 4–8 hours round-trip

Distance 2.2 miles round-trip; 6.2 miles round-trip

Difficulty Difficult

Start/Finish Grandview Trailhead (Grandview Point)

Nearest Town Grand Canyon Village

Transportation Car

Summary The unmaintained Grandview (map p61) plummets about 2600ft over 3.1 miles from the rim to Grandview Mesa.

One of the steepest trails in the park – dropping 1200ft in the first 0.75 miles – Grandview is also one of the finest day hikes. The payoff following the stunning (and grueling) descent is an up-close look at one of the inner canyon's sagebrush-tufted mesas and a wonderful sense of solitude. The trail spirals down to a sprawling horseshoe-shaped mesa, where Hopi people once collected minerals.

In 1892 miner Pete Berry improved the former Native American route and constructed the current trail to access his Last Chance Mine at Horseshoe Mesa. For the next 15 years mules carted high-grade copper from there to the rim, even after Berry established his Grand View Hotel in 1897 and guided mule tours into the canyon.

Because there is no water on the very exposed trail, and the climb out is a doozy, do not day-hike to Horseshoe Mesa in the summer. Instead, hike to Coconino Saddle and turn around there. Though it's only a 1.5-mile round-trip, it packs a quick and precipitous punch as you plunge 1600ft over about 1 mile. With the exception of a few short level sections, the Grandview is a rugged, narrow and rocky trail, and the steep drop-offs can be a bit scary. This is not a good choice for those skittish of heights.

Steep from the start, the trail first winds down the north end of Grandview Point, passing through Kaibab limestone along cobbled and cliff-edged rock stairs fringed with occasional flowers like fiery orange Indian paintbrush, straw-yellow arnica and blue delphinium. The views from the trailhead and just below are extraordinary, so even if you don't plan to hike, do walk down the trail a short way to take in the vistas. After about 30 minutes, you'll reach the **Coconino Saddle**, where the trail crosses the slender spur between Hance and Grapevine Canyons.

The saddle is a stunning overlook and a nice leafy spot for a snack and a rest in the shade. From here the trail is more exposed and eventually narrows to a ribbon as it traverses the ruddy Supai sandstone. A little over 2 miles past Coconino you'll hit a second saddle, connecting to **Horseshoe Mesa**, then a short dip later you reach pit toilets and remnants of an old miners' camp cookhouse. There are traces of mining all over the mesa, from the speckled soil to old machinery and mine shafts. Although the many hollowed-out caves may look enticing, it's forbidden, not to mention very dangerous, to enter them.

The trailhead is at Grandview Point, 12 miles east of the village on Desert View Dr, with year-round parking.

🕍 Tonto Trail: Down South Kaibab, up Bright Angel

Duration 7–9 hours one-way

Distance 13.1 miles one-way

Difficulty Very difficult

Start South Kaibab Trailhead

Finish Bright Angel Trailhead

Nearest Town Grand Canyon Village

Transportation Shuttle

Summary A stellar choice for strong hikers seeking solitude, this full-day excursion links two popular corridor trails along a peaceful, winding section of the Tonto Trail (map p61) – but time it right to avoid charring your epidermis and brain. Distance and duration given for this hike are from start to finish; the hike description, however, details only the section linking the South Kaibab and Bright Angel trails.

This 4.1-mile section of the Tonto linking the South Kaibab and Bright Angel trails jumps up and down as it follows the contours and canyon faults. The segment described here – from the Tipoff on South Kaibab to Indian Garden on Bright Angel – is considered the central portion and is officially referred to as the Tonto Trail.

From the South Kaibab Trailhead it's a bone-jarring, hot 4.4-mile descent beyond Skeleton Point to the Tonto Trail junction, dropping 3260ft in elevation to the edge of the Tonto Platform. Just past the junction there's an emergency telephone and a toilet, a final reminder you're about to set foot on wilder terrain.

Heading west on the Tonto, you'll hug the contours as the trail crosses the agave-dotted plateau and darts in and out of gulches. Deep in a canyon fold, the trail skirts through a canopy of cottonwoods near a drainage; just past here on the left is a terrific spot for camping.

The trail remains in shade through mid-morning. As the day progresses, however, the Tonto bakes and the surrounding landscape is completely parched – you don't want to be caught here at midday, so it's imperative you time your start accordingly.

After about two hours you'll stumble into lush **Indian Garden**, the perfect shady oasis for cooling off before the 4.6-mile haul up to the rim (or, with advanced reservation and a backcountry permit, you can camp at Indian Garden).

Though technically a day hike, this is a long, difficult backcountry haul that is not suited for summer, regardless of skill-level or experience.

🏃 OVERNIGHT HIKES

Overnight stays in the canyon require an advanced reservation at Phantom Ranch or a backcountry permit for camping. If you didn't secure a permit in advance, swing by the Backcountry Information Center (p89) behind Maswik Lodge; if one is not available, you'll be put on a wait-list and you must return at 8am daily until you snag one. Typically, it's a few days' wait. Contact the Bright Angel Transportation Desk (p89) for last-minute reservations at Phantom Ranch – it takes reservations 13 months in advance, and books out within days, but if you're lucky there will be a cancellation.

There are no overnight hikes above the rim.

Below the Rim

🏃 Rim to Rim

Duration 2–3 days one-way

Distance 21 miles one-way

Difficulty Difficult

Start South Kaibab Trailhead (South Rim)

Finish North Kaibab Trailhead (North Rim)

Nearest Town Grand Canyon Village

Transportation Shuttle, car

Summary Descend 6.9 miles along the panoramic ridge of the South Kaibab, sleep in the canyon depths and climb 14 miles back out the canyon to the North Rim.

The three-day South Kaibab to North Kaibab trek is the classic Grand Canyon rim-to-rim hike and one of the finest trips in the

> ℹ If hiking the two- or three-day Rim-to-Rim, you need to make advanced reservations for the 4½-hour shuttle return to your starting point, and it can be stressful to huff it out of the canyon when you know you have to be on the rim in time to catch your ride. Avoid this stress by beginning your Rim-to-Rim with a shuttle (p236) to the North Rim – spend the night before your descent at the lodge or campground there, and emerge from the canyon to your starting point at your leisure.

canyon. For those hikers beginning on the South Rim, most descend the South Kaibab 6.9 miles and across the Colorado River to **Bright Angel Campground** (or another 0.3 up to **Phantom Ranch**). From Bright Angel Campground, it's 7.2 miles up the North Kaibab to **Cottonwood Campground** for the second night, and a final 6.8-mile climb up to the North Rim, 1000ft higher in elevation than the South Rim.

Alternatively, descend from the South Rim 9.3 miles to Phantom Ranch along the Bright Angel Trail, or begin the hike from the North Rim. Because the climb up the South Kaibab is the hottest and most exposed in the park, it's best to ascend via the Bright Angel Trail when hiking from north to south.

For details on hiking down the South Kaibab and up Bright Angel, see the walking tour on p66; and p144 for North Kaibab.

You'll need a backcountry permit to camp below the rim (or, if you plan on hiking down one day and out the second, reservations at Phantom Ranch, p84) and will need to arrange a ride back to your starting point. Between mid-May and mid-October, the nifty Trans-Canyon Shuttle (p236) departs twice daily (7am and 2pm) from Grand Canyon Lodge (p148) on the North Rim for the 4½-hour drive to the South Rim. From South Rim to North Rim, it departs Bright Angel Lodge at 8am and 1:30pm; there is only one shuttle daily, weather permitting, from mid-October through November 30. They also offer private custom shuttle services, as does Flagstaff Shuttle & Charter (p92).

Think through your schedule carefully. If you emerge from the canyon without a pre-arranged, same-day shuttle pick-up, you'll need a place to spend the night, and the only accommodations on the North Rim is Grand Canyon Lodge or the North Rim Campground (p232). Kaibab Lodge (p154), about 16 miles away from the North Rim, is the closest alternative, and they offer shuttle pick-up at the North Kaibab Trailhead.

Facilities on the North Rim are closed between mid-October and mid-May, and the weather is unpredictable – you could leave warm, sunny skies on the South Rim and walk into a blizzard on the North Rim. There is a year-round ranger station that can provide shelter if you turn left at the North Kaibab Trailhead and walk about a mile, but if you turn right at the trailhead, you will encounter a whole lotta nothing for 43 miles.

There is no public transportation from the North Kaibab Trailhead to Grand Canyon Lodge (12 miles) and cell phone service is unreliable.

Hermit Trail to Hermit Camp and Hermit Rapid

Duration 2 days round-trip

Distance 15.4 miles round-trip (to Hermit Camp); 18.4 miles round-trip (to Hermit Rapid)

Difficulty Difficult

Start/Finish Hermit Trailhead

Nearest Town Grand Canyon Village

Transportation Shuttle, car

Summary Tracing the path of the Hermit, this steep but rewarding out-and-back hike leads to a backcountry campground on the site of one of the park's earliest tourist accommodations.

DAY 1: HERMIT TRAILHEAD TO HERMIT CAMP
4–6 HOURS / 7.7 MILES

From the Hermit Trailhead, a steep, rocky path descends 2 miles to **Santa Maria Spring** (p62), a lovely day hike. Backpackers continue past the spring as the trail levels

Hermit Trail
0 ——— 1 km
0 ——— 0.5 miles

Overnight Hike
South Kaibab Ranch to Phantom Ranch, up Bright Angel

START SOUTH KAIBAB TRAILHEAD
END BRIGHT ANGEL TRAILHEAD
LENGTH 19.5 MILES

If you only have time to spend one night in the canyon, or you want to start and finish on the South Rim, this hike is an ideal choice. It's 6.9 miles down the South Kaibab to Bright Angel Campground, just beyond the Colorado River, and 9.3 miles back up along Bright Angel. Phantom Ranch sits 0.3 miles beyond Bright Angel Campground. Reserve a tent site or ranch accommodation up to 13 months in advance of your descent.

From the mule corral by the South Kaibab Trailhead (7000ft) the trail starts out deceptively gentle, with a long, well-graded switchback that leads to the end of a promontory about 20 minutes from the top. Here the cliff-hugging trail opens up to **1** **Ooh Aah Point**, a shaggy promontory, which juts off the elbow of a switchback and offers a sweeping panorama of the purplish Tonto Platform far below. The ledge is a nice spot for rest and refreshment.

Soon after, things turn serious, as the trail takes a sharp nosedive and begins to zigzag down a series of steep, tight switchbacks, making its way down the red sandstone. After about 30 minutes, the trail straightens out some when it hits the gorgeous Cedar Mesa and its namesake **2** **Cedar Ridge** (6060ft), a striking red-tinged mesa. Stop long enough for a snack and perhaps a visit to the pit toilet, and linger to enjoy the lovely vast views of Bright Angel Canyon, Devil's Corkscrew and the North Rim.

The trail then meanders off the mesa toward O'Neill Butte, wraps around to the east, then levels out onto another plateau known as **3** **Skeleton Point** (5200ft), where you can enjoy views of the Colorado River while you refuel with a snack. From here, the trail continues its precipitous drop over scree and through the Redwall cliffs, eventually opening up onto the Tonto Platform.

Traverse the agave-studded plateau past the Tonto Trail junction, then take a long pause and a deep breath at the **4** **Tipoff**

(3870ft), which provides an emergency phone and pit toilet, and marks the beginning of the steep descent into the inner gorge. After hiking another challenging 1.5 miles and drinking in pretty views of Phantom Ranch, you'll reach the intersection of the River Trail, which skirts the south side of the Colorado River and connects up with the Bright Angel Trail. Soon you'll go through a short tunnel and cross the river via the skinny black **5** **Kaibab Suspension Bridge**, built in 1928 by the NPS and spanning 440ft across the Colorado.

At the other side of the river, turn left past an ancient Puebloan dwelling (do not enter the site), Boat Beach below and the grave of Rees B Griffiths, who died building the Tipoff, and head less than a mile to the intersection with the River Trail. Here you'll find drinking water, a restroom and a ranger station (circa 1934) now used as a residence. Follow Bright Angel Creek north a few minutes to **6** **Bright Angel Campground**, and just past that is **7** **Phantom Ranch**. Designed by Mary Colter in 1922, the lovely stone lodge is the only developed facility in the inner canyon. Riders heading into the canyon on mules, as well as hikers with advanced reservations, spend the night at Phantom Ranch, and the canteen here is welcomed air-conditioned bliss. Relax over a beer and board games, or kick back in the cool, clear waters of Bright Angel Creek.

From May through September, you'll want to start the return to the rim at dawn to avoid hiking in the searing sun. It's 9.6 miles from the ranch to the South Rim via Bright Angel. Cross the Colorado River on the **8** **Silver Bridge**, and take the River Trail just over 1 mile to Bright Angel Trail; from here, the 7.7-mile ascent takes between six and nine hours.

The River Trail's desert vegetation and slogging sand soon give way to willows and cottonwoods as the trail follows loosely along Pipe Creek, and then begins the grueling and exposed switchbacks of **9** **Devil's Corkscrew**. As the name implies, this is one of the most daunting stretches – the trail winds up and up 1000ft through the desert landscape

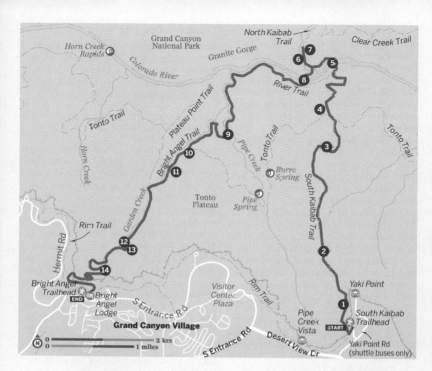

of the Vishnu schist, ending in another sweet sigh of riparian landscape surrounding Garden Creek.

In about 30 minutes, the trail passes through **10 Tapeats Narrows**. Here, where the Vishnu schist meets the Tapeats, the rocks sit atop one another like a pile of flapjacks. Continuing up the canyon, you soon arrive at **11 Indian Garden Campground** (3760ft), 5 miles from Phantom Ranch, where you'll find water, toilets, a ranger station and a popular campground. Provided you have planned ahead, you could break up your climb from Bright Angel Campground (or Phantom Ranch) to the South Rim with a night here. It's a popular and lovely spot, with plenty of shade and the cool waters of Garden Creek.

You'll want to relax and refuel at Indian Garden, as the final stretch to the rim is a doozy. The trail stretches 1.6 miles through the upper Tonto Platform to **12 Jacob's Ladder**, another set of grueling switchbacks, and through the distinctive Redwall Limestone to the stone **13 Three-Mile Resthouse**. From May through September, there is drinking water, but because of increasingly frequent waterline breaks it's best not to depend on it. Wander behind the building to take in the view out over the Redwall to Indian Garden and Plateau Point.

The **14 Mile-and-a-Half Resthouse**, 1.5 miles later, offers another welcome respite in the cool of the 1936 stone cottage, as well as seasonal water and compost toilets, before the final 1.5 miles to the South Rim. You'll pass under two tunnels – at the second one, look to the right for Native American pictographs painted onto the canyon wall.

Upon emerging on the bustling rim, take a moment to congratulate yourself, and head left to El Tovar for a well-deserved beer and bison chile on the rim-side patio.

for a mile or so before zigzagging over loose rocks. Note that the Hermit Trail hasn't seen a maintenance crew in over 80 years, and it's showing signs of the same erosion that created the canyon. The Supai section of the trail (just below Santa Maria Spring) has deteriorated to the point where hikers will need to scramble over rocks and it can be difficult to find the trail.

Soon after descending the Redwall via a series of extremely steep, compressed switchbacks known as the Cathedral Stairs (keep an eye out for fossils in the bottom sections of this formation), the Hermit eventually hits the cross-canyon Tonto Trail (6.4 miles from the trailhead, at 3210ft).

Turn left (west) to merge with the Tonto; in 1 mile you'll reach the stone remnants of the old Hermit Camp (2800ft), one of the original Fred Harvey tent accommodations. Just beyond the ruins, the cliff-rimmed backcountry campground (with pit toilets and seasonal water) makes a glorious place to sleep.

From the campground it's another 1.5 miles to the Colorado River, which you can reach by following your nose down the creek right from the campground; alternatively, the river is a bit closer if you turn down Hermit Creek just before Hermit Camp.

Down at the river, the canyon walls are exquisite black Vishnu schist shot through with veins of pink Zoroaster granite. Hermit Rapids, a major Colorado River rapid, marks the confluence of Hermit Creek and the Colorado. There's a backcountry campground, but no facilities.

DAY 2: HERMIT CAMP TO HERMIT TRAILHEAD
6–8 HOURS / 7.7 MILES

To return to Hermits Rest, retrace your steps for the arduous climb back to the trailhead. For a longer wilderness excursion, with advanced backcountry permits, you can pick up the eastbound Tonto and intercept the Bright Angel.

🦌 Tonto Trail: Down the Hermit Trail, Up Bright Angel

Duration 3–4 days one-way

Distance 26.9 miles one-way

Difficulty Difficult

Start Hermit Trailhead

Finish Bright Angel Trailhead

Nearest Town Grand Canyon Village

Transportation Shuttle

Summary For experienced canyon hikers, this stunning trek may require some route finding – particularly along the undulating and unmaintained Tonto – but you'll find plenty of backcountry camping spots.

DAY 1: HERMIT TRAILHEAD TO MONUMENT CREEK
5–7 HOURS / 9.3 MILES

Descend the Hermit Trail 4.4 miles past Santa Maria Spring (p62), and turn right at the Tonto Trail junction for the 14.5-mile eastbound passage to the Bright Angel Trail. From the junction it's just over 4 miles to Monument Creek (3640ft below the rim), providing water and designated trail-side campsites. Alternatively, you can spend the first night at Hermit Camp Campground, (p65) just over a mile beyond the junction, then backtrack to embark on the Tonto your second morning. Do not hike the Tonto without securing an NPS map and guide.

For a side trip, head 2 miles down the drainage to Granite Rapids, one of the bigger rapids on the Colorado and a designated backcountry campsite.

DAY 2: MONUMENT CREEK TO INDIAN GARDEN
4–6 HOURS / 10.7 MILES

The Tonto snakes along the contour with a mild elevation change of 600ft, reaching Cedar Spring after 1.3 miles and Salt Creek in another 30 minutes; both are approved for backcountry camping. From there it's just under 5 miles to Horn Creek – don't even think about drinking the water here (even after filtering it), as it's been found to be highly radioactive. You can backcountry camp at Horn Creek, but in under an hour you'll be at verdant Indian Garden (p84), a popular corridor campground with treated water available year-round and a ranger station.

DAY 3: INDIAN GARDEN TO BRIGHT ANGEL TRAILHEAD
3–5 HOURS / 4.6 MILES

Load up on water at the campground before beginning the hot grind on the Bright Angel 4.6 miles back to the South Rim. The trail meanders along Garden Creek for a couple of miles, and two resthouses between the campground and the rim provide drinking water from June through August. Get a very early start so that you're still in the shade for the grueling Jacob's Ladder switchbacks.

CYCLING

Bicycles are allowed on paved roads and the Greenway Trail only.

Hermit Rd offers a scenic ride west from Grand Canyon Village to Hermits Rest, about a 16-mile round-trip from the village. Shuttles are not permitted to pass cyclists, so you'll have to pull over each time one drives by, but the road is closed to cars from March through November and shuttles only run every 15 minutes or so. Hermit Rd shuttles are equipped to carry up to three bicycles, making it possible to cycle one way, and catch a shuttle for the other, or to simply hop on at any of the nine shuttle stops anytime you get tired.

Alternatively, you could ride out to the East Entrance along Desert View Dr, a 50-mile round-trip from the village.

For details on sights along the way, see Hermit Road (p72) and Desert View Drive (p70) driving tours.

Bright Angel Bicycles & Cafe at Mather Point   BICYCLE RENTAL
(Map p76; ☎928-814-8704, 928-638-3055; www.bikegrandcanyon.com; Visitor Center Plaza, Grand Canyon Village; 24hr rental adult/child under 16yr $40/30, 5hr rental $30/20, wheelchair $10, single/double stroller up to 8hrs $18/27; ☺Apr-Nov; 🚐Village, 🚐Kaibab/Rim) Half-or full-day bicycle rentals, with helmets and add-on pull-along trailer option, can be reserved in advance online or by phone; with the exception of the peak stretch from July through mid-August, however, walk-ins can usually be accommodated. Hermit Rd bicycle/shuttle packages allow you to ride past overlooks one way, and hop on one of their private shuttles the other.

On the one-way package (adult/child $37/25; 10.5 miles, five to seven hours), you ride from the rental shop west through busy Grand Canyon Village, on Hermit Rd to Monument Creek Vista, and finally along the multi-use Greenway Trail to Hermits Rest. From there, a shuttle returns you to the Visitor Center Complex. The round-trip package (adult/child $34/23; 5.5 miles, two hours) includes a shuttle from the shop straight to Hopi Point, allowing you to focus your time and energy on the most beautiful stretch and to avoid cycling through the village and the uphill leg.

For folks with limited time or small children, the Orange Route is a moderate ride that heads west on a 7-mile round-trip from Bright Angel Bicycles to the South Kaibab Trailhead and Yaki Point. It's a lovely winding cruise through the piñon, past some canyon-view picnic spots and spectacular overlooks. The only traffic is the short stretch of Yaki Rd shuttles.

Guided tours of Yaki Point (adult/child $48/38) or Hermit Rd ($58/45) are offered multiple times daily.

Greenway Trail   CYCLING
(http://www.nps.gov/grca) A multi-use trail open to cyclists and hikers. From Monument Creek Vista 2.8 miles west to Hermits Rest and from Visitor Center Plaza 1.9 miles east to the South Kaibab Trailhead, the Greenway Trail and the Rim Trail are the same thing. These stretches wind gently through piñon-dotted landscape and offer several lovely trail-side picnic spots.

You can also ride along the Greenway Trail from Visitor Center Plaza 6.6 miles south to the IMAX in Tusayan, but note that the final 4 miles are not paved.

HERMITS REST

The railway commissioned Mary Colter to design a resthouse on the canyon rim and in 1913 completed the 8.5-mile trail from the rim down to Hermit Camp. A predecessor to Phantom Ranch 10 years later, Hermit Camp, which closed in 1930, offered intrepid travelers tent cabins, restrooms, showers and meals cooked by a Fred Harvey chef. Colter's Hermits Rest, a beautiful stone and wood shelter, gave tourists a place to freshen up before descending by mule into the canyon or after the arduous journey back to the rim.

Today, Hermits Rest features a small gift shop and snack bar, and you can still hike Hermit Trail to the remnants of Louis Boucher's home and ranch. Somewhat ironically, given the crowds here, the flat rocks just a few steps down from the trailhead make one of the most peaceful and easily accessible spots in the South Rim to pause in the silence of the canyon wind.

🚗 DRIVING

Two scenic drives follow the contour of the rim on either side of the village: Hermit Rd to the west and Desert View Dr to the east. The canyon dips in and out of view as the road passes through the piñon-juniper and ponderosa stands of Kaibab National Forest. Pullouts along the way offer spectacular views and interpretive signs that explain the canyon's history and geology.

Millions of visitors drive up, jump out of their cars and snap a photo – but photos don't do justice to the vastness of this place. The marvel of the canyon is in the sounds and smells, the silence of the wind, the dust, the emptiness that a photograph can never reveal. Especially along Hermit Rd, where the Rim Trail stretches between the rim and the road, you can easily wander east or west from any given overlook and find silence and solitude within minutes.

You might expect bumper-to-bumper traffic, but this is generally not the case. Yes, there's a constant stream of cars, but you'll rarely come to a standstill and can usually find plenty of parking at the viewpoints. The road to Yaki Point and the South Kaibab Trailhead is closed year-round to all traffic except bicycles and the Kaibab/Rim Route Shuttle. From March 1 to November 30, Hermit Rd is closed to all traffic except bicycles and the Hermits Rest Route Shuttle. Both scenic drives may close due to snow or ice buildup from November through March; call ☎928-638-7888 for current road and weather conditions.

Bus tours (p74) offering scenic drives leave several times daily year-round. Bicycles are allowed on both Hermit Rd and Desert View Dr; Bright Angel Bicycles (p69) offers cycle rental with private shuttle service and tours.

There is no public transportation to Desert View overlooks east of Pipe Creek Vista.

The Grand Canyon Association Park Store at Visitor Center Plaza (p87) sells an audio guide with more information on what you'll see along the rim. Some overlooks offer good river views, while others are best for sunrises or sunsets.

🚗 Driving Tour
Desert View Drive

START GRAND CANYON VILLAGE (VISITOR CENTER PLAZA)
END DESERT VIEW (EAST ENTRANCE)
LENGTH 25 MILES; FOUR HOURS

Desert View Dr winds through the desert woodlands past several panoramic overlooks and a Native American ruin on its way to the 1932 Mary Colter classic, the stone Watchtower. A leisurely drive, with plenty of time for every stop, takes about four hours, but you could zip along in much less. Desert View Dr could also make an excellent one-way bike ride if you can be dropped off or picked up at one end, or if you don't mind the 50-mile round-trip. There is parking at every stop, six designated picnic areas along the road and bathrooms at Grandview Point, Tusayan Museum & Ruin, and Desert View.

As it sits beside the Grand Canyon Visitor Center parking lot (300 yards away), **❶ Mather Point** can be the most crowded of all the viewpoints. However, its roomy overlooks extend to two promontories that jut out over the canyon, providing views of the Bright Angel and South Kaibab trails ribboning down into the canyon. From here, it's a short drive or 1.3-mile walk along the Rim Trail east to **❷ Pipe Creek Vista**. Views from this overlook take in Brahma Temple and O'Neill Butte, as well as Pipe Creek, naturally, and it tends to be less of a traffic circus than Mather Point. From Pipe Creek you can catch a Kaibab/Rim Route Shuttle back to your car at the Visitor Center Plaza to continue the tour, or continue east.

If you don't see many cars as you drive by the unsigned **❸ Shoshone Point Trailhead**, make time for the wonderful 1-mile walk along a dirt road to this peaceful picnic spot and viewpoint. It's a mostly flat stroll, and the overlook is one of the quietest and best on the South Rim.

They didn't call the next overlook **❹ Grandview Point** for nothing. Peter Berry (another prospector-turned-entrepreneur) and his partners built the Grandview Toll Trail in 1893 to access copper claims more than 2000ft below on Horseshoe Mesa. In 1897 he built the

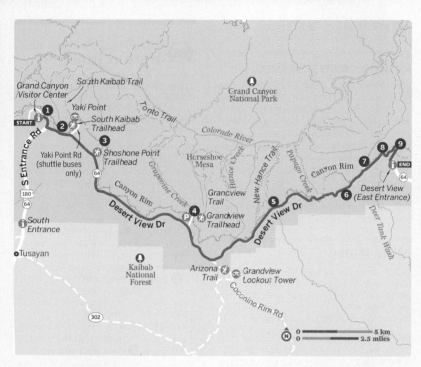

Grandview Hotel here on the rim, and when he wasn't hauling copper, he led tourists into the canyon on foot and by mule. When the railroad arrived 13 miles west of here in 1901, tourists naturally gravitated toward those facilities, forcing Berry to close up shop in 1908. Today thousands make a steep descent into the canyon via Berry's Grandview Trail, while others enjoy impressive canyon views from the spot where his hotel once thrived.

The oft-visited ⑤ **Moran Point** is named after Thomas Moran, the landscape painter who spent just about every winter at the canyon from 1899 to 1920 and whose romantically dramatic work was instrumental in securing the canyon's national-park status. From here you can see down the river in both directions, and peer onto the reddish-orange Hakatai shale of Red Canyon below. A few miles past Moran Point is ⑥ **Tusayan Museum & Ruin** (p79).

One of the most spectacular viewpoints on the South Rim, ⑦ **Lipan Point** gives a panoramic eyeful of the canyon and makes a magnificent spot to watch the sunset. From here, you'll get an unobstructed view of Un-kar Rapid just to the west; to the northeast,

the sheer cliffs called the Palisades of the Desert define the southeastern wall of the Grand Canyon, beyond which the Echo and Vermilion Cliffs lie in the distance.

The Escalante and Cardenas Buttes are the immediate features that you'll see from ⑧ **Navajo Point** (7498ft), beyond which you'll get good views of several miles of the Colorado River. Finish your drive at ⑨ **Desert View Watchtower**, where you'll want to take the time to climb up the winding staircase to the highest point in the South Rim. On the way up from the gift shop, look for an unmarked door on the left; you can wander outside onto a rooftop terrace here, and it makes a nice spot to relax with a drink and a sandwich.

Outside the Watchtower, a bronze plaque marks the spot as a National Historic Landmark. Just below the rim is the site of the 1956 TWA plane crash that killed 128 people and marked the beginning of modern regulations in air safety.

Exit the park at the East Entrance or retrace your steps back to Grand Canyon Village.

OTHER ACTIVITIES

Cross-country Skiing

From November through March, depending on snowfall, the surrounding national forest offers several trails for cross-country skiing and snowshoeing, and there's a groomed cross-country skiing loop 0.3 miles north of the Grandview Lookout Tower (p92). Contact the **Tusayan Ranger Station** (☑928-638-2443; www.fs.usda.gov/kaibab) for current information. You can rent skis from Peace Surplus (p108) in Flagstaff, where you'll also find plenty of cross-country and downhill trails and the Flagstaff Nordic Center (p102).

Mule Rides

Mosey into the canyon the way tourists traveled a century ago, on the back of a sure-footed mule. Overnight mule trips into the canyon depart every day of the year from the corral west of Bright Angel Lodge.

Grand Canyon Mule Rides GUIDED TOUR
(☑888-297-2757, same day/next day reservations 928-638-3283; www.grandcanyonlodges.com; Bright Angel Lodge; 3hr mule ride $120, 1-/2-night mule ride inc meals and accommodation $533/758; ☺rides available year-round, hours vary; ♿) The **Canyon Vistas Mule Ride** takes groups of up to 20 mules 4 miles along the East Rim Trail. If you want to descend into the canyon, the only option is an overnight trip to Phantom Ranch. These trips follow the Bright Angel Trail 10.5 miles (5½ hours) down, spend one or two nights in Phantom Ranch, and return 7.8 miles (five hours) along the South Kaibab Trail.

Reservations can be made up to 13 months in advance. If rides are booked, and they often fill up within weeks of availability, call or show up at the Bright Angel Transportation Desk (p89) no earlier than 5am on the day before you want to ride and put your name on a waiting list. On the day of the ride, you must show up at the transportation desk at 7am, and if there are any no-shows they will accept those on the waiting list. Check the website for age and weight restrictions.

Driving Tour
Hermit Road

START GRAND CANYON VILLAGE
(BRIGHT ANGEL TRAILHEAD)
END HERMITS REST
LENGTH 7 MILES

Hermit Rd is closed to private vehicles from March through November, but the Hermits Rest Route Shuttle will take you to all the sites detailed here; alternatively, the western 7.8-mile leg of the Rim Trail parallels Hermit Rd, so you can walk from overlook to overlook and hop on the shuttle whenever you'd like. This drive also makes a great bike ride. Cycle along Hermit Rd to Monument Creek Vista, and ride the Greenway Trail from there 2.8 miles to Hermits Rest.

❶ **Trailview Overlook** offers a great view of Bright Angel Trail, the lush vegetation at Indian Garden and Grand Canyon Village on the rim to the east.

In 1890 prospector Daniel Lorain Hogan discovered what he believed to be copper 1100ft below ❷ **Maricopa Point**. He filed a mining claim for the area, including 4 acres on the rim, and set about making his fortune. After more than 40 years of minimal success, Hogan realized that the real money at the canyon was in tourism, so in 1936 he built tourist cabins, a trading post and a saloon on the rim. In 1947 he sold the property to Madelaine Jacobs for $25,000.

Ironically, it was Jacobs who would make her fortune off mining interests here. Learning that the gray rock Hogan had ignored in his quest for copper was rich in uranium, she sold out to Western Gold & Uranium. During the height of the atomic era, in the 1950s and 1960s, the Orphan Mine just southwest of this point was one of country's most prolific producers of uranium. Tourists still visited the point during the mining, though the experience must have been somewhat marred by the noise and radioactive dust.

Perched at Powell Point, the ❸ **Powell Memorial** was erected in 1915 in honor of John Wesley Powell, the intrepid one-armed Civil War veteran, ethnologist and geologist who led the first run through the canyon on the Colorado in 1869. The park was officially dedicated here in 1920. The monument makes a dramatic spot to pause and consider the massive chasm as

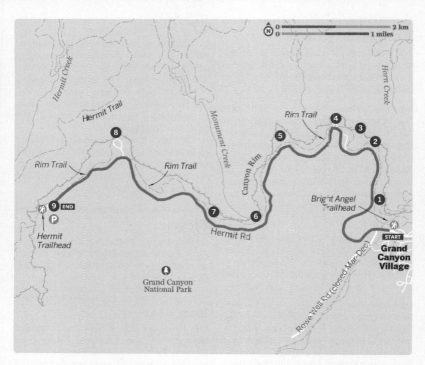

it may have appeared to Powell way back before the canyon became a tourist destination.

One of the park's best viewpoints, **4 Hopi Point** juts out further than any other overlook along Hermit Rd and offers huge, spectacular views of plateau upon plateau and the Colorado River a mile below. Notable canyon features here include the Isis and Osiris Temples. Until the completion of Hermit Rd in 1912, Hopi Point was the westernmost spot on guided tours. Nowadays, it's a popular place to watch the sunset and is often crowded on summer evenings. If you're here during shuttle season, walking the 0.3-mile segment of the Rim Trail between Powell Point and Hopi Point is a pleasant alternative to the bus.

5 Mohave Point offers cliff views in all directions. It's also a particularly good place to see the Colorado, as three rapids – Salt Creek, Granite and Hermit – are visible below.

Aptly named, the **6 Abyss** is a beautiful example of how steep some canyon drop-offs can be. If you're acrophobic, consider stopping at a different viewpoint – sheer cliffs drop 2600ft to the Redwall limestone below. If heights don't bother you, walk about a quarter-mile westward along the Rim Trail and (carefully) check out the dizzying drop. The next overlook, **7 Monument Creek Vista**, marks the beginning of the

paved Greenway Trail; from here 2.8 miles west to the road's end, there are five overlooks and a handful of picnic tables that are not accessible by car or shuttle.

From **8 Pima Point** you can see for miles to the west, north and east, and it's one of the best places to view the Colorado River. In 1912 the Atchison, Topeka & Santa Fe Railway completed Hermit Camp, a tourist hub 3000ft below Pima Point, accessible from a trailhead at Hermits Rest. The camp was a popular mule-train destination, and a 6300ft tramway was built in 1925 to transport supplies. By 1930, tourists favored Phantom Ranch, and Hermit Camp was abandoned. In 1936 the railway intentionally torched the camp; the remains are visible from the rim.

9 Hermits Rest (p69) is named after Louis Boucher, who came to the canyon from Canada in 1891 with hopes of finding his fortune as a prospector. He lived at Dripping Springs, several miles below the rim, and offered tourists guided trips to his home there. He never did strike it rich, and after 20 years he sold the upper portions of his trail to the Santa Fe Railroad and Fred Harvey Company, and moved to Utah.

Look for the picnic grounds and trailhead just beyond the the snack bar.

Ranger Programs

The Guide provides a schedule of current ranger programs, including Junior Ranger Programs designed specifically for children, and details on evening events.

Into the Canyon Hike
HIKING

(www.nps.gov/grca; Grand Canyon Village; ☉7am Tue, Thu, Sat, Sun Jun-Aug) **FREE** The most strenuous ranger talk on the South Rim involves a challenging 3-mile hike (three to four hours round-trip) 1120ft below the rim on the South Kaibab Trail. While you can take this trail by yourself, the ranger will explain canyon geology and history as you hike.

Rim View Walk
HIKING

(Map p76; www.nps.gov/grca; Grand Canyon Village; ☉8:30am Mon, Wed & Fri Jun-Aug) **FREE** Two-hour walk along a paved 2-mile section of the Rim Trail examines the natural history and contemporary Grand Canyon issues.

Fossil Discovery Walk
HIKING

(Map p76; www.nps.gov/grca; Grand Canyon Village; ☉9:30am Jun-Aug) **FREE** An easy 0.2-mile, one-way, ranger-led walk to exposed fossil beds along the rim, a particularly nice activity if you plan on hiking into the canyon from Hermits Rest and great for kids. If you attend the ranger talk, you'll be able to recognize fossils that lie about 10 minutes down the trail. The tour begins at the Bright Angel Trailhead restrooms.

☞ TOURS

In addition to the following tours offered within the park, dozens of independent companies provide guided cycling, driving and hiking tours to the South Rim ranging from day trips to multiday backpacking adventures (p40). Some include transportation from Williams, Flagstaff and beyond, and some meet inside the park.

The highly recommended Grand Canyon Field Institute (p229), part of the non-profit Grand Canyon Association, offers all kinds of guided hikes, overnight backpacking and 'rim-based learning adventures'.

Bicycle

Guided bicycle tours are available from April 1 through October 31, and beyond as weather permits, through Bright Angel Bicycles (p69).

Bus

Five bus tours offer a natural and human history of the park and depart daily from Maswik, Yavapai and Bright Angel Lodges. You can reserve tickets in advance online at www.grandcanyonlodges.com. Otherwise three days in advance, you can book via phone ☑928-638-2631, or in person at the transportation desks inside Bright Angel Lodge and Maswik and the concierge at El Tovar.

DAY TRIPS ON THE COLORADO RIVER

From the South Rim, day trips on the river require several hours' drive (or a combination of helicopter and bus transport) and take at least 12 hours start to finish. A handful of adventure companies offer variations on the basic itinerary.

Smooth Water Float

Colorado River Discovery (p163), offers smooth water floats along the stunningly beautiful 15-mile stretch from Glen Canyon Dam down Marble Canyon to Lee's Ferry; Xanterra (☑888-297-2757, 303-297-2757, 928-638-3283; www.grandcanyonlodges.com), National Geographic Visitor Center (☑928-638-2468; www.explorethecanyon.com; 450 Hwy 64, Tusayan; adult/child $14/11; ☉8am-10pm Mar-Oct, 10am-8pm Nov-Feb) and Grand Canyon Airlines (☑866-235-9422, 702-835-8484; www.grandcanyonairlines.com) offer combination tours that include the float trip and transport to/from the South Rim to the river via bus and/or helicopter. Some tours include a side trip to Antelope Canyon (p162).

White-Water Trip through the Hualapai Reservation

Guided tours offered by independent companies include various combinations of bus and helicopter for a 20-minute white-water trip in a motorized raft. Visit www.grandcanyon.com for options, or contact Hualapai Tourism (p117). Some itineraries begin in Flagstaff or Williams.

Children under 16 ride free when accompanied by an adult, and wheelchair-accessible vehicles are available with a day's advance notice.

➡ **Hermits Rest** ($30) Two-hour tour to Hermit Rd overlooks.

➡ **Desert View Dr** ($50) Four-hour tour includes a stop at Lipan Point and about an hour at Desert View Watchtower.

➡ **Sunrise** ($23) This 90-minute tour can leave as early as 4am in the summer.

➡ **Sunset** ($23) Two-hour tour.

➡ **Combination** ($65) Take in both western and eastern reaches of the South Rim, in one day or over two days. It combines a Desert View Dr tour with Hermits Rest, Sunrise or Sunset, and saves a few bucks.

Hiking

Several Park Ranger Programs include moderate to strenuous guided hikes. Check *The Guide* or ask at any lodge or visitor center for seasonal offerings and times.

Train

An early-morning shuttle takes guests one hour south to the train depot in Williams where you hop on the historic Grand Canyon Railway (p94) back to the South Rim.

Make reservations by 3pm on the day before departure at the transportation desks inside Maswik and Bright Angel, or through the El Tovar concierge.

⊙ SIGHTS

While you'll obviously want to marvel at the main attraction, the South Rim is also the site of notable buildings and museums. Many of the historic buildings on the South Rim were designed by visionary architect Mary Colter, painstakingly researched to complement the landscape and reflect the local culture. Both Bright Angel and Verkamp's Visitor Center house small but excellent museums.

Consider purchasing the self-guided *Walking Tour of Grand Canyon Village Historical District* brochure ($1) at park bookstores. Hours vary seasonally. Admission to all museums and historic buildings is included in the park admission.

HISTORY OF THE BRIGHT ANGEL

In one form or another, the Bright Angel Trail has been in continuous use for thousands of years. It was originally forged by the Havasupai people to access present-day Indian Garden, where they grew crops and farmed until the early 20th century. In the early 1890s prospectors Ralph Cameron and Pete Berry – who built the Grand View Hotel – improved the trail, eventually extending it to the river. Seeing a golden opportunity, in 1903 Cameron imposed a $1 toll on anyone using the trail, a widely criticized decision. In response, the Atchison, Topeka & Santa Fe Railway and others constructed toll-free alternative trails, such as the Hermit, to draw the burgeoning mule-tourism trade. In 1928 the park service took the reins of the Bright Angel and lifted the toll.

⊙ Grand Canyon Village

Hopi House   HISTORIC BUILDING
(Map p76; www.nps.gov/grca; Grand Canyon Village; ☺8am-8pm mid-May–Aug, 9am-6pm Sep–mid-Oct, 9am-5pm mid-Oct–mid-May; ⊛; ☒Village) A beautiful Mary Colter–designed stone building, Hopi House has been offering high-quality Native American jewelry, basketwork, pottery and other crafts since its 1904 opening. The structure was built by the Hopi from native stone and wood, inspired by traditional dwellings on their reservation. Be sure to walk upstairs for the Native American Art Gallery.

★ Trail of Time   INTERPRETIVE DISPLAY
(Map p76; www.nps.gov/grca; Grand Canyon Village; ⊛; ☒Village) This interpretive display traces the history of the canyon's formation, and each meter equals one million years of geologic history. From the trail's start at the Yavapai Geology Museum just over a mile to Verkamp's Visitor Center, you pass about 2.1 billion years. Rock samples from within the canyon line the trail immediately west from the geology museum; look through specially positioned metal cylinders to view these rocks on the far canyon wall. Brass placards continue beyond Verkamp's. It's located on the Rim Trail, west from Yavapai Geology Museum.

Grand Canyon Village

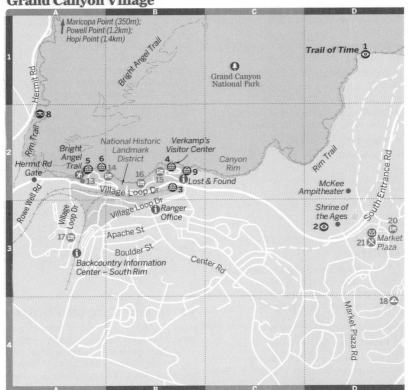

SOUTH RIM GRAND CANYON VILLAGE

Bright Angel Lodge   HISTORIC BUILDING
(Map p76; www.nps.gov/grca; National Historic Landmark District, Grand Canyon Village; ⚐; ⌨ Village) **FREE** Commissioned by the Fred Harvey Company, designed by Mary Colter, and completed in 1935, the log-and-stone Bright Angel Lodge offered canyon travelers alternative accommodations to the luxurious El Tovar. Just off the lobby is the History Room, a small museum devoted to Harvey, who, in conjunction with the Atchison, Topeka & Santa Fe Railway, transformed Grand Canyon into a popular tourist destination.

Today's Bright Angel is the latest in a series of incarnations that began after the first stagecoach arrived at the South Rim from Flagstaff on May 19, 1892. When train service to the canyon looked inevitable, James Thurber relocated his Flagstaff–Grand Canyon stagecoach line to the head of the Bright Angel Trail and opened Bright Angel Hotel and Camps. He sold the property to Wil-

liams hotelier Martin Buggein in 1901, but because neither man made a formal claim to the land upon which the hotel stood, the Atchison, Topeka & Santa Fe Railway enveloped the site as part of its 20-acre depot; upon completion of the railroad's luxury El Tovar in 1905, the railroad bought Buggein's share of Bright Angel and upgraded his accommodations.

On the lodge grounds is the Buckey O'Neill Cabin. Built in the 1890s by William Owen O'Neill, the cabin is the longest continually standing building on the rim. Nicknamed 'Buckey' because he 'bucked the odds' in a card game, O'Neill moved to Arizona in 1879 and worked as an author, journalist, miner, politician and judge. In 1897 he raised money for and became president of the Santa Fe and Grand Canyon Railroad Co, and was a significant force behind the railroad's arrival at the South Rim in 1901. In 1898 he joined Teddy Roosevelt's Rough Riders in the

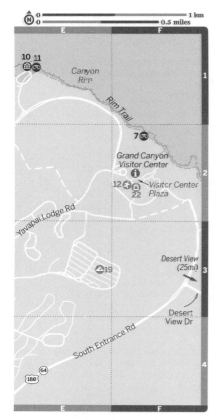

Spanish-American War and died at age 38, the day before the assault on San Juan Hill. Today, the lucky few who make reservations well in advance can stay in his cabin.

El Tovar
HISTORIC BUILDING

(www.nps.gov/grca; National Landmark Historic District, Grand Canyon Village; 🚌 Village) Built in 1905 as a railroad hotel, El Tovar was designed by architect Charles Whittlesey as a blend between a Swiss chalet and the more rustic style that would come to define national park lodges in the 1920s. With its unusual spires and dark wood beams rising behind the Rim Trail, elegant El Tovar remains a grande dame of national park lodges.

The public spaces look much as they did when the lodge opened, and wide, inviting porches with rocking chairs offer travelers a comfortable and elegant place to relax after a long journey to the park. Moose and elk trophy heads, reproduction Remington bronzes and Craftsman-style furniture

lend the interior a classic Western feel. The lodge sits about 100 yards from the rim, and though it's thronged with tourists by day, the scene mellows considerably in the evening. The bench swing on the side porch is the best spot on the South Rim to relax with a cocktail and watch the comings and goings along the canyon rim.

Kolb Studio
HISTORIC BUILDING

(Map p76; 📞 928-638-2771; www.nps.gov/grca; National Historic Landmark District, Grand Canyon Village; ⊙8am-7pm Mar-May & Sep-Nov, to 6pm Dec-Feb, to 8pm Jun-Aug ♿; 🚌 Village) FREE In 1905 Ellsworth and Emery Kolb built a small photography studio on the edge of the rim, which has since been expanded and now holds a bookstore and museum.

The brothers arrived at the canyon from Pennsylvania in 1902 and made a living photographing parties descending the Bright Angel Trail. Because there was not enough water on the rim to process the film, they had to run 4.5 miles down the trail to a spring at Indian Garden, develop the film and race back up in order to have the pictures ready when the party returned.

By 1924 the brothers' dynamic and conflicting personalities challenged their business relationship, and they flipped a coin to decide who got to stay to run the photography business at Grand Canyon. Ellsworth lost and headed to California, and Emory remained until his death in 1976 at the age of 95. Today, an original Kolb brothers 1911 silent film runs continuously, offering incredible footage of their early exploits exploring the Colorado River, and a museum displays momentos and photographs from their careers on the South Rim. In January and February, the NPS offers tours of the brothers' original Craftsman home in a lower level of the studio.

Yavapai Geology Museum
MUSEUM

(Map p76; www.nps.gov/grca; Grand Canyon Village; ⊙8am-7pm Mar-May & Sep-Nov, to 6pm Dec-Feb, to 8pm Jun-Aug; ♿; 🚌 Kaibab/Rim) FREE Views don't get much better than those unfolding behind the plate-glass windows of this little

ℹ️ Kolb Studio, right next to Bright Angel Trailhead, sells last-minute hiking gear including Yaktrax ($24) for walking on ice, neck cloths that stay cool for hours ($10), flashlights, sun hats and small bottles of sunscreen.

Grand Canyon Village

stone building at Yavapai Point. Handy panels identify and explain the various formations before you, and displays highlight the canyon's multilayered geologic history.

Lookout Studio HISTORIC BUILDING
(Map p76; www.nps.gov/grca; National Historic Landmark District, Grand Canyon Village; ☉ 8am-sunset mid-May–Aug, 9am-5pm Sep–mid-May; 🚻; 🚌 Village) FREE Like Mary Colter's other canyon buildings, Lookout Studio was modeled after stone dwellings of the Southwest Pueblo Native Americans. Made of rough-cut Kaibab limestone, with a roof that mirrors the lines of the rim, the studio blends into its natural surroundings. Inside is a small souvenir shop and a tiny back porch that offers coin-operated telescopes and spectacular canyon views.

Grand Canyon Train Depot HISTORIC BUILDING
(Map p76; www.thetrain.com; National Historic Landmark District, Grand Canyon Village; 🚌 Village, 🚂 Grand Canyon Railway) FREE This train depot, designed by Francis Wilson and completed in 1910, was built nine years after the first train arrived in the village from Williams. It's one of only 14 log depots ever constructed in the US, and is the only train station inside a US national park.

The 1st floor was used for passenger services, and the 2nd floor was a two-bedroom apartment for the ticket agent. Today, a Grand Canyon Railway train pulls into the station daily from Williams.

Verkamp's Visitor Center HISTORIC BUILDING
(Map p76; www.nps.gov/grca; National Historic Landmark District, Grand Canyon Village; ☉ 8am-7pm; 🚻; 🚌 Village) FREE In 1898 John G Verkamp sold souvenirs from a tent outside Bright Angel Lodge to persevering travelers arriving after long, arduous stagecoach rides. He was a little before his time, however, as there weren't yet enough customers to make a living, and he closed down his operation after only a few weeks. The arrival of the railroad in 1901 opened up the canyon to more and more tourists, and in 1905 Verkamp returned to build the modified Mission-style Verkamp's Curios.

After running the shop for more than 100 years, Verkamp's descendants closed down the business, and the NPS revamped the building as a small visitor center in 2008. It maintains an old-fashioned, dusty feel, and the tiny museum gives a timeline of Grand Canyon pioneer history in the context of other national events.

Grand Canyon Pioneer Cemetery CEMETERY
(Map p76; www.nps.gov/grca; Market Plaza, Grand
Canyon Village; ⊞; ⊡ Village) More than 300
people are buried at Grand Canyon Cemetery, the lives of many of them are intricately
woven into the history of the canyon. They
include the Kolb brothers, John Verkamp,
Ralph Cameron and John Hance, who ran
a hotel a few miles from Grandview Point.

⊙ Desert View

In the summer months from 9am to 4:30pm,
Desert View hosts cultural demonstrations
that highlight Native American weaving,
pottery, jewelry and other crafts. Check *The
Guide* for times.

★**Desert View Watchtower** HISTORIC BUILDING
(www.nps.gov/grca; Desert View, East Enrance;
⊗ 8am-sunset mid-May–Aug, 9am-6pm Sep–
mid-Oct, 9am-5pm mid-Oct–Feb, 8am-6pm Mar–
mid-May; ⊞) The marvelously worn winding
staircase of Mary Colter's 70ft stone tower,
built in 1932, leads to the highest spot on the
rim (7522ft). From here, unparalleled views
take in not only the canyon and the Colorado River, but also the San Francisco Peaks,
the Navajo Reservation and the Painted
Desert. Murals depicting the snake legend,
a Hopi wedding and other scenes grace the
interior walls and there's a small gift shop
on the 1st floor.

Tusayan Museum & Ruin MUSEUM, RUIN
(www.nps.gov/grca; Desert View Dr; ⊗ 9am-5pm;
⊞) Just west of Desert View and 22 miles
east of Grand Canyon Village, these small
ruins and museum examine the culture
and lives of the Ancestral Puebloan people
who lived here 800 years ago. Only partially
excavated to minimize erosion damage, it's
less impressive than other such ruins in the
Southwest, but still interesting and worth a
look. Pottery, jewelry and split-twig animal
figurines on display date back 2000 to 4000
years, and ranger-led tours are offered at
11am and 1:30pm daily.

OVERLOOKS
Nineteen overlooks, spread across roughly 40 miles, dot the Hermit Rd and Desert
View scenic drives and Grand Canyon Village and serve as the canyon's primary
points of interest. The **Rim Trail** (www.nps.
gov/grca; Grand Canyon National Park, South Rim;
⊞⊠; ⊡ Hermits Rest, ⊡ Village, ⊡ Kaibab/Rim)
connects overlooks from Hermits Rest to the

South Kaibab Trailhead (13 miles), and all
but Shoshone Point are accessible by shuttle or car and have small parking lots. From
March through November, however, Hermit
Rd is closed to private vehicles. During this
time, you can walk the Rim Trail, catch a
shuttle or ride a bike to the nine overlooks
along Hermit Rd.

To reach Yaki Point, you must either catch
the Kaibab/Rim Shuttle from the Visitor
Center Plaza or cycle. Yaki Rd is closed to
private vehicles year-round and the Rim
Trail does not stretch east from South Kaibab Trailhead to Yaki Point.

The best times of day to watch the light
and shadow bring out the canyon's sculpted features are at sunrise and sunset – of
course, these are also prime times for busloads of like-minded visitors to pull up and
pile out for photo-ops at the most popular
overlooks. Hiking a few minutes along the
rim from any overlook, however, is usually
all it takes to get you to a secluded spot.

Overlooks, with the exception of the westernmost Hermits Rest (p72) and the easternmost Desert View Watchtower, are listed
here west to east.

Pima Point VIEWPOINT
(www.nps.gov/grca; Hermit Rd; ⊞⊠; ⊡ Hermits
Rest) Good views of Hermit Camp on the
Tonto Platform and Hermit Rapids on the
Colorado River as well as some sections of
the Hermit Trail. A great spot to watch a
sunrise or a sunset.

OVERNIGHT EXPEDITIONS ON THE GRANDVIEW TRAIL

For experienced overnight backpackers, three different spur trails descend
1000ft from Grandview Trail's Horseshoe Mesa (3.1 miles below the rim) to
the inner-canyon east–west Tonto Trail:
**Horseshoe Mesa West, Horsehoe
Mesa North** and **Horseshoe Mesa
East.** The easiest to follow is the one
that heads west near the pit toilets. Take
it to hike a 7-mile loop around the foot of
the mesa, following the Tonto and East
Horseshoe Mesa Trails and rejoining
Grandview a little ways up from the
mesa. Secure a backcountry permit, as
well as an NPS park map and a detailed
guide, before overnight backpacking
expeditions, and note that there are no
water sources.

South Rim (Hermit Rd)

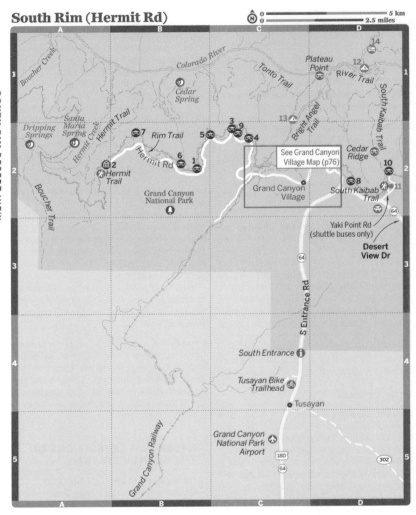

Monument Creek Vista VIEWPOINT
(www.nps.gov/grca; Hermit Rd; 📶🏠; 🚌 Hermits Rest) From here, the bicycle- and wheelchair-friendly Greenway Trail west overlaps with the Rim Trail, offering multiple informal overviews and resting areas along its 2.8-mile route west to Hermits Rest.

Abyss VIEWPOINT
(www.nps.gov/grca; Hermit Rd; 📶🏠; 🚌 Hermits Rest) Good place to see sheer canyon walls.

Mohave Point VIEWPOINT
(www.nps.gov/grca; Hermit Rd; 📶🏠; 🚌 Hermits Rest) Great spot to watch a sunrise or sunset.

Hopi Point VIEWPOINT
(www.nps.gov/grca; Hermit Rd; 📶🏠; 🚌 Hermits Rest) Juts further into the canyon than any other South Rim overlook, offering magnificent east–west views. During the summer peak, there can be more than 1000 people waiting for shuttle pick-up after sunset.

Powell Point VIEWPOINT
(www.nps.gov/grca; Hermit Rd; 📶🏠; 🚌 Hermits Rest) The rocky peninsula cuts out over the canyon, offering some of the South Rim's most dramatic vistas. Similar to Hopi Point but not as crowded, Powell makes a magnificent spot to catch the sunset.

South Rim (Hermit Rd)

Maricopa Point   VIEWPOINT
(www.nps.gov/grca; Hermit Rd; 🚹🚻; 🚌Hermits Rest) Look carefully and you may be able to see hikers winding their way down the canyon along the Bright Angel Trail. Maricopa, an easy walk along the paved section of the Rim Trail, makes a lovely sunrise spot.

Trailview Overlook   VIEWPOINT
(Map p76; www.nps.gov/grca; Hermit Rd; 🚹🚻; 🚌Hermits Rest) With an excellent view of most of the Bright Angel Trail, this is a good spot to watch hikers and mule trains ascending and descending the trail.

Yavapai Point   VIEWPOINT
(Map p76; www.nps.gov/grca; Grand Canyon Village; 🚹🚻; 🚌Kaibab/Rim) Yavapai Point shares a spot with the geology museum, with views of Phantom Ranch (on the canyon bottom – look carefully!), Bright Angel Canyon and Tonto Platform, among many other iconic canyon features. Best place for an overview of canyon geology.

Mather Point   VIEWPOINT
(Map p76; www.nps.gov/grca; Visitor Center Plaza, Grand Canyon Village; 🚹🚻; 🚌Kaibab/Rim) The busiest and most popular overlook, due in part to its proximity to the visitor center. It's named after Stephen Mather, the first director of the National Park Service.

Pipe Creek Vista   VIEWPOINT
(www.nps.gov/grca; Desert View Dr; 🚹🚻; 🚌Kaibab/Rim) A quieter alternative to Mather Point on the same section of the South Rim.

Yaki Point   VIEWPOINT
(www.nps.gov/grca; Yaki Rd, off Desert View Dr; 🚹; 🚌Kaibab/Rim) Dramatic views to both the east and west, Yaki Point is one of the best spots to catch a sunrise. Because it's accessible year-round by shuttle or bicycle only, it tends to be a quieter overlook.

★Shoshone Point   VIEWPOINT
(www.nps.gov/grca; Desert View Dr; 🚹) Walk 1 mile along the mostly level dirt road to marvelously uncrowded Shoshone Point, a rocky promontory with some of the canyon's best views. This viewpoint is unmarked; look for the small parking lot about 1.2 miles east of Yaki Point.

Grandview Point   VIEWPOINT
(www.nps.gov/grca; Desert View Dr; 🚹🚻) Take in expansive views of the canyon from the overlook, one of the highest points on the South Rim, or hike down a short way for solitude. John Hance built the park's first hotel here in 1886, followed soon after by Pete Berry's Grandview Hotel. With the arrival of the railroad in 1901, the tourist hub shifted to Bright Angel and the hotels here closed in 1908.

William Randolph Hearst bought Berry's land, tore down the Grandview Hotel in 1928 and planned to build a new hotel, but the park service bought him out in 1939.

Moran Point   VIEWPOINT
(www.nps.gov/grca; Desert View Dr; 🚹🚻) Excellent view down both directions of the Colorado River and of the colorful walls of Red Canyon.

Lipan Point   VIEWPOINT
(www.nps.gov/grca; Desert View Dr; 🚹🚻) Expansive views and an excellent perch for sunset.

Navajo Point   VIEWPOINT
(www.nps.gov/grca; Desert View Dr; 🚹🚻) At 7461ft, Navajo Point is the South Rim's highest overlook.

ℹ HIKING OUT OF THE CANYON

When hiking out of the canyon, it helps to gauge your progress by stopping occasionally to look back at how far you've climbed – instead of only up toward the rim, which can feel daunting and overwhelming, especially when you're tired. Remember, the hike up generally takes twice as long as the hike down, so plan accordingly.

SLEEPING

There are five lodges, two campgrounds and one RV park on the South Rim. All but Desert View Campground are located in the tourist hub around Grand Canyon Village, within walking distance of restaurants and sights and easily accessed by park shuttle transportation. El Tovar, Bright Angel, Kachina and Thunderbird sit along the Rim Trail in the National Landmark Historic District, a stone's throw from the canyon abyss. Both Maswik and Yavapai, however, sit rather depressingly in the Ponderosa forest. Maswik is five-minute walk from the canyon and Yavapai is a mile away, across from the grocery store, bank and post office.

While convenient, don't expect the historic charm that many associate with national park lodges. With the exception of El Tovar and rim-side cabins at Bright Angel Lodge, South Rim accommodations is not much more than a basic highway motel.

Lodging reservations are accepted up to 13 months prior to your stay, and can be canceled up to 48 hours in advance with no penalty (☎888-297-2757, Yavapai ☎877-404-4611).

Call the South Rim switchboard (☎928-638-2631) to make day-before and same-day reservations; for Yavapai, call ☎928-638-6421.

For photos and details of El Tovar, Bright Angel, Thunderbird, Kachina, Maswik and Phantom Ranch, go to www.grandcanyonlodges.com; for Yavapai, go to www.visitgrandcanyon.com.

Children 16 and under stay free with adults, and cots and cribs can be rented for $10 per night.

If there are no rooms available, consider Tusayan (p92), a few miles south of the rim and connected during the summer with free regular park shuttles, or the roadside motel in Valle (p94). Note that summer Tusayan accommodations rates soar upward from $250, and the town is just a short strip of mediocre restaurants and uninspiring hotels.

For more than just a place to lay your head, head to Flagstaff (p99), Williams (p94) or Sedona (p111).

Camping

There's a seven-day limit at above-the-rim campgrounds and a two-night limit at below-the-rim campgrounds (four nights November 15–February 28). If you don't find a spot in the park, you can always pitch your tent free of charge in the surrounding Kaibab National Forest.

NPS campgrounds below the rim require a backcountry permit. Requests are processed by fax or mail only beginning on the first of the month, four months prior to the start of the trip. Within 21 days of departure, you must go to the Backcountry Information Center (p89) in person to secure a permit.

Above the Rim

Both Mather and Trailer Village are about a mile along the bicycle-friendly Greenway

SOUTH RIM CAMPGROUNDS

CAMPGROUND	LOCATION	DESCRIPTION	ELEVATION
Desert View Campground (p83)	Desert View	Well-dispersed sites on the peaceful eastern side of the South Rim, 26 miles from Grand Canyon Village. No showers, hot water or hookups.	7463ft
Grand Canyon Camper Village (p93)	Tusayan	Large, utilitarian campground located outside park's south entrance. Has laundry facilities. Full hookups.	6612ft
Mather Campground (p83)	Grand Canyon Village	Park's biggest campground, centrally located with wooded, well-dispersed sites; no hookups; trailers & RVs limited to 30ft. RV dump station closed in winter.	6971ft
Ten-X Campground (p92)	2 miles south of Tusayan	Spacious USFS campground with pit toilets; no hookups, showers or hot water.	6650ft
Trailer Village (p83)	Grand Canyon Village	Trailer park near Mather Campground; hookups and pull-through sites for vehicles up to 50ft; RV dump station closed in winter.	7028ft

 Drinking Water

 Flush Toilets

 Ranger Station Nearby

 Great for Families

 Wheelchair Accessible

Trail to the canyon rim. Desert View sits at Desert View (East Entrance), 25 miles east of Grand Canyon Village.

Desert View Campground CAMPGROUND **$**
(www.nps.gov/grca; Desert View (East Entrance); campsites $12, reservations not accepted; ⊘ mid-April–mid-Oct; ☀) In a piñon-juniper forest near the East Entrance, this first-come, first-served 50-site NPS campground is quieter than campgrounds in the Village, with a nicely spread-out design that ensures a bit of privacy. The best time to secure a spot is mid-morning, when people are breaking camp. It usually fills by mid-afternoon. Facilities include toilets and drinking water, but no showers or hookups.

Mather Campground CAMPGROUND **$**
(Map p76; ☎877-444-6777, late arrival 928-638-7851; www.recreation.gov; Market Plaza, Grand Canyon Village; sites $18; ⊘year-round; ☎☀; ☐Village) South Rim's primary campground has shaded and fairly well-dispersed sites set in the ponderosa forest, 1 mile from the canyon rim. You'll find pay showers and laundry facilities, drinking water, toilets, grills and a small general store; a full grocery store is a short walk away. Reservations are accepted from March to mid-November; the rest of the year it's first-come, first-served. No hookups.

Trailer Village CAMPGROUND **$**
(Map p76; ☎877-404-4611, same-day 928-638-3047; www.visitgrandcanyon.com; Market Plaza, Grand Canyon Village; hookups $36; ⊘year-round;

OVERNIGHTS ON BRIGHT ANGEL

Bright Angel, the park's most popular corridor trail, offers the only patrolled inner-canyon campground between the South Rim and the Colorado River. From the trailhead on the rim, it's 4.6 miles down to Indian Garden Campground, and then 4.7 and 5 miles to Bright Angel Campground and Phantom Ranch respectively (p66).

☀; ☐Village) A trailer park with RVs lined up tightly at paved pull-through sites amid a barren patch of ground. You'll find picnic tables, barbecue grills and full hookups, but coin-operated showers and laundry are a quarter-mile away at Mather Campground.

Below the Rim

In addition to these maintained corridor campgrounds, with water, toilets and a ranger station, there are multiple designated backcountry campsites along inner-canyon trails. For details and maps, check the park website or go to the backcountry office.

The third and final corridor campground (Cottonwood) is about 7 miles up the North Kaibab, halfway up the canyon's north face between the Colorado River and the North Rim.

NO. OF SITES	OPEN	RESERVATIONS	DAY FEE	FACILITIES
50	mid-April–mid-Oct	no	$12	
300	Mar–Oct	no	$35-50	
317	year-round	yes, up to 6 months in advance	$18	
70	May–Sep	yes (15 sites)	$10	
84	year-round	yes	$36	

 Dogs Allowed (On Leash)   Grocery Store Nearby   Snack Shop Nearby   Showers   RV Dump Station

Bright Angel Campground CAMPGROUND $
(Backcountry Information Center ☑928-638-7875; www.nps.gov/grca; Colorado River, Phantom Ranch; campsite $10, plus $8 per person per night; ⊙year-round) Located between the Colorado River and Phantom Ranch and perched along the inviting Bright Angel Creek, this is a lovely spot to hunker down after the arduous trek to the canyon bottom. Each of the 32 campsites has a picnic table and fire ring. Make reservations for meals at Phantom Ranch or just pop into the canteen for a cold drink and snack – it's just a few minutes' walk from the campground.

Indian Garden Campground CAMPGROUND $
(☑Backcountry Information Center 928-638-7875; www.nps.gov/grca; Bright Angel Trail; campsite $10, plus $8 per person per night; ⊙year-round) Located 4.6 miles below South Rim, Indian Garden

is surrounded by cottonwoods, with a ranger station, toilets and year-round drinking water. Each of the campground's 15 sites offers a picnic table shaded by an open-walled, roofed enclosure. This is the only spot to spend the night until you reach Bright Angel Campground and Phantom Ranch on the canyon bottom, about 5 miles further.

Lodging

★**Bright Angel Lodge** LODGE $$
(Map p76; ☑888-297-2757, front desk & reservations within 48hr 928-638-2631 ext 6285; www.grandcanyonlodges.com; National Historic Landmark District, Grand Canyon Village; r with bath $100, r without bath $77-89, ste $426, cabins $128-197; �℗☎; ☐Village) This 1935 log-and-stone lodge on the ledge delivers simple historic

---

PHANTOM RANCH

Hikers heading to the canyon bottom can spend the night at **Phantom Ranch** (☑888-297-2757, same day or next day reservations ☑928-638-3283; www.grandcanyonlodges.com; Grand Canyon National Park, canyon bottom; dm $48, d cabin $135; ❄), a picturesque cluster of stone buildings built in the 1920s by the Fred Harvey Company and designed by Mary Colter that sits just north of the Colorado River, 0.3 miles up from Bright Angel Campground. Fringed with towering cottonwoods and fruit orchards planted more than a century ago, Phantom Ranch is a marvelously inviting low-key oasis. Folks mingle over a beer and board games in its air-conditioned canteen, cool off in its clear, cold stream, and share the trials and delights of their hike into the canyon depths.

Four single-sex dormitories, available to hikers only, each include five bunks with bedding and towels, toilets and showers. Cabins, accommodating two to 12 people and often filled with folks descending the Bright Angel on mule, provide bedding, a cold-water sink, toilet and towels, but showers are at a central location. Reservations must be made up to 13 months in advance, and you must check in at the transportation desk at Bright Angel Lodge by 4pm on the day prior to your hike. Without a reservation, put yourself on the waiting list at the **Bright Angel Transportation Desk** (p89) the day before you want to go (starting at 5am) and then show up again at 6:15am the next morning and hope to snag a canceled bed.

Communal family-style meals at Phantom Ranch are fun – but not for the faint of heart. The hikers here are a hungry bunch, and they tend to eat fast, so grab the bacon when you can! The set dinner menu offers three choices: steaks or stew ($45/$29; 5pm) and vegetarian chili ($29; 6:30pm). Breakfast ($21) is served at 5am and 6:30am, and sack lunches ($13) are prepared for the trail. You must make meal reservations in advance, ideally at the same time as you book your lodgings. Note that you do not have to be staying at Phantom Ranch to reserve breakfast or dinner – folks camping at nearby Bright Angel Campground can eat here as well (with advanced reservation).

The canteen is open for cold lemonade, hot drinks, beer, wine and packaged snacks from 8am to 4pm and 8pm to 10pm. It also sells a limited supply of gear, including first-aid supplies and flashlights. Phantom Ranch and NPS campgrounds are the only below-the-rim accommodations within the national park. Hours change seasonally.

From the South Rim, it's 9.6 miles down Bright Angel or 7.2 miles down the much steeper South Kaibab to Phantom Ranch; from the North Rim, 1000 miles higher in elevation than the South Rim, it's 13.6 miles down the North Kaibab. Mules go to Phantom Ranch from the South Rim only (p72).

charm by the bucketload. Small public spaces bustle with activity, and the transportation desk in the lobby is the central contact for hiking services, mule rides and guided trips. Though the lodges are an excellent economy option, historic cabins are brighter, airier and have tasteful Western character.

Most are scattered in the piñon behind the main building, but Rim Cabins and the two suites are some of the best accommodations in the South Rim and well worth the extra bucks. Cabins number 6157 and 6158 offer the quietest views and a gas fireplace. Only the Red Horse Suite has air-conditioning.

Kachina & Thunderbird Lodges LODGE $$

(Map p76; ☎888-297-2757, reservations within 48hrs 928-638-2631; www.grandcanyonlodges.com; National Historic Landmark District, Grand Canyon Village; r streetside/rimside $216/232; P❄🛜; 🖥Village) These institutional-looking lodges, built in the late 1960s, offer standard motel-style rooms with two queen beds or one king, full bath, flat-screen TV and a refrigerator. Though ugly on the outside, rooms are bright and comfortable, and you're steps away from the historic charms of El Tovar and the canyon rim. Location, location!

Yavapai Lodge MOTEL $$

(Map p76; ☎877-404-4611, reservations within 48hrs 928-638-6421; www.visitgrandcanyon.com; Market Plaza, Grand Canyon Village; r West/East $140/174; ⊙year-round; P❄@🛜🐾; 🖥Village) Basic one- and two-story motel-style lodgings cluster in the piñon and juniper forest about a mile from the rim. Air-conditioned rooms at Yavapai East sleep four to six, and offer two queen beds or a king and bunk beds. Rooms in Yavapai West sleep up to four and do not have air-conditioning.

Note that Yavapai Lodge and Trailer Village are the only South Rim accommodations that are not run by Xanterra, and Yavapai West is the only South Rim accommodations that allows pets.

Maswik Lodge MOTEL $$

(Map p76; ☎888-297-2757, front desk & reservations within 48hrs 928-638-2631 ext 6784; www.grandcanyonlodges.com; Grand Canyon Village; r south/north $107/205; P❄@🛜; 🖥Village) The Maswik Lodge includes 18 modern two-story buildings set in the woods a quarter-mile from the canyon rim. Standard motel rooms at Maswik North feature private patios, air-con, cable TV and forest views. Those at Maswik South are smaller, with fewer amenities, no air-con and more forgettable views.

TONTO TRAIL

Tonto Trail is a 95-mile east–west trail along the entire length of the Tonto Platform, from Red Canyon to Garnet Canyon, the longest in the canyon and a primary vein for complicated inner-canyon treks. It parallels the Colorado River on the south side of the canyon, intersecting with several rim-to-river trails. Unlike the corridor trails, the Tonto does not extend to the rim, and it does not involve significant elevation change, remaining around 4000ft. Most folks hike specific sections of the Tonto, descending the South Rim on, for example, the Bright Angel, cutting west on the Tonto, and ascending back to the South Rim on the Hermit. There are several backcountry campsites along the way, as well as spurs to the river.

The Tonto is an unpatrolled wilderness area with no facilities along its undulating, sun-baked desert terrain – under no circumstances is this route an option for moderate hikers.

★ El Tovar LODGE $$$

(Map p76; ☎888-297-2757, front desk & reservations within 48hrs 928-638-2631 ext 6380; www.grandcanyonlodges.com; National Historic Landmark District, Grand Canyon Village; r $187-305, ste $381-465; ⊙year-round; P❄🛜; 🖥Village) Stuffed mounts. Pine walls. Sturdy fireplaces. Is this the fanciest hotel on the South Rim or a backcountry hunting lodge? Despite renovations, this rambling 1905 wooden lodge hasn't lost a lick of its genteel historic patina, or its charm.

The concierge can help with any questions and arrange tours, even if you're not a guest. It's also the only place beyond the post office and grocery store in Market Plaza, 1 mile from the rim, where you can buy stamps.

🍴 EATING & DRINKING

Grand Canyon Village has all the eating options you will need, from a pizza to venison, icy pints to pink cocktails. The vast majority of dining, however, is in the form of cafeterias and walk-up snack bars. The only table-service options are the El Tovar Dining Room, the Arizona Room and Bright Angel Restaurant, which are all in the National Historic Landmark District.

SOUTH RIM EATING & DRINKING

PICNIC PICKS

Find terrific picnic spots simply by roaming the rim along Hermit Rd, away from the shuttle-stop overlooks. Below the rim, Cedar Ridge (1.5 miles down South Kaibab Trail) and Indian Garden (4.6 miles down Bright Angel Trail) offer idyllic picnic surrounds.

Greenway Trail (p69) Between Visitor Plaza and Pipe Creek Vista, this flat-topped hill is perfect for a blanket and a cooler of goodies.

Shoshone Point (p81) Wander under the shade to this off-the-beaten-path South Rim picnic site.

Hermits Rest (www.nps.gov/grca; Hermit Rd; 🚻; 🚌 Hermits Rest) Walk past the stone gift shop and snack bar to the handful of peaceful tables by the trailhead.

There are two grocery stores; the full-scale Canyon Village Market is centrally located in Grand Canyon Village, and the much smaller **Desert View Market** (📞928-638-2393; Desert View; ⊗8am-8pm Jun-Aug, varies rest of year; 🚌Village) sits at the East Entrance. Both Desert View and Hermits Rest offer a snack bar (9am to 4pm). From May through September, the walk-up hot-dog stand in Market Plaza, just outside the grocery store, serves tasty dogs with all the fixin's.

The walk-up counter inside **Bright Angel Bicycle** (p69) at the Visitor Center Plaza offers the best fast-food in the park and makes an excellent spot to pick up a last-minute bite to enjoy on the Rim Trail hike east to South Kaibab Trailhead. Fare includes breakfast burritos, simple peanut-butter-and-jelly sandwiches, salads, wraps and a large selection of quirky drinks and snacks (grass-fed bison, bacon-and-cranberry bar?)

All South Rim bars close at 11pm, and drinks are prohibited along the rim itself. Expect slightly reduced hours September through May.

✗ Grand Canyon Village: National Historic Landmark District

Maswik Pizza Pub   PIZZA $
(Map p76; 📞928-638-4044, 928-638-2631; www.grandcanyonlodges.com; Maswik Lodge, Grand Canyon Village; slice $3, pie from $14; ⊗11am-11pm May-Aug, varies rest of year; 🚻; 🚌Village) Pick up a slice or pie to enjoy over a Grand Canyon Pilsner, or call in advance for to-go orders. Bright and open, the pizzas here have basic toppings and there's a vegetarian pesto pizza, too.

Bright Angel Ice-Cream Fountain   FAST FOOD $
(Map p76; 📞928-638-2631; Bright Angel Lodge, National Historic Landmark District, Grand Canyon Village; mains $3-5; ⊗10am-5pm May-Aug; varies rest of year; 🚻; 🚌Village) Hot dogs, sandwiches, ice cream and coffee. Cash only.

Maswik Food Court   CAFETERIA $
(Map p76; 📞928-638-2631; www.grandcanyonlodges.com; Maswik Lodge, Grand Canyon Village; mains $7-13; ⊗6am-10pm May-Aug, varies rest of year; 🚻; 🚌Village) Though fairly predictable, the food encompasses a nice variety and isn't too greasy. Various food stations serve burgers, pasta, Mexican food, chile bowls and comfort food. A deli, grab-and-go sandwiches, beer and wine are also available.

Bright Angel Restaurant   AMERICAN $$
(Map p76; 📞928-638-2631; www.grandcanyonlodges.com; Bright Angel Lodge, National Historic Landmark District, Grand Canyon Village; mains $9-26; ⊗6-10:45am, 11:15am-4pm & 4:30-10pm; 🚻; 🚌Village) With uninspired, windowless surrounds, Bright Angel offers a standard menu of burgers, fajitas, salads and pasta. The original graphic from the Bright Angel's 1920s menu, shown on the back of today's menu and available as notecards in the gift shop, may be the best part. Reservations not accepted.

★ El Tovar Dining Room & Lounge   AMERICAN $$$
(Map p76; 📞928-638-2631; www.grandcanyonlodges.com; El Tovar, National Historic Landmark District, Grand Canyon Village; mains $17-35; ⊗restaurant 6:30-10:45am, 11:15am-2pm & 4:30-10pm, lounge 11am-11pm; 🚻; 🚌Village) Dark-wood tables are set with china and white linen, eye-catching murals spotlight Native American tribes and huge windows frame views of the Rim Trail and canyon beyond. Breakfast

options include El Tovar's pancake trio (buttermilk, blue cornmeal and buckwheat pancakes with pine-nut butter and prickly-pear syrup) and blackened trout with two eggs.

Reservations are required for dinner. To avoid lunchtime crowds, eat before the Grand Canyon Railway train arrives at 11.45am. The adjacent cocktail lounge is busy for afternoon cocktails and after-dinner drinks. Parties of six or more can request the intimate Teddy Roosevelt Room across from the hostess desk – pop your head in to check out the mustache motif carved into the wood-paneling.

Arizona Room   AMERICAN $$$

(Map p76; www.grandcanyonlodges.com; Bright Angel Lodge, National Historic Landmark District, Grand Canyon Village; mains $12-29; ☺11:30am-3pm & 4.30-10pm Jan-Oct; 👶; 🚌 Village) Antler chandeliers hang from the ceiling and picture windows overlook the Rim Trail and canyon beyond. Try to get on the waitlist when doors open at 4:30pm, because by 4:40pm you may have an hour's wait – reservations are not accepted. Bison and black-bean chile, oven-roasted squash and ribs with prickly-pear barbecue give a Western vibe.

You can pick up a drink from the bar and take it outside to the small, informal deck and watch passersby on the Rim Trail while you wait, and they'll buzz you in when your table is ready.

Bright Angel Lounge   BAR

(Map p76; www.grandcanyonlodges.com; National Historic Landmark District, Grand Canyon Village; ☺11am-11pm May-Aug, varies rest of year; 👶; 🚌 Village) The dark, windowless bar inside Bright Angel Lodge doesn't offer much character, but it's a cozy and friendly spot for a beer and occasionally live music. Serves coffee, yogurt and pastries in the morning.

✕ Grand Canyon Village: Market Plaza

Canyon Village Market   SUPERMARKET

(Map p76; 📞 928-638-2262; Market Plaza, Grand Canyon Village; ☺8am-7pm May-Aug, varies rest of year; 🚌 Village) The biggest source for supplies on either rim, this market offers everything you'd expect from your local grocery store, including a fair selection of organic items, fresh produce, liquor and over-the-counter medications. Also sells hiking gear, including boots, water sandals and apparel.

Canyon Village Deli   CAFETERIA $

(Map p76; 📞 928-638-2262; Canyon Village Market, Market Plaza, Grand Canyon Village; mains $3-9; ☺8am-6pm May-Aug, varies rest of year; 👶; 🚌 Village) Fresh-made sandwiches, hot dogs and grab-and-go meals inside the grocery store.

Yavapai Lodge Restaurant   AMERICAN $

(Map p76; 📞 928-638-6421; www.visitgrandcanyon.com; Yavapai Lodge, Market Plaza, Grand Canyon Village; breakfast $7-12, lunch & dinner $8-22; ☺6:30am-9pm May-Aug, varies rest of year; 👶; 🚌 Village) Place your order, pick up your drinks and they'll call your number when the food is ready; barbecue and sandwiches, as well as beer and wine.

Yavapai Lodge Tavern   BAR

(Map p76; 📞 928-638-6421; www.visitgrandcanyon.com; Yavapai Lodge, Market Plaza, Grand Canyon Village; ☺11am-10pm May-Aug, varies rest of year; 🚌 Village) Specialty cocktails and bar menu, 1 mile from the rim.

🛍 SHOPPING

Gift shops in historic buildings and lodges sell souvenirs ranging from vintage posters, prickly-pear licorice, hiking guides, over-the-counter toiletries and basic outdoor supplies such as raincoats and sunscreen. For high-end Native American crafts and quality jewelry, head to Hopi House (p75).

The best selection of camping and hiking supplies is at Canyon Village Market.

Grand Canyon Association Park Store at Visitor Center Plaza   BOOKS

(Map p76; Visitor Center Plaza, Grand Canyon Village; ☺8am-8pm Jun-Aug, varies rest of year; 🚌 Village, Kaibab/Rim) An extensive collection of adult and children's books about the canyon, plus canyon prints and T-shirts. The store is run by the Grand Canyon Association, which supports education and research at the park.

SOUTH RIM SHOPPING

INDIAN GARDEN VIEW

Peer over the rim outside El Tovar for a bird's-eye view of Indian Garden. You can clearly see the lush green of this inner-canyon oasis and at night campers' flashlights look like giant fireflies buzzing about the vast darkness of the canyon interior.

GETTING AWAY FROM IT ALL

It's easy to get away if you know how.

➡ Arrive through the East Entrance.

➡ Walk the 1-mile, mostly level trail for a picnic at Shoshone Point.

➡ Catch the sunset along the Rim Trail stretch between Pima Point and Hermits Rest – a handful of benches make a perfect perch.

➡ Avoid the Rim Trail through Grand Canyon Village between 9am and 5pm.

➡ Hike into the canyon on the steep and narrow Hermit Trail to Santa Maria Spring.

➡ Camp at Desert View Campground rather than Mather Campground.

❶ Orientation

MAJOR REGIONS

Grand Canyon South Rim is comprised of four distinct sections:

Grand Canyon Village (South Entrance) Divided into the National Historic Landmark District, clustered along and close to the rim: Market Plaza, the park's commercial hub with a grocery store, bank and post office set into the woods about a mile from the rim; and the Visitor Center Plaza, with the bulk of the parking, bike rental and an excellent bookstore. You'll find most services in Grand Canyon Village, including all above-the-rim lodges and two of the three developed campgrounds. Shuttles loop year-round through the village.

Hermit Rd Stretches west along the rim 8 miles from Grand Canyon Village to Hermits Rest, at the South Rim's western edge, offering nine overlooks along the way. From March 1 through November 30, this road is closed to private vehicles. During this time, you can access Hermit Rd via bicycle or the Hermits Rest Route Shuttle, or you can walk along the Rim Trail.

Desert View Dr & Desert View (East Entrance) This scenic road passes several overlooks, picnic areas and the Tusayan Ruins and Museum, but does not hug the rim as it winds east 25 miles from the village to Desert View. At Desert View there's a market, seasonal gas station and a first-come, first-served camp ground. There is no shuttle-service beyond the first few miles of this road.

Below-the-Rim Backcountry Accessible by foot or mule only along established trails, with backcountry campsites and one lodge.

The 13-mile Rim Trail (p79) winds along the canyon rim from Hermits Rest east to the South Kaibab Trailhead, passing multiple overlooks, the Bright Angel Trail, historic buildings in Grand Canyon Village, the geology museum and the Visitor Center Plaza.

MAJOR ROADS

Hwy 180/64 runs north to the South Entrance from Tusayan (2 miles), Valle (22 miles), Williams (60 miles) and Flagstaff (80 miles). In Valle, the highway splits off, with Hwy 64 cutting southwest to Williams and Hwy 180 heading southeast to Flagstaff.

Hwy 89 runs north from Flagstaff 44 miles to Cameron, where Hwy 64 heads west to the park's East Entrance. It is 25 miles from the East Entrance to Grand Canyon Village.

❶ Information

Almost all services on the South Rim are in Grand Canyon Village, easily accessible via the Village Route Shuttle. Limited hours go into effect between October and March.

INTERNET ACCESS

Wi-fi is available 24-hours-a-day in hotel lobbies (fees may apply). A computer in the lobby of Yavapai Lodge offers free internet access even if you're not a guest, and there's free wi-fi in Canyon Village Market.

Grand Canyon Community Library (Grand Canyon Village; ⊗10:30am-5pm Mon-Fri; ⊙; ⊟ Village) Free wi-fi and and several terminals with free internet access.

Park Headquarters Library (Grand Canyon Village; ⊗8am-4:30pm Mon-Fri; ⊙; ⊟ Village) At the back of the courtyard at Park Headquarters, the small library offers free internet access and free wi-fi.

KENNELS

South Rim Kennel (⊡928-638-0534, for retrieval after 5pm 928-638-2631; www.nps.gov/grca; behind Maswik Lodge, Grand Canyon Village; overnight dog $22-26, cat $15, day boarding dog/cat $22/15; ⊗7:30am-5pm) Convenient for one or two days, but not recommended for extended stays (for that, Flagstaff offers several good options). There are no large play areas for the dogs, and individual walks are limited to one five-minute walk per day. Rates include meals. Proof of vaccinations required. Maswik Lodge is the only South Rim accommodations that allows dogs in rooms.

LOST & FOUND

Lost & Found (☑928-638-2631, 928-638-7798; www.nps.gov/grca; Grand Canyon Village)

MEDICAL SERVICES

Clinic (☑928-638-2551; ☺8am-6pm, reduced hours mid-Oct–mid-May)

MONEY

The only ATMS outside the bank are in the grocery store at Desert View and in the lobby of Maswik Lodge.

Chase Bank (☑928-638-2437; Market Plaza, Grand Canyon Village; ☺9am-5pm Mon-Thu, 9am-6pm Fri; ☐Village) Currency-exchange for Chase Bank members only and a 24-hour ATM.

POST

Post Office (☑928-638-2512; Market Plaza, Grand Canyon Village; ☺9am-4:30pm Mon-Fri, 11am-1pm Sat) Stamps and walk-up window. To send gear to yourself, address it to yourself, General Delivery, Grand Canyon, AZ, 86023.

TELEPHONE

There is reliable cell phone service on the South Rim. Because a Verizon tower sits on the South Rim, travelers who use this carrier can count on the most consistent coverage, and all service is spotty along Hermit Rd. Do not depend on service below the rim.

TOURIST INFORMATION

Backcountry Information Center – South Rim (☑928-638-7875; www.nps.gov/grca; Grand Canyon Village; ☺8am-noon & 1-5pm, phone staffed 1-5pm Mon-Fri; ☐Village) Come here to get waitlisted for a backcountry permit if you haven't reserved one ahead of time. Also posts alerts and weather reports, and provides detailed information on below-the-rim hiking.

Bright Angel Transportation Desk (☑928-638-3283; Bright Angel Lodge, National Historic Landmark District, Grand Canyon Village; ☺5am-8pm summer; ☐Village) Books same- or next-day mule trips and Phantom Ranch accommodations; if these are full, this is the go-to spot for the waiting list. They can also arrange bus tours, scenic flight, smooth-water float trips and hikers' duffel service (mule transport for bags). There are satellite transportation desks in the lobbies of Maswik and Yavapai. Check in here for mule rides.

Grand Canyon Visitor Center (☑928-638-7888; www.nps.gov/grca; Visitor Center Plaza, Grand Canyon Village; ☺8am-5pm Mar-Nov, 9am-5pm Dec-Feb; ☐Village, ☐Kaibab/Rim) The South Rim's main visitor center. On the plaza here, bulletin boards and kiosks display information about ranger programs, the weather, tours and hikes. Inside is a ranger-staffed information desk, a lecture hall and a theater screening a 20-minute movie, *Grand Canyon: A Journey of Wonder*.

Verkamp's Visitor Center (National Historic Landmark District, Grand Canyon Village; ☺8am-8pm Jun-Aug, shorter hours rest of year; ☐Village)

ⓘ Getting There & Away

The closest Greyhound (p236) bus stop is in Flagstaff; Amtrak (p99) stops at Flagstaff and Williams.

TRAIN

Historic Grand Canyon Railway connects Williams and Grand Canyon Village (p238).

SHUTTLE

A handful of shuttle services (p92) provide regularly scheduled and custom transport to the South Rim from Flagstaff, Sedona, Williams and the North Rim. Grand Canyon Tour Company (p125) offers daily shuttle from Las Vegas.

Tusayan Route Shuttle (Purple) (www.nps.gov/grca; Tusayan & Grand Canyon Visitor Center; ☺8am-9:30pm mid-May–early Sep) Seasonal shuttle runs every 15 minutes between Grand Canyon Visitor Center, inside the park, and Tusayan, a few miles south; about 20 minutes each way. In Tusayan, it stops at the National Geographic Visitor Center (IMAX) and a handful of hotels.

ⓘ Getting Around

Though the park can seem overwhelming when you first arrive, it's actually quite easy to navigate. *The Guide* contains a color-coded shuttle-route map in the centerfold.

BICYCLE

Bicycles are allowed on paved roads and the Greenway Trail only; Hermit Rd shuttles are equipped to carry up to three bicycles. Bright Angel Bicycles (p69) rents cycles, provides shuttle service independent of NPS shuttles and offers guided trips.

> ⓘ You can arrange for the **Mule Duffel Service** to carry your gear from the South Rim to Phantom Ranch (one-way $70). Call ☑888-297-2757 (up to three days in advance) or ☑928-638-3283 (day before) for required reservations. Go to www.grandcanyonlodges.com for size and weight restrictions and details.

PARKING IN GRAND CANYON VILLAGE

You'll find four large parking lots at Grand Canyon Visitor Center, where you can catch shuttles or walk to the historic village. Other lots are located at Market Plaza (by the grocery store), at the Backcountry Office and at Park Headquarters (by Shrine of the Ages).

El Tovar and Bright Angel Lodge parking lots, conveniently located next to the rim in the historic village and open to all park visitors, make a sweet parking spot. They generally open up when guests check out between 9am and 11am. Alternatively, check the unmarked lot behind Verkamp's Visitor Center; follow the gravel drive behind the El Tovar lot.

Parking lots are free and open to all guests; once parked, your car can remain there for the duration of your visit.

CAR

From March through November, cars are not allowed on Hermit Rd, which heads west from the village to Hermits Rest. The closest gas station to Grand Canyon Village is in Tusayan, a few miles south.

Desert View Service Station (p239) is the only gas station on the South Rim; credit card service available 24-hours-a-day. There's also a garage (p239) offering emergency repair and tow service.

SHUTTLE

Free shuttle buses holding a maximum of 70 people connect South Rim points of interest and tourist facilities. In the pre-dawn hours, shuttles are every half-hour or so and typically begin running about an hour before sunrise; from early morning until after sunset, buses depart every 15 minutes. *The Guide* features exact seasonal operating hours relevant to your visit, sunrise and sunset times, and a map of shuttle stops.

The Hermits Rest Route Shuttle operates only from March through November, when cars are not allowed on Hermit Rd, and the Kaibab/Rim Route Shuttle is the only public transport to the South Kaibab Trailhead after 7am.

Be sure that the shuttle you hop on is going the direction you want to go; several stops service shuttles going in both directions.

Shuttle service to the North Rim is available through Trans Canyon Shuttle (p236) and **Flagstaff Shuttle & Charter** (www.flagshuttle.com).

Village Route Shuttle (www.nps.gov/grca; Grand Canyon Village) Loops through Grand Canyon Village facilities (Market Plaza, the National Historic Landmark District and the Visitor Center Plaza), including the Backcountry Office and all hotels. It also connects to the Hermits Rest Route and Kiabab/Rim Route. An express bus runs between Hermits Rest Route Transfer (east end of village) to the Visitor Center Plaza (west end of village). Fifty minutes round-trip.

Hermits Rest Route Shuttle (Red) (www.nps.gov/grca; Hermit Rd; ☉ Mar-Nov) Runs west from Grand Canyon Village along Hermit Rd to Hermits Rest. You can hop off at any of the eight overlooks along the way, enjoy the view and a hike along the Rim Trail, then catch another shuttle further west or back to the village. It's 80 minutes roundtrip. Note that the shuttle stops at all eight overlooks heading west, but only Pima Point, Mohave Point and Powell Point heading east.

Kaibab/Rim Route Shuttle (Orange) (www.nps.gov/grca; Visitor Center Plaza, Grand Canyon Village) Stops at the Yavapai Geology Museum, several overlooks, the Visitor Center Complex and South Kaibab Trailhead. Fifty minutes round-trip.

Hikers' Express Bus (www.nps.gov/grca; Bright Angel Lodge, National Historic Landmark District, Grand Canyon Village; ☉ Departs 5am, 6am & 7am in May & Sep, 4am, 5am & 6am June-Aug, 6am, 7am & 8am Apr & Oct, 8am, 9am & 10am Nov-Mar) Early-bird transport from Bright Angel Lodge to South Kaibab Trailhead, with stops at the Backcountry Information Center and the Visitor Center Plaza.

TAXI

Grand Canyon South Rim Taxi Service (☐ 928-638-2822; Tusayan & South Rim; ☉ 24hr) Offers taxi service to and from Tusayan (one-way $14 for two people) and within the park. Service is available 24 hours, but there are only a couple of taxis, so you may have to wait. Each person in the taxi must pay $6 (what is known as 'local regularly scheduled transit' fee) to enter the park.

WHEELCHAIR & STROLLER RENTAL

Rent wheelchairs and strollers at Bright Angel Bicycles (p69) in the Visitor Center Plaza.

Around South Rim

Best Places to Eat

➡ Sophie's Mexican Kitchen (p93)

➡ Tourist Home Urban Market (p104)

➡ Proper Meats + Provisions (p105)

➡ Brix Restaurant & Wine Bar (p106)

Best Places to Stay

➡ Lodge on Route 66 (p97)

➡ Little America Hotel (p104)

➡ L'Auberge de Sedona (p116)

➡ Hotel Monte Vista (p104)

Why Go?

Carved into the stunning landscape of the Southwest, Grand Canyon has more than its own unique splendor to offer visitors. Stretching both north and south of the canyon is the Kaibab National Forest, and to the west of the park's South Rim are the Hualapai and Havasupai Reservations that encompass thousands of acres of desert and rim-to-river Canyon lands. Further west, where the Colorado River has been reined in by the massive engineering feat that is Hoover Dam, Lake Mead is a popular recreation area for desert dwellers thirsting for fishing, houseboating and water sports. Bordering the national park to the east, and spanning mile-upon-mile of the rim-to-rim drive, is the Navajo Reservation.

The gateway towns leading to the South Rim are destinations in their own right: Las Vegas for its slick excess and cardinal sins, Flagstaff for its cool, outdoorsy feel, Sedona for day-hiking and red-rock landscape, and Williams for its small-town, Route 66 atmosphere.

When to Go
Las Vegas

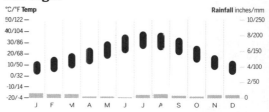

Jan Ski near Taos and Flagstaff. In Park City, hit the slopes and the Sundance Film Festival.

Jun–Aug High season for exploring national parks in New Mexico, Utah and northern Arizona.

Sep–Nov Hike to the bottom of the Grand Canyon or gaze at bright leaves in northern New Mexico.

Kaibab National Forest (South Rim)

The park's South Rim is bordered by the piñon-juniper and ponderosa-pine woodland of Kaibab National Forest, offering several great mountain-biking trails, unlimited camping, hiking and cross-country skiing. Its Tusayan Ranger Station (p72), just outside the park's South Entrance, has maps and details. One of the best and most popular rides is the 16-mile Arizona Trail (www.aztrail.org), which stretches from Grandview Lookout Tower to Tusayan.

The main road through the forest is Hwy 64/180, which connects Williams and Flagstaff with the canyon.

◉ Sights & Activities

Grandview Lookout Tower LOOKOUT
Built by the Civilian Conservation Corps in 1936 as a fire tower, the 80ft Grandview Lookout Tower offers great views of the region for those willing and able to climb all those stairs. From the park's Desert View Dr, turn at the sign for 'Arizona Trail' between mileposts 252 and 253, about 2 miles east of Grandview Point. You can hike or cycle 1.3 miles on a dirt road to the lookout.

REGIONAL SHUTTLE SERVICES
···

The **Trans Canyon Shuttle** (p236) runs twice-daily between the North and South Rims from mid-May through November 30.

Arizona Shuttle (☑928-226-8060, 800-888-2749; www.arizonashuttle.com; ⊙year-round) Vans run regular routes between Flagstaff, Grand Canyon's South Rim, Williams, Sedona and Phoenix Sky Harbor Airport, departing multiple times throughout the day. To Grand Canyon from Flagstaff, it's $30 per person one-way; to Phoenix, it's $45.

Flagstaff Shuttle & Charter (☑888-215-3105; www.flagshuttle.com; ⊙year-round) Door-to-door customized shuttle transport and tours. Services Las Vegas and Phoenix airports, as well as Sedona, Flagstaff, Grand Canyon South Rim, Grand Canyon North Rim, Marble Canyon and Bryce and Zion National Parks.

Apache Stables HORSEBACK RIDING
(☑928-638-2891; www.apachestables.com; Moqui Dr/Forest Service Rd 328; 1/2hr ride $49/89, wagon/trail ride $26/59; ⊙vary seasonally) Trail and wagon rides through the forest (no canyon views). The stables are about 1 mile north of Tusayan.

Tusayan

☑928 / POP 573 / ELEV 6612FT

The little town of Tusayan, situated just outside of the park's South Entrance along Hwy 64, is basically a half-mile strip of hotels and restaurants that caters to Grand Canyon visitors and serves as over-flow accommodations a few minutes drive from the canyon rim. Beyond that, and the IMAX Grand Canyon film, there's no reason to come here.

In summer, to avoid traffic jams and parking hassles inside the park, you can catch the Tusayan shuttle from here into the park.

◉ Sights

National Geographic Visitor Center & IMAX Theater MUSEUM
(☑928-638-2203; www.explorethecanyon.com; 450 Hwy 64; adult/child $14/11; ⊙visitor center 8am-10pm Mar-Oct, 10am-8pm Nov-Feb, theater 8:30am-8:30pm Mar-Oct, 9:30am-6:30pm Nov-Feb; ▣Tusayan) Hourly, on the half-hour, the IMAX theater here screens a terrific 34-minute film called *Grand Canyon – The Hidden Secrets*. The recommended film plunges you into the history and geology of the canyon through the eyes of ancient Native Americans, John Wesley Powell and a soaring eagle, and is a safer, cheaper alternative to a canyon flyover.

⊨ Sleeping

Camping

Ten-X Campground CAMPGROUND $
(☑877-444-6777, 928-638-2443; www.recreation.gov; Hwy 64; RV & tent sites $10; ⊙May-Sep) Woodsy and peaceful, this USFS campground, 2 miles south of Tusayan, has 70 sites and can fill up early in the summer. You'll find large sites, picnic tables, fire rings and barbecue grills (the campground host sells firewood), cold water and toilets, but no showers. Fifteen sites are reservable up to six months in advance; the rest are first-come, first-served. No hookups.

Grand Canyon
Camper Village CAMPGROUND $
(☑ 928-638-2887; www.grandcanyoncampervillage.
com; 549 Camper Village Ln; tent sites $29, RV
sites in summer $46-56; ☎) This private camp-
ground will never be called pretty, with
many spots lacking shade or natural surroundings. On the plus side? There are a
ton of sites and pay showers, and the campground is only 1 mile south of the park on
Hwy 64. Reservations not accepted for tent
sites; full hookups.

Lodging
A handful of chain and independent motels
offer clean and friendly accommodations,
but don't expect anything memorable. Folks
stay here because it's conveniently located
a few miles from Grand Canyon, and that's
it – location, location, location. Rates soar
along with demand during the busy summer
months, and it's not unusual to find doubles
peaking upwards from $250.

Seven Mile Lodge MOTEL $
(☑ 928-638-2291; Hwy 64; r $99; ✳ ☎) Friend-
ly and basic motel accommodations that
doesn't take reservations; rooms are usually
filled by early afternoon in the summer.

Holiday Inn Express MOTEL $$
(☑ 928-638-3000; 266 Arizona 64; r $120-175;
✳ ☎ ≋) Built in 1995 and renovated in 2013.

Canyon Plaza Resort MOTEL $$
(☑ 800-995-2521, 928-638-2673; www.grand
canyonplaza.com; 406 Canyon Plaza Lane; d/ste
$160/210; ✳ @ ☎ ≋ ☷) Popular with tour
groups, this is less a resort than your standard chain motel. All suites have two rooms;
king-bed suites include pullout couches in
the sitting area. Look for it behind the National Geographic Visitor Center.

Red Feather Lodge MOTEL $$
(☑ 928-638-2414; www.redfeatherlodge.com; 300
Hwy 64; r $107-128; ✳ @ ☎ ≋ ☷) The Red
Feather Lodge offers rooms in two buildings,
as well as laundry facilities and an outdoor
pool. Built in 1997, the three-story hotel features elevators and interior doors; the older
two-story motor lodge (c 1964) has outside
entrances and stairs. Pets are $25 per stay.

Best Western Grand Canyon
Squire Inn HOTEL $$$
(☑ 928-638-2681; www.grandcanyonsquire.com;
74 Hwy 64; r $220-351; ✳ @ ☎ ≋; ☐ Tusayan)
Rooms range from standard doubles in a

two-story 1973 annex, sans elevator, to spacious interior and rooms in the main hotel,
with elevator. Amenities include the most
upscale dining in town, a bowling alley, pool
tables, game room, coin laundry and seasonal outdoor pool.

Grand Hotel HOTEL $$$
(☑ 888-634-7263, 928-638-3333; www.grand
canyongrandhotel.com; 149 Hwy 64; r from $259;
✳ ☎ ≋; ☐ Tusayan mid-May–mid-Sept) The giant stone fireplace, antler light fixtures and
nightly live cowboy-and-country music in
the lounge give this hotel's public spaces a
distinct Western vibe. The rooms, however,
are your basic chain hotel.

Eating & Drinking
Considering the annual number of tourists that pass through Tusayan, the village
manages to retain a sort of old-fashioned,
roadside-hub pace. There's an OK variety of
eateries to choose from, but nothing worth
seeking out.

Nightlife in Tusayan is mostly limited to
the popular sports bar in the Best Western
Grand Canyon Squire Inn or live country-
and-western music at the Grand Hotel.

RP's Stage Stop CAFE $
(www.rpsstagestop.com; 400 Hwy 64; breakfast under $5, lunch $3-11; ⊙ 7am-6pm; ☎ ☷) The only
place in Tusayan to grab an espresso and
pick up a sandwich for your picnic lunch;
also offers wi-fi.

★ Sophie's Mexican Kitchen MEXICAN $$
(☑ 928-638-4679; mains $10-16; ⊙ 11am-9pm;
☷) Festooned with colorful *papel picado*
(cut paper banners), this cheery restaurant
offers Mexican food like street-style tacos,
fajitas and a few vegetarian options.

We Cook Pizza & Pasta PIZZA $$
(☑ 928-638-2278; 605 Hwy 64; mains $10-29;
⊙ 11am-9pm; ☷) This cavernous, busy pizza
joint is the kind of place where you order,
take a number and unceremoniously chow
it down at one of the big tables. The pizza
isn't particularly compelling, but it's good
and no-nonsense, just like its name.

Coronado Room AMERICAN $$$
(☑ 928-638-2681; Best Western Grand Squire Inn,
100 Hwy 64; mains $15-32; ⊙ 5-10pm; ☎ ☷) The
Best Western Grand Squire Inn serves the
most upscale cuisine in town, offering bison,
elk and boar as well as salmon and steak.

ℹ️ Information

The National Geographic Visitor Center & IMAX Theater (p92) sells park entrance permits, arranges tours and is an excellent resource for all things Grand Canyon. Permits are also available at the Grand Canyon Trading Post, next to McDonalds, Red Feather Lodge, Best Western Grand Canyon Squire Inn, RP's Stage Shop and Canyon Plaza Resort.

ℹ️ Getting There & Around

You can walk to most places along the highway through Tusayan. The free Tusayan Route Shuttle (p89) loops between Tusayan and Grand Canyon Visitor Center on the canyon rim from mid-May to early September.

Commercial flights do not fly into Grand Canyon Airport; it services scenic flights and tours.

Valle

About 25 miles south of the park, middle-of-nowhere-feeling Valle marks the intersection of Hwy 64 to Williams and Hwy 180 to Flagstaff. There isn't much to it apart from a couple of curiosities, as well as a gas station and minimart. The only reason to stay in Valle is its proximity to the park.

There are rooms at the **Grand Canyon Inn & Motel** (☑928-635-9203, 800-635-9203; www.grandcanyoninn.com; 317 S Hwy 64; r $90-150; ☉closed early-Jan–Feb; ✳🖥🐾). This family-run motel offers standard rooms and a restaurant; the less expensive rooms in the motel section across the highway from the lobby are a bit nicer, with Southwestern flair, but they are smaller and don't have refrigerators or telephones. **Flintstones Bedrock City** (☑928-635-2600; www.bedrockaz.com; adult $5, child under 5yr free; ☉6am-8.30pm, hours vary seasonally), a kitschy 1972 roadside attraction, offers tent sites ($12) and RV hookups ($14).

Williams

☑928 / POP 3014 / ELEV 6780FT

A pretty slow spot by day, tiny Williams comes to life in the evening when the Grand Canyon Railway train returns with passengers from the South Rim...and then closes down again on the early side. It's a friendly town and caters to canyon tourists. Route 66 passes through the main historic district as a one-way street headed east; Railroad Ave parallels Route 66, and heads one-way west.

Williams is 35 miles west of Flagstaff on I-40 and 55 miles south of the park via Hwy 64.

👁️ Sights & Activities

Ask at the visitor center or at the ranger station for maps and information on hiking and biking in the surrounding Kaibab, Coconino and Prescott national forests. You can also cycle to the canyon on the historic Grand Canyon Railways (p238).

Grand Canyon Deer Farm PETTING ZOO
(☑800-926-3337, 928-635-4073; www.deerfarm.com; 6769 E Deerfarm Rd; adult/child/under 3yr $11.50/7.75/free; ☉9am-6pm) Blanketed in wood chips, a trail leads through an open area where the deer roam free and gather eagerly around visitors with outstretched hands full of tasty pellets. A smaller pen is home to goats (quite the loud-mouthed personalities here, mischievously reaching to munch on food, shirts, strollers, whatever). Just $3 buys enough deer food to keep kids busy for a while. Among the more exotic animals in residence are marmosets and wallabies, while the resident parrot chats sassily.

It's 8 miles east of Williams, off I-40's exit 171.

Bearizona ZOO
(☑928-635-2289; www.bearizona.com; 1500 E Route 66; adult/child 4-12yr $20/10; ☉8am-6pm Jun-Aug, hours vary rest of year) While the main attraction here is the wildlife park, where visitors drive themselves slowly along a road that winds through 160 acres inhabited by roaming gray wolves, bison, bighorn sheep and black bears, the real draw is the small zoo dubbed Fort Bearizona. Here, under ponderosa shade, you can see tiny baby bears sidle up the trees, playful otter brothers slide and bob through the water, porcupines, badgers and a handful of other small animals indigenous to the area.

Check the website for scheduled Birds of Prey shows, otter feeding and animal meet 'n' greets.

Grand Canyon Railway HISTORIC RAILWAY
(reservations ☑800-843-8724; www.thetrain.com; Railway Depot, 233 N Grand Canyon Blvd; round-trip adult/child from $65/25; 🚃) Following a 9am **Wild West show** by the tracks, this historic train departs for its 2¼-hour ride to the South Rim. If you're only visiting the rim for the day, this is a fun and hassle-free way to travel. Once at the South Rim, you can ex-

plore by foot, shuttle or tour bus. Arrive back in Williams at 5:45pm.

Route 66 Zipline
ZIPLINE

(www.ziplineroute66.com; $12-15; ☺ Mar 15-Oct 31, & select days Nov-Dec; 🚻) Only 1400ft round-trip, this kitschy Route 66–inspired ride zips over the parking lot downtown. More like a carnival attraction than a zipline, it's a lot of fun on a summer evening when you're poking around town.

🛏 Sleeping

Camping

Free dispersed camping is allowed in the national forest provided you refrain from camping in meadows, within a quarter-mile of the highway or any surface water, or within a half-mile of any developed campground.

Three lovely wooded USFS campgrounds (Dog Town Lake, Kaibab Lake, White Horse Lake; open May to September) near Williams offer seasonal camping without hookups. Swimming is not allowed in any of the lakes, but they are popular for fishing and hiking.

Kaibab Lake Campground
CAMPGROUND $

(📞 928-699-1239, reservations 877-444-6777; www.recreation.gov; tent & RV sites $20-32; ☺ April–mid-Oct; 🚻) Large campsites in ponderosa shade with fire rings and picnic tables. It sits 4 miles northeast of Williams; take exit 165 off I-40 and go north 2 miles on Hwy 64. Offers both reservable and first-come, first-served campsites.

White Horse Lake Campground
CAMPGROUND $

(www.recreation.gov; tent & RV sites $18; ☺ May-Sep; 🚻) Nineteen miles southeast of town, this 94-unit campground offers a hiking trail and fishing. From town, drive 8 miles on 4th St and turn left on FR 110. Reservations accepted.

Dogtown Lake Campground
CAMPGROUND $

(www.recreation.gov; $20; ☺ May-Sep) Wooded USFS camping 6 miles southeast of Williams. Turn south on 4th St for 3.5 miles to FR 140 and follow the signs.

Railside RV Ranch
CAMPGROUND $

(📞 888-635-4077, 928-635-4077; www.railsiderv.com; 877 Rodeo Rd; RV sites $36-38, cabin 4 people daily/weekly $159/890; 🚻) A few blocks' walk to restaurants and shops of downtown Williams, with 96 RV hookups, a cabin sleeping

---

ℹ If you're traveling with a pet and want to catch the train **Railway Pet Resort** (p49) sits steps away from the train depot with opening hours that coordinate with train departure and return; the best pet-friendly accommodations in town is **Best Western Plus Inn** (p49) at I-40 exit 161.

---

four and a handful of tent sites. It's a pleasant and friendly spot, with clean bathrooms, 24-hour laundry, complimentary breakfast, hot tubs and a dog play area. They can also help arrange tours and shuttles to the Grand Canyon.

Lodging

Grand Canyon Hotel
HOTEL $

(📞 928-635-1419; www.thegrandcanyonhotel.com; 145 W Route 66; hostel dm/r $28/32, r with shared bath $70, r with private bath $75-125; ☺ Mar-Nov; 🏧@🛜) This rambling European-style hotel first welcomed guests in 1891. Perched on the corner of Route 66 and S 2nd St downtown, the welcoming hotel struts its quirky stuff with themed rooms (giraffe room, anyone?) and eclectic decor. Overnight options include a hostel-style dorm, rooms with shared baths, en-suite rooms and units in a separate carriage house ($165).

Grand Canyon Hotel Hostel
HOSTEL $

(📞 928-635-1419; www.grandcanyonhotelhostel.com; 145 W Route 66; dm/s/d with shared bath $25/31/62; 🅿🛜) Clean, sunny and airy, this small and friendly adobe-style hostel offers shared bath and free wi-fi. There's one mixed dorm with six beds (no bunks); private rooms have walls and doors, but no ceilings. Sheets and bright Mexican-style blanket are provided. Check in at the Grand Canyon Hotel; the hostel sits a few blocks up the road.

Check in between 3pm and 9pm only; note that Amtrak arrives too late for hostel check in. There's a small fridge, microwave and hot-plate, while laundry facilities are a half-block away.

Canyon Country Inn
MOTEL $

(📞 928-635-2349; 422 W Route 66; r $90; 🏧🛜) Rooms at this small family-run motel are a step up from typical motel rooms and give you more of a B&B feel. Country-style decor includes frilly curtains, floral bedspreads and a teddy bear on the bed.

HISTORIC ROUTE 66

Arizona claims bragging rights for having the longest remaining continuous stretch of Route 66, running east to west from Seligman to Topock. When the Mother Road re-routed here in 1933, roadside businesses thrived, but once the I-40 bypass was completed in 1978, this snake of a road through the desert scrub almost died away. Angel Delgadillo, a local barber, spearheaded the successful effort to designate the road an Historic Highway in 1987, and in 2005 it was listed on the National Register of Historic Places.

Getting off I-40 for part of a long road trip can be a beautiful alternative to simply blowing through this part of the country, but the tiny pockets of businesses that dot the dusty surrounds along the way are more a constructed kitschy tourist trinket than a preserved stretch of something real. There's a melancholy echo here, with the iconic romance of Route 66 boiled down to Little Debbie pastries, Route 66 mugs, T-shirts and keyrings, and vintage gas pumps.

Nineteen miles west of Williams and just off I-40 is **Ash Fork**, founded in 1882 when the Atlantic and Pacific Railroad established a stop here. These days its claim to fame is as the 'Flagstone Capital of the World,' as smooth vermilion slabs of Coconino sandstone are quarried in the area. You can stay for the night at **Ash Fork Inn** (☎ 928-637-2514; 859 W Route 66; r $30-50) and poke around the free **Ash Fork Route 66 Museum** (☎ 928-637-0204; www.ashforkrt66museum.com; 901 W Route 66).

From Ash Fork, the Mother Road hugs I-40 24 miles to **Seligman**. Juan Delgadillo once reigned supreme as an infamous prankster at his famous **Delgadillo's Sno Cap Drive-In** (☎ 928-422-3291; 301 Route 66, Seligman; mains $2-6; ⏰ 10am-6pm Mon-Sat, to 5pm Sun, reduced hours Sep-May), and you can still line up for shakes and cheeseburgers. Along both sides of Seligman's stretch of Route 66 are the historic buildings that have survived over the years, as well as cafes, restaurants and souvenir shops where they lay the kitsch on thick. One of Seligman's handful of clean, basic budget motels is the non-descript **Historic Route 66 Motel** (☎ 928-422-3204; 500 W Route 66; r $47-57; ✳ 🛜).

Getting back on the westward highway, the road veers north from I-40, through miles upon miles of rolling hills and canyon country towards tiny **Peach Springs** and **Grand Canyon Caverns & Inn** (☎ 928-422-3223; www.grandcanyoncaverns.com; milepost 115, Route 66; adult/child $15/10; ⏰ 8am-6pm May-Sep, call for off-season hours), where you can escape the desert heat in the cool subterranean caverns 21 stories below ground via elevator. Stay the night at the cavern inn (double $77 to $86) or the very quiet, underground suite ($800) within the caverns. The caverns and the modern and recommended **Hualapai Lodge** (☎ 928-769-2230; www.grandcanyonwest.com; 900 Route 66; r $109-119; ⏰ Diamond Creek Restaurant 6am to 8pm; ✳ 🛜 🏊) in Peach Springs are the closest accommodation to Hualapai Hilltop – the windswept trailhead for the 10-mile hike down to **Havasu Canyon** (camping reservations ☎ 928-448-2180, lodge reservations ☎ 928-448-2111; www.havasuwaterfalls.net; Havasu Canyon, Havasupai Reservation; $35; $22 per person for camping, $145 for a quad in the lodge) on the Havasupai Reservation. Both motels arrange day and overnight trips into the canyon, offering various combinations of helicopter, mule and hiking to get down and back up.

Moving westward, you'll come to teeny **Hackberry**, whose 1934 **Hackberry General Store** (☎ 928-769-2605; www.hackberrygeneralstore.com; 11255 E Route 66, Hackberry; ⏰ 9am-6pm Apr-Oct, 10am-5pm Oct-Mar) lures passersby with its eccentrically decorated gas station, vintage cars in faded disrepair and rusted-out ironwork. It's run by a Route 66 memorialist and makes the best spot on this stretch to stop for a cold drink and souvenirs.

For more information on the history of this old highway as well as details on annual events, check out the **Historic Route 66 Association of Arizona** (www.azrt66.com).

Canyon Motel & RV Park　MOTEL $
(☎ 928-635-9371; www.thecanyonmotel.com; 1900 E Rodeo Rd; tent/RV sites $31/43, r $88-94, train cars $94-192; ✳ 🛜 🏊 🐾) Stone cottages (c 1940s) and rooms in two 1929 railroad-cabooses and a former Grand Canyon Railway coach-car offer a quirky alternative to a standard motel. Children especially love the

cozy caboose rooms, with bunks and modern conveniences; rates for the larger one include up to six guests, while five people can fit into the smaller one.

★ **Lodge on Route 66**　　　MOTEL **$$**
(☑ 877-563-4366, 928-635-4534, Rodeway Inn & Suites 4041; www.thelodgeonroute66.com; 200 E Route 66; r incl breakfast $100-190, ste $155-190; ❄ ✆) This smart drive-up motel embraces its Route 66 and Southwest heritage with low-key style, carved vigas and loads of handsome charm. Rooms feature sturdy dark-wood furniture, wrought-iron accents and sumptuous linens. Most suites have kitchenettes, and there's a pleasant sitting area outside each room.

Unlike the bulk of accommodations cashing in on Route 66 nostalgia, the Lodge doesn't feel lonely and depressing. Rooms across the street in the sister Rodeway Inn & Suites are more contemporary in feel, with cool colors, stone soaking tubs and Warholesque portraits of iconic America on the wall. Rates include continental breakfast.

**Grand Canyon
Railway Hotel**　　　HOTEL **$$**
(☑ 928-635-4010; www.thetrain.com; 235 N Grand Canyon Blvd; r $175-200, ste $249; ❄ ✆ ❄) This sprawling 297-room hotel caters primarily to Grand Canyon Railway passengers. An elegant lobby with chandelier, stone fireplace and plush leather chairs is designed to take travelers back to the romance of train travel, but the rooms are basic upscale roadside hotel. It's spacious and comfortable, and centrally located, with a glass-enclosed indoor pool.

Trappers Rendezvous　　　B&B **$$$**
(☑ 928-635-1002; www.trappersrendezvous.com; 1019 Airport Rd; r/ste $195/247) Handsome Western-style cabins sit in a half-circle, with barbecue grills and a fire pit. Despite being a stone's throw from the highway and only a few minutes' drive from downtown Williams, it's a peaceful spot and an excellent choice.

A friendly low-key breakfast is served family style, and there's a prairie dog colony just beyond the cabins. It's fun to sit on a rock with morning coffee and watch the vigilant critters scurry about the desert flatland.

✗ Eating & Drinking

★ **Grand Canyon Winery**　　　BAR
(☑ 855-598-0999; www.thegrandcanyonwinery.com; 138 W Route 66) You just gotta try a place that produces wines with names like Traveler, Wanderlust and Dreamer, and sports the motto, 'Travel far, drink local.' But Grand Canyon Winery is more than just branding. It has excellent wines, produced with local grapes, and craft beer from their sister Historic Brewing Co, served by the mason glass or hefty-portioned flight.

It's a friendly low-key spot, with a handful of stools along the tiny bar and a few tables. Kids play Jenga, folks wander in from the Western-themed shenanigans outside, while travelers share canyon stories. A limited menu includes a huge plate of cheese and meats.

Cafe 326　　　CAFE **$**
(www.cafe326.com; 326 W Route 66; breakfast under $5, lunch $5-7; ❨ 7:30am-3:30pm; ✆) A friendly and homey spot with wi-fi, bagels, pastries and breakfast sandwiches in the morning, and a healthy array of salads and sandwiches at lunch – all from scratch. Nothing fancy and weak coffee, but a good spot for a quick meal.

Pine Country Restaurant　　　AMERICAN **$**
(☑ 928-635-9718; www.pinecountryrestaurant.com; 107 N Grand Canyon Blvd; breakfast $4-17, lunch $7-10, dinner $10-25; ❨ 6:30am-9pm) Though the menu offers few surprises, there's a wide variety from pork chops to taco salad that keeps everyone happy and the price is right. If nothing else, swing by for a slice of one of their gigantic pies, made fresh in-house daily, and an Annie Oakley (that's Williams-talk for cappuccino) at the GidcyUp 'n' Go Coffee Bar.

Dara Thai Cafe　　　THAI **$**
(☑ 928-635-2201; 145 W Route 66, Suite C; mains $3-15; ❨ 11am-2pm & 5-9pm Mon-Sat; ✎) An unassuming spot tucked down a quiet side street, this is your only option for a lighter alternative to meat-heavy menus elsewhere

---

ⓘ Swing by the **Safeway** (pharmacy ☑ 928-635-0500; 637 W Route 66; ❨ 5am-10pm), just southwest of the tourist hub on old Route 66, for groceries and supplies before heading up to the Grand Canyon. Inside there's a pharmacy and a Starbucks, Williams' best bet for a strong cup of brew.

in town. Despite its address, look for the front door along S 2nd St.

Station 66 Italian Bistro
ITALIAN $$

(☑ 928-635-3992; www.thestation66.com; 144 W Route 66; mains $8-18; ⏱ 11am-10pm) Housed in an old Route 66 building, here you'll find live music in the sidewalk café and rooftop dining. Wood-fire pizza toppings include fresh mozzerella, feta and prosciutto, and the $12 Butcher's Board appetizer is big enough for a meal. Owned by the same folk who run neighboring Grand Canyon Winery, Station 66 serves locally produced wine and beer.

Red Raven Restaurant
AMERICAN $$

(☑ 928-635-4980; www.redravenrestaurant.com; 135 W Route 66; mains $10-22; ⏱ 11am-2pm & 5-9pm, hours vary seasonally) The most upscale dining experience you'll find in Williams. There's a vague sense that you're eating what might be served in the first-class cabin of an American-based airline, but it's fresh and tasty, and quite satisfying.

Pancho McGillicuddy's Mexican Cantina
MEXICAN $$

(☑ 928-635-4150; www.vivapanchos.com; 141 W Railroad Ave; mains $10-15; ⏱ 11am-10pm) Housed in an 1893 tavern with a lively bar serving local microbrews on tap, Pancho's serves up big plates of American-style Mexican fare (don't expect any kick to the 'authentic' New Mexico green chile) and locally sourced grass-fed-beef burgers.

Rod's Steak House
STEAK $$

(☑ 928-635-2671; www.rods-steakhouse.com; 301 E Route 66; mains $13-26; ⏱ 11am-9pm Mon-Sat) The cow-shaped sign and menus spell things out – if you want steak and potatoes, this has been the place to come since 1946. A dark and old-school Route 66 classic with iceberg wedge salad and prime rib.

Cruisers Café 66
AMERICAN $$

(www.cruisers66.com; 233 W Route 66; mains $10-20; ⏱ 3-10pm; 🚗) Decorated with vintage gas pumps and old-fashioned Coke ads, this former Route 66 gas station is a fun place for kids. Expect barbecue fare such as burgers, spicy wings, pulled-pork sandwiches and mesquite-grilled ribs (cooked on the outdoor patio).

World Famous Sultana Bar
BAR

(☑ 928-635-2021; 301 W Route 66; ⏱ 10am-2am, shorter hours winter) Expect the once-over when you walk in, as this place seems to spook most tourists. But this 100-year-old bar is pretty darn cool, especially if you like the sort of place that's kitted out with dusty taxidermied animals and crusty locals. It was a speakeasy during Prohibition. No food.

ℹ Information

Visitor Center (☑ 928-635-1418, 800-863-0546; www.experiencewilliams.com; 200 Railroad Ave; ⏱ 8am-6pm summer) Inside the 1901 train depot, with a small but interesting museum on Williams' history, and bookstore selling titles on the canyon, Kaibab National Forest and other areas of interest. You can purchase Grand Canyon entrance passes here.

Police Station (☑ 928-635-4461; 501 W Route 66)

Post Office (☑ 928-635-4572; 120 S 1st St; ⏱ 9am-4:30pm Mon-Fri)

North Country HealthCare (☑ 928-635-4441; www.northcountryhealthcare.org/williams.htm; 301 S 7th St; ⏱ 8am-8pm) Emergency care.

FLAGSTAFF AND WILLIAMS FOR KIDS

➡ Feed the fawns at Grand Canyon Deer Farm (p94).

➡ Picnic and play at Thorpe Park (p101).

➡ Browse books in the children's section of the library (p108).

➡ Ride the scenic chairlift at Arizona Snowbowl (p102).

➡ Hike through lava flows at Sunset Crater Volcano National Monument (p109).

➡ Board the Grand Canyon Railway (p94) to the South Rim.

➡ Check out the playful otters and baby bears at Bearizona (p94).

➡ Pick up a gelato at the Sweete Shoppe (Map p102; ☑ 928-255-4919; www.sweetshoppecandy.com; 15 E Aspen Ave; ⏱ 10am-10pm Mon-Sat, to 9pm Sun).

➡ Glide along the kitschy Route 66 Zipline (p95) in downtown Williams.

➡ Pull up a chair in Heritage Sq and catch a family-friendly flick on a summer weekend.

Williams Ranger Station (☑928-635-2633; www.fs.usda.gov/kaibab; 742 S Clover Rd; ☺8am-4:30pm Mon-Fri) Maps and details for hiking, biking, fishing and camping in the surrounding national forest. It sits just beyond the parking lot of the Best Western Plus, off I-40 west of downtown.

❶ Getting There & Around

Williams sits 60 miles southwest of the South Rim and 34 miles west of Flagstaff; Arizona Shuttle (p92) offers multiple daily runs to the canyon ($29) and to Flagstaff ($22).

Amtrak (☑800-372-7245; www.amtrak.com; 233 N Grand Canyon Blvd) Trains stop at Grand Canyon Railway Depot.

Flagstaff

☑928 / POP 67,458 / ELEV 7000FT

Flagstaff's laid-back charms are myriad, from its pedestrian-friendly historic downtown crammed with vernacular architecture and vintage neon to its high-altitude pursuits like skiing and hiking. Locals are generally a happy, athletic bunch, skewing more toward granola than gunslinger. Northern Arizona University (NAU) gives 'Flag' its college-town flavor, while its railroad history still figures firmly in the town's identity. Throw in a healthy appreciation for craft beer, freshly roasted coffee beans and an all-around good time and you have the makings of a town you want to slow down and savor. In Flag, Northern Arizona students, tourists and locals mingle seamlessly, and it makes an excellent base to hunker down for days or weeks.

From downtown, I-17 heads south toward Phoenix; a few miles south of town, Hwy Alt 89 (89A) splits off and parallels I-17 as a scenic and winding road through Oak Creek Canyon for 28 miles to Sedona. Hwy 180 north leads to Grand Canyon's South Entrance, and Hwy 89 beelines north to Cameron to meet Hwy 64, leading westward to the recommended East Entrance.

◉ Sights

⭐**Museum of Northern Arizona**   MUSEUM
(Map p100; ☑928-774-5213; www.musnaz.org; 3101 N Fort Valley Rd; adult/senior/child 10-17yr $10/9/6; ☺10am-5pm Mon-Sat, noon-5pm Sun; ⊞) An attractive Craftsman-style stone building amid a pine grove, this small but excellent museum spotlights local Native American archaeology, history and culture, as well as geology, biology and the arts. It's on the way to the Grand Canyon, and makes

FLAGSTAFF URBAN TRAIL SYSTEM (FUTS)

The envy of any town, Flagstaff's **Urban Trail System** is a 50-mile city-wide interconnected network of trails reserved for walking, hiking and cycling. The trails, about 50% of which are paved, pass through the urban center, climb gently through ponderosa forest and wind through meadows. When completed, the system will include a total of 130 miles of trails. Pick up a free map at shops throughout town, including downtown's **Pay 'n' Take** (p107), or access it online at www.flagstaff.az.gov.

a wonderful introduction to human and natural history of the region.

Lowell Observatory   OBSERVATORY
(Map p100; ☑928-774-3358, recorded information 928-233-3211; www.lowell.edu; 1400 W Mars Hill Rd; adult/child 5-17yr $12/6; ☺9am-10pm Jun-Aug, shorter hours Sep-May; ⊞) Sitting atop a hill just west of downtown, this national historic landmark was built by Percival Lowell in 1894. The first sighting of Pluto occurred here in 1930. Weather permitting, visitors can stargaze through on-site telescopes, including the famed 1896 Clark Telescope, the impetus behind the now-accepted theory of an expanding universe.

Riordan Mansion
State Historic Park   HISTORIC SITE
(Map p100; ☑928-779-4395; www.azstateparks.com/parks/rima; 409 W Riordan Rd; adult/child 7-13yr $10/5; ☺9:30am-5pm daily May-Oct, 10:30am-5pm Thu-Mon Nov-Apr) Having made a fortune from their Arizona Lumber Company, brothers Michael and Timothy Riordan built this sprawling duplex in 1904. The Craftsman-style design was the brainchild of architect Charles Whittlesey, who also designed El Tovar on the South Rim. The exterior features hand-split wooden shingles, log-slab siding and rustic stone. Filled with Edison, Stickley, Tiffany and Steinway furniture, the interior is a shrine to arts and crafts.

Arboretum   GARDENS
(☑928-774-1442; www.thearb.org; 4001 S Woody Mountain Rd; adult/child $8.50/3; ☺9am-4pm Wed-Sun, May-Oct; ⊞) More than just an attraction for gardeners and plant lovers, this 200-acre arboretum is a lovely spot to take a

Flagstaff

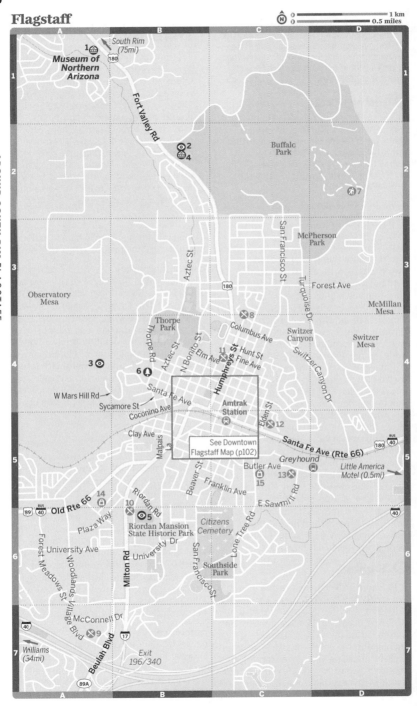

0 ——————— 1 km
0 ——————— 0.5 miles

1 Museum of Northern Arizona

South Rim (75mi)

180

Fort Valley Rd

Buffalo Park

2
4

7

San Francisco St

McPherson Park

Forest Ave

Observatory Mesa

McMillan Mesa

Thorpe Park

180

Columbus Ave

8

Switzer Canyon

Switzer Mesa

Aztec St

Thorpe Rd

Aztec St

N Bonito St

Elm Ave

Humphreys St

Hunt St

Fine Ave

11

Turquoise Dr

Switzer Canyon Dr

3

6

W Mars Hill Rd

Santa Fe Ave

Sycamore St

Coconino Ave

Amtrak Station

Elden St

12

Santa Fe Ave (Rte 66)

BUS 180 40

Clay Ave

Malpais La

See Downtown Flagstaff Map (p102)

Greyhound

Little America Motel (0.5mi)

89 BUS 40

Old Rte 66

14

Beaver St

Franklin Ave

Butler Ave

15

13

40

Plaza Way

Riordan Rd

10

5

Riordan Mansion State Historic Park

University Dr

E Sawmill Rd

Lone Tree Rd

Citizens Cemetery

17

Milton Rd

University Rd

University Ave

San Francisco St

Southside Park

Forest Meadows St

Woodlands Village Blvd

McConnell Dr

40

9

Beulah Blvd

17

Williams (34mi)

Exit 196/340

89A

Flagstaff

break and rejuvenate your spirits. Two short trails hug a meadow and wind beneath ponderosa pines, passing a herb garden, native plants and wildflowers. A longer loop makes an easy amble through the woods.

Thorpe Park FARK

(Map p100; 191 N Thorpe Rd; 🚸 🐕) A great playground, plenty of shade, and a dog park.

Pioneer Museum MUSEUM

(Map p100; ☎928-774-6272; www.arizonahistorical society.org/museums/flagstaff.asp; 2340 N Fort Valley Rd; adult/child $5/free; ☺9am-5pm Mon-Sat) Built in 1908 from volcanic remains of the nearby Mt Eldon eruptions, this stone house served as the county hospital for the indigent and was known as the 'poor farm' until its closure in 1936. John Hance, a colorful Grand Canyon character who built its first tourist trail, died here in 1919. Today, it is a small and quirky museum of Flagstaff's early history, with photographs and an eclectic mix of pioneer and medical memorabilia.

Coconino Center for the Arts ARTS CENTER

(Map p100; ☎928-779-2300; www.culturalpartners. org; 2300 N Fort Valley Rd; ☺vary) Behind the Pioneer Museum, this center exhibits work by local artists and hosts various performances and programs. Check its website for current exhibitions and events.

🏃 Activities

If you can't guess by glancing around at the physically fit townsfolk, Flagstaff is a mecca for outdoor pursuits. For details on hiking and swimming in Oak Creek Canyon, about a half-hour south of Flagstaff, see p113.

Hiking & Biking

Pop into the USFS ranger station or any of Flagstaff's outdoor shops for maps and information about the scores of hiking and mountain-biking trails in and around Flagstaff. For cycle rental, local expertise and trailmaps, head to **Absolute Bikes** (Map p100; ☎928-779-5969; www.absolutebikes.net; 202 E Route 66; bike rentals per day from $39; ☺9am-7pm Mon-Fri, 9am-6pm Sat, 10am-4pm Sun Apr-Dec, shorter hours Jan-Mar).

Buffalo Park HIKING

(Map p100; ☎928-774-2868; 2400 N Gemini Rd; 🚸🐕) This easily accessible and mostly flat 2-mile trail winds around a lovely open expanse of grassland, dips into the ponderosa and offers beautiful views of the San Francisco Peaks. Several exercise stops (stretch, hang, balance) pepper the wide dirt path, and it's popular with joggers, dog-walkers and families. Bicycles allowed.

Kachina Trail HIKING

(Arizona Snowbowl) A gentle 5-mile one-way hike through ponderosa forest and meadows offers lovely views. The trail begins at 9500ft and descends 700ft.

Humphrey's Peak HIKING

(www.fs.usda.gov; Arizona Snowbowl) The state's highest mountain (12,633ft) is a reasonably straightforward, though strenuous, hike in summer. The trail, which begins in the Arizona Snowbowl, winds through forest, eventually coming out above the beautifully barren tree line. The total distance is 4.5 miles one-way; allow six to eight hours round-trip.

> ### DISC GOLF
>
> As you might expect from an outdoorsy college town, disc golf (much like golf, but played with frisbees and also known as frisbee golf) is quite popular. There are four 18-hole courses in the Flagstaff area – our favorite is **Snowbowl** (p102), where you can while away a high desert afternoon or the quiet slopes of the ski basin. Buy discs and get details on all four courses at downtown's **Aspen Sports** (p108).

Downtown Flagstaff

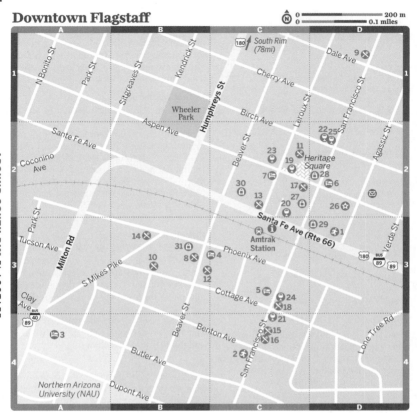

Arizona Trail Walnut Canyon Rim   CYCLING
This stretch of the Arizona Trail (6.7 miles to Fisher Point) winds through pine and oak, and follows a tributary of Walnut Canyon. You may want to walk your bike along some tight turns. Take I-40 for 5 miles east to the Walnut Canyon exit, and look for the signed dirt road leading 1.7 miles to the trailhead.

Skiing
Flagstaff sees an annual average of 108in of snow. Go to Peace Surplus (p108) for ski rental.

Arizona Snowbowl   SKIING
(☎928-779-1951; www.arizonasnowbowl.com; 9300 N Snowbowl Rd, Hwy 180 & Snowbowl Rd; lift ticket adult/youth 13-18yr/child 8-12yr $59/55/35; ⊙9am-4pm mid-Dec–mid-Apr) About 14 miles north of downtown, Arizona Snowbowl is small but lofty, with four lifts that service 32 ski runs between 9200ft and 11,500ft.

Flagstaff Nordic Center   SKIING
(☎928-220-0550; www.flagstaffnordiccenter.com; Mile Marker 232, Hwy 180; weekend/weekday from $18/12; ⊙9am-4pm Dec-Mar) Fifteen miles north of Flagstaff, the Nordic Center offers 25 miles of groomed trails for cross-country skiing, as well as lessons and rentals. Also has snowshoe and multi-use trails. Near the Nordic Center off Hwy 180 you can ski – no permit required – across forest service land.

Other Activities
**Flagstaff Climbing
(Downtown Crag)**   ROCK CLIMBING
(Map p102; ☎928-556-9909; www.flagstaffclimbing.com; 205 S San Francisco St; $15; ⊙10am-10pm Mon-Fri, noon-8pm Sat & Sun) Provides 7000-sq-ft of indoor climbing walls, and offers indoor and outdoor classes, camps, guided trips and information on local climbing routes. There is a second location (☎928-699-4246; 1519 Main St), with a smaller climbing gym.

Downtown Flagstaff

◎ Activities, Courses & Tours
1 Absolute Bikes	D3
2 Flagstaff Climbing (Downtown Crag)	C4

◉ Sleeping
3 Drury Inn & Suites	A4
4 Dubeau Hostel	C3
5 Grand Canyon International Hostel	C3
6 Hotel Monte Vista	D2
7 Weatherford Hotel	C2

⊗ Eating
8 Beaver Street Brewery	B3
9 Brix Restaurant & Wine Bar	D1
10 Cottage Place	B3
11 Diablo Burger	C2
La Bellavia	(see 12)
12 Macy's	B3
13 McMillan Bar & Kitchen	C2
14 Pizzicletta	B3
15 Proper Meats + Provisions	C4
16 Sugar Mama's Bakery	C4
17 Sweete Shoppe	C2
18 Tourist Home Urban Market	C3

◎ Drinking & Nightlife
19 Cuvee 928 Wine Bar & Cafe	C2
20 Flagstaff Brewing Company	C2
21 Historic Brewing Co Barrel & Bottle House	C4
22 Hops on Birch	D2
Monte Vista Cocktail Lounge	(see 6)
23 Pay 'n' Take	C2
24 Tinderbox Annex	C3
25 Vino Loco	D2
Zane Grey Bar & Ballroom	(see 7)

◎ Entertainment
Charly's Pub & Grill	(see 7)
26 Flagstaff Symphony Orchestra	D2

◎ Shopping
27 Aspen Sports	C2
28 Babbitt's Backcountry Outfitter	D2
29 Painted Desert Trading Co	D3
30 Peace Surplus	C2
The Artists' Gallery	(see 27)
31 Zani	B3

Hitchin' Post Stables   HORSEBACK RIDING
(☑928-774-1719; www.hitchinpoststables.com; 4848 Lake Mary Rd) Trail, wagon and sleigh rides through the ponderosa of Coconino National Forest, with options to include Cowboy breakfasts and steak dinners.

🛏 Sleeping

Camping

There are nine USFS campgrounds in the surrounding area, and the four USFS Red Rock Ranger District campgrounds stretch along Hwy 89A through lovely Oak Creek Canyon, 15 miles south of town. Free dispersed camping is permitted in the Coconino National Forest surrounding Flagstaff.

Bonito Campground   CAMPGROUND $
(www.fs.usda.gov/coconino; Sunset Crater & Wupatki National Monument; $18; ☺May-Sep) This USFS campground has 43 tent-only sites conveniently located next to the entrance of Sunset Crater and Wupatki National Monuments. It's just off Hwy 89 from Flagstaff, between Flagstaff and the turn-off for the South Rim's East Entrance.

Flagstaff KOA   CAMPGROUND $
(☑800-562-3524, 928-526-9926; www.flagstaffkoa.com; 5803 N Hwy 89; tent sites $26-34, RV sites $34-68, cabins $70, tepee $55; ☺year-round;

🛜🐕) This big campground lies a mile north of I-40 off exit 201, 5 miles northeast of downtown. A path leads from the campground to trails at Mt Elden. It's family-friendly, with banana-bike rentals, family weekend movies and a splash park. Four one-room cabins sleep up to four, but you must bring your own bedding.

Lodging

Dozens of nondescript, independent motels, with rates ranging from $40 to $60, line Old Route 66 and the railroad tracks east of downtown (exit 198 off I-40). Check the room before you pay – some are much worse than others. For the money, you're far better off at one of the hostels or historic hotels downtown.

★**Dubeau Hostel**   HOSTEL $
(Map p102; ☑928-774-6731; www.grandcanyonhostel.com; 19 W Phoenix Ave; dm $27, r $50-130; 🅿❄@🛜) Built in 1929 and Flagstaff's first motel, this independent hostel offers the same friendly service and clean, well-run accommodations as its sister property, Grand Canyon International Hostel. The private rooms are like basic, but handsome, hotel rooms, with refrigerators, cable TV and private baths. The on-site Nomads serves beer, wine and light snacks. Also has kitchen and laundry facilities.

SCENIC CHAIRLIFT

From May through mid-October, Flagstaff's Arizona Snowbowl opens a **scenic chairlift** (adult/child 6-12yrs $19/10; ⊙10am-4pm Mon-Fri). The 30-minute ride takes folks to 11,500ft, where you'll find marvelously cool temperatures and panoramic views of Sedona's red rocks, Grand Canyon and more; they say that on a clear day you can see as far as the North Rim. Children under six years of age ride free.

Grand Canyon International Hostel   HOSTEL $

(Map p102; ☑928-779-9421; www.grandcanyon hostel.com; 19½ S San Francisco St; dm $25, r with shared bath $52-60; ✳@🖘) Housed in a historic building with hardwood floors and Southwestern decor, this bright, homey and immaculate hostel offers eight private rooms and dorms with a four-person maximum. There's also a kitchen and laundry, and complimentary coffee, pastries and instant oatmeal.

★Little America Hotel   HOTEL $$

(☑928-779-7900;   http://flagstaff.littleamerica. com; 2515 E Butler Ave; r $119-225, ste $269-349; ✳🖘☒) When you reach the Sinclair truck stop just off I-40, don't drive away thinking you have the wrong place. A little further down the side driveway behind an unassuming exterior and hugging 500 acres of ponderosa forest, is a sprawling two-story hotel with spacious French Provincial–styled rooms, upscale bedding with goose-down pillows and large retro-tiled bathrooms.

Part of a hotel chain that first opened in 1952, this quiet and friendly oasis feels like stepping into a time warp. Take your martini out back, relax on the lawn and take a stroll through the woodland path.

★Hotel Monte Vista   HISTORIC HOTEL $$

(Map p102; ☑928-779-6971; www.hotelmontevista. com; 100 N San Francisco St; r $85-160, ste $145-180; ✳🖘) A huge, old-fashioned neon sign towers over this allegedly haunted 1926 landmark hotel, hinting at what's inside: feather lampshades, vintage furniture, bold colors and eclectic decor. Rooms are named for the movie stars who slept in them, such as the Humphrey Bogart room, with dramatic black walls, yellow ceiling and gold-satin bedding. Several resident ghosts supposedly make regular appearances.

Comfi Cottages   BUNGALOW $$

(☑928-774-0731; www.comficottages.com; cottages $145-285; 🖘🐾) All but one of the these well-kept bungalows are within a mile of the historic district. Most were built in the 1920s and '30s and have a comfortable homey feel, with wood floors, Craftsman-style kitchens, board games in the cabinet and little lawns. The friendly owners have lived in Flagstaff for many years, and they're a wonderful source for tourist information.

Weatherford Hotel   HISTORIC HOTEL $$

(Map p102; ☑928-779-1919; www.weatherfordhotel. com; 23 N Leroux St; r $95-145, without bath $85; ✳🖘) This charming historic hotel in downtown Flagstaff opened its doors in 1900, and the rooms maintain a pared down turn-of-the-20th-century authenticity. Three of the rooms incorporate modern amenities such as TVs and air-conditioning, and there's a lovely wraparound porch on the 3rd floor.

The hotel hosts four bars and weekend live music; if you need silence in the evening, consider staying elsewhere. The real bargain here is the $55 room across from the bar.

Drury Inn & Suites   HOTEL $$

(Map p102; ☑928-773-4900; www.druryhotels. com; 300 S Milton Rd; r $170-200, ste $215-225; 🅿✳🖘☒🐾) Stylish rooms with a microwave and refrigerator make this a dependable chain hotel within walking distance of Flagstaff's historic downtown. Included in the rate is happy hour with beer, wine (with a limit) and a hearty spread of appetizers, and breakfast.

Starlight Pines   B&B $$

(☑928-527-1912; www.starlightpinesbb.com; 3380 E Lockett Rd; r $135-189; ✳@🖘) Low-key and friendly Starlight Pines offers four spacious rooms in a Victorian-style home, each decorated in simple, homey style with Tiffany-style lamps, antique clawfoot tubs and other lovely touches.

✕ Eating

Flagstaff loves good food and drink, and it's the best place in the region for independently owned and creative dining.

★Tourist Home Urban Market   CAFE $

(Map p102; ☑928-779-2811; www.touristhome urbanmarket.com; 52 S San Francisco St; mains $7-12; ⊙6am-6pm; 🐾) Housed in a beautifully renovated 1926 house that was originally home to Basque sheepherder immigrants, this upscale market café serves up the best breakfast in a town full of excellent morning vittles. Try delicious poached eggs served on cheese grits with Applewood smoked bacon and a homemade donut, or pop in for a carne asada sandwich with spicy gunslinger mayo at lunch.

The small market features local and organic products, homemade side salads and a wide assortment of juices, including quirky twists like dandelion and burdock, and old-school bottled sodas. The outdoor seating shares space with the Tinderbox Annex (p107).

★ **Proper Meats + Provisions** MARKET
(Map p102; ☑928-774-9001; www.propermeats. com; 110 S San Francisco St; ☺10am-7pm Tue-Sun)
🐾 Come here for salami, local grass-fed beef for the barbecue, house-made pancetta and other meat-lover delights. There's also wine, an eclectic selection of non-alcoholic drinks, cheese and fresh-baked rustic bread. Pick up a sandwich, meat-heavy or veggie-friendly, for the road. And for your canine companion, the Proper Meats' commitment to organic and local extends to their dog food.

Macy's CAFE $
(Map p102; www.macyscoffee.net; 14 S Beaver St; mains under $8; ☺6am-8pm; 🛜🖋) The delicious house-roasted coffee at this Flagstaff institution has kept the city buzzing for more than 30 years now. The vegetarian menu includes many vegan choices, along with traditional café grub like pastries, steamed eggs, waffles, yogurt and granola, salads and veggie sandwiches.

McMillan Bar & Kitchen AMERICAN $
(Map p102; ☑928-774-3840; www.themcmillan flagstaff.com; 2 W Route 66; mains $8-12; ☺11am-2am) Housed in an historic bank, here the menu features excellent lamb sliders, posole soup and pub fare with a local twist. Creative cocktails pack a punch.

Diablo Burger BURGERS $
(Map p102; ☑928-774-3274; www.diabloburger. com; 120 N Leroux St; mains $11-14; ☺11am-9pm Sun-Wed, 11am-10pm Thu-Sat) A locally sourced gourmet burger joint with hefty burgers on English-muffin buns and delicious Herbes de Provence seasoned fries. The cheddar-topped Blake gives a nod to New Mexico with Hatch chile mayo and roasted green chiles. The place is tiny, so come early or plan to sit outside and people-watch. Beer and wine are also served.

La Bellavia BREAKFAST $
(Map p102; 18 S Beaver St; mains $4-9; ☺6:30am-2pm) Be prepared to wait in line at this popular breakfast spot. The seven-grain French toast with bananas, apples or blueberries is excellent; or try one of their egg dishes, such as eggs sardo, with sautéed spinach and artichoke hearts. Lunch includes a grilled portobello-mushroom sandwich and a grilled salmon salad, as well as standard options like grilled cheese, burgers and a tuna melt.

AROUND SOUTH RIM FLAGSTAFF

PICNIC SUPPLIES

Pick up a loaf of rustic bread and fill a cooler with house-cured meats, locally sourced cheese and homemade pastries for a rim-side picnic. Regardless of picnic plans, eating options at the park veer towards food court or high-end so a cooler of goodies in the room is a good idea.

Whole Foods (Map p100; ☑928-774-5747; 320 S Cambridge Lane; ☺8am-9pm; 🖋) Focus on organic and a large selection of ready-made fare.

Bashas' (Map p100; ☑928-774-3882; www.bashas.com; 2700 S Woodlands Village Blvd; ☺6am-11pm) Local chain grocery; there's a second location at Humphrey St.

Proper Meats + Provisions Upscale sandwiches, salami and grass-fed meat.

Tourist Home Urban Market Side salads, gourmet condiments and quirky drinks.

Sugar Mama's Bakery (Map p102; ☑928-221-8440; www.sugarmamasflagstaff.com; 116 S San Francisco St; pastries $2-4; ☺10am-4pm Wed-Sat) Old-school bakery with tasty cookies, pies, cupcakes and pastries.

Simply Delicious Cafe Daily Fare (p106) Sandwiches and salads.

La Fonda
MEXICAN $

(☎ 928-779-0296; www.lafondaflg.com; 1900 N 2nd St; mains $7-14; ☺ 10am-9pm) Big plates of simple and tasty Mexican fare in a residential neighborhood.

★ Pizzicletta
PIZZA $$

(Map p102; ☎ 319-774-3242; www.pizzicletta. com; 203 W Phoenix Ave; pizzas $10-15; ☺ from 5pm Tue-Sun) Tiny Pizzicletta, where the excellent thin-crusted wood-fired pizzas are loaded with gourmet toppings like arugula and aged prosciutto, is housed in a sliver of a white-brick building lined with handsome paned windows. Inside there's an open kitchen, one long table with iron chairs, Edison bulbs and industrial surrounds. It's located just south of the Amtrak station. Try a gelato for dessert.

Coppa Cafe
CAFE $$

(Map p100; ☎ 928-637-6813; www.coppacafe.net; 1300 S Milton Rd; lunch & brunch $8-15, mains $21-31; ☺ 11am-7pm Wed & Thu, 11am-8pm Fri & Sat, 10am-4pm Sun) Brian Konefal and Paola Fioravanti, who met at an Italian culinary school, are the husband-and-wife team behind this tiny European-styled locally sourced café. The polenta shepard's pie and seasonal quiche, served as individual casseroles, are excellent, but the real stars are the homemade desserts including s'more lollipops and tiny dark-chocolate brownies.

Unmatched chairs and simple wooden tables, a white-tin ceiling and bright orange walls give Coppa an airy, homey feel; more like you're sitting in someone's kitchen rather than a strip-mall café.

Simply Delicious Cafe Daily Fare
CAFE $$

(Map p100; ☎ 928-774-2855; www.simplydeliciousflagstaff.com; 408 E Route 66; mains $8-15; ☺ 11am-4pm Mon-Sat) Hefty and creative sandwiches, homemade soups and tasty salads, as well as fresh spins on Mexican fare such as fish tacos and quesdaillas with blue corn, brie and pear. It's difficult to find this tiny gem, hidden in the back of an industrial strip – look for the inviting orange awning jutting out from a stone wall behind the used-car lot.

They also do frozen oven-ready enchiladas ($32), lasagna ($32) and stuffed poblanos ($52) that serve eight to 10 people; perfect for quick and easy meals.

Beaver Street Brewery
BREWPUB $$

(Map p102; www.beaverstreetbrewery.com; 11 S Beaver St; lunch $8-23, dinner $13-23; ☺ 11am-11pm Sun-Thu, to midnight Fri & Sat; ⊞) Families, river guides, ski bums and businesspeople – everybody is here or on the way. The menu is typical brewpub fare, with pizzas, burgers and salads. Relax with a season brew on the small outdoor terrace, or head to the cozy old-fashioned feeling-Brews & Cues (21 years and older) for a round of pool.

★ Brix Restaurant & Wine Bar
MODERN AMERICAN $$$

(Map p102; ☎ 928-213-1021; www.brixflagstaff.com; 413 N San Francisco St; mains $23-34; ☺ from 5pm Tue-Sat) Brix brings a breath of fresh, unpretentious sophistication to Flagstaff's dining scene. It offers locally sourced seasonal fare in handsome intimate surrounds punctuated with exposed brick walls and an intimate copper bar. Options include coffee-and-chile roast duck and chicken with collard greens, and there's a leafy patio in the back.

Cottage Place
MODERN AMERICAN $$$

(Map p102; ☎ 928-774-8431; 126 W Cottage Ave; mains $24-36; ☺ dinner Wed-Sun) Housed in an understated bungalow on a quiet street south of the tracks, Cottage Place has pleasant courtyard dining and a cozy interior. It's a hot commodity with dating couples, birthday celebrants and other special-occasion types.

Josephine's
AMERICAN $$$

(Map p100; ☎ 928-779-3400; www.josephines restaurant.com; 503 N Humphreys St; mains $18-30; ☺ 11am-2:30pm & 5-9pm Mon-Fri, 8am-2pm & 5-9pm Sat & Sun) Josephine's feels more like someone's home than a restaurant, occupying a 1911 Craftsman bungalow. There's pleasant patio dining, a great old stone bar, a fireplace and Craftsman light fixtures. Consider stopping for lunch – pecan-encrusted fish tacos or a fried-green-tomato-and-turkey-sandwich are welcome changes from typical lunch fare.

SUMMER NIGHTS ON THE SQUARE

On summer weekends, people gather on blankets at Heritage Sq, in the center of Flagstaff's historic downtown, for live music (6:30pm) and a kid-friendly movie projected on an adjacent building (9pm). See www.flagdba.com/movies-on-the-square for a schedule.

🍷 Drinking

⭐ Tinderbox Annex
COCKTAIL BAR

(Map p102; ☑ 928-226-8440; www.tinderboxkitch en.com; 34 S San Francisco St; ⊙ from 4pm) Craft cocktails that don't slack on flavor or punch. We can't vouch for the TBOX (cola over red wine?) but the Moscow Mule with mint and cucumber might just be the best cocktail in Flagstaff. The outdoor patio, which is in fact a handball court built by Basque immigrants in 1926, attracts a low-key local crowd.

It's quintessential Flag, where families with babies in jogging strollers and toddling little ones mingle seamlessly with students, business-folk and outdoor types.

⭐ Hops on Birch
PUB

(Map p102; ☑ 928-774-4011; www.hopsonbirch. com; 22 E Birch Ave; ⊙ 1:30pm-2am; 🐾) Simple and handsome, Hops on Birch has 28 rotating beers on tap, weekend live music and a friendly local-crowd vibe. In classic Flagstaff style, dogs are as welcome as humans.

Historic Brewing Co Barrel & Bottle House
MICROBREWERY

(Map p102; www.historicbrewingcompany.com; 110 S San Francisco St; ⊙ 11am-10pm Sun-Thu, to 11pm Fri & Sat) The taproom for the Historic Brewing Co, Flagstaff's local microbrew, has 26 craft beer taps, wine flights and bottles of locally crafted Grand Canyon Winery. There's also a massive wall-refrigerator lined with a dizzying selection of beer by the bottle or can.

This is the most sophisticated and low-key of Flagstaff's many brewpubs, with an industrial-hip vibe and a limited menu of meat-heavy delights from Proper Meats + Provisions next door (grass-fed-beef burgers, warm pastrami and beef barbecue).

Vino Loco
WINE BAR

(Map p102; ☑ 928-226-1764; www.vinolocoflag. com; 22 E Birch Ave; ⊙ 11am-9pm Sun-Wed, to midnight Thu-Sat) An intimate under-the-radar hangout with a handful of outdoor tables, wines by the flight, glass or bottle, plus beer, snacks and a small retail shop.

Zane Grey Bar & Ballroom
BAR

(Map p102; ☑ 928-779-1919; www.weatherford hotel.com; Weatherford Hotel, 23 N LeRoux) When the weather is nice, the 3rd-floor wraparound porch of the Weatherford Hotel, just wide enough to hold one row of tables, makes a delightful perch above the bustle of downtown Flag.

Monte Vista Cocktail Lounge
BAR

(Map p102; ☑ 928-779-6971; www.hotelmontevista. com; 100 N San Francisco St, Hotel Monte Vista; ⊙ from 4pm) This hopping lounge in the historic Monte Vista Hotel has a tin ceiling, pool table and weekend live music ranging from country and hip-hop to rock.

Flagstaff Brewing Company
BREWERY

(Map p102; ☑ 928-773-1442; www.flagbrew.com; 16 E Route 66; ⊙ 11am-2am) Popular with students and outdoors types, this downtown brew-pub offers a small and convivial outdoor patio, dependable fare, ping-pong and live music on the weekend.

Pay 'n' Take
BAR

(Map p102; www.payntake.com; 12 W Aspen Ave; ⊙ 7am-10pm Mon-Wed, 7am-1am Thu-Sat, 9am-10pm Sun; 🐾) As much a bar as a 7-Eleven-style market, the Pay 'n' Take is a local institution for midday imbibing. Help yourself to whatever you'd like from the wall refrigerators and take it to the back patio, or sit at the bar. There's an excellent beer selection, and you can have pizza delivered or bring takeout. Cash only; ATM on-site.

Cuvee 928 Wine Bar & Cafe
BAR

(Map p102; ☑ 928-214-9463; www.cuvee928wine bar.com; 6 E Aspen Ave, Heritage Sq; ⊙ 11:30am-9pm Mon-Thu, to 10pm Fri & Sat, 10am-5pm Sun) Wine by the flight and by the glass, and excellent craft cocktails including the classic Pimm's Cup made with fresh cucumber and lime juice. It's a great place to relax outside and people-watch; full menu and Sunday brunch.

Museum Club
BAR

(☑ 928-526-9434; www.themuseumclub.com; 3404 E Route 66; ⊙ 11am-2am) This honky-tonk roadhouse on Route 66 has been kicking up its heels since 1936. Inside what looks like a huge log cabin, you'll find a large wooden dance floor, animal mounts and a sumptuous elixir-filled mahogany bar. The origins of the name? In 1931 it housed a taxidermy museum.

☆ Entertainment

For a complete listing of Flagstaff's many festivals, outdoor music concerts and special events, including the monthly **First Friday ArtWalk**, go to www.flagstaff365.com.

Flagstaff Symphony Orchestra
CLASSICAL MUSIC

(Map p102; ☑ 928-774-5107; www.flagstaffsym phony.org; 113 E Aspen Ave, Suite A; ⊙ 10am-3pm)

Holds eight annual performances in the Ardrey Memorial Auditorium, on the NAU campus.

Charly's Pub & Grill
LIVE MUSIC

(Map p102; ☑928-779-1919; www.weatherford hotel.com; 23 N Leroux St; ⊘8am-2am) Inside the Weatherford Hotel, with regular live blues, jazz and folk.

🛍 Shopping

The hands-down best place in the area for Native American jewelry is the gift shop inside the Museum of Northern Arizona (p99).

The Artists' Gallery
ARTS & CRAFTS

(Map p102; ☑928-773-0958; www.flagstaffartists gallery.com; 17 N San Francisco St; ⊘9:30am-7:30pm Mon-Sat, to 5:30pm Sun) This art co-op, locally owned and operated since 1992, carries the work of over 40 northern Arizona artists, including two-dimensional art, jewelry, ceramics and glasswork.

Painted Desert Trading Co
HANDICRAFTS

(Map p102; ☑928-226-8313; www.painteddesert trading.com; 2 N San Francisco St; ⊘10am-6pm) Carries quality Native American crafts and an excellent selection of books on regional topics.

Zani
GIFTS

Map p102; ☑800-294-9409, 928-774-9409; www.zanicardsandgifts.com; 107 W Phoenix Ave; ⊘10:30am-6pm Mon-Sat) Zani carries beautiful handmade paper, locally made jewelry of silver or fused glass, stamped leather goods and Asian-inspired gifts and homewares.

Outdoor Equipment

Flagstaff is a good place to get last-minute advice and gear before your Grand Canyon backpacking adventure. With the exception of REI, these locally owned outdoor shops sit in the heart of downtown Flagstaff.

Babbitt's Backcountry Outfitter
OUTDOOR EQUIPMENT

(Map p102; ☑928-774-4775; www.babbittsback country.com; 12 E Aspen Ave; ⊘9am-8pm Mon-Sat, 10am-6pm Sun) Rents only backpacks and tents, but sells quality outdoor gear, books and USGS maps.

> ℹ The best way to get to Flagstaff by air is to fly into Phoenix Sky Harbor International Airport, a hub for both major and budget airlines. From here drive the easy two-hour straight shot north to Flagstaff.

Peace Surplus
OUTDOOR EQUIPMENT

(Map p102; ☑928-779-4521; www.peacesurplus. com; 14 W Route 66; ⊘8am-9pm Mon-Fri, to 8pm Sat, to 6pm Sun) Sells and rents a huge array of outdoor clothing and equipment, including snowboards, and downhill and cross-country skis.

Aspen Sports
OUTDOOR EQUIPMENT

(Map p102; ☑928-779-1935; 15 N San Francisco St; ⊘10am-6pm Mon-Sat) Head here for gear that's more climbing- and backpacking-oriented; no rentals.

REI
OUTDOOR EQUIPMENT

(Map p100; ☑928-213-1914; www.rei.com/stores/flagstaff; 323 S Windsor Lane; ⊘9am-8pm Mon-Sat, 10am-6pm Sun) National chain with a wide selection of outdoor gear, including camping supplies, bikes, books and clothes. There's also on-site bike repair and tuning.

ℹ Information

Visitor Center (☑928-774-9541, 800-842-7293; www.flagstaffarizona.org; 1 E Route 66; ⊘8am-5pm Mon-Sat, 9am-4pm Sun) Inside the Amtrak station, the visitor center has a great Flagstaff Discovery map and tons of information on things to do.

Flagstaff Medical Center (☑928-779-3366; www.flagstaffmedicalcenter.com; 1200 N Beaver St; ⊘emergency 24hr)

Library (☑928-779-7670; 300 W Aspen Ave; ⊘10am-9pm Mon-Thu, 10am-7pm Fri, 10am-6pm Sat; 🛜) Free internet and wi-fi.

Police Station (emergency ☑911, general information 928-556-2316, non-emergency dispatch 928-774-1414; 911 E Sawmill Rd; ⊘emergency 24hr)

Post Office (☑928-779-2371; 104 N Agassiz St; ⊘10am-4pm Mon-Fri, 9am-1pm Sat)

USFS Flagstaff Ranger Station (☑928-526-0866; 5075 N Hwy 89; ⊘8am-4pm Mon-Fri) Provides information on the Mt Elden, Humphreys Peak and O'Leary Peak areas north of Flagstaff.

ℹ Getting There & Away

The regional Flagstaff Pulliam Airport is 4 miles south of town off I-17; **US Airways** (☑800-428-4322; www.usairways.com), the only commercial airline to Flagstaff, offers several daily flights from Phoenix Sky Harbor International Airport.

The regional shuttle service is another option. **Amtrak** (☑928-774-8679, 800-872-7245; www.amtrak.com; 1 E Route 66; ⊘3am-10:45pm) Amtrak's Southwest Chief stops at Flagstaff on its daily run between Chicago and Los Angeles, arriving at 8.51pm heading west and 4.36am heading east. The historic station sits in Flag-

WORTH A TRIP

FLAGSTAFF NATIONAL MONUMENTS

Three small but excellent national monuments highlighting the interconnected volcanic and Native American history of the region sit within a roughly 10-mile radius of Flagstaff.

Covered by a single $5 entrance fee (valid for seven days), both **Sunset Crater Volcano** and **Wupatki** lie along Park Loop Rd 545, a well-marked 36-mile loop that heads east off Hwy 89 about 12 miles north of Flagstaff on the way to the North Rim. **Walnut Canyon** sits 8 miles east of Flagstaff, just off I-40.

Each site offers an interpretive visitor center, pleasant picnic grounds, ranger talks and guided walks (summer only).

Sunset Crater Volcano National Monument (928-526-0502; www.nps.gov/sucr; Park Loop Rd 545; $5; 9am-5pm Nov-May, from 8am Jun-Oct) In AD 1064 a volcano erupted on this spot, spewing ash across 800 sq miles, spawning the Kana-A lava flow and leaving behind the 8029ft Sunset Crater. The eruption forced farmers to vacate lands they had cultivated for 400 years, and subsequent eruptions continued for more than 200 years. A 1-mile trail winds through the blacker than black Bonito lava flow (formed c 1180), and another 1-mile round-trip hike climbs Lenox Crater (7024ft).

More ambitious hikers and mountain bikers can ascend O'Leary Peak (8965ft; 8 miles round-trip), and there is a 0.3-mile wheelchair-accessible loop that offers views of the lava flow.

Wupatki National Monument (928-679-2365; www.nps.gov/wupa; Park Loop Rd 545; adult/child 15yr & under $5/free; visitor center 9am-5pm, trails sunrise-sunset) The first eruptions of Sunset Crater (AD 1040–1100) enriched the surrounding soil, luring ancestors of today's Hopi, Zuni and Navajo to the rich agriculture land. By AD 1180, it was home to roughly 100 people, and 2000 more peppered the immediate area. By 1250, however, their pueblos stood abandoned. About 2700 of these structures lie within Wupatki National Monument, though only a few are open to the public.

Walnut Canyon (928-526-3367; www.nps.gov/waca; I-40 exit 204, 8 m les east of Flagstaff; adult/child under 17yr $5/free; 8am-5pm May-Oct, from 9am Nov-Apr; entry to trails close 1hr before park closing;) The Sinagua cliff dwellings here are set in the nearly vertical limestone walls of a small piñon-studded canyon. The mile-long Island Trail steeply descends 185ft (more than 200 stairs), passing 25 rooms built under the natural overhangs and a shorter, wheelchair-accessible Rim Trail affords views of the cliff dwelling from across the canyon.

staff's pedestrian downtown, across the street from restaurants, historic hotels and hostels.

Greyhound (800-231-2222, 928-774-4573; www.greyhound.com; 880 E Butler Ave; midnight-6:30am & 10am-midnight) Stops in Flagstaff multiple times daily en route to/from Albuquerque, Las Vegas, Los Angeles and Phoenix.

Getting Around

Several major car-rental agencies operate from the airport and downtown. A handful of local taxis service the city.

Mountain Line Transit (928-779-6624; www.mountainline.az.gov; adult/child one-way fare $1.25/0.60) Services eight fixed bus routes daily; pick up a user-friendly map at the visitor center. Exact change required; day passes cost adult/child $2.50/1.25.

Uber Flagstaff (www.uber.com/cities/flag staff) App-based members-only car service.

Havasupai Reservation

The 185,000-acre Havasupai Reservation encompasses thousands of acres below the rim and borders Kaibab National Forest and Grand Canyon National Park. The highlights are its stunning, spring-fed waterfalls and inviting azure swimming holes of **Havasu Canyon**, one of the Grand Canyon's greatest treasures. Parts of the canyon floor, as well as the rock underneath the waterfalls and pools, are made up of limestone deposited by flowing water. These limestone deposits are known as travertine, and they give the famous blue-green water its otherworldly hue. The most famous of the waterfalls, Havasu Falls, tumbles 100ft past red rock into a sparkling pool. Mooney Falls tumbles 190ft, while the cascading waters of Beaver Falls tumble gently from pool to pool.

VISITING THE WATERFALLS OF HAVASU CANYON

Far from any hub of tourist services and inaccessible by car, a visit to Havasu Canyon requires a bit of planning and determination. Note, however, that just becasue it's isolated doesn't mean you'll be alone – thousands upon thousands of visitors find their way to Havasu Canyon every year.

First off, don't let place names confuse you: **Hualapai Hilltop**, the access point for Havasu Canyon, is on the Havasupai Indian Reservation, *not* the Hualapai Reservation, as one might think. The Hualapai Reservation, several long and dusty hours west, is home to Grand Canyon West (p117) and the glass skywalk.

From Grand Canyon South Rim, it is a four-hour drive to the middle-of-nowhere-feeling Hualapai Hilltop parking lot. From Hualapai Hilltop, you must hike, ride a horse or fly in a helicopter the 8 miles down into the canyon to the Havasupai village of **Supai**. Supai, the only village within the Grand Canyon and basically just one packed dirt 'road', is the most remote village in the lower 48 states.

Finally, from the village, it's about a 1-mile hike to the first of five waterfalls in Havasu Canyon. The trail to see all five of them involves scrambling, steep inclines, ropes and chain footholds. The descent to the pools below Mooney, in particular, can be treacherous. Before heading down to Supai for the night, you must have reservations at either **Havasu Campground** or **Supai Lodge**. If you camp without a reservation, you will be charged double. Consider spending the night before your descent at the recommended **Hualapai Lodge** (p96), a modern motel that serves as the primary tourist desk for canyon sojourns to both the Hualapai and the Havasupai reservations. Or otherwise the roadside motel **Grand Canyon Caverns & Inn** (p96) in tiny Peach Springs, 67 miles from Hualapai Hilltop.

Despite its popularity, the trail from Supai to Havasu Falls can be tough hiking through unpredictable desert conditions. Use caution when swimming, as there are dangerous currents. Bring plenty of water, and check weather conditions in the region. Flash floods can sweep through the canyon with no warning, even on a beautiful sunny day. The Havasupai Tribe does not allow day trips to Supai or Havasu Falls.

Go to www.havasuwaterfalls.net for details on guided tours, reservations and updated conditions.

Photographs of the striking blue waters are standard on Grand Canyon calenders and postcards, but the falls in fact do not lie within the national park.

🛏 Sleeping

It is essential that you make reservations in advance; if you hike in without a reservation, you will not be allowed to stay in Supai and will have to hike 8 miles back up to your car at Hualapai Hilltop. There are only two overnight options at Havasupai.

Havasu Campground CAMPGROUND $
(☏ 928-443-2137, 928-448-2121, 928-448-2141, 928-448-2180; www.havasuwaterfalls.net; Havasu Canyon, Havasupai Reservation; per night per person $53) Two miles past Supai, the campground stretches 0.75 miles along Havasu Creek between Havasu and Mooney Falls. Sites have picnic tables and the campground features several composting toilets and spring water (treat before drinking). Fires are not permitted but gas stoves are allowed. Reservations required, but sites are first-come, first-served.

Supai Lodge LODGE $$
(☏ 928-448-2201, 928-448-2111; www.havasuwater falls.net; Supai; r for up to 4 people $145; ❄) The only lodging in Supai offers bare-bone white-walled motel rooms, each with two double beds and private showers. Reservations are accepted by phone only.

🍴 Eating

The only eating options in Supai are a mediocre café, a small and overpriced market, and a walk-up window with ice-cream and fry-bread. The following is not a list of the best options, it's a list of the only options.

Sinyella Store FAST FOOD
(Supai, Havasupai Reservation; ⊙ 7am-7pm) The first shop you'll see as you walk through the village. Take off your pack for a minute and lounge on the lawn with fry-bread and an ice-cream float.

Havasupai Tribal Cafe   CAFE

(☑928-448-2981 Supai, Havasupai Reservation; ⊙7am-6:15pm) Basic fare includes hamburgers and fry-bread – but no one comes to Havasupai for the dining.

Havasupai Trading Post   MARKET

(☑928-448-2951 Supai; ⊙8am-5pm) Sells basic but expensive groceries and snacks.

ℹ Information

Entrance to the Havasuapai Reservation is $40 per person. Contact the **Havasupai Tourist Office** (Camping Office; ☑ 928-448-2141, 928-448-2237; www.havasuwaterfalls.net; Supai, Havasupai Reservation; ⊙5:30am-7pm) for all information, including options for guided tours, updated conditions, camping reservations, and horse and mule arrangements. You must call the lodge directly to make a reservation or inquire about a room.

Liquor, recreational drugs, pets, bicycles and nude swimming are not allowed.

ℹ Getting There & Around

Seven miles east of Peach Springs on historic Route 66, a signed turnoff leads to the 62-mile paved road ending at Hualapai Hilltop. Here you'll find the parking area, stables and the trailhead into the canyon, but no services. The closest services are in Peach Tree, and there is no public transportation to Hualapai Hilltop.

Helicopter

Airwest Helicopters (☑ 623-516-2790; www. havasuwaterfalls.net; Hualapai Hilop & Supai, Havasupai Reservation; one-way Hualapi Hilltop to Supai $85; ⊙10am-1pm Mon, Thu, Fri & Sun weather permitting, closed for federal & tribal holidays) Helicopter service from Hualapai Hilltop to Supai, 8 miles below the rim. Reservations are not accepted, and first-come first-served priority is given to Havasupai tribal members. To ensure a flight out of the canyon, you must arrive at the landing area in Supai by 1pm. Call to confirm flights are running, as service may be canceled for all kinds of reasons.

Horse & Mule

You can ride a horse from Hualapai Hilltop to the lodge (one-way/round-trip $70/120), the Havasu Campground (one-way/roundtrip $94/187) or from the lodge to the waterfalls ($60). You can also arrange for a mule, for the same price, to carry your pack into and out of the canyon.

If you're staying at Supai Lodge, call them directly to arrange a ride; otherwise, call the Havasupai Tourist Office. Arrangements are accepted within a week of departure.

Tours

Several companies, including **Wildland Trekking** (p38) and **Papillon Grand Canyon Helicopters** (☑ 702-736-7243, 888-635-7272; www. papillon.com), offer multiday guided hiking and camping tours, sometimes combining helicopter and horseback travel in itineraries. For the package, count on around $500.

Sedona

☑928 / POP 10,111 / ELEV 4500FT

Nestled amid dramatic sandstone formations, Sedona's a stunner. From the small pedestrian-friendly tourist hub, spectacular expanses of red-and-orange-rock landscape stretch south, west and east, and the riparian lushness of Oak Creek Canyon winds north to Flagstaff.

Many New Age types believe that this area is the center of vortexes that radiate Earth's power, and Sedona's combination of scenic beauty, outdoor activities and mysticism draws throngs of tourists year-round. Unlike nearby Flagstaff, 30 miles to the north, Sedona's economy is almost entirely driven by tourism, and in summer the traffic and the crowds in town and on the trails can be stressful.

Sedona is divided into three distinct districts. The roundabout at the intersection of Hwys Alt 89 (89A) and 179, referred to locally as the 'Y', leads to each district. Directly northeast of the Y is **Uptown Sedona**, the pedestrian and tourist center and a hub for souvenir shopping. From here, Hwy 89A continues north to Midley Bridge and through Oak Creek Canyon to Flagstaff. Turning south at the Y on Hwy 179 leads a half-mile to **Tlaquepaque Village**, with many of the town's galleries and a bit less tourist bustle and mayhem.

TRAVEL SMART

Don't be lulled into complacency by the idyllic surrounds of Havasu Canyon. Like anywhere else, the Havasupai Reservation suffers from poverty, drug abuse and crime, and the campground is not patrolled by night. In 2007, the canyon made headlines after the stabbing murder of tourist Tomomi Hanamure on her hike from the lodge to the falls. Do not travel alone, do not travel with valuables and avoid travel after dark.

Sedona

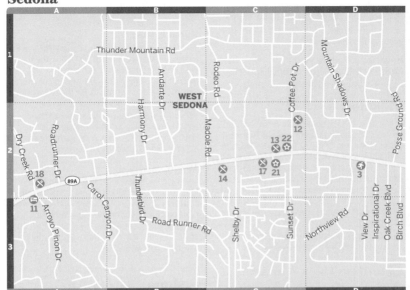

West of the Y is **West Sedona**, where Hwy 89A heads past Airport Rd and a few miles of strip malls and chain hotels to some of Sedona's best spots. These include Dry Creek Rd (Boynton Canyon), Red Rock Loop Rd (with Red Rock State Park and Red Rock Crossing) and Page Springs Rd (to the winery).

A **Red Rock Pass** (per day/week/year $5/15/20) is required to park anywhere in the surrounding national forest and several cultural sites. You can buy one at the visitor centers, various local businesses and hotels, and at some trailheads.

Endless roundabouts on Hwy 179 and stoplights on Hwy 89A through West Sedona make driving through town tricky and frustrating.

◉ Sights

★ Red Rock Crossing/
Crescent Moon Ranch   PARK
(Upper Red Rock Loop Rd; day-use per vehicle $10, cash only; 🎣🐕) Splash in Oak Creek, swim in its deep swimming holes and relax on the wide, flat, red slabs that dot the water. Famous for its splendid views of Cathedral Rock, blazoned on postcards all over town, this picnic area is a lovely place to while away an afternoon. Provides access to Templeton, Baldwin and Cathedral Rock hiking trails.

Red Rock Crossing is 7 miles southwest of town, on the same road as Red Rock State Park. To get here, head west on US 89A to FR 216 (Upper Red Rock Loop Rd), turn south, drive 1.5 miles and follow the signs. If the parking lot is full, turn around and park at the pullout where Red Rock Crossing Rd intersects Chavez Ranch Rd.

Red Rock State Park   PARK
(☑928-282-6907; www.azstateparks.com/Parks/rero; 4050 Red Rock Loop Rd; adult/child 7-13yr/6yr & under $5/3/free; ⊙8am-5pm, visitor center 9am-4:30pm; 🎣) Not to be confused with Slide Rock State Park, this low-key 286-acre park includes an environmental education center, picnic areas and 5 miles of well-marked, interconnecting trails in a riparian habitat amid gorgeous red rock surrounds. Trails range from flat creek-side saunters to moderate climbs to scenic ridges. Ranger-led activities include nature walks and bird walks. Swimming in the creek is prohibited.

The park, 9 miles west of downtown Sedona off Hwy 89A, is the eastern edge of the 15-mile Lime Kiln Trail.

Chapel of the Holy Cross   CHURCH
(☑928-282-4069; www.chapeloftheholycross.com; 780 Chapel Rd; ⊙9am-5pm Dec-Feb, until 6pm Mar-Nov) **FREE** Situated between spec-

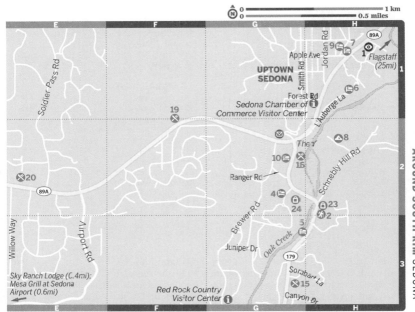

tacular, statuesque natural stone columns 3 miles south of town, this modern 1956 Roman Catholic chapel soars from the rock like a slice of the land itself. Architect Marguerite Brunwig Staude followed the tradition of Frank Lloyd Wright – its wall of glass and the perch it occupies offer a dramatic perspective on the landscape, and the architecture is stunning. Though there are no traditional services, the church offers a 'Taize prayer service' on Mondays at 5pm.

This is one of Sedona's most popular tourist destinations; to avoid summer crowds, come first thing in the morning. Not only is the church itself tiny, just a skinny rectangle designed to blend into and look like the surrounding red rock, but parking is difficult. Follow the signs and keep going past the small parking lots until the winding road dead-ends at the parking lot directly below the chapel; if there's no room, turn around and park wherever you can and hoof it up.

Sedona Arts Center
ARTS CENTER

(☏928-282-3809, 888-954-4442; www.sedona artscenter.com; 15 Art Barn Rd; ☉10am-5pm) The arts center features changing exhibits of local and regional artists, a gift shop, classes in performing and visual arts, and a variety of cultural events like the Sedona Plein Air Festival – featuring local artists in an outdoor festival.

🏃 Activities

Hiking and mountain-biking trails crisscross the surrounding red-rock country and the woods and meadows of green Oak Creek Canyon. The free *Red Rock Country Recreation Guide*, available at the visitor center and ranger station, describes hiking and biking trails for all skill levels and includes a map of scenic drives.

From Midgley Bridge, just over a mile north of town on Hwy 89A, you can hike a mile or so down the Huckaby Trail to a swimming hole and stretch of creek particularly popular with University of Northern Arizona students and locals. It's also a great view of the canyon, and a trailhead for Wilson Canyon and Wilson Mountain trails.

West Fork Trail
HIKING

(☏928-527-3600; Hwy 89A, Oak Creek Canyon; day-use $10) This deservedly popular trail crosses Oak Creek several times as it winds through the ponderosa and the canyon, where walls soar more than 200ft in some places. The trail is marked for the first 3 miles, but you can scramble along the stream bed for the 14-mile length of the canyon.

Sedona

Most people head straight into the canyon, but if you cut over to the creek within the first 50ft just beyond the parking lot, you'll find a particularly nice, sunny stretch with a swimming hole and shallow waters for splashing. It's an excellent hike for fall colors. It's located 9.5 miles north of Sedona (a few miles north of Slide Rock State Park) and 17.5 miles south of Flagstaff on Hwy 89A; look for the signed parking lot.

Boynton Canyon   HIKING

A moderate 3-mile one-way hike through spectacular red-rock Boynton Canyon includes shaded stretches and petroglyphs. From Sedona, head a couple miles west on Hwy 89A to Dry Creek Rd; turn north and follow signs to Boynton Canyon and Enchantment Resort. For a shorter stretch, access the trail from the gated resort.

Ask at the Hike Shop for other hiking and mountain-biking trails in Boynton Canyon.

Slide Rock State Park   SWIMMING

(☑ 928-282-3034; www.azstateparks.com/parks/slro; 6871 N Hwy 89A, Oak Creek Canyon; per car Jun-Sep $20, Sep-May $10; ☺ 8am-7pm Jun-Aug, shorter hours rest of the year; ⛹ ♿) One of Sedona's most popular and most crowded spots, this state park features an 80ft natural sandstone chute that whisks swimmers through Oak Creek. In addition to the main attraction, you can slide along from shallow plateau to shallow plateau along the park's half-mile stretch of creek, or splash in the cool, clear waters. Bring a blanket and a cooler, or buy drinks and snacks at the small park store. It's 7 miles north of downtown Sedona.

Huckaby Trail   HIKING

From the signed trailhead a few miles up from the roundabout on Schnebley Rd to Midgley Bridge, just north of town on Hwy 89A, this trail cuts across the desert scrub, along a ridge with panoramic views of Sedona, and down to Oak Creek. It's a great one-way hike if you can arrange a pickup at Midgley Bridge.

Grasshopper Point   SWIMMING

(Hwy 89A, Oak Creek Canyon; per car $8; walk-ins and bicycles $2; ☺ 9am-dusk) This well-marked national forest park, 3 miles north of Sedona, offers easy access to the siren call of Oak Creek's cool, clear waters. Swim in the marvelously shaded and delightfully deep swimming hole or simply splash along the creek. Though crowds aren't as packed in summer as nearby Sliding Rock, it's a popular escape from the searing rays and can get packed by midday.

In addition to swimming, the park serves as a trailhead for three hiking trails (Allen's Bend, Casner Canyon and Huckaby).

Hi Line Trail   CYCLING

(Hwy 179, off Yavapai Vista parking lot) This triple black-diamond, single-track mountain-bike trail runs along a ridge to Cathedral Rock view. It also makes a beautiful hike; 2 miles one-way.

Over the Edge Sports   BICYCLE RENTAL

(www.otesports.com; 1695 W Hwy 89A; per day $50-80; ☺ 9am-6pm) Mountain-bike rental and trail information.

⚡ Festivals & Events

Sedona International Film Festival FILM
(📞928-282-1177; www.sedonafilmfestival.org;
⊗mid-Feb) International film festival features art and documentary films and film-inspired special events.

🛏 Sleeping

As you might expect from such a scenic town, Sedona is rich with beautiful B&Bs and full-service resorts, for which you should also expect to pay accordingly. Rates at chain motels range from $80 to $180, reasonable by Sedona standards.

Apart from camping, Sedona doesn't have many options for the budget traveler. The little Old West town of Cottonwood, 19 miles southwest of Sedona on Hwy 89A and a famous bootlegging center in its day, has a handful of motels and well-recommended B&Bs that are generally much less expensive.

Camping

Dispersed camping in Red Rock Canyon is limited to designated camping corridors only; the best for red-rock views are along FR 525 in Boynton Canyon. Head west on Hwy 89A, 3 miles past Lower Red Rock Loop Rd to FR 525; dispersed camping is allowed from 2 miles north of Hwy 89A to Boynton Pass Rd.

The **USFS** (📞877-444-6777; www.fs.usda.gov/coconino; Hwy 89A; campsites $16-20) runs campgrounds along Hwy Alt 89 in Oak Creek Canyon between Sedona and Flagstaff. All are nestled in the woods just off the road and along the Oak Creek. Reservations are accepted for a limited number of sites at each campground; otherwise, it's first-come, first-served. All three campgrounds provide drinking water, but only Cave Springs has coin-operated showers.

Manzanita (📞877-444-6777; www.fs.usda.gov/coconino; Hwy 89A, Oak Creek Canyon; camping $20) Has 18 sites; open year-round; 6 miles north.

Cave Springs (📞877-444-6777; www.fs.usda.gov/coconino; Hwy 89A, Oak Creek Canyon; camping $20) Has 82 sites; showers; 11.5 miles north.

Pine Flat (📞877-444-6777; www.fs.usda.gov/coconino; Hwy 89A, Oak Creek Canyon; camping $20) Has 56 sites; 13 miles north.

Rancho Sedona RV Park CAMPGROUND $
(📞928-282-7255, 888-641-4261; www.ranchosedona.com; 135 Bear Wallow Lane; RV sites $35-71;

🐕🌳) Offers a laundry, showers and more than 60 RV sites, most with full hookups. No tent camping.

Lo Lo Mai Springs Outdoor Resort CAMPGROUND $
(📞928-634-4700; www.lolomai.com; 11505 E Lo Lo Mai Rd, Cornville; tent sites $42, RV sites $43-60, cabins $80-85; 🐕🌳) Pretty, clean and friendly spot west of Sedona, with a swimming pool, easy access to swimming and splashing in Oak Creek, and an honor-code DVD library. It gets busy on weekends, but quietens down during the week. Cabins have toilets but no shower; bring your own linens. Take Hwy 89A for 7 miles southwest of Sedona; turn left onto Page Springs Rd.

Lodging

Sedona Motel MOTEL $
(📞928-282-7187; www.thesedonamotel.com; 218 Hwy 179; r $90-150; 🌳) Though it doesn't look like much more than an old-school one-story roadside motel from the outside, updated rooms include flat-screen TVs, handsome grey interiors and small refrigerators. Patio chairs sit outside each room, and it's within walking distance to both the tourist center of uptown Sedona and the shops and restaurants of Tlaquepaque.

DAY HIKING IN SEDONA

With over 100 trails within a 20-mile radius, Sedona is a day-hiking (and mountain-biking) paradise. Options range from creek-side ambles to challenging uphill grinds, and the rewards can be as simple as an afternoon frolicking in a shallow creek or as dramatic as panoramic vistas of red rock surrounds.

With so many choices, the best place to start is the 'Sedona Trail Finder' tab at **Hike House** (📞928-282-5820; www.thehikehouse.com; 431 Hwy 179, Suite B-1; ⊗9am-6pm). This online resource rates trails on difficulty and views, gives specifics on elevation change, length and location, provides photographs and offers a platform for traveler reviews. Once in town, the professionals at the Hike House have personally tested every trail – the small but uber-cool spot offers maps, books, gear and coffee shop with smoothies, massive oatmeal cookies and other tasty fuel for hiking delights.

Page Springs Winery (☑928-639-0004; www.pagespringscellar.com; 1500 Page Springs Rd, Cornville; tours $10; ⊘11am-7pm Mon-Wed, to 9pm Thu-Sun, tours Fri & Sun 10am & 2pm) A beautiful spot above Oak Creek in the quiet desert surrounds 20 minutes west of uptown Sedona, friendly Page Springs offers winery tours, wine tasting and delicious picnic-basket meals. Though it can get busy on weekends, it's a lovely drive and the wine is excellent.

There are a couple of other wineries nearby, and it's worth taking a few minutes to check out the tiny fish at the fish hatchery on the way here. From Sedona, take Hwy 89A south about 10 miles, turn left onto Page Springs Rd and drive 3 5 miles. Thirsty Thursday offers $3.33 flights and glasses from 6pm to 9pm, and 13% off bottles and meals.

Sedona Real Inn & Suites   MOTEL $$
(☑928-212-1414; www.sedonareal.com; 95 Arroyo Pinon Dr; r $90-140; ☎☀✉) Set just off the strip on a quiet end, this is the best bet for reasonably priced, conveniently located and modern motel accommodations in Sedona. Complimentary breakfast.

Sky Ranch Lodge   MOTEL $$
(☑928-282-6400; www.skyranchlodge.com; 1105 Airport Rd; r $130-180; ☀☎✉☀) At the top of winding Airport Rd, Sky Ranch has spectacular views of the town and surrounding red-rock country. It's a quiet respite from the flurry of activity that defines Sedona, with spacious motel rooms scattered among 6 landscaped acres. It's free from fancy frills, with a low-key wine bar off the lobby

Inn on Oak Creek   B&B $$
(☑928-282-7896, 800-499-7896; www.innonoakcreek.com; 556 Hwy 179; r $125-290; ☀@☎) Though this bright and immaculate inn sits right on Hwy 179, its back sits above Oak Creek and the Pottery Barn–styled rooms are peaceful and lovely. Some face the water and have fireplaces and massive Jacuzzi tubs, and the tiny $80 'bonus room' is excellent value. Complimentary bagels, pastries and coffee can be enjoyed on the small deck overlooking the creek.

Matterhorn Inn   MOTEL $$
(☑928-282-7176; www.matterhorninn.com; 230 Apple Ave; r $140-150; ☀☎✉☀) Set just above the main drag along Sedona's tourist epicenter, this friendly motel offers clean and simple rooms with patios and refrigerators. You can walk to uptown's restaurants and bars, and though it's hectic in the peak of summer days, during winter and evenings it quietens down. It overlooks the T-shirt, fudge and rock shops that define the town's tourist melee.

Rose Tree Inn   MOTEL $$
(☑928-282-2065, 888-282-2065; www.rosetreeinn.com; 376 Cedar St; r $109-150; ☀@☎) The five homey rooms make you feel as though you're settling in at a friend's place. Some rooms have fireplaces, and all have kitchenettes. It's much cozier and more personable than a hotel and feels a world away from busy Hwy Alt 89 just a block south. Guests are free to use the washer and dryer; ask about weekly rates.

★ Briar Patch Inn   CABIN $$$
(☑928-282-2342; www.briarpatchinn.com; 3190 N Hwy 89A; cottages incl breakfast $240-325 ; ☎) Nestled in 9 wooded and grassy acres above Oak Creek, this bucolic and peaceful bed-and-breakfast hideaway offers 19 handsome cottages with Southwestern decor and Native American art. All cottages include patios and full or partial kitchens, many have fireplaces and several sit just above the gurgling waters.

★ Enchantment Resort   RESORT $$$
(☑888-250-1690; www.enchantmentresort.com; 525 Boynton Canyon Rd; r/studio from $425/450; ⊘11am-11pm; ☀@☎✉) Chic, exclusive and tucked within the beautiful Boynton Canyon, this country club–style resort lives up to its name. Stylish and spacious Southwestern-inspired rooms, with private patios and big views, sprawl across the expansive grounds. Active travelers can hike in the canyon, splash in the pool or play tennis or golf. Or utterly unwind in Mii Amo Spa.

L'Auberge de Sedona   BOUTIQUE HOTEL $$$
(☑928-282-1661; www.lauberge.com; 301 L'Auberge Lane; ste $250-350, cottages $412-560; ☀☎✉) With well-appointed cabins amid the shady green lawns, immaculate public spaces, an intimate spa and easy access to the clear and cool waters of Oak Creek, L'Auberge de Sedona blends elegance with classic low-key Sedona style. The least expensive rooms are in the lodge rather than individual cottages, and dogs are welcomed with a gift bag. Activities include a creek-

side yoga stretch, morning duck feedings and stargazing.

★ El Portal
B&B $$$

(☎928-203-9405, 800-313-0017; www.elportal sedona.com; 95 Portal Lane; r $259-459; @☎) ◍ This discreet little inn is a beautiful blend of Southwestern- and Craftsman-style. It's a pocket of relaxed luxury tucked away in a corner across from the galleries and restaurants of Tlaquepaque and marvelously removed from the chaos of Sedona's tourist-heavy downtown. The look is rustic but sophisticated, incorporating reclaimed wood, Navajo rugs, river rock and thick adobe walls.

Garland's Oak Creek Lodge
CABIN $$$

(☎928-282-3343; www.garlandslodge.com; Hwy 89A; cabins $180-295; ☉closed Sun & mid-Nov–Apr

HUALAPAI RESERVATION: GRAND CANYON WEST & THE GLASS SKYWALK

Bordering many miles of the Colorado River between Hoover Dam and Grand Canyon National Park, the roughly 1-million-acre Hualapai Reservation is home to Grand Canyon West (also known as the West Rim). This canyon-viewing alternative to the national park lies completely within the confines of the reservation and includes the much-hyped glass Skywalk (☎928-769-2636; www.grandcanyonwest.com; West Rim, Hualapai Reservation; per person $88; ☉7am-7pm Apr-Sep, 8am-5pm Oct-Mar), a slender see-through glass horseshoe that juts 70ft into the canyon. Note that Grand Canyon West sits at an elevation of 4825ft, 2000ft higher and 3000ft lower than the South Rim and North Rim respectively, and the views here are far less dramatic.

Driving to Grand Canyon West from the South Rim is a four-hour delight through some of the most eerily beautiful desert landscape in the region. Endless expanse of dusty flat leads to horizon-hugging mountains, and the road winds mile after Seussian mile through a spectacular 900-year-old Joshua Tree forest. Upon arrival, however, the magic falls apart.

All visitors must check in at the visitor center, a massive window ess white tent with tour desks, souvenirs and busloads of people piling through. From here purchase either a Hualapai Legacy Package ($44) or the Legacy Gold Package ($81); both include the hop-on, hop-off shuttle loop to the three overlooks (Guano Point, Hualapai Ranch and Eagle Point), but the Legacy Gold adds access to the glass skywalk at Eagle Point. The only access to the overlooks is via shuttle, and there are no hiking trails at Grand Canyon West.

In addition to serving as the overlook shuttle hub, the visitor center functions as Grand Canyon West's airport. Helicopters whirl in and out all day long, transporting folk down to the river for scenic flights and 20-minute smooth-water pontoon rides on the Colorado.

The Hualapai Ranch, a minute's drive from the visitor center, is the only overnight accommodation. Billed as Western-styled rim-side cabins, they offer basic housing with one window and no canyon views. From guest check-in at the trailer, it's a short drive past dumpsters and rubble piles to the cabins. There is no compelling reason to stay here.

The Hualapai Nation also offers white-water day trips along the Colorado River. These trips, however, do not depart from Grand Canyon West. They leave from the modern and friendly chain-hotel-style Hualapai Lodge (p96) in tiny Peach Springs, a two-hour drive southeast from the West Rim, and a two-hour drive southwest from Grand Canyon Village. It includes a 22-mile drive along unpaved Diamond Creek Rd, the only road within the Grand Canyon.

At the end of Diamond Creek Rd is the first-come, first-served Diamond Creek Campground (www.grandcanyonwest.com; along the Colorado River, Hualapai Reservation; sites incl entrance fee $25), offering 10 tent sites along the Colorado River. Popular with multiday river trips, the campground has minimal shade and no drinking water, and the road here is not recommended without a 4WD vehicle. Call the lodge for road conditions.

For details and all reservations, contact Hualapai Tourism (☎928-769-2636; www.grand canyonwest.com). Note that Grand Canyon West is particularly popular as a day-trip from Las Vegas and several operators offer scenic flights, and Jeep, Hummer and bus tours; go to www.lasvegas.com/tours/grand-canyon for a listing. From Vegas, it's a two-hour drive.

1; 🐦) 🏄 Set back from Oak Creek on 8 secluded and verdant acres with broad lawns, woods and an apple orchard, this friendly lodge 8 miles north of uptown Sedona offers nicely appointed Western log cabins, many with fireplaces. Rates include a full hot breakfast, 4pm tea and a gourmet dinner. If you can't stay overnight, booking dinner is a delicious alternative.

🍴 Eating & Drinking

Pick up groceries and supplies at **Whole Foods** (🖉 928-282-6311; 1420 W Hwy 89A; ⊘8am-9pm Mon-Sat, to 8pm Sun; 🗲), with a wide selection of pre-made options, or **Bashas'** (🖉 928-282-5351; 160 Coffee Pot Dr; ⊘6am-11pm).

★ Indian Gardens
Oak Creek Market   CAFE $
(🖉 928-282-7702; www.indiangardens.com; 395 Hwy 89A, Oak Creek; mains $6-10; ⊘7am-5pm, kitchen closes 4pm) Featuring local and organic, little Indian Gardens is an Oak Creek Canyon hub for locals and passersby alike. Sit in the back courtyard (complimentary wool blankets for chilly nights) for a Canyon Breakfast Bowl, with eggs, bacon, cilantro, avocado and red chile, or swing by for a post–Oak Creek swim Happy Hipster kale salad.

There's grab 'n' go sandwiches, perfect for last-minute picnics, and a small bar with Flagstaff-brewed craft beer.

★ Local Juicery   HEALTH FOOD $
(🖉 928-282-8932; 3150 Hwy 89A; mains $8-12) Contemporary fast-food spot in West Sedona, with salads, smoothies and tantalizing veggie and fruit cold-pressed juices to cure what ails you. Try the Bright Eyes (orange, carrot, strawberry) or Black Water (with 'activated charcoal'). You feel healthier just walking in here.

Java Love   CAFE $
(www.javalovesedona.com; 2155 Hwy 89A; ⊘6am-3pm) Best coffee shop in town and a local hangout, with earthy eclectic surrounds. It has ready-made breakfast burritos, baked french toast, oatmeal, sandwiches and wraps, and made-to-order items as well. Look for it in the strip mall across from Coffee Pot, set back a bit from the main drag.

Hideaway   ITALIAN $
(🖉 928-282-4204; 251 Hwy 179; mains $7-15; ⊘11am-9pm) The best reason for coming to the Hideaway is to dine on the deck at sunset, when gorgeous red-rock views serve as the appetizer. As the name suggests, this hidden-away, casual spot is easy to get to and equally easy to miss. Retreat from uptown madness and enjoy a glass of wine with down-home, American-style Italian food and specialty pizzas.

Coffee Pot Restaurant   BREAKFAST $
(🖉 928-282-6626; www.coffeepotsedona.com; 2050 W Hwy 89A; breakfast $5-10, lunch $5-14; ⊘6am-2pm; 🖟) A go-to breakfast and lunch joint for decades. Nothing fancy but it gets the refueling job done, with massive plates of reasonably priced fare and a huge selection – 101 types of omelets for starters, including peanut butter, jelly and banana perhaps?

Mesa Grill at the
Sedona Airport   AMERICAN $$
(🖉 928-282-2200; www.mesagrillsedona.com; 1185 Airport Rd; mains $13-18; ⊘7am-9pm) Removed from the mayhem of 89A and Hwy 179, Mesa Grill sits at the dead of the winding Airport Rd. Yes, it's a bit odd to eat in an airport, on the patio next to airplanes, but 'airport' is a misnomer – it's really more of a landing strip for scenic flights. It has contemporary surrounds, an outdoor patio and panoramic windows.

Oak Creek Brewery & Grill   AMERICAN $$
(🖉 928-282-3300; www.oakcreekpub.com; 336 Hwy 179; mains $10-23; ⊘11:30am-8:30pm; 🐦) This spacious brewery at Tlaquepaque Village will satisfy your post-hike drinking needs, with upmarket pub-style dishes like a grilled mahi mahi salad and 'fire-kissed' pizza. It has outdoor seating and beer flights.

★ Elote Cafe   MEXICAN $$$
(🖉 928-203-0105; www.elotecafe.com; Arabella Hotel, 771 Hwy 179; mains $19-26; ⊘5pm-late Tue-Sat) Come here for some of the best, most authentic Mexican food in the region. It serves unusual traditional dishes you won't find elsewhere, like the namesake *elote* (fire-roasted corn with spicy mayo, lime and cotija cheese) or tender, smoky pork cheeks.

L'Auberge Restaurant on
Oak Creek   AMERICAN $$$
(🖉 928-282-1661; www.lauberge.com; 301 L'Auberge Lane; mains $34-52; ⊘7am-9pm Mon-Sat, 9am-2pm & 5:30-9pm Sun) Featuring refined American cuisine with a French accent, the menu at L'Auberge changes seasonally (you might find spring onions and morels in the

spring, and roast duck and beets in the fall). The creek-side spot is a local favorite for celebrating special occasions in elegant environs, with a select wine list to complement your meal.

Dahl & DiLuca Ristorante ITALIAN $$$
(☑ 928-282-5219; www.dahlanddiluca.com; 2321 Hwy 89A; mains $13-33; ☺ 5-10pm) Though this lovely Italian place fits perfectly into the groove and color scheme of Sedona, at the same time it feels like the kind of place you'd find in a small Italian seaside town. It's a bustling, welcoming spot serving excellent, authentic Italian food.

Mariposa LATIN AMERICAN $$$
(☑ 928-862-4444; www.mariposasedona.com; 700 W Hwy 89A; tapas $6-14, mains $26-50; ☺ 5-9pm) Though not yet opened at time of research, word in town is that Mariposa, the latest restaurant by local celebrity chef Lisa Dahl, will be the town's best hot spot. Look for Latin-inspired steak and seafood with a focus on fresh, local fare and lovely patio dining.

Enchantment Resort BAR
(525 Boynton Canyon Rd) Head to the terrace margarita bar in the Enchantment Resort, several miles west of town in stunning Boynton Canyon, for sunset cocktails.

☆ Entertainment

For Hollywood blockbusters, head to **Harkins Theatres Sedona 6** (☑ 928-282-2211; 2081 Hwy 89A).

Mary D Fisher Theater THEATER
(☑ 928-282-1177; www.sedonafilmfestival.org; 2030 Hwy 89A) A Sedona Film Festival venue in February, but screens documentaries and art-house films year-round.

🛍 Shopping

Tlaquepaque Village MALL
(☑ 928-282-4838; www.tlaq.com; 336 Hwy 179; ☺ 10am-5pm) Just south of Hwy 89A on Hwy 179, this is a series of Mexican-style interconnected plazas home to dozens of high-end art galleries, shops and restaurants.

Garland's Navajo Rugs HANDICRAFTS
(☑ 928-282-4070; www.garlandsrugs.com; 411 Hwy 179; ☺ 10am-5pm) This 38-year-old institution offers the area's best selection of rugs, and sells other Native American crafts. It's an interesting shop to visit, displaying naturally dyed yarns with their botanical sources of color, as well as descriptions of how many hours it takes to create a handwoven rug.

❶ Information

Several Sedona visitor centers sell Red Rock passes and provide hiking, cycling and recreation information for Oak Creek Canyon and red-rock country. In addition, most hotels offer concierge service for booking Sedona and Grand Canyon tours and scenic flights.

Sedona Chamber of Commerce Visitor Center (☑ 928-282-7722, 800-288-7336; www.visitsedona.com; 331 Forest Rd; ☺ 8:30am-5pm) Located in the pedestrian center of uptown Sedona; pick up free maps and buy a Red Rock Pass.

Red Rock Country Visitor Center (☑ 928-203-2900; www.redrockcountry.org; 8375 Hwy 179; ☺ 9am-4:30pm) Get a Red Rock Pass here, as well as hiking guides, maps and local national forest information.

Oak Creek Canyon Visitor Center (Indian Gardens, Oak Creek Canyon (Hwy 89A); 8am-4:30pm) Fishing licenses and information on recreation in Oak Creek Canyon; located about 4 miles north of uptown Sedona.

Police Station (emergency ☑ 911, non-emergency 928-282-3100; www.sedonaaz.gov; 100 Roadrunner Dr)

Post Office (☑ 928-282-3511; 190 W Hwy 89A; ☺ 8:45am-5pm Mon-Fri, 9am-1pm Sat)

Sedona Public Library (☑ 928-282-7714; www.sedonalibrary.org; 3250 White Bear Rd; ☺ 10am-6pm Mon, Tue & Thu, to 8pm Wed, to 5pm Fri & Sat; 🖥)

Verde Valley Medical Center (☑ 928-204-3000; www.verdeval eymedicalcenter.com; 3700 W Hwy 89A; ☺ 24hr) Has 24-hour emergency services.

❶ Getting There & Away

The closest commercial airports are Phoenix (two hours) and Flagstaff (30 minutes; US Air from Phoenix only). Reserve door-to-door shuttle service from the Phoenix Sky Harbor Airport at **Ace Xpress** (☑ 800-336-2239, 928-649-2720; www.acexshuttle.com; one-way/round-trip adult $68/109, child $60/40; ☺ office hours 7am-8pm Mon-Fri, 8am-8pm Sat & Sun). There's also regional shuttle services (p92), including regularly scheduled services from the Phoenix airport and Flagstaff.

Amtrak (☑ 800-872-7245; www.amtrak.com) and **Greyhound** (☑ 800-231-2222; www.greyhound.com) stop in nearby Flagstaff.

❶ Getting Around

Barlow Jeep Rentals (☑ 928-282-8700, 800-928-5337; www.barlows.us; 3009 W Hwy 89A; half-/full-/3-day $195/295/589; ☺ 8am-6pm) Great for rough road exploring. Maps and trail information provided.

Enterprise (✆ 928-282-2052; www.enterprise.com; 2090 W Hwy 89A; per day $35-50; ⏰ 8am-6pm Mon-Fri, 9am-1pm Sat & Sun)

Bob's Taxi (✆ 982-282-1234; www.sedonataxi bobs.com) Taxi service, flat-rate to surrounding areas, grocery delivery and guided tours.

Cameron

A tiny, windswept community 32 miles east of the park's East Entrance and 54 miles north of Flagstaff, Cameron sits on the western edge of the Navajo Indian Reservation.

There's not much to it; the town basically is just the Cameron Trading Post & Motel. In the early 1900s, Hopis and Navajos came to the trading post to barter wool, blankets and livestock for flour, sugar and other goods. Today, visitors can browse a large selection of quality Native American crafts, including Navajo rugs, basketry, jewelry and pottery. Of course, you'll also find roadrunner knick-knacks and other canyon kitsch.

If you're driving to the North Rim and need a place to stay en route or if rooms in the park are booked, this is a great option. It also makes a good lunch spot if you're driving rim-to-rim.

BOOTLEG CANYON

With 35 miles of single-track cross-country and downhill trails, dramatic rocky desert landscape and panoramic views of Lake Mead and beyond, popular Bootleg Canyon Mountain Bike Park is a mountain-biking mecca. It can be unbearably hot in the summer, so come prepared with plenty of water and consider early morning or night rides. In the grand spirit of Vegas-style living, it's open 24/7.

Bootleg Canyon is on the northwest side of Boulder City. Take Veterans Memorial Drive off Hwy 93, and turn north on Yucca St. For tours, bicycle rental and detailed information on this and other area trails, head to All Mountain Cyclery (✆ 702-453-2453; www.allmountain cyclery.com; 1404 Nevada Hwy, Boulder City; ⏰ 10am-6pm Tue-Fri, 11am-6pm Mon, 9am-6pm Sat, 9am-4pm Sun). On weekends they offer a shuttle service to the top of the canyon ($5 per run, $30 per day) so you can ride down again and again and again. There's also a zipline and hiking trails.

🛏 Sleeping & Eating

Cameron Trading Post & Motel　　MOTEL $$
(✆ gift shop 928-679-2231, motel 800-338-7385; www.camerontradingpost.com; Hwy 89; r $109, ste $179; ⏰ 6am-9:30pm summer, 7am-9pm winter; ❋ 🛜) The spacious rooms, many with balconies, feature hand-carved furniture and a Southwestern motif spread out in three two-story, adobe-style buildings. The nicest is the Hopi, set around a lovely, lush garden with fountains and benches. Ask for a room with a garden view or a view of the Little Colorado River Gorge, which winds around the back of the hotel. RV sites offer hookups. Pets stay for $15.

Cameron Trading Post Dining Room　　NATIVE AMERICAN $$
(✆ 928-679-2231; www.camerontradingpost.com; breakfast $7-14, lunch $9-13, dinner $11-27; ⏰ 6am-close) A good place to try the Navajo taco (fried dough with whole beans, ground beef, green chile and cheese).

Lake Mead & Hoover Dam

The Lake Mead National Recreation Area (www.nps.gov/lake) encompasses 110-mile-long Lake Mead, 67-mile-long Lake Mohave, many miles of bone-dry desert around the lakes, and the 726ft art-deco-style Hoover Dam. Quiet Boulder City is the central town for tourist services in and around Lake Mead.

At the height of the Depression, thousands of men and their families migrated here to build the dam. They worked in excruciating conditions, dangling hundreds of feet above the canyon in 120°F (about 50°C) desert heat. Hundreds of people lost their lives. Today, standing on its edge offers a dramatic perspective on both the dam itself and the startling drop in Lake Mead water levels, as evidenced by the swaths of white bathtub rings on the canyon sides.

Guided tours begin at Alan Bible Visitor Center (✆ 702-293-8990; Lakeshore Scenic Dr, off US Hwy 93; ⏰ 9am-4:30pm) with a video of original construction footage. An elevator takes visitors 50 stories below to view the dam's massive generators, which could each power a city of 100,000 people. Children under eight years of age are not permitted on the more extensive dam tour (first-come, first-served) that visits the dam passageways. The 3.7-mile Historic Railroad Trail connects the visitor center to the parking area, passing through five tunnels each 25ft in diameter and offering panoramic views of Lake Mead.

Inside the Boulder Dam Hotel, the **Boulder City/Hoover Dam Museum** (☎702-294-1988; www.bcmha.org; 1305 Arizona St, Boulder Dam Hotel, Boulder City; adult/child & student $2/1; ⊙10am-5pm Mon-Sat; ☀) is worth popping into for exhibits focusing on the tough living conditions endured by the people who came to build the dam. A 20-minute film features historic footage of the project.

Despite falling water levels, the lake remains a popular place to explore by boat. Call ☎702-451-2992 for speedboat, pontoon and watersport equipment rental; for houseboat rental, contact **Callville Bay Resort and Marina** (☎800-255-5561; www.callvillebay.com; per day from $560). To kayak Lake Mead or the Colorado River, talk to **Desert Adventures** (☎702-293-5026; http://kayaklasvegas.com; 1647-A Nevada Hwy, Boulder City; ⊙9am-6pm summer, to 4pm winter). They also rent camping equipment, offer guided smooth-water kayak tours down the Colorado River's 30-mile **Black Canyon** (www.blackcanyonwatertrail.org), and lead hiking and cycling trips to Grand Canyon, Zion and Bryce.

🛏 Sleeping & Eating

Boulder Dam Hotel   HOTEL **$**
(☎702-293-3510; www.boulderdamhotel.com; 1305 Arizona St; r incl breakfast $89-94, ste $99; ☀@☎) For a peaceful night's sleep worlds away from the madding crowds and neon of Vegas, this gracious Dutch Colonial-style hotel (listed on the National Register of Historic places) has welcomed illustrious guests since 1933. Relax with a cocktail at the art-deco jazz lounge on site.

Milo's Cellar   CAFE **$$**
(☎702-293-9540; www.miloswinebar.com; 534 Nevada Hwy, Boulder City; mains $9-14; ⊙11am-10pm Sun-Thu, to 11pm Fri & Sat) The unassuming Milo's Cellar just down the street from the Boulder Dam Hotel makes a relaxing spot for tasty sandwiches, salads, soups, gourmet cheese plates and wine flights. There's sidewalk seating and a small wine shop.

Las Vegas
☎702 / POP 596,425 / ELEV 2000FT

Las Vegas, an oasis of neon and famous worldwide for its gambling, drinking and shows, is a city of multi-personalities that aims to offer all things to all people.

The city's multiple personalities are evident in the city landscape itself. From the airport and the vintage 'Welcome to Las Vegas' sign 6 miles north, massive casinos, luxury hotels and contemporary fast-food joints line Las Vegas Blvd aka 'the Strip'. This is where you'll find, from south to north, Mandalay Bay, the landmark pyramid-inspired Luxor, the Belagio, Caesar's Palace and Circus Circus. Throngs of tourists mill about, eyes to the sky ingesting postcard-perfect Vegas eye candy, absent-mindedly accepting brochures for topless dance shows and Grand Canyon West Rim helicopter tours, in between pausing for street performers. There's McDonalds and Walgreens, Four Seasons and Mandarin Oriental, billboards blazoned with exotic dancers, Venice-style gondola rides, an indoor amusement park and windowless shopping malls with recreated thunderstorms. This is the Strip of the contemporary imagination.

Continuing north, the mood shifts dramatically; high-rises give way to pawn shops and little wedding chapels, and the neon sizzle fizzles. There are residential stretches with bungalows and tiny yards: a different Vegas altogether; a slower, quieter, everyday place, dotted with ghost-like reminders of yesterday's sin city.

At the northern edge, about 10 miles from the airport, are classic old-school Vegas casinos. These are worn but still charming in their authentic vintage style, including the 1941 El Cortez and the 1946 Golden Nugget, which sit next to hipster industrial restaurants and low-rise apartment complexes. This is downtown Las Vegas, where you'll find the Fremont Experience (popular with tourists), East Fremont (more popular with locals), the Arts District and a handful of art-and-culture destinations.

Whether walking or driving, distances on the Strip are deceiving, and a walk to what looks like a nearby casino usually takes much longer than expected. Major tourist areas are safe. However, Las Vegas Blvd between downtown and Circus Circus gets shabby, and east from downtown's East Fremont St is rather unsavory.

Las Vegas Strip

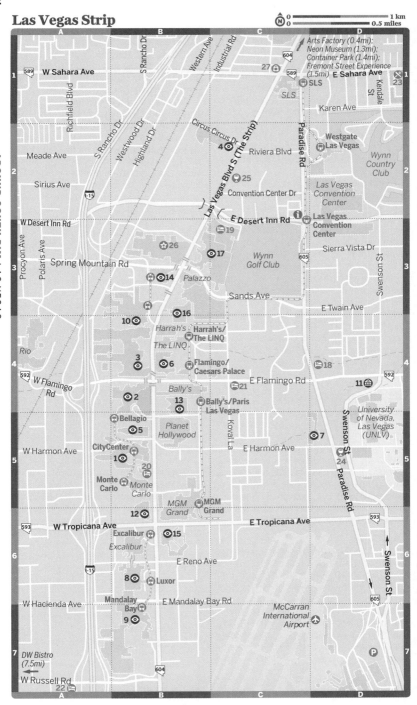

Las Vegas Strip

◉ Sights

Other Attractions

National Atomic Testing Museum MUSEUM
(☑ 702-794-5151; www.nationalatomictesting museum.org; 755 E Flamingo Rd, Desert Research Institute; adult/child 7-17yr $14/12; ⊗ 10am-5pm Mon-Sat, noon-5pm Sun; ☐ 202) Fascinating multimedia exhibits focus on science, technology and the social history of the 'Atomic Age', which lasted from WWII until atmospheric bomb testing was driven underground in 1961 and a worldwide ban on nuclear testing was declared in 1992. View historical footage of atomic testing and examine southern Nevada's past, present and future, from Native American ways of life to the environmental legacy of atomic testing. Don't miss the cool museum shop near the ticket booth, a Nevada Test Site guard station replica.

Neon Museum – Neon Boneyard MUSEUM
(☑ 702-387-6366; www.neonmuseum.org; 770 Las Vegas Blvd N; 1hr tour adult/child 7-17yr daytime $18/12, after dark $25/22; ⊗ tours daily, schedules vary; ☐ 113) This nonprofit project is doing what almost no one else does: saving Las Vegas' history. Book ahead for a fascinating guided walking tour of the 'neon boneyard,'

where irreplaceable vintage neon signs – Las Vegas' original art form – spend their retirement. Start exploring at the visitor center inside the salvaged La Concha Motel lobby, a mid-century modern icon designed by African-American architect Paul Revere Williams. Tours are usually given throughout the day, special events and weather permitting.

Fremont Street Experience OUTDOORS
(www.vegasexperience.com; Fremont St, btwn Main St & Las Vegas Blvd; ⊗ hourly dusk-midnight; ☐ Deuce, SDX) **FREE** A five-block pedestrian mall topped by an arched steel canopy and filled with computer-controlled lights, the Fremont Street Experience, between Main St and Las Vegas Blvd, has brought life back to downtown. Every evening, the canopy is transformed by hokey six-minute light-and-sound shows enhanced by 550,000 watts of wraparound sound and a larger-than-life screen lit up by 12.5 million synchronized LEDs. Soar through the air on ziplines strung underneath the canopy from **Slotzilla** (☑ 844-947-8342; rides from $20; ⊗ noon-midnight Sun-Thu, to 2am Fri & Sat), a 12-story, slot-machine-themed platform.

LAS VEGAS CASINOS

The big-hitter and most recognized casinos, listed from south, by McCarran International Airport, to north, in downtown Las Vegas.

Mandalay Bay (702-632-7777; www.mandalaybay.com; 3950 Las Vegas Blvd S; 24hr) Home to Shark Reef Aquarium, a walk-through aquarium with thousands of tropical fish and a shallow pool where you can pet pint-sized sharks.

Luxor (702-262-4000; www.luxor.com; 3900 Las Vegas Blvd S; 24hr) Iconic Pyramid-shaped casino with a mildly themed Egyptian interior.

Tropicana (800-462-8767; www.troplv.com; 3801 Las Vegas Blvd S; 24hr) Open since 1957; the tropically inspired pool complex has multilevel lagoons, streaming waterfalls and classic swim-up blackjack tables.

New York–New York (702-740-6969; www.newyorknewyork.com; 3790 Las Vegas Blvd S; 24hr) Statue of Liberty, the Brooklyn Bridge and, wrapped around the hotel's flashy facade, the Big Apple roller coaster, with cars resembling NYC taxicabs.

Aria (702-590-7111; www.aria.com; 3730 Las Vegas Blvd S; 24hr) Contemporary resort with a deluxe, design-savvy casino surrounded by tempting restaurants.

Hard Rock (702-693-5000; www.hardrockhotel.com; 4455 Paradise Rd; 24hr; 108) Original rock 'n' roll casino houses an impressive collection of rock-star memorabilia. It's just east of the Strip at Planet Hollywood, on Harmon.

Cosmopolitan (702-698-7000; www.cosmopolitanlasvegas.com; 3708 Las Vegas Blvd S; 24hr) Elegant and hip.

Paris (702-946-7000; www.parislasvegas.com; 3655 Las Vegas Blvd S; 24hr) Mini-version of the French capital, including a 34-story Hotel de Ville replica and replicas of famous facades from the Paris Opera House and the Louvre.

Bellagio (888-987-6667; www.bellagio.com; 3600 Las Vegas Blvd S; 24hr) Airy and lovely, with elaborate gardens and the Gallery of Fine Art; don't miss the fountain show out front.

Caesars Palace (702-731-7110; www.caesarspalace.com; 3570 Las Vegas Blvd S; 24hr) Out front are the same spritzing fountains that daredevil Evil Knievel made famous when he jumped them on a motorcycle on December 31, 1967 (and ended up with a shattered pelvis and a fractured skull).

Flamingo (702-733-3111; www.flamingolasvegas.com; 3555 Las Vegas Blvd S; 24hr) Its original owners – all members of the East Coast mafia – shelled out millions in 1946 to build this unprecedented tropical gaming oasis in the desert.

Mirage (702-791-7111; www.mirage.com; 3400 Las Vegas Blvd S; 24hr) Rainforest atrium and 20,000-gallon saltwater aquarium.

Venetian (702-414-1000; www.venetian.com; 3355 Las Vegas Blvd S; 24hr) Gondola rides, Canyon Ranch Spa and Madame Tussauds interactive Vegas-centric wax museum.

Treasure Island (www.treasureisland.com; 3300 Las Vegas Blvd S) Traces of the original swashbuckling skull-and-crossbones theme linger.

Wynn & Encore (702-770-7000; www.wynnlasvegas.com; 3131 S Las Vegas Blvd; 24hr) Lavish, sprawling, gorgeous.

Circus Circus (702-734-0410; www.circuscircus.com; 2880 Las Vegas Blvd S; 24hr;) Trapeze artists, high-wire workers, jugglers and unicyclists perform excellent free circus acts above the casino floor.

Golden Nugget (702-385-7111; www.goldennugget.com; 129 E Fremont St; 24hr; Deuce, SDX) Downtown classic, with an outdoor pool featuring a three-story waterslide through a 200,000-gallon shark tank.

El Cortez (702-385-5200; www.elcortezhotelcasino.com; 600 E Fremont St; 24hr; Deuce) Vegas' oldest continuously operating casino, on the National Register of Historic Places and going strong since 1941. It's one of the few remaining joints where the slot machines use actual coins.

Arts Factory
ARTS CENTER

(☎702-383-3133; www.theartsfactory.com; 107 E
Charleston Blvd; ⊙9am-6pm daily, to 10pm 1st Fri
of month; ⊟Deuce, SDX) Las Vegas' fractured
art scene received an enormous boost in the
late 1990s, when commercial photographer
Wes Isbutt accidentally established this arts
complex downtown. Today, the Arts Facto-
ry is the lynchpin for **First Friday** (www.first
fricaylasvegas.com; ⊙5-11pm) events, with as
many as 10,000 people stepping inside the
vibrant collective to see gallery exhibits on
the first Friday evening of every month. Next
door, **Art Square** (☎702-483-8844; www.
artsquarelv.com; 1025 S 1st St; ⊙most galleries
1-7pm Wed-Fri, to 4pm Sat) has even more galleries, eclectic shops, an experimental theater
space and an arty bar.

Activities

Red Rock Canyon National Conservation
Area (www.redrockcanyonlv.org), 16 miles
west of downtown Las Vegas, offers rock
climbing and hiking, and there's good
mountain biking, hiking and swimming to
be had in Lake Mead National Recreation
Area (p120), a half-hour's drive east.

Red Rock Climbing Center
ROCK CLIMBING

(☎702-254-5604; www.redrockclimbingcenter.
com; 8201 W Charleston Blvd; day pass $15, belay
check $5, equipment rental $8; ⊙9am-9pm Sat &
Sun, to 11pm Mon & Fri, 9am-11pm Tue-Thu) Run
by climbers, this outdoor-adventure shop
rents bouldering crash pads and carries
all-weather apparel and brand-name hiking,
rock-climbing, camping and backpacking
equipment. The indoor **Red Rock Climbing
Center** is next door.

Sleeping

Rates rise and fall dramatically depending
on demand. During the dog days of summer
rates can plummet – Vegas is the place to
check out luxury resorts at bargain prices.
For upscale digs without having to battle casino mayhem, consider the Four Seasons or
Mandarin Oriental.

Most hotel websites feature calendars
with day-by-day room rates listed. Listed
rates, however, do not include mandatory
resort fees ($20 to $30 per night).

First-come, first-served campsites are
available at **Red Rock Canyon Campground**, 16 miles west of downtown, from
late May to early September only. Call ☎702-
515-5350 for details.

The Strip

Mandalay Bay
CASINO HOTEL $$

(☎877-632-7300, 702-632-7777; www.mandalaybay.
com; 3950 Las Vegas Blvd S; weekday/weekend r from
$105/130; P❉@☎≋; ⊟Deuce) The upscale
Mandalay Bay casino hotel, exclusive **Four
Seasons** (☎702-632-5000; www.fourseasons.
com/lasvegas; weekday/weekend r from $229/289;
P❉@☎≋) hotel and boutique **Delano**
(www.delanolasvegas.com; P❉@☎≋) hotel of-
fer variety at the Strip's southernmost resort.

Tropicana
CASINO HOTEL $$

(☎800-462-8767, 702-739-2222; www.troplv.com;
3801 Las Vegas Blvd S; weekday/weekend r from
$75/120; P❉@☎≋; ⊟Deuce) Keeping its
tropical vibe going since the 1950s, the Trop's
multimillion-dollar renovation pays off with
Miami-chic rooms painted in sunset hues.

Mandarin Oriental
LUXURY HOTEL $$$

(☎888-881-9578, 702-590-8888; www.mandarin
oriental.com/lasvegas; 3752 Las Vegas Blvd S; r/ste
from $225/435; P❉@☎≋; ⊟Deuce) Busi-
ness travelers and couples book the swanky
Mandarin Oriental, with its staggering views
and sumptuous design.

Cosmopolitan
CASINO HOTEL $$$

(☎855-435-0005, 702-698-7000; www.cosmopoli-
tanlasvegas.com; 3708 Las Vegas Blvd S; r/ste from
$160/220; P❉@☎≋❉; ⊟Deuce) Frequent-
ed by style-conscious clientele, the arty, cool
Cosmo has the Strip's hippest hotel rooms.

Bellagio
CASINO HOTEL $$$

(☎702-693-7111, 888-987-6667; www.bellagio.com;
3600 Las Vegas Blvd S; weekday/weekend r from
$169/239; P❉@☎≋; ⊟Deuce) Romantic
and artistically designed, Bellagio is a lake-
side monument to nouveau-riche opulence.

Encore
CASINO HOTEL $$$

(☎877-321-9966, 702-770-7100; www.wynnlas
vegas.com; 3131 Las Vegas Blvd S; weekday/week-
end ste from $199/249; P❉@☎≋; ⊟Deuce)
Newer than its sister resort Wynn, Encore
offers similarly lavish yet even more spacious suites amid gorgeous surrounds.

ⓘ Grand Canyon Tour Company
(☎702-655-6060, 800-222-6966; www.
grandcanyontourcompany.com) provides a
shuttle service between most Las Vegas
hotels and the South Rim's Bright Angel
Lodge ($99 per person; five hours).
Departure from Las Vegas is at 7:30am;
departure from Bright Angel Lodge is at
9:30am.

📖 Downtown & Off Strip

Candlewood Suites
Extended Stay   BUSINESS HOTEL **$**
(📞 702-836-3660; 4034 Paradise Rd; r $65-120; 🛜 🍽) Set just a mile from the Strip. The free wi-fi, free laundry machines and a kitchenette in every room to save on food costs more than makes up for the occasional taxi ride for big nights out. With lots of business travelers calling this place home, count on quiet nights.

El Cortez Cabana Suites   HOTEL **$**
(📞 800-634-6703, 702-385-5200; http://elcortez hotelcasino.com; 651 E Ogden Ave; weekday/weekend r from $40/80; P ⊛ @ 🛜) Across the street from the 1940s casino, mod suites decked out in mint green hide fab retro tiled bathrooms with walk-in showers.

Platinum Hotel   HOTEL **$$**
(📞 877-211-9211, 702-365-5000; www.theplatinum hotel.com; 211 E Flamingo Rd; weekday/weekend ste from $135/170; P ⊜ ⊛ @ 🛜 🍽 🏊) This nongaming and nonsmoking hotel near the Strip charms guests with a wellness spa and sanctuary-like suites with kitchens and whirlpool tubs.

Red Rock   CASINO HOTEL **$$**
(📞 702-797-7777, 866-767-7773; www.redrock.sclv. com; 11011 W Charleston Blvd; weekday/weekend r from $95/140; P ⊛ @ 🛜 🏊) At this upscale casino hotel, forget about the faraway Strip and spend your time outdoors by the resort pool or at nearby Red Rock Canyon.

Staybridge Suites Las Vegas   HOTEL **$$**
(📞 702-259-2663; www.staybridge.com; 5735 Dean Martin Dr; ste $120-150; P 🛜 🍽 🏊) Convenient to McCarran International Airport and I-15,

---

---

with spacious and immaculate suites, balconies with views, complimentary breakfast, shuttle service to the Strip and airport, and free parking.

🍴 Eating

Sin City is an unmatched eating adventure. Since Wolfgang Puck brought Spago to Caesars in 1992, celebrity chefs have taken up residence in nearly every megaresort, and you'll find everything from noodle shops to multi-course dining extravanganzas.

⭐ Carson Kitchen   AMERICAN **$$**
(📞 702-473-9523; www.carsonkitchen.com; 124 S 6th St; tapas & mains $8-19; ☺ 11am-11pm Thu-Sat, to 10pm Sun-Wed; 🚌 Deuce) Tiny industrial space hops with downtowners looking to get away from Fremont Street mayhem and big-scale Vegas eateries. Excellent shared plates include rainbow cauliflower, watermelon and feta salad and bison meatloaf sliders. Pair with a creative 'libations' menu, 'because no good love story started with someone ordering a salad.'

Yellowtail   JAPANESE **$$$**
(📞 702-693-8300; http://yellowtaillasvegas. com; Bellagio; shared plates $10-55, tasting menu without/with sake pairings $150/205; ☺ 5-10pm Mon-Thu, to 11pm Fri-Sun, lounge closes 1hr later; 🚌 Deuce) The entrance to this sleek sushi bar is heralded by a massive bronze sculpture of a yellowtail fish. Local maverick chef Akira Back buys top-drawer seafood and ingredients imported from markets all over the globe. Dip into an extensive sake cellar and savor a long list of cold and hot shared dishes. Reservations recommended.

Lotus of Siam   THAI **$$**
(📞 702-735-3033; www.saipinchutima.com; 953 E Sahara Ave; mains $9-30; ☺ 11:30am-2:30pm Mon-Fri, 5:30-10pm daily; 🍴; 🚌 SDX) Saipin Chutima's authentic northern Thai cooking has won almost as many awards as her distinguished European and New World wine cellar. Renowned food critic Jonathan Gold once called it 'the single best Thai restaurant in North America.' Reservations essential.

Container Park   FAST FOOD **$**
(📞 702-637-4244; http://downtowncontainerpark. com; 707 E Fremont St; menu $3-9; ☺ 11am-11pm Sun-Thu, to 1am Fri & Sat; 🚌 Deuce) With food-truck-style menus, outdoor patio seating and late-night hours, various food vendors inside the cutting-edge Container Park sell something to satisfy everyone's appetite.

O Face Doughnuts BAKERY

(📞702-476-3223; www.ofacedoughnuts.com; 124 S 6th, #140; doughnuts from $1.25; ⏰7am-5:30pm Mon-Fri, 8am-5pm Sat & Sun; 🚌Deuce) Traditional, vegan and gluten-free in-hand donuts, as well as specialty flavors (try the Hibiscus Tea Glazed) and fork and knife delights like Mexican Chocolate with Horchata Pudding. Go to their website for doughnut delivery – the $35 doughnut and coffee box special, with a dozen glazed doughnuts, is perfect for early morning departures to Grand Canyon.

Chicago Joe's ITALIAN $$

(📞702-382-5637; www.chicagojoesrestaurant.com; 820 S 4th; mains $15-24; ⏰11am-10pm Tue-Fri, from 5pm Sat; 🚌Deuce) Chicago Joe's, a little brick house nestled incongruously right off the downtown strip, is like stepping into a time warp. Inside there are red-and-white checkered tablecloths, year-round twinkling Christmas lights and black-and-white photographs. Nothing fancy, nothing trendy, just big plates of simple Italian fare in intimate old-school surrounds.

Bacchanal BUFFET $$$

(Caesars Palace; buffet per adult $26-54, child 4-10yr $15-27; ; 🚌Deuce) This is the Strip's most expansive and expensive buffet. An all-you-can-eat feast of king crab legs, housemade sushi and dim sum, oak-grilled barbecue, baked-to-order souffles and so much more goes beyond what you could ever possibly taste in just one sitting.

🍸 Drinking

🍸 The Strip

Mandarin Bar & Tea Lounge LOUNGE, BAR

(Mandarin Oriental; ⏰lounge 10am-10pm daily, bar 5pm-2am Fri & Sat, to 11pm Sun; 🚌Deuce) With glittering Strip views from the panoramic windows of the hotel's 23rd-floor 'sky lobby,' this sophisticated lounge serves exotic teas by day and champagne cocktails by night. Make reservations for afternoon tea (from $36, available 1pm to 5pm daily).

Parasol Up & Parasol Down COCKTAIL BAR

(Wynn; ⏰11am-4am Sun-Thu, to 5am Fri & Sat, Parasol Down 11am-2am; 🚌Deuce) Stepping into the whimsical jewel-hued Parasol Up feels something like walking into a glamorous version of *Alice in Wonderland*. Cozy up on a plush ruby-red loveseat and gaze out at the glassy Lake of Dreams. Down the fairytale-like curved escalator, Parasol Down's seasonal

WORTH A TRIP

DW BISTRO

From Mandalay Bay, at the bottom of the Las Vegas Strip, it's a straight shot 8 miles west through residential neighborhoods to **DW Bistro** (📞702-527-5200; www.dwbistro.com; 6115 S Fort Apache Rd; ⏰11am-9pm Tue-Thu; 🚌Deuce 120). Offering an eclectic mix of Jamaican and New Mexican fare, this bright and modern bistro feels worlds away from the claustrophobic chaos of Sin City's neon strip. The New Mexican–style slow pork, served on rice with over-easy eggs, is excellent, as is the boneless fried chicken dusted with jerk-seasoned flour.

Take Hacienda Ave west over I-15; cut south two blocks on Durango Ave, continue west a few blocks on Russell Rd and turn south on S Fort Apache. The bistro sits in a strip mall on the west side. If you're zipping through Vegas on Hwy 215, take Russell Rd exit west.

outdoor patio is the perfect spot for cucumber and ginger-infused martinis.

Red Square BAR

(📞702-632-7407; Mandalay Bay; ⏰4:30-10pm Sun-Thu, to midnight Fri & Sat; 🚌Deuce) How very post-*perestroika*: a headless Lenin invites you to join your comrades for a tipple behind the blood-red curtains of this Russian restaurant. Behind the solid-ice bar are caviar bowls and more than 200 vodkas mixed with infusions and into cocktails. Sable coats are kept on hand for visiting the private vodka vault. Happy hour runs from 4pm to 7pm daily.

Chandelier Bar COCKTAIL BAR

(Cosmopolitan; ⏰24hr; 🚌Deuce) Towering high in the center of Cosmopolitan, this ethereally designed cocktail bar is inventive yet beautifully simple, with three levels connected by romantic curved staircases, all draped with glowing strands of glass beads. The second level is headquarters for molecular mixology (order a martini made with liquid nitrogen), while the third specializes in floral and fruit infusions.

🍸 Downtown & Off Strip

Fireside Lounge LOUNGE

(www.peppermilllasvegas.com; 2985 Las Vegas Blvd S, Peppermill; ⏰24hr; 🚌Deuce) Don't be blinded by the outlandishly bright neon outside. The Strip's most spellbinding retro hideaway awaits at the pint-sized Peppermill casino. Courting couples adore the sunken fire pit, fake tropical foliage and 64oz goblet-sized 'Scorpion' cocktails served by waiters in black evening gowns.

Double Down Saloon
BAR

(www.doubledownsaloon.com; 4640 Paradise Rd; ⊗24hr; 108) This dark, psychedelic gin joint appeals to the lunatic fringe. It never closes, there's never a cover charge, the house drink is called 'ass juice' and it claims to be the birthplace of the bacon martini. When live bands aren't playing, the jukebox vibrates with New Orleans jazz, British punk, Chicago blues and surf-guitar king Dick Dale.

Commonwealth
BAR

(☑702-445-6200; www.commonwealthlv.com; 525 E Fremont St; ⊗6pm-2am Wed-Fri, 8pm-2am Sat & Sun; Deuce) It might be a little too cool for school but, whoa, that Prohibition-era interior is worth a look: plush booths, softly glowing chandeliers, Victorian-era bric-a-brac and a saloon bar. Imbibe your cocktails on the rooftop patio overlooking the Fremont East scene. They say there's a secret cocktail bar within the bar, but you didn't hear that from us.

Downtown Cocktail Room
LOUNGE

(☑702-880-3696; www.thedowntownlv.com; 111 Las Vegas Blvd S; ⊗4pm-2am Mon-Fri, 7pm-2am Sat; Deuce) With a serious list of classic cocktails and house-made inventions, this low-lit speakeasy is undeniably romantic. The entrance is ingeniously disguised: the door looks like just another part of the wall until you discover the sweet spot you have to push to get in. Happy hour runs 4pm to 8pm weekdays.

Griffin
BAR

(☑702-382-0577; 511 E Fremont St; ⊗usually 7pm-2am; Deuce) Escape from the casinos' clutches and imbibe craft beers and cocktails at this darkly lit lounge, an arty twist on the dive bar. Glowing fireplaces, leather booths and an almost unbearably cool jukebox make it popular with hipster sweethearts and rebels alike.

☆ Entertainment

There are hundreds of shows to choose from in Vegas. Any Cirque du Soleil show tends to be an unforgettable experience. **Ticketmaster** (☑800-745-3000; www.ticketmaster.com) sells tickets for pretty much everything.

O
THEATER

(☑888-488-7111, 702-693-8866; www.cirquedusoleil. com; Bellagio; tickets $99-155; ⊗7:30pm & 10pm Wed-Sun) Phonetically speaking, it's the French word for water (eau). With a lithe international cast performing in, on and above water, Cirque du Soleil's O tells the tale of theater through the ages. It's a spectacular feat of imagination and engineering, and you'll pay dearly to see it – it's one of the Strip's few shows that rarely sells discounted tickets.

Beatles LOVE
THEATER

(☑702-792-7777, 800-963-9634; www.cirquedu soleil.com; Mirage; tickets $79-180; ⊗7pm & 9:30pm Thu-Mon;) Another smash hit from Cirque du Soleil. Using Abbey Road master tapes, the show psychedelically fuses the musical legacy of the Beatles with Cirque's high-energy dancers and signature aerial acrobatics. Come early to grab drinks at Abbey Road bar, next to Revolution Lounge.

🛍 Shopping

Writers' Block
BOOKS

(☑702-550-6399; www.thewritersblock.org; 1020 Fremont St; ⊗10am-8pm Mon-Sat, 11am-6pm Sun) A marvelously eclectic and spirited independent bookstore with an excellent collection of good reads, board games and kids' books. They also have stationery, a resident rabbit and an in-house 'print and craft lab'. Check the website for details on Codex workshops, where artists can 'write, design and construct' their own multimedia creations.

Bonanza Gift Shop
SOUVENIRS

(www.worldslargestgiftshop.com; 2440 Las Vegas Blvd S; ⊗8am-midnight) The self-proclaimed 'purveyors of Las Vegas pop culture' brag about running the world's largest gift shop. Whether or not it's true, it's a blast wading through the truly terrible, 100% tacky selection of souvenirs. Beware that prices for kitsch are higher here than at downtown's Fremont Street Experience.

Grand Canal Shoppes
at the Venetian
MALL

(www.grandcanalshoppes.com; Venetian; ⊗10am-11pm Sun-Thu, to midnight Fri & Sat) Wandering, painted minstrels, jugglers and laughable living statues perform in Piazza San Marco, while gondolas float past in the canals and mezzo-sopranos serenade shoppers. In this airy Italianate mall adorned with frescoes, cobblestone walkways strut past Burberry, Godiva, Sephora and 85 more luxury shops.

ℹ️ Information

EMERGENCY & MEDICAL SERVICES

Sunrise Hospital & Medical Center (☑702-731-8000; http://sunrisehospital.com; 3186 S Maryland Pkwy; ⊘24hr) Specialized children's trauma services available at a 24-hour emergency room.

University Medical Center (UMC; ☑702-383-2000; www.umcsn.com; 1800 W Charleston Blvd; ⊘24hr) Southern Nevada's most advanced trauma center has a 24-hour ER.

INTERNET RESOURCES & MEDIA

Las Vegas Weekly (http://lasvegasweekly.com) Free weekly with good entertainment and restaurant listings.

Las Vegas (www.lasvegas.com) Travel services.

Las Vegas How To (www.lasvegas-how-to.com) How to do Vegas, from booking shows to getting around to getting married.

Las Vegas Kids (www.lasvegaskids.net) The lowdown on what's up for the wee ones.

Cheapo Vegas (www.cheapovegas.com) Rundown of casinos with low table limits and their insider's guide to cheap eating.

Eater Vegas (www.vegas.eater.com) Posts a regularly updated list of the city's top 38 eateries.

TOURIST INFORMATION

Las Vegas Convention & Visitors Authority (LVCVA; ☑702-892-7575, 877-847-4858; www.lasvegas.com; 3150 Paradise Rd; ⊘8am-5:30pm Mon-Fri; 🚍Las Vegas Convention Center)

ℹ️ Getting There & Away

AIR

Just south of the major Strip casinos and easily accessible from I-15, McCarran International Airport (p235) has direct flights from most US cities, and some from Canada and Europe. Though relatively small, pleasant and easy to navigate, it's notoriously crowded so allow plenty of time to catch your flight.

BUS

Greyhound (☑800-231-2222; www.greyhound.com) Its Lucky Streak Casino Service runs from Los Angeles, San Diego and Phoenix to Las Vegas. Bus 6362 departs Phoenix at 11:15am, stops in Flagstaff at 2:10pm and arrives in Las Vegas at 8:20pm ($26 to $62).

See the website for routes, schedules and rates for Greyhound service to Las Vegas.

CAR

Most major car-rental agencies can be found at McCarran International Airport, but note that lines can stretch for hours.

Jucy Rentals (☑800-650-4180; www.jucyrentals.com) These pop-up camper vans have started appearing in the Southwest. They have rental locations in Las Vegas and Los Angeles.

Train

Amtrak (www.amtrak.com) offers the **Thruway Bus Service** from its west-bound Southwest Chief stop in Kingman, Arizona. Arriving from the east, the train arrives at Kingman at 11:39pm; a bus dedicated to Amtrak passengers only, coordinated with the train, departs at 11:50pm for a 3:10am arrival in Las Vegas.

ℹ️ Getting Around

TO/FROM AIRPORT

Group shuttles are located outside baggage claim in Terminal 1 and Terminal 3. Go to www.mccarran.com for details. It costs about $8 to $15 per person to area hotels, and private car shuttle is available.

There are also regional shuttles (p92).

Bus

The **Deuce** (☑702-228-7433; www.rtcsnv.com; 2hr/24hr/3-day pass $6/8/20), a local double-decker bus, runs 24 hours daily from Mandalay Bay to downtown's Fremont Street Experience. Look for bus stops every 0.25 miles all along the strip.

Car

All of the mega-casinos in Vegas have free self-parking and valet parking. East Fremont has streetside parking and outdoor lots.

Monorail

Las Vegas Monorail   MONORAIL (☑702-699-8299; www.lvmonorail.com; single-ride $5, 72hr pass $40; ⊘7am-midnight Mon, to 2am Tue-Thu, to 3am Fri-Sun) A private monorail links some Strip casino resorts, zipping between the MGM Grand, Bally's/Paris Las Vegas, the Flamingo Harrah's/The Quad, the city's convention center, LVH and the SLS. Children under six years old ride free.

Taxi

It's illegal to hail a cab on the street. Taxi stands are found at casino, hotel and shopping-mall entrances; call **Yellow/Checker/Star** (☑702-873-2000) for off-strip cab service. From one end of the strip (McCarran Airport) to the other (Fremont St), expect to pay about $30.

The Nevada State Legislature approved Uber Las Vegas at time of research. Taxis protested its arrival, but Uber had not yet set a start date for operations.

1. Grandview Point (p81)
It's not called that for nothing! The views here are extraordinary.

2. Bright Angel Lodge (p76)
Designed by Mary Colter, this log-and-stone building contains a museum and accommodations.

3. South Kaibab Trail (p61)
Enjoy panoramic views on this sun-drenched trail.

4. Ooh Aah Point (p66)
This is a great spot for a rest while hiking the South Kaibab Trail.

North Rim

Best Hikes

➜ Bright Angel Point (137)
➜ North Kaibab (p144)
➜ Widforss Trail (p138)
➜ Cape Final (p140)
➜ Cliff Springs (p139)

Best Places to Stay

➜ Grand Canyon Lodge (p148)
➜ Kaibab Lodge (p154)
➜ Parry Lodge (p158)
➜ Cliff Dwellers Lodge (p167)
➜ Canyons Lodge (p157)

Why Go?

On the quiet North Rim, an elegant stone and timber lodge with floor-to-ceiling windows is perched directly on the edge of the canyon. Nearby, miles of trails wind through old forests of towering ponderosa pines, past meadows thick with wildflowers, and down through layers of ancient rock. The lodge's sun porch fills with hikers as the sun goes down. Dusty and weary, they settle into Adirondack chairs, comparing notes and sharing experiences, toasting the day with drinks from the nearby saloon. Later, when children have gone back to the lodge's cabins and darkness has subdued the canyon's ferocity, people bundle up in fleeces and sit quietly, studying the stars, breathing in the canyon's emptiness, listening to the silence. This is the kinder, gentler Grand Canyon, and once you've been here you'll never want to see the canyon from anywhere else.

Road Distances (miles)

	North Rim	North Rim Entrance Gate	Kanab	Page	Vermilion Cliffs
North Rim Entrance Gate	15				
Kanab	80	70			
Page	125	110	75		
Vermilion Cliffs	85	75	80	75	
Fredonia	75	60	7	80	70

Note: Distances are approximate

Entrances

The North Rim Entrance sits 30 miles south of Jacob Lake on Hwy 67. A park pass of $30 per car (or $25 per motorcycle), good for seven days on both rims, can be purchased at the gate. Those entering on foot, by bicycle or on a shuttle bus pay $15 per person. If you arrive after-hours, a posted note will direct you – remember to pay the fee when you depart. From here, it is 14 miles to Grand Canyon Lodge.

DON'T MISS

If you think the views from Grand Canyon Lodge (p148) are nice, wait until you see the canyon from Point Imperial and Cape Royal. These are two of several drives you'll want to make time for when visiting the North Rim. Wear your hiking boots – many of the overlooks are connected to easy (and family-friendly) trails – and **pack a picnic**, as you won't find many services after pulling away from the North Rim General Store (p149). Popular day-trip destinations include the aptly named **Point Imperial** (p141): at an altitude of 8803ft, it's the highest lookout on either rim, and a prime spot to watch cloud shadows moving across the canyon below. The second essential drive takes you to the spectacular **Cape Royal** (p146) lookout. Stop for lunch at one of the picturesque picnic spots along the way, and don't miss the once-in-a-lifetime photo-op at the striking natural arch known as **Angels Window** (p146).

When You Arrive

➜ Upon entry, you'll receive a map and a copy of *The Guide*, a National Park Service (NPS) newspaper with information on ranger programs, hikes and park services

➜ Do not lose your entrance receipt, as you'll need it if you intend on leaving and re-entering the park. If you have an annual pass, senior pass, or access pass, display it from your rearview mirror using the hangtag provided.

➜ The road dead-ends at Grand Canyon Lodge. At the lodge entrance you'll find the North Rim Visitor Center (p150) as well as a cafeteria, a saloon and coffee shop, and various other amenities.

Tip: Bring Your Own Water Bottle

In an ongoing effort to go green, Grand Canyon National Park no longer sells disposable plastic water bottles. Bring your own reusable container and fill it up at a water station at one of three locations on the North Rim: at the North Kaibab Trailhead, at the North Rim Visitor Center (adjacent to the restrooms) and at the North Rim Backcountry Office. The backcountry water station stays open year-round.

PLANNING TIPS

Park accommodations are limited to Grand Canyon Lodge and the campground. All facilities at the Grand Canyon North Rim are closed mid-October through mid-May.

NORTH RIM

Fast Facts

➜ Rim trail length: 25 miles

➜ Highest elevation: 8803ft

➜ Elevation change from rim to Colorado River: 5850ft

Reservations

➜ Grand Canyon Lodge (p148) takes reservations up to 13 months in advance: accommodations book up quickly Reservations are often required for dinner at the Grand Canyon Lodge Dining Room (p149). Reach the lodge operator at ☏ 877-386-4383.

➜ North Rim Campground (p148) takes reservations up to six months in advance and stays open through late October. Hiker/cyclist sites are usually available without reservation.

Resources

➜ **Grand Canyon National Park** (www.nps.gov/grca)

➜ **Grand Canyon Lodge** (www.grandcanyon lodgenorth.com) A one-stop resource for all dining, mule rides and services affiliated with the lodge.

➜ **Visit Southern Utah** (www.visitsouthernutah.com) An online travel planner with interactive maps.

North Rim

KAIBAB NATIONAL FOREST

Outside the National Park, Kaibab National Forest offers hiking trails with alternative views of the canyon and the Colorado River – and less traffic. (p152)

KEN PATRICK TRAIL

A challenging hike that winds through ravines and dark forests en route to Point Imperial. (p142)

POINT IMPERIAL

A high-elevation hike through a charred old forest takes you to the fabulous vistas of Point Imperial, the highest point on either rim of the Grand Canyon. (p141)

Canyon Rim

Saddle Mountain Trail

Nankoweap Trail

Saddle Canyon

Buck Farm Canyon

South Canyon

Kaibab National Forest

Nankoweap Creek

Bourke Point

Grand Canyon National Park

Point Imperial (8803ft)

Point Imperial

Point Imperial Trail

Point Imperial Rd

Bright Angel Canyon

Canyon Rim

Greenland Lake

Thompson Canyon

Arizona Trail

Point Sublime R...

...on Patrick Trail

...tyo Point Trail

Canyon Rim

67

North Rim Entrance Gate

Lower Little Park

67

5 miles — 10 km

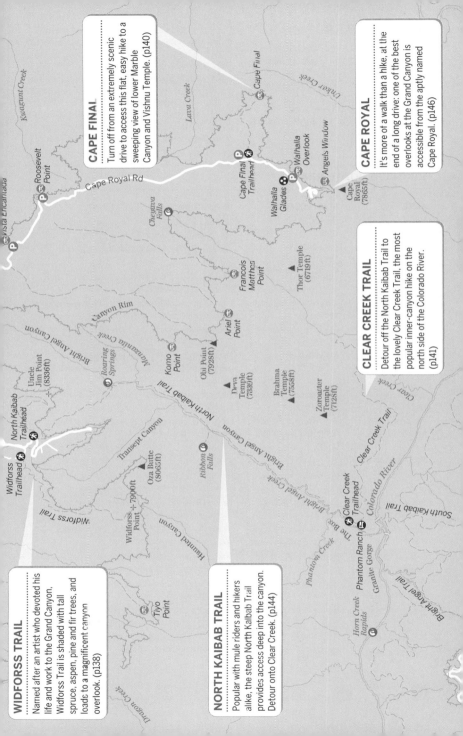

WIDFORSS TRAIL

Named after an artist who devoted his life and work to the Grand Canyon, Widforss Trail is shaded with tall spruce, aspen, pine and fir trees, and leads to a magnificent canyon overlook. (p138)

NORTH KAIBAB TRAIL

Popular with mule riders and hikers alike, the steep North Kaibab Trail provides access deep into the canyon. Detour onto Clear Creek. (p144)

CAPE FINAL

Turn off from an extremely scenic drive to access this flat, easy hike to a sweeping view of lower Marble Canyon and Vishnu Temple. (p140)

CAPE ROYAL

It's more of a walk than a hike, at the end of a long drive: one of the best overlooks at the Grand Canyon is accessible from the aptly named Cape Royal. (p146)

CLEAR CREEK TRAIL

Detour off the North Kaibab Trail to the lovely Clear Creek Trail, the most popular inner-canyon hike on the north side of the Colorado River. (p141)

Kwagunt Creek

Vista Encantada

Roosevelt Point

Cape Royal Rd

Chuar Creek

Unkar Creek

Lava Creek

Cape Final

Cape Final Trailhead

Walhalla Overlook

Angels Window

Walhalla Glades

Cape Royal (7865ft)

Chegiza Falls

Francois Matthes Point

Thor Temple (6719ft)

Ariel Point

Canyon Rim

Manzanita Creek

Roaring Springs

Komo Point

Obi Point (7928ft)

Deva Temple (7339ft)

Brahma Temple (7556ft)

Zoroaster Temple (7126ft)

Clear Creek

North Kaibab Trail

Bright Angel Canyon

Uncle Jim Point (8336ft)

North Kaibab Trailhead

Widforss Trailhead

Widforss Trail

Bright Angel Creek

Transept Canyon

Oza Butte (8065ft)

Ribbon Falls

Widforss Point 7900ft

Haunted Canyon

Tiyo Point

Clear Creek Trailhead

Colorado River

Clear Creek Trail

South Kaibab Trail

Phantom Creek

The Box

Phantom Ranch

Granite Gorge

Horn Creek Rapids

Bright Angel Trail

Dragon Creek

🚶 DAY HIKES

From Grand Canyon Lodge or the North Rim Campground, you'll have to drive to access most trails: some trailheads are a few miles down the road, others require an hour or more in the car. The only maintained rim-to-river trail from the North Rim is the North Kaibab (p146), a steep 14-mile haul to the river that's often busy with mule riders. Day hikers will find multiple turnaround spots, plus restrooms and a water fountain midway down. Do not attempt to hike to the Colorado River and back in one day, and do not underestimate the effect of altitude: if you can, spend a few days acclimatizing with scenic drives, short walks and lazy days before conquering longer trails.

In addition to the official trails, a number of old unmarked and unmaintained fire roads off Cape Royal Rd lead several

HIKING IN NORTH RIM

NAME	START LOCATION	DESCRIPTION
Bright Angel Point (p137)	Grand Canyon Lodge	Short, easy paved hike to a narrow peninsula with canyon views on three sides
Cape Final (p140)	Cape Royal Rd	Flat, easy hike along the Kaibab Plateau to a nice overlook
Cliff Springs (p139)	Cape Royal Rd	Perfect for kids, this short trail passes ancient ruins and ends at a verdant spring
Ken Patrick Trail (p142)	North Kaibab Trailhead parking lot	Point-to-point wooded trail opening up to spectacular views at Point Imperial
Point Imperial (p141)	Point Imperial Trailhead	Short rim trail with views of the eastern canyon
Transept Trail (p140)	Grand Canyon Lodge	Enjoyable amble along a path rimming the canyon, connecting Grand Canyon Lodge with the campground
Uncle Jim Trail (p142)	North Kaibab Trailhead parking lot	A loop atop the Kaibab Plateau, with views of Roaring Springs Canyon
Widforss Trail (p138)	Signed turnoff 2.7 miles north of Grand Canyon Lodge	Lovely forested walk with some of the finest canyon views on the North Rim
North Kaibab Trail		
Bridle Trail (p143)	Grand Canyon Lodge	Flat, utilitarian trail provides access between lodge, campground and North Kaibab trailhead
To Coconino Overlook (p144)	North Kaibab Trailhead	Views of Roaring Springs and Bright Angel Canyon at the end of this short hike
Clear Creek Trail (p141)	North Kaibab, 0.3 miles north of Phantom Ranch	Off the North Kaibab, the most popular inner canyon hike on the Colorado's north side
To Supai Tunnel (p144)	North Kaibab Trailhead	Steep, spectacular hike to red sandstone tunnel with sweeping views of the inner canyon chutes
To Cottonwood Campground (p144)	North Kaibab Trailhead	Last 2 miles of this trail traces Bright Angel Creek to the campground
To Redwall Bridge (p144)	North Kaibab Trailhead	Challenging descent along switchbacks leads to Redwall Bridge, which crosses Roaring Springs Canyon
To Roaring Springs (p144)	North Kaibab Trailhead	A favorite for strong hikers, featuring pools in a green oasis on the otherwise hot trail

 Drinking Water   *Flush Toilets*   *Ranger Station Nearby*   *Great for Families*   *Wildlife-Watching*

miles to rarely visited **Komo Point**, **Ariel Point** and **Francois Matthes Point**. They don't have the sweeping views of the North Rim's standard overlooks, but they promise solitude.

Ask at the visitor center for current conditions and details.

🚶Bright Angel Point

Duration 30 minutes round-trip
Distance 0.5 miles round-trip
Difficulty Easy
Start/Finish Grand Canyon Lodge
Transportation Car
Summary More a walk than a hike, this

NORTH RIM DAY HIKES

DIFFICULTY	DURATION	ROUND-TRIP DISTANCE	ELEVATION CHANGE	FEATURES	FACILITIES
easy	30min	0.5 miles	150ft		
easy	2hr	4 miles	150ft		
easy–moderate	1hr	1 mile	600ft		
moderate–difficult	6–7hr (one-way)	10 miles (one-way)	800ft		
easy	2hr	4 miles	100ft		
easy	1½hr	3 miles	200ft		
easy–moderate	3hr	5 miles	600ft		
moderate	6hr	10 miles	350ft		
easy	45min (one-way)	1.2 miles (one-way)	25ft		
easy–moderate	1hr	1.5 miles	800ft		
moderate–difficult	10hr	16.8 miles	1500ft		
moderate–difficult	3–4hr	4 miles	1410ft		
difficult	4½hr (one-way)	6.8 miles (one-way)	4170ft		
difficult	4–5hr	5.2 miles	2150ft		
difficult	7–8hr	9.4 miles	3050ft		

 Views   Grocery Store Nearby   Restaurant / Snack Shop Nearby   Waterfall   Backcountry campsite

North Rim – Day Hikes

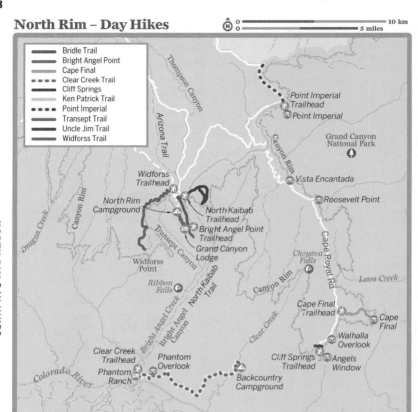

paved trail (map p138) wraps up, down and out along a narrow finger of an overlook that dangles between Transept Canyon and Roaring Springs Canyon.

This is one of the few trails on the North Rim where you feel like you're walking along a precipice, with the canyon dropping off from either side of the trail. Anyone with a fear of heights should think twice before strapping on their walking shoes. There are few guardrails, and the edges are crumbling rock and sand – hold onto your children's hands and do not veer from the established trail. While it is officially paved and easy, the few steep inclines, rocky spots and narrow path make this dangerous for strollers and prohibitive to wheelchairs. A few benches and boulders offer pleasant spots to rest along the way.

The overlook gives unfettered views of the mesas, buttes, spires and temples of Bright Angel Canyon, as well as a straight shot of the South Rim, 10 miles across the canyon as the crow flies, and the distant San Francisco Peaks towering over Flagstaff. Listen carefully and you can hear Roaring Springs below. The trail begins on the left side of the sun porch, or you can start at a second trailhead in the log shelter in the parking area by the visitor center.

Widforss Trail

Duration 6 hours round-trip

Distance 10 miles round-trip

Difficulty Moderate

Start/Finish Widforss Trailhead

Transportation Car

Summary A moderate hike (map p138) through woods and meadows with peeping canyon views leads to a spectacular canyon overlook.

Named after Gunnar Widforss, an early-20th-century artist who lived, worked, died and was buried at the Grand Canyon, the Widforss Trail meanders through stands of spruce, white fir, ponderosa pine and aspen to **Widforss Point**. Tall trees offer shade, fallen limbs provide pleasant spots to relax, and you likely won't see more than a few people along the trail. To reach the trailhead, turn onto the dirt road just south of the Cape Royal Rd turnoff, continuing a mile to the Widforss Trail parking area.

After a 15-minute climb, the canyon comes into view. For the next 2 miles, the trail offers wide views of the canyon to one side and meadows and woods to the other. Halfway into the hike, the trail jags away from the rim and dips into gullies of lupines and ferns; the canyon doesn't come into view again until the end. From Widforss Point (elevation 7900ft), take the small path to the left of the picnic table to a flat rock, where you can enjoy a sandwich, the classic view and the silence. Though the total elevation change is only 350ft, rolling terrain makes the first few miles a moderate challenge. The park service offers a self-guided trail brochure for the first half of this hike; available at the trailhead and the visitor center. Follow the guided walk as listed in the brochure, then turn around, and, though you'll miss the overlook at the point, you'll have hiked the best part of the trail. This is a really pretty hike in late September or early October when the leaves are golden, and the point makes an excellent backcountry campsite.

Cliff Springs

Duration 1 hour round-trip

Distance 1 mile round-trip

Difficulty Easy–moderate

Start/Finish Cliff Springs Trailhead, Cape Royal Rd

Transportation Car

Summary While this sweet little trail (map p138) leads to a lovely hidden dell, stretches can be tricky to negotiate — it's not a particularly pleasant hike, but it can be rewarding.

Look for the trailhead directly across the road from a small pullout on a curve 0.3 miles from Cape Royal. The trail immediately heads sharply downhill, over loose rock and through the woods. In about five minutes, you'll come to a stone **Ancestral Puebloan granary**, used by the Ancestral Puebloans to store corn, beans and squash. The path then makes its way through dry, barren pines and along a short, rocky descent into a ravine. It hugs the wall of a narrow side canyon, passing under the shade of a boulder overhang, for about 10 minutes to its end. At **Cliff Springs**, a tiny trickle emerges from the ground, forming a large puddle fringed with ferns and verdant thistle, and a huge, flat rock, cooled by steady breezes, offers a shaded spot to sit. The view here is strikingly different from other North Rim trails. You are actually hidden in the canyon, as opposed to sitting on the

NORTH RIM DAY HIKES

WILDERNESS EXPEDITIONS

Experienced hikers with extensive wilderness experience and GPS navigational systems will find several unmaintained and roughly marked North Rim trails to tackle. These are intense, interior-canyon death traps that should not be attempted by the average canyon visitor.

The **Nankoweap Trail** descends from Marble Canyon 5240ft to the Colorado River. Considered by many to be the toughest hike in the canyon, the grueling 14-mile trail can be tricky to follow and requires a fair amount of maneuvering along steep ledges. Nankoweap Creek, 10.6 miles below the rim provides a resplendent green oasis for backcountry camping.

From Toroweap, the **Lava Falls Route** plummets 2540ft over a distance of 1.5 miles to the Colorado River. Do not try this treacherous, shadeless hike, described by the park service as 'one of the hottest, steepest, loosest, scariest chutes in the canyon' in the summer, when temperatures can reach upward of 115°F (46°C).

Other trails include the **Tuckup Trail, Bill Hall Trail, Thunder River Trail** and **North Bass Trail**. Good day-hike options include Bill Hall 1 mile down to Muav Cabin, or North Bass 1.3 miles to Monument Point. Contact the backcountry office for maps, guides and current conditions.

canyon's edge, and you don't get a sense of the massive vista that so many overlooks boast.

Do not drink from the spring: the water may be contaminated.

🏃 Cape Final

Duration 2 hours round-trip

Distance 4 miles round-trip

Difficulty Easy

Start/Finish Cape Final Trailhead, Cape Royal Rd

Transportation Car

Summary Forested walk (map p138) to jutting rock over the canyon, with spectacular views of the canyon and the Painted Desert.

Hike this trail for the destination, not the hike. It's so dry, with nothing but brown ponderosa and brittle needles for most of the hike, that it feels like you're walking through a box of kindling, and what you see at the trailhead is what you'll see for just about the entire hike. But it's almost completely flat, quite easy and you're rewarded with an amazing canyon overlook.

After the initial, moderate 10-minute incline, the trail levels off. In about a half hour, a short side trail veers left to a beautiful view – take a few minutes to rehydrate, and return to the main trail. There is one more view before the trail narrows, turns rocky and heads a couple of minutes downhill. The ponderosas give way to piñons, sagebrush and cliff rose, and a flat, rocky triangle roughly 25ft by 25ft extends into the canyon with incredible views. Hike five more minutes through cactus and scramble up some boulders to **Cape Final**. Here, a small, rocky overlook sits at the edge of the canyon, offering a 270-degree view of lower Marble Canyon and one of the Grand Canyon's most famous formations, Vishnu Temple. The ease of this hike makes it great for children, but it's a frighteningly dangerous overlook and there are no guardrails.

🏃 Transept Trail

Duration 45 minutes one-way

Distance 1.5 miles one-way

Difficulty Easy

Start Grand Canyon Lodge

Finish North Rim Campground

Transportation Car

Summary Conveniently connecting Grand Canyon Lodge to the campground, this rocky dirt path (map p138) with moderate inclines follows the rim and meanders through the aspen and ponderosa pines.

From the bottom of the steps off the Grand Canyon Lodge sun porch, follow the trail along the rim to the right. This is particularly nice in the evening, as you can relax in the woods and watch the sun set across a side canyon. In about 15 minutes, you'll come to a log bench with a quiet, lovely view of the canyon. With plenty of room to run, this is a nice spot for a picnic with children. From here, the trail veers from the edge and the path becomes relatively level, more a walk through the woods than a hike. The trail passes a small **Ancient Puebloan site** and several viewpoints before reaching the rim-view tent sites of the campground, and the general store beyond. If hiking the trail from the campground to the lodge, look for the trailhead behind the general store.

HIDDEN SPOTS ON THE NORTH RIM

Just coming to the North Rim is getting away from it all, but once you're here there are a few easily accessible hideaways. **Uncle Jim's Cave**, once used as a ranger residence, lies in the rocks on the far side of **Harvey Meadow** on the way to the Widforss Trailhead. Easy to get to and free of crowds, the meadow and cave make a great spot to hang out, particularly for children. The stone **Moon Room** below the sun porch of Grand Canyon Lodge offers a cool and quiet rimside refuge. Look for small, unmarked stairs along the trail that runs between the lodge and the canyon. On the road to Cape Royal, few folks bother stopping at **Greenland Lake**, and it's a peaceful place for a picnic. Unmaintained forest roads off Cape Royal Rd and the road to Point Sublime lead miles through the woods and meadows to **backcountry overlooks**. Ask at the visitor center for details, and secure a backcountry permit if you plan on primitive camping.

⚑Point Imperial

Duration 2 hours round-trip

Distance 4 miles round-trip

Difficulty Easy

Start/Finish Point Imperial Trailhead

Transportation Car

Summary Forested walk (map p138) to jutting rock over the canyon with great views.

From the Point Imperial parking lot this trail heads northeast along the rim, veers through areas burned by the 2000 fire and ends at the park's northern border, where it connects with the backcountry Nankoweap Trail and US Forest Service (USFS) roads. Expect to see a haunting landscape of blackened remains of burned forest mixed with tender regrowth and emerging meadows, and keep an eye out for the white-tailed Kaibab squirrel and mule-deer. Though this quiet trail rolls gently along the rim and through the woods, the high elevation (8800ft) can make it seem more difficult. Unlike other trails on the North Rim, it doesn't lead to a spectacular overlook and doesn't form a loop. You'll need to retrace your steps to return to the Point Imperial parking lot.

⚑Clear Creek Trail

Duration 5 hours one-way

Distance 8.4 miles one-way

Difficulty Moderate–difficult

Start North Kaibab Trail, 0.3 miles north of Phantom Ranch

Finish Clear Creek

Transportation Foot

Summary Side hike (map p138) off the North Kaibab offers spectacular views and backcountry camping.

In excellent condition and easy to follow, the enjoyable Clear Creek Trail is one of few inner-canyon trails on the north side of the Colorado River and easily the most popular inner-canyon hike. Built in 1935, it was originally created as a mule trail so visitors to Phantom Ranch could access a side canyon and do some trout fishing in the stocked creek. The views into the gorge and across the canyon are magnificent. Even the first few miles provide gorgeous views, so hik-

---

TOP FIVE OVERLOOKS

Every drive and hike on the North Rim includes a canyon overlook, but unlike the South Rim there is no extended stretch of trail with panoramic canyon views.

Grand Canyon Lodge (p148) Steps lead from the lodge's sun porch to two rocky overlooks.

Bright Angel Point (p137) An easy amble along a precipitous rocky outcrop.

Cape Royal (p146) Primarily paved trail leads from the parking lot to one of the park's best overlooks.

Point Imperial Highest overlook on either rim.

Cape Final Quiet, uncrowded and spectacular, well worth the wooded 2-mile hike.

---

ing a couple of miles and turning around it makes a lovely day hike from Phantom Ranch or Bright Angel Campground. Be warned, however, that because it lies on the south-facing slope the entire trail bears the brunt of the sun from sunrise to sunset. It is unspeakably hot during the summer, and there's no shade or water anywhere. Bring plenty of water and get an early start.

Pick up the trail 0.3 mile north of Phantom Ranch. Heading east off the North Kaibab, the trail switchbacks up to the base of Sumner Butte, and in just under 1 mile stone benches at **Phantom Overlook** offer a pleasant rest and view of Phantom Ranch. The trail levels for a bit, offers spectacular views of the river, then ascends to the Tonto Platform, climbing just over 1000ft over the first 1.7 miles. It then meanders the contours and canyon folds, passing beneath Zoroaster and Brahma Temples on the left, before dropping to the streambed and ending at a dry tributary creek. You need to hike the drainage about 100ft down to the lovely little cottonwood-fringed **backcountry campground** alongside tiny Clear Creek. You can spend the night with a backcountry permit, or retrace your steps to Phantom Ranch.

Several rough trails follow the creek's tributaries from the campground, and there's a 6-mile scramble along the creek to the Colorado River. The northeast fork of Clear

Creek leads up to **Cheyava Falls**, but it only flows in the spring after heavy snowfall and it's 10 miles round-trip from Clear Creek. Do not attempt any side-hikes without a map, and always check conditions with rangers before setting out.

Ken Patrick Trail

Duration 6 hours one-way

Distance 10 miles one-way

Difficulty Moderate–difficult

Start North Kaibab Trail parking area

Finish Point Imperial

Transportation Car

Summary Offering rim and forest views, the challenging Ken Patrick Trail (map p138) ascends and descends numerous ravines as it winds through an old, deep forest, crosses Cape Royal Rd after 7 miles and continues for another 3 miles to Point Imperial.

The trail starts with a gentle climb into the woods and winds through gambel oaks,

TASTE OF THE CANYON INTERIOR

Except for the handful of hard-core wilderness trails into the canyon, the only option for hiking the canyon interior on the North Rim is the overnight North Kaibab Trail. For a day hike you can stop at various points and turn around. Even a short jaunt gives a feel for the distinct world below the rim.

Coconino Overlook (one hour round-trip, 1.5 miles) Flat Coconino Sandstone on the canyon edge.

Supai Tunnel (three to four hours round-trip, 4 miles) Red-rock tunnel with seasonal water.

Redwall Bridge (four to five hours round-trip, 5.2 miles) Wooden bridge crosses Roaring Springs Canyon.

Eye of the Needle (six to seven hours round-trip, 7 miles) Steep cliffs soar high above hikers in this dramatic section of the trail.

Roaring Springs (seven to eight hours round-trip, 9.4 miles) Primary source of water for both rims.

ponderosa pines, white firs and aspen woodland. Views are intermittent, offering quick glimpses of Roaring Springs Canyon. The trail sees a lot of mule traffic, and it shows – particularly on the first mile, where the soft dirt path, worn into sandy grooves by hooves and softened by mule urine, can be smelly and hard on the feet. After a mile the mules head off on the Uncle Jim Trail, while the Ken Patrick veers to the left. Beyond this junction the trail grows increasingly serene, at times faint but still discernible, and involves several difficult uphill stretches.

For excellent views and a shorter, easier, mule-free walk, start at Point Imperial and hike 3 miles to Cape Royal Rd, and turn around. This stretch is the steepest but also the prettiest and the quietest. The trail alternates between shady conifer forests and panoramic views of Nankoweap Canyon, the Little Colorado River gorge, Marble Platform and the Painted Desert, and the San Francisco Peaks far to the south. Allow four hours for this round-trip journey.

Uncle Jim Trail

Duration 3 hours round-trip

Distance 5 miles round-trip

Difficulty Easy–moderate

Start/Finish North Kaibab Trail parking area

Transportation Car

Summary Wooded loop (map p138) to a canyon overlook.

This spur trail – named for a hunting advocate and forest-service warden who shot hundreds of mountain lions on the North Rim to protect resident deer – shares the Ken Patrick Trailhead. The two trails are the same for the first mile, then Uncle Jim heads right. After a bit of down and up, the trail soon reaches the 2-mile loop out to the point – it makes little difference if you go left or right. Near the tie-up area for mules at **Uncle Jim Point**, you'll have a terrific view of the North Kaibab switchbacks, Roaring Springs, the Walhalla Plateau and the South Rim. Tree trunks carved into chairs and stools offer a perfect resting spot before your return. Note that this trail is also used by mules.

TOROWEAP

One of the park's most impressive overlooks, **Toroweap** (also known as Tuweep) offers a landscape and views unlike anywhere else on the North Rim. Its 4552ft elevation, lower than either rim, supports piñons, junipers, cacti and small flowering desert plants, and sheer cliffs drop directly into the canyon and the Colorado River below. But Toroweap is not for everyone. It sits 150 miles from the North Rim Entrance Gate and requires at least two hours' drive in a high clearance vehicle on a rough desert road. Facilities are non-existent, and it's almost unbearably hot and dry during the summer. (Toroweap is, in fact, a Paiute term meaning 'dry or barren valley.')

For those who venture out here, however, Toroweap promises a Grand Canyon experience unlike any other. You literally have to crawl on your belly to see the river below, and there are no guardrails. Lava Falls, perhaps the roughest water in the canyon, is visible 1.5 miles downstream, and Vulcans Throne, basalt remnants of a cinder cone eruption 74,000 years ago, rises from the Esplanade Platform. Across the canyon is the Hualapai Reservation and 25 miles east sits the mouth of Havasu Canyon, home to the Havasupai.

Forget the GPS: you'll need the BLM Arizona Strip Visitor Map for this trip. The best way to arrive is to drive 8 miles west of Fredonia on Hwy 389 and look for a dirt road and the sign 'Toroweap.' Take this road 55 miles south to the **Tuweep Ranger Station**, which is staffed year-round. **Tuweep Campground**, a free, first-come first-served primitive campground offering nine sites, lies 5.4 miles beyond the ranger station and a mile before the rim. Call up to four months in advance to reserve the group site that sleeps between seven and 11 people. A backcountry permit is required for camping beyond the designated camping area, but Toroweap does not require a park entrance fee.

About 46 miles after the turn onto BLM 109 from Hwy 389, turn west onto Mt Trumbull Rd and head 3 miles to **Nampaweap Petroglyphs**, inside **Grand Canyon-Parashant National Monument**. A small parking lot marks the short walk to the petroglyphs. Once at Toroweap, a few moderate and sparsely marked hikes offer chances to stretch your legs. The 2.9-mile **Esplanade Loop Trail** begins at the campground. For a shorter hike, try the easy **Saddle Horse Canyon Trail**, a 1.6-mile round-trip to the canyon rim. The easy-to-miss trailhead is 0.3 miles south of the Tuweep Campground.

The road to Toroweap, notorious for flattening tires, keeps garages in Kanab in business, and a tow can cost as much as $2000. Drive under 25mph to minimize your chances, have at least one spare tire, and bring plenty of water (there is none at Toroweap, and shade is scarce). The ranger is not always available, and cell service is spotty at best. Log onto www.nps.gov/grca/planyourvisit/tuweep.htm for more information.

🚶Bridle Trail

Duration 45 minutes one-way

Distance 1.2 miles one-way

Difficulty Easy

Start Grand Canyon Lodge

Finish North Kaibab Trailhead

Transportation Car

Summary Hard-packed utilitarian trail and the only one in the park that allows dogs and bicycles.

The uninspiring Bridle Trail (map p138) offers visitors a means of walking from the lodge to the campground, and on to the North Kaibab Trailhead. It hugs the road for 1 mile to the campground before climbing a bit up through the woods to the North Kaibab parking area.

🚶 OVERNIGHT HIKES

Even the most able-bodied hikers emerge from the pines after a day hike on the North Kaibab and collapse, exhausted and hot, on the stone wall by the trailhead. The 3 miles just below the rim are steep switchback after steep switchback of grinding haul, with no shade and no relief from the heat, made all the more draining by the pools of mule urine blocking the trail. It's not so bad going down, but coming back up is tough – time your hike so you're not tackling this section during the heat of the day. You can overnight about halfway down the trail. With a dawn

Overnight Hike
North Kaibab Trail

START NORTH KAIBAB TRAILHEAD
END COLORADO RIVER
LENGTH 14.2 MILES ONE-WAY; 9 HOURS DOWN, 12 HOURS UP

This spectacular inner-canyon trek, featuring creekside stretches, strenuous switchbacks and a cottonwood-fringed campground, takes a few days to complete, depending on how you pace it. The sandy trail begins at 8250ft, under the shade of aspens and pines. The first part of the trail is perhaps the least pleasant, as hikers share the path with mules and their riders — and, as backpackers quickly learn when they're pressed against the edge of the trail, waiting for a long line of riders to pass, mules have the right of way. Watch your step: the trail gets muddy here even when the weather is dry. Further along the trail, however, the mules turn back, and the rest of the journey downward is easier to manage.

Just 10 minutes' walk from the trailhead, the path emerges from the trees and opens up to canyon views. At ❶**Coconino Overlook** (7450ft), about 25 minutes from the trailhead, a flat ledge offers clear views of Roaring Springs and Bright Angel Canyon. Forty minutes or so later, the trail comes to a tree-shaded glen with a seasonal water tap and pit toilets, the turn-around for half-day mule trips. Just around the bend is ❷**Supai Tunnel** (6800ft), a short red corridor blasted through the rock when the trail was built in the 1930s. On the other side of the tunnel, views open to an intimidating set of switchbacks beside a knuckle-biting drop-off. It's a tough descent along the switchbacks to ❸**Redwall Bridge** (6100ft). The bridge, built in 1966 when more than 14in of rain fell over 36 hours and washed away huge sections of the North Kaibab Trail, crosses Roaring Springs Canyon. Once you cross the bridge, the trail thins. It hugs the canyon wall to the right and hovers above dramatic sheer drops to the left.

A little over a mile after the bridge, you'll reach the cascading waterfall of ❹**Roaring Springs** (5200ft) itself; take the short detour to the left, where you'll find picnic tables and a pool to cool your feet. Seasonal water is available at the restrooms or 10 minutes down the trail at the ❺**Pumphouse Residence**. New York City–born Grand Canyon artist Bruce Aiken (www.bruceaiken.com) lived and worked here as the pump operator from 1973 until his retirement in 2006. Park rangers now live here during the summer only; hikers report that rangers aren't always on duty, so come prepared with information instead of relying on their resources.

From Roaring Springs, the trail follows the small and inviting ❻**Bright Angel Creek** 2.1 miles to ❼**Cottonwood Campground** (4080ft). Here, tall cottonwoods offer a shaded spot to relax along the creek. It's a beautiful spot and a welcome oasis after the scorching canyon descent, but the campsites themselves are not shaded. The campground provides drinking water (May 15 to October 15), pit toilets, a phone, a ranger station and an emergency medical facility.

From the campground, the trail levels off considerably. The steepest grind is over, and it's a gentle downhill walk along Bright Angel Creek to the Colorado River – a feature that only intrepid hikers get to see up close when they visit the Grand Canyon. After about 30 minutes, you'll see a turn-off on the right for ❽**Ribbon Falls** (3720ft; 8.3 miles one-way from rim). Take this 0.3-mile spur across the bridge and up to the falls. Here, water mists 100ft over moss-covered stone to a small pool surrounded by ferns, columbines and monkeyflowers, creating a hidden fairyland. Standing underneath feels like a cold shower, and it's an ideal spot to rest. Retrace your steps to the main trail, and continue to the ❾**Box**, a narrow passage between 2000ft walls that tower over the trail. For about 4 miles, the trail, shaded by canyon walls but with no breeze, follows the stream along almost flat ground. It passes over several bridges before opening up about 20 minutes before ❿**Phantom Ranch** (2546ft), ⓫**Bright Angel Campground** and, a few minutes later, the ⓬**Colorado River** (2400ft).

departure, you could hike down to the river in one day. Note that the trail drops 4170ft over 7.4 miles from the rim to Cottonwood Campground, but from Cottonwood it levels off to a pleasant 1680ft decline over 7.4 miles.

The clearly marked trailhead lies about 2 miles north of Grand Canyon Lodge. The modest parking lot often fills soon after dawn; you can also walk from the lodge or campground on the Bridle Trail or reserve a spot on the hikers' shuttle. Potable water is available mid-May through mid-October at Supai Tunnel, Roaring Springs and Cottonwood Campground (6.8 miles from the rim), and year-round at Phantom Ranch (at the canyon bottom). Rangers staff Phantom Ranch year-round, and Cottonwood Campground from mid-May through mid-October. The trail remains open year-round, even though the North Rim closes. Snowshoes may be necessary for the upper elevations, and the trail can be dangerous due to ice and snow. If you emerge from the canyon when the North Rim is closed, turn left out of the parking lot toward seasonal rangers – otherwise it's more than 40 miles to civilization.

Backcountry permits ($10 per permit, plus $8 per camper below the rim and $8 per group above the rim) are required for overnight hiking, overnight camping at rim sites beyond North Rim Campground, and camping below the rim. Passes are available on the first of the month, four months prior to the proposed start month. The North Rim Backcountry Office reserves a limited number of last-minute walk-up permits for Cottonwood Campground, and maintains a waiting list for other sites, available in person only. Go to www.nps.gov/grca/planyourvisit/backcountry-permit.htm for the rather complicated details on securing passes and the various regulations.

🚗 DRIVING

Driving is required to reach most trailheads and overlooks, including many of the region's most spectacular lookout points, on the North Rim. Expect miles of slow roads through dense stands of evergreens and aspen. To reach Cape Royal and Point Imperial Rds, head 3 miles north from Grand Canyon Lodge to the signed right turn. From here, it is 5 miles to the Y-turn for Point Imperial and Cape Royal Rds. The road to Point

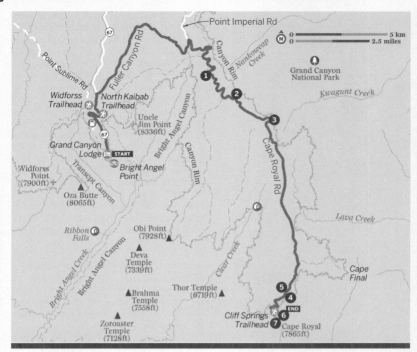

Driving Tour
Cape Royal

START GRAND CANYON LODGE
END CAPE ROYAL
LENGTH 23 MILES (45 MINUTES) ONE-WAY

From the Y-turn for Point Imperial and Cape Royal Rds, it's 2.5 miles to **1 Greenland Lake**. Look for the small parking lot on the right. A two-minute walk leads to a meadow and alpine pond and, a few minutes further, an old, empty salt cabin. This is the only stop on the drive without rim views, and it makes an excellent spot for a picnic.

Cape Royal Rd continues 2 miles to **2 Vista Encantada**. Views from this overlook extend from Nankoweap Creek within the canyon to the Vermilion Cliffs and Painted Desert in the distance. You'll find a few picnic tables, but because the tables are right next to the road and parking lot it's not a particularly nice spot to eat. After taking in the view, continue 1.6 miles to **3 Roosevelt Point**. From here, you can see the confluence of the Little Colorado and Colorado Rivers,

the Navajo Reservation, the Painted Desert and the Hopi Reservation. The easy 0.2-mile round-trip rimside Roosevelt Point Trail loops through burnt-out forest to a small bench at the canyon edge.

The next stop is **4 Walhalla Overlook**, 6.5 miles past Roosevelt Point. Just below the rim lies Unkar Delta, a plateau composed of sand and rocks deposited by Unkar Creek. This was the winter home of Ancestral Puebloans from AD 850 to 1200. On the north side of the parking lot, a path crosses the street and leads to **5 Walhalla Glades**, the Ancestral Puebloans' summer home. Because this area sits below most of the North Rim, snow here melted earlier and enabled villagers to grow beans, corn and squash. A short self-guided walk leads past six small ruins; pick up a walking-tour brochure from a small box at the trailhead just off the road.

The road ends 1.5 miles past Walhalla Overlook at the Cape Royal parking lot. From here, a 0.3-mile paved path, lined with piñons, cliff rose and interpretive signs, leads

A view from Cape Royal

to **6 Angels Window**, a natural arch, and **7 Cape Royal Point**, arguably the best view from this side of the canyon. The path splits at the view of Angels Window, a few minutes from the trailhead. To the left, a short path leads to a precipice overlook that juts into the canyon and drops dramatically on three sides – here, you are literally standing atop Angels Window. To the right, the path continues to the rocky outcrop of Cape Royal Point. The Colorado River – 70 miles downstream of Lees Ferry, 18 miles upstream of Phantom Ranch and 207 miles upstream of Lake Mead – can be seen directly below the point.

While the path is plenty wide enough for strollers and wheelchairs, they can't access Angels Window and the point itself is rocky. Several pleasantly shaded picnic tables sit at the far end of the parking lot.

This road may be closed in the late fall and early spring, and during heavy wind. The only bathrooms are at the Cape Royal parking lot.

Sublime offers amazing views, but requires at least four hours round-trip navigating a treacherous dirt road. Note that vehicles longer than 30ft are not recommended on the roads to Cape Royal and Point Imperial.

OTHER ACTIVITIES

Like everything on the North Rim, activities here are friendly, low-key affairs.

Mule Rides

Unless you're planning to hike the North Kaibab, a mule ride is your best bet for discovering a taste of life below the canyon rim – and unlike mule trips on the South Rim, you can usually book a mule ride on the North Rim when you arrive at the park. Just duck inside the Grand Canyon Lodge (p148) to the Mule Desk. Family-run **Canyon Trail Rides** (Map p149; ☎ 435-679-3665; www.canyonrides.com; North Rim; 1hr/half-day mule ride $40/80; ☺ schedules vary mid-May–mid-Oct) will also take advance reservations.

Mule rides from the North Rim don't go into the canyon as far as the Colorado River. On the plus side, they're suitable for all ages (above 10 years of age, and within a 220lb weight limit), and the guided excursions don't follow precipitous canyon ledges, making them appropriate even for those a bit shy around horses.

On offer are a one-hour rim tour – a wooded ride to an overlook with several departures daily - a half-day trip to Uncle Jim's Point and a half-day trip to Supai Tunnel, which descends 1450ft into the canyon along the North Kaibab Trail. The half-day trips depart at 7.30am and 12.30pm.

Ranger Programs

A word to the wise: don't miss park ranger programs on the North Rim. These informal gatherings, led by the region's official outdoor experts, are a highlight of any visit – they're free to join, reflect the summer-camp atmosphere and add a valuable dimension to your understanding of the park. Several afternoon and evening talks are held on the sun porch or in the auditorium of Grand Canyon Lodge; when skies are clear, guests gather to gaze through telescopes while a ranger describes the night sky. Other programs are conducted at the campground

NORTH RIM OTHER ACTIVITIES

amphitheater or at the Walhalla Overlook parking lot. *The Guide* publishes a seasonal schedule, and daily events are posted at the visitor center and at the campground.

Cycling

Because bikes are allowed on blacktop roads only, options for cycling on the North Rim are limited to Hwy 67 into the park, Point Imperial Rd and Cape Royal Rd. The two exceptions are the 17-mile dirt road to Point Sublime and the utilitarian Bridle Trail that follows the highway from the lodge to the North Kaibab Trailhead. Bring your own bicycle, or, if you're coming from the South Rim, rent one at Bright Angel Bicycles (p237) near the Visitor Center.

In the surrounding Kaibab National Forest just outside the park entrance, bikes are allowed on a seemingly endless network of forest roads and all trails, including the spectacular 18-mile **Rainbow Rim Trail** (p152) connecting five remote overlooks.

Cross-Country Skiing

Once the first heavy snowfall closes Hwy 67 into the park (as early as late October or as late as January), you can cross-country ski the 44 miles to the rim and camp at the campground (no water, pit toilets). There's a water bottle filling station with a frost-free valve open year-round at the North Rim Backcountry Office. Camping is permitted elsewhere with a backcountry permit, available from rangers year-round. You can ski any of the rim trails, though none are groomed. The closest ski rental is in Flagstaff (p102).

ℹ TACKLING THE ELEVATION

Hikes and overlooks on the North Rim range from 8000ft to almost 9000ft in elevation, and it can take a couple days to acclimate. Simply drinking lots of water can often prevent headaches, nausea, shortness of breath and exhaustion, all symptoms of elevation sickness. There is an ice-maker (free) and water-bottle filling stations behind the visitors center and near the lodge's front door. Pick up bagged ice to fill your cooler at the **North Rim General Store**.

🛏 SLEEPING

Your best bet for exploring the North Rim is to stay at Grand Canyon Lodge or the North Rim Campground. Outside the park, the closest lodging is Kaibab Lodge, 18 miles from the rim, or Jacob Lake Inn, 44 miles from the rim. Beyond that, you'll have to drive 78 miles north to Kanab, Utah, 85 miles northeast to Marble Canyon or 125 miles northeast to Page, Arizona. Contact the North Rim Backcountry Information Center (p150) for permits to camp at remote North Rim overlooks or at backcountry sites below the rim; you can camp for free without a permit anywhere in the bucolic North Kaibab National Forest, just outside the park gate.

★ **Grand Canyon Lodge**   HISTORIC HOTEL $$
(Map p149; ✉ advance reservations 877-386-4383, reservations outside USA 480-337-1320, same-day reservations 928-638-2611; www.grandcanyon lodgenorth.com; r $130, 2-person per cabin $138-191; ⊘ mid-May–mid-Oct) 🐾 Walk through the front door of the lodge, and here, framed by picture windows, is the canyon in all its glory. Built in 1937 with wood, Kaibab limestone and glass, the lodge features a spacious rimside dining room and sun porches lined with Adirondack chairs. Guest rooms are not in the lodge itself; most accommodations are cozy log cabins nearby.

North Rim Campground   CAMPGROUND $
(Map p149; ✉ 928-638-7814, 877-444-6777; www. recreation.gov; tent sites $18, RV sites $18-25; ⊘ mid-May–mid-Oct by reservation, first-come, first-served Oct 16-31; 🖥) Operated by the National Park Service, this campground, 1.5 miles north of the lodge, offers shaded sites on level ground blanketed in pine needles. Sites 11, 14, 15, 16 and 18 overlook the Transept (a side canyon) and cost $25. There's water, a store, a snack bar, coin-op showers and laundry facilities, but no hookups. Make reservations online.

✕ EATING & DRINKING

There's only one restaurant, one cafeteria and one saloon on the North Rim – and that's part of the charm of staying up here. Luckily, the Grand Canyon Lodge's dining and drinking venues are all appealing, just steps away from sweeping vistas of the vast canyon below. There's a short menu and

North Rim Visitor Area

North Rim Visitor Area

◎ Sights
    Bright Angel Point......................(see 1)

⊕ Activities, Courses & Tours
    Canyon Trail Rides ....(see 1)

⊟ Sleeping
    1 Grand Canyon Lodge B3
    2 North Rim Campground.....................A2

⊗ Eating
    Deli in the Pines...................(see 1)
    3 Grand Canyon Cookout
       Experience............................... A1
    Grand Canyon Lodge
       Dining Room...............(see 1)
    North Rim General Store............(see 2)

⊜ Drinking & Nightlife
    The Coffee Shop & Rough
       Rider Saloon ....(see 1)

⊚ Shopping
    4 Gift Shop B3

waiters serving the lodge's living room in the afternoon. but it's quicker to help yourself – whether for sunset cocktails or breakfast with an unforgettable view, simply order what you like from the coffee shop or saloon, then carry it to one of the Adirondack chairs or tables on the lodge's sun porch. Reservations are required for dinner in the elegant Grand Canyon Lodge Dining Room; visitors can contact the restaurant and all the following establishments through the North Rim Switchboard (☏928-638-2612).

Deli in the Pines   CAFETERIA $
(Map p149; Grand Canyon Lodge; lunch & dinner $7-15; ⊙10.30am-9pm, mid-May–mid-Oct) The name is a bit misleading: this isn't a deli, but a small cafeteria adjacent to the lodge serving takeaway salads and sandwiches to pack for a hike or picnic. There's also pizza, ice cream, and a handful of daily specials such as chili and pulled pork.

North Rim General Store   MARKET $
(Map p149; Grand Canyon Lodge; ⊙7am-8pm mid-May–mid-Oct; ☏) Pick up basic groceries and supplies at the General Store, adjacent to the campground and just over a mile from the lodge. It's the only place around the North Rim with a wi-fi signal: grab a coffee from the small café kiosk and take a seat to use it.

★ **Grand Canyon Lodge**
Dining Room   AMERICAN $$
(Map p149; ☏928-638-2511, off-season 928-645-6865; www.grandcanyonlodgenorth.com; mains breakfast $6-13, lunch $10-15, dinner $13-33; ⊙6.30-10am & 11.30am-2.30pm & 4.45-9.45pm mid-May–mid-Oct; ☻) Although the seats beside the window are wonderful, views from the dining room are so huge it doesn't matter where you sit. While the solid dinner menu includes buffalo steak, western trout and vegetarian options, don't expect culinary memories – the view's the thing. Book ahead for dinner.

Grand Canyon Cookout
Experience   AMERICAN $$$
(Map p149; ☏928-638-2611; Grand Canyon Lodge; adult/child 6-15yr $30/15; ⊙5.45pm Jun 1-Sep 30; ☻) Feast on smoked beef brisket, roasted chicken, skillet cornbread and all the fixings – served with a side of Western songs and jokes. It might sound cheesy, but it's a lot of fun, old-school national-park-style, and it's great for kids. Take the Bridle Trail to the cookout site, or catch the complimentary train or shuttle van.

The Coffee Shop &
Rough Rider Saloon   BAR
(Map p149; Grand Canyon Lodge; pastries $3, breakfast burritos $5, cocktails $8-10; ⊙5.30am-10.30am & 11.30am-10.30pm) If you're up for an early-morning hike, stop for breakfast at the cozy

Coffee Shop – a space that morphs into a saloon by midday, serving beer, wine and mixed drinks, plus sandwiches, wraps and pizza. Teddy Roosevelt memorabilia lines the walls, honoring his role in the history of the park.

ℹ Information

All services on the North Rim are closed from mid-October through mid-May, but rangers are always on hand. Day-trippers are welcome year-round (no charge). You can stay at the campground (with water and a bathroom but no services) until the first heavy snowfall closes the road from Jacob Lake; after that you'll need a backcountry permit (available directly from winter rangers after the backcountry office closes). Public showers and laundry facilities are next to the campground.

EMERGENCY

Emergency Dial 🕿 911 from your cabin. EMT-certified rangers respond.
North Rim Switchboard 🕿 928-638-2612

INTERNET ACCESS

The only place to pick up a wireless signal is a mile away from Grand Canyon Lodge at the North Rim General Store (p149). Look for the small café area with tables and electrical outlets on the far side of the store.

MEDIA

Pick up a copy of *The Guide: North Rim Information and Maps* when you arrive at the gate or in the visitor center.

MEDICAL SERVICES

The closest hospital is Kane County Hospital (p241) in Kanab, UT.

MONEY

There are ATMs at the Rough Rider Saloon (p149) and the North Rim General Store (p149).

POST

Post office (⊙ 8am-noon & 1-5pm Mon-Fri, closed mid-Oct–mid-May) Offers post and parcel services from a window next to the Coffee Shop & Roughrider Saloon.

TOURIST INFORMATION

North Rim Backcountry Information Center (🕿 928-638-7875; Administrative Building; ⊙ 8am-noon & 1-5pm mid-May–Oct 31) Backcountry permits for overnight camping on and below the rim, at Tuweep Campground, or camping anytime between November 1 to May 14.
North Rim Visitor Center (🕿 928-638-7864; www.nps.gov/grca; North Rim; ⊙ 8am-6pm) Beside Grand Canyon Lodge, this is the place to get information on the park, and the starting point for ranger-led nature walks.

ℹ Orientation

Walking from the parking lot to the entrance of Grand Canyon Lodge, you'll pass the North Rim Visitor Center – find restrooms and a water bottle filling station behind the building. Approaching the lodge itself, you'll see the **Gift Shop** (Map p149; ⊙ 8am-9pm mid-May–mid-Oct), post office and Coffee Shop & Rough Rider Saloon on the left. On the right, find the Deli in the Pines cafeteria and another set of public restrooms. Just over a mile up the road, next to the campground, there are laundry facilities, the North Rim General Store, fee showers, a gas station and the North Rim Backcounry Office. Both the 1.2-mile Transept Trail and a 1-mile leg of the Bridle Trail link the lodge and campground.

ℹ Getting There & Around

The only public transportation to the North Rim is provided by Trans Canyon Shuttle (p150), whose vans make the trip from the South Rim to the North Rim (and vice versa) twice dailly. Once on the North Rim, you'll get around on foot, or in your own car or motorcycle. Both the 1.2-mile Transept Trail and a 1-mile leg of the Bridle Trail link the lodge and campground, and the Bridle Trail continues a mile or so to the North Kaibab Trailhead.

CAR & MOTORCYCLE

Service station (⊙ 8am-5pm, 24hr pay at the pump, mid-May–mid-Oct) Next to the campground, the service station only sells gas and oil: there aren't garage or towing services. The closest full-service garage and 24-hour towing is located in Kanab, 78 miles north of Grand Canyon Lodge.

SHUTTLES

Hikers' Shuttle (⊙ 5:30am & 6am, seasonal variations) Complimentary shuttle takes hikers from the Grand Canyon Lodge to the North Kaibab Trailhead twice daily. Sign up 24 hours in advance. Note that there's no service from North Kaibab Trailhead back to the lodge, but it's only a couple of miles down the road.
Trans Canyon Shuttle (🕿 877-638-2820, 928-638-2820; www.trans-canyonshuttle.com; one-way rim-to-rim $85, one-way South Rim to Marble Canyon $70; ⊙ mid-May–mid-Oct) From mid-May through mid-October, the shuttle van (or vans, depending on demand) departs from Grand Canyon Lodge twice daily, at 7am and 2.30pm, to make the 4½-hour journey to Bright Angel Lodge on the South Rim. The shuttle also offers a single daily departure from October 17th to November 30th, weather permitting. Reserve in advance.

The shuttle also serves Marble Canyon, Arizona, from the South Rim, and will transport unaccompanied luggage ($20 for up to 20lbs) on request.

Around North Rim

Best for Western Movie Buffs

➡ Frontier Movie Town & Trading Post (p155)

➡ Western Legends Roundup (p157)

➡ Old Barn Playhouse (p158)

➡ Kane County Office of Tourism (p159)

➡ Paria Townsite (p160)

Best for Families

➡ East Rim View (p152)

➡ Seldom Seen Adventures (p157)

➡ Antelope Canyon (p162)

➡ Angel Canyon (p158)

➡ Best Friends Animal Sanctuary (p155)

Why Go?

The North Rim sits on the southern edge of the spectacular 1010-sq-mile North Kaibab Plateau, refreshingly cool and green at 8000ft and surrounded below by red-rock scenery, miles of trails and vast expanses of desert wilderness. You can easily spend a week exploring the dramatic diversity of the region, boating on Lake Powell one day, hiking a slot canyon the next and cycling through the aspen and meadows of the Kaibab another. Combine a visit to the North Rim with Zion and Bryce National Parks (see Lonely Planet's *Zion & Bryce Canyon National Parks*), both within a few hours' drive north of the park.

When to Go
North Rim

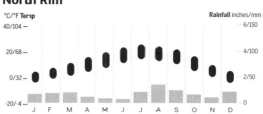

Oct Cottonwoods and aspen display magnificent fall color.

Jul North Rim altitude offers relief from the canyonlands' summer sizzle.

Sep The desert sun softens and meadows tease with autumn delights.

Kaibab National Forest (North Rim)

📞 928 / ELEV 7900FT-9000FT

Hwy 89A (also known as Alt 89) winds 5000ft up from the burning canyons of the Paria Canyon-Vermilion Cliffs Wilderness, past the Kaibab National Forest boundary and through the eerie black-timbered remains of a 2001 forest fire, to the outpost of Jacob Lake. Nearly everyone heading up to the canyon stops here, piling out of dusty vehicles to breathe in the mountain air, shop for canyon souvenirs, grab a cookie or an extra-thick milkshake – the inn is famous for both. They then continue south on Hwy 67 through the meadows, rolling hills, aspen and ponderosa pine trees of the Kaibab National Forest on their way to the North Rim.

On the 30 miles between Jacob Lake and the park entrance, dirt forest-service roads on either side lure curious travelers, offering yellow canopies in the fall, wildflowers in the summer and miles of opportunities for hiking, cycling, snowmobiling and cross-country skiing. While most folk simply pass through on their way to the rim, the Kaibab is an idyllic setting in its own right and a worthwhile stop for a couple of days.

⊙ Sights & Activities

The 107-sq-mile Kanab Creek Wilderness, comprised of classic canyonland formations cut by Kanab Creek, lies in the southwestern corner of the Kaibab and abuts the western edge of the Kaibab Plateau. Here you'll find many desert trails for experienced hikers; the 21.5-mile Snake Gulch rewards hikers with loads of incredible petroglyphs. On the southeast corner, abutting the eastern edge of the Kaibab Plateau, is the Saddle Mountain Wilderness. Stop by the Kaibab Plateau Visitor Center in Jacob Lake for maps and information on the network of hiking trails throughout the region. In the winter, you can cross-country ski or snowmobile throughout the Kaibab. The Jacob Lake Inn is open year-round, but the 44-mile road from Jacob Lake to the North Rim Lodge (which is closed from mid-October through mid-May) is not plowed and there are no services north of Jacob Lake.

Dirt roads veer off Hwy 67 in both directions to overlooks on the edge of the plateau. The drives are lovely, particularly in the fall when the aspens turn or in late summer when wildflowers and tall grass

burst out of the meadows, but they are long and bumpy. Even in a 4WD, be prepared to drive at a snail's pace in some spots. Consider tackling the roads to Fire Point, Crazy Jug, Indian Hollow and the recommended Jumpup Point overlooks, all of which make nice backcountry camping sites. The five overlooks connected by Rainbow Rim Trail may see a few more people, but they have the advantage of excellent hiking and mountain-biking from each point.

While they're certainly beautiful, don't expect classic canyon vistas at any of the Kaibab's overlooks; for that, head to the park itself.

★ Marble View   VIEWPOINT
A favorite of the many Kaibab Forest overlooks, this viewpoint makes a spectacular picnic or camping spot. From the 1-acre meadow, covered with Indian paintbrush and hiding Coconino sandstone fossils, views extend over the eastern edge of the canyon to the paper-flat expanse beyond. This is not a quintessential Grand Canyon overlook that you see in postcards and Grand Canyon books. Instead, you're looking down where the Colorado first cuts into the rocks from Lees Ferry.

East Rim View   HIKING
With views east into the Saddle Mountain Wilderness, Marble Canyon and the Vermilion Cliffs, this easily accessible overlook (elevation 8810ft) is suitable for strollers and wheelchairs. In fact, it's so easy to reach, it's amazing there aren't more people out here. East Rim doesn't offer the inviting views, picnic and camping opportunities of Marble View, but it's a beautiful spot. From the overlook you can hike the East Rim Trail 1.5 miles down, and from there connect to longer hikes.

Arizona Trail: Park Boundary
Trailhead to Crystal Spring   HIKING
This narrow meander through wide meadows bordered by aspens and ponderosas is a hidden gem of the North Kaibab. There are no big views or cliffs, but plenty of room to run and scramble. Keep your eye out for fossils in the rocks along the trail. Perfect for families, this hike can be shortened considerably by hiking 2.3 miles to Sourdough Wells and turning around, or lengthened by hiking an added 1.5 miles to East Rim View.

Rainbow Rim Trail   MOUNTAIN BIKING
The Rainbow Rim Trail connects Parissawampitts, Fence, Locust, North Timp

Kaibab National Forest (North Rim)

0 ——— 10 km
0 ——— 5 miles

Jacob Lake (15mi)

Kane Canyon

Pleasant Valley Outlet

Dog Canyon

Saddle Mountain Wilderness

Marble View

Arizona Trail 219

Park Boundary Trailhead

610

Sowdough Walls

East Rim View

611

North Rim Country Store

Crystal Spring

610

67

North Rim Entrance Gate

Kaibab Lodge

DeMotte Campground

270

Kaibab Plateau

241

240

67

462

22

223

Kaibab National Forest

Lookout Canyon

Dry Park

206

214

Shinumo Creek

Snake Gulch

22

425

Burnt Corral Ridge

Rainbow Rim Trail

Parissawampitts Point

Fence Point

Locust Point

North Timp Point

Timp Point

Fire Point

White Creek

Swamp Ridge

Tapeats Creek

Tapeats Amphitheater

Tapeats Creek

Tapeats Terrace

425

232

Indian Hollow

Monument Point

Crazy Jug Point

Indian Hollow

Deer Creek

Galloma Terrace

Bedrock Canyon

Colorado River

701

Kaibab Plateau

Sowats Canyon

Sowats Point

Kanab Creek Wilderness

Jumpup Point

Kanab Creek

Grand Canyon National Park

Havasupai Reservation

and **Timp Points**, each a finger of the Kaibab Plateau that sticks out over the Grand Canyon. While the ride is beautiful – meandering through meadows, winding up and down with an elevation change of no more than 250ft and following the canyon edge for stretches at each overlook – none of the viewpoints stand out from one another and each point-to-point stretch drops into a steep side canyon.

Allen's Outfitters
HORSEBACK RIDING

(📞435-689-1660; www.jallenoutfitters.com; half-/full-day trail ride $100/130, two-hour trail ride $70) Offers one-hour, two-hour, half-day, full-day and custom-designed overnight or multiday horseback rides through the woods and to overlooks. Children must be at least five years old. Reservations are not required for short rides – just stop by the corrals just south of Jacob Lake Lodge.

🛏 Sleeping & Eating

You can camp for free anywhere in the national forest, including canyon overlooks.

DeMotte Campground
CAMPGROUND $

(📞877-444-6777, visitor center 928-643-7298; www.recreation.gov; Hwy 67; campsite $18; ☺mid-May–mid-Oct; 🐾) Near Kaibab Lodge (on Hwy 6 about 6 miles north of the park entrance) is the first-come, first-served DeMotte Campground with 23 primitive sites.

DON'T MISS

JACOB LAKE INN
•••

Traveling to or from the Grand Canyon's North Rim, it's hard to miss the pull-off for this high-elevation roadside inn, 44 miles north of the national park entrance. It's one of the only places to stop for gasoline, restrooms and snacks – but not just any snacks. Jacob Lake Inn is rightly famous for its fantastic freshly baked cookies and extra-thick milkshakes. It's also a good place to stock up on snacks for the next day's hike, such as dried fruit and almonds. Take the time to look around the Native American–themed gift shop: if you happen to be passing through in the evening, you might even catch a quick lecture by a naturalist or a member of one of the region's tribes.

Kaibab Lodge
LODGE $

(📞928-638-2389; www.kaibablodge.com; Hwy 67; cabin $90, cabin for 4 $130-185; ☺mid-May–mid-Oct; 🐾) Located 18 miles from the North Rim, surrounded by meadows and ponderosa and aspen forest, Kaibab Lodge is a simple, quiet, low-key place, where the biggest excitement comes from counting deer that wander from the woods to graze. It's a place to get away from it all, and a good option if Grand Canyon Lodge is booked.

Kaibab Camper Village
CAMPGROUND $

(📞928-643-7804; www.kaibabcampervillage.com; tent/RV sites $18/36; ☺closed mid-Oct–mid-May) Set back a half-mile from Hwy 67 on a forest-service road just south of Jacob Lake Inn, this privately run campground offers the only RV hookups on the North Kaibab Plateau. It's friendly, but with so many idyllic (and free) spots in the surrounding national forest, there's no reason to camp here except the shower and laundry facilities.

Jacob Lake Inn
MOTEL $$

(📞928-643-7232; www.jacoblake.com; intersection of Hwys 89A & 67, 44 miles north of North Rim; r $126-144, cabins $94-144; ☺6.30am-9pm mid-May–mid-Oct, 8am-8pm mid-Oct–mid-May; 🐾) Jacob Lake Inn is a minor landmark: nearly everyone stops here on the way to the Grand Canyon's North Rim entrance, 44 miles south. But the inn is better known for its famous cookies and milkshakes (and a great Native American–themed gift shop) than for its basic accommodations – cabins, motel-style rooms, or larger doubles in a newer building.

North Rim Country Store
MARKET $

(📞928-638-2383; www.northrimcountrystore.com; Hwy 67; ☺7.30am-7pm, closed late-Oct–mid-May) This small and friendly store and gas station sells a limited selection of groceries, including sandwiches, fruit, cereal, coffee, tea, cheese, wine and beer. There's also camping supplies and tire repair. It's located across Hwy 67 from Kaibab Lodge and DeMotte Campground, 18 miles north of the North Rim.

ℹ Information

The Kaibab Lodge, North Rim Country Store and DeMotte Campground, the only facilities between Jacob Lake and Grand Canyon Lodge, cluster together 18 miles north of the North Rim and 26 miles south of Jacob Lake. Jacob Lake itself is nothing more than a lodge and restaurant, visitor center, campground and gas station.

Kaibab Plateau Visitor Center (☑928-643-7298; cnr Hwys 89A & 67; ☉8am-4pm mid-May–mid-Oct) The United States Forest Service visitor center features a small museum and bookstore, and has maps on the region's many trails and forest roads.

❶ Getting There & Around

There is no public transportation or shuttle service to or around Jacob Lake and the Kaibab National Forest.

Jacob Lake Inn Chevron (☑928-643-7232; ☉7.30am-8pm, credit-card sales 24hr) Services flat tires and can do basic mechanical work, but the closest towing services are in Fredonia and Kanab.

Fredonia

☑435 / POP 1145 / ELEV 4672

Tiny blink-and-you-miss-it Fredonia lies along Alt 89, 72 miles northwest of the rim. There's not much here for the traveler except the **Grand Canyon Motel** (☑928-643-7646; http://grand-canyon-motel.com/; 175 S Main St; r $44; ☎). If you're looking for a last-minute, cheap place to stay, it's an option, but otherwise head to Kanab.

Stop by the **Kaibab National Forest District Headquarters** (☑928-643-7395; 430 S Main St; ☉8am-4.30pm Mon-Fri) for info on hiking and camping in the forest.

If you need it, **Judd Auto Service** (☑928-643-7726; 623 S Main St) does towing, tire repair and simple mechanical work.

Kanab

☑435 / POP 4468 / ELEV 4925FT

In 1874 Mormons settled remote Kanab, Utah. Hollywood followed in the 1920s, drawn by the desert backdrop and stunning red-rock formations. It has since served as a location for hundreds of movies and TV shows, including numerous Westerns and episodes of *The Lone Ranger* and *Gunsmoke*. Though the filmmaking craze here faded, the town still flaunts its silver-screen past.

Small-town Kanab offers a tidy, pedestrian-friendly downtown, peaceful surroundings and a handful of good dining options. It's a quiet, sleepy place that closes up early, and while not a destination in itself, Kanab offers a quirky taste of the American West. It also makes a good base to explore the area, as it's located within relatively easy proximity of the Grand Canyon's North Rim, Zion National Park, Bryce Canyon National Park, Coral Pink Sand Dunes State Park and Lake Powell.

OFF THE BEATEN TRACK

HISTORIC FIRE LOOKOUTS

In addition to various hikes, the region has a unique historic feature: three steel towers, all on the National Register of Historic Places, and still used as fire lookouts. Built in 1934, the towers in Big Springs and Jacob Lake stand 100ft tall, while the one in Dry Park, built in 1944, is 120ft tall. You can drive out to any of them and climb up and up and up for great views of the national forest and the Arizona Strip beyond. But be warned that they sway in any kind of wind – not for the faint of heart! Though the lookout rooms at the top are locked, someone staffs them May through October and they'll usually let you in. The easiest to reach is Jacob Lake, as it's on Hwy 67 about 1 mile south of Jacob Lake Inn.

◉ Sights & Activities

Best Friends
Animal Sanctuary RESCUE CENTER
(☑435-644-2001; www.bestfriends.org; Hwy 89, Angel Canyon; ☉9:30am-5:30pm; ⊞) FREE Kanab's most famous attraction is outside of town. Surrounded by more than 52 mostly private square miles of red-rock desert 5.5 miles north of Kanab, Best Friends is the largest no-kill animal-rescue center in the country. The center shows films and gives facility tours four times a day; call ahead for times and reservations. The 1½-hour tours let you meet some of the more than 1700 horses, pigs, dogs, cats, birds and other critters on site.

Pipe Spring
National Monument PARK
(☑928-643-7105; www.nps.gov/pisp; adult/child $5/free; ☉8am-5pm) Fourteen miles southwest of Fredonia on Hwy 389, **Pipe Spring** is quite literally an oasis in the desert. Visitors can experience the Old West amid cabins and corrals, an orchard, ponds and a garden. Tours let you peek inside the stone Winsor Castle, and there's also a small museum that examines the turbulent history of local Paiutes and Mormon settlers.

Frontier Movie Town &
Trading Post FILM LOCATION
(297 W Center St; ☉7.30am-11pm Apr-Oct, 10am-5pm Nov-Mar) FREE Wander through a bunkhouse, saloon and other buildings used in Western movies filmed locally, including *The*

Kanab

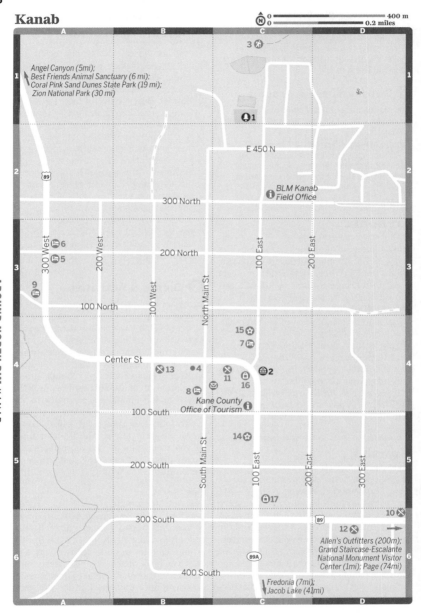

Angel Canyon (5mi);
Best Friends Animal Sanctuary (6 mi);
Coral Pink Sand Dunes State Park (19 mi);
Zion National Park (30 mi)

E 450 N

BLM Kanab
Field Office

300 North

200 North

100 North

Center St

100 South

Kane County
Office of Tourism

200 South

300 South

Allen's Outfitters (200m);
Grand Staircase-Escalante
National Monument Visitor
Center (1mi); Page (74mi)

400 South

Fredonia (7mi);
Jacob Lake (41mi)

Outlaw Josey Wales, and learn some tricks of the trade (such as short doorways to make movie stars seem taller). This classic roadside attraction sells all the Western duds and doodads you could care to round up.

Squaw Trail   HIKING

Accessed just north of **Jacob Hamblin Park** at the end of 100 East St, this short but steep 800ft scramble leads to spectacular views of Kanab and the surrounding desert wilderness. It's about a mile to the city overview;

Kanab

you can continue another 0.5 miles to the top, with 360-degree views, or retrace your steps.

Kanab Heritage Museum MUSEUM
(☏435-644-3966; www.kanabheritagemuseum.com; 13 S 100 East St; admission by donation; ◉10am-5pm Mon-Fri 1 May-30 Sep) For a glimpse into the region's popular history, this small museum is worth a stop. While the few pieces of historical memorabilia aren't particularly riveting, it's fun to browse the 30-plus spiral-bound notebooks filled with movie newspapers, magazine articles, written histories and photographs.

☞ Tours

★**Dreamland Safari** TOURS
(www.dreamlandtours.net; 3hr tour $90) Hikes with naturalist tour guides to gorgeous backcountry sites and slot canyons by 4WD. It also offers nature photography and multiday backpacking trips.

Seldom Seen Adventures ADVENTURE TOUR
(☏888-418-9908; www.seldomseenadventures.net; day hike $129) Family-oriented, personalized tours of the national parks, Grand Staircase-Escalante National Monument (GSENM) and wilderness areas, with canyoneering, 4WD tours, super fat-tire biking and hiking. Also offers transfers.

Terry's Camera TOUR
(☏435-644-5981; www.terryaldermanphotography.com) Customized area photo tours and workshops.

✾ Festivals & Events

Kaibab Paiute
Tribal Heritage Days CULTURAL
(◉Aug) Tribes of Southern Paiute celebrate with dancing, songs, competition, food and crafts and children's activities. All events are open to the public.

Western Legends Roundup FILM
(☏800-733-5263; www.westernlegendsroundup.com ◉late Aug) The town lives for the annual Western Legends Roundup in late August. There are concerts, gunfights, cowboy poetry, dances, quilt shows, a film festival and more. Take a bus tour to all the film sites, or sign up for a Dutch-oven cooking lesson.

⌂ Sleeping

Tiny Kanab serves as overflow accommodations not only for the North Rim but for Zion and Bryce National Parks to the north as well, and during the high season of summer it can be surprisingly difficult to find a room. If the accommodations below are booked, try one of the chain hotels or independently run motels in the vicinity.

Hitch'n Post Campground CAMPGROUND $
(☏435-644-2142; www.hitchnpostrvpark.com; 196 E 300 South St; tent/RV sites with hookups $18/29, camping cabins $32-36; ☎☀) Friendly 17-site campground near the town center; has laundry and showers.

★**Canyons Lodge** MOTEL $$
(☏435-644-3069, 800-644-5094; www.canyonslodge.com; 236 N 300 West St; r incl breakfast $89-179; ✳@☎☀☀) ✿ A renovated motel with an art-house Western feel. There's a warm welcome, free cruiser bikes and good traveler assistance. In summer, guests enjoy twice-weekly live music and wine and cheese by the fire pit. Rooms feature original artwork and whimsical touches. Recycles soaps and containers.

Parry Lodge
MOTEL $$

(☑ 888-289-1722, 435-644-2601; www.parrylodge.
com; 89 E Center St; r $109-139; ❄ 🐕 ♿ 🐾) The
aura of bygone Westerns is the best feature
of this rambling old classic motel. Some
rooms bear the names of movie stars who
stayed here, such as Gregory Peck or Lana
Turner. If quality is your concern, opt for the
L-shaped double queen room, nicely refur-
bished in cottage decor.

Purple Sage Inn
B&B $$

(☑ 435-644-5377, 877-644-5377; www.purplesage
inn.com; r incl breakfast $135-165; ❄ 🐕) A for-
mer Mormon polygamist's home, this later
became a hotel, where Western author Zane
Grey stayed. Now it's a B&B with exquisite
antique details. Zane's namesake room –
with its quilt-covered wood bed, sitting
room and balcony access – is our favorite.

Canyons Boutique Hotel
BOUTIQUE HOTEL $$

(☑ 435-644-8660; www.canyonshotel.com; 190 N
300 West St; r incl breakfast $149-169; ❄ 🐕 🐾)
From the architecture to appointments,
the inn is a modern-day remake of period
Victoriana. Ethan Allen furnishings, gas
fireplaces and jetted tubs grace every room,
but it all looks a little stiff in these parts.
Look for the new on-site restaurant.

WORTH A TRIP

ANGEL CANYON

During Kanab's Hollywood heyday, **An-
gel Canyon** became the site of scores
of movies and TV shows, including *The
Lone Ranger*, Disney's *Apple Dumpling
Gang* and *The Outlaw Josey Wales*. A
dirt and gravel road winds up and down
through Best Friends Animal Sanctu-
ary, offering quintessential red-rock
scenery and desert views. Just across
from the Best Friends Animal Sanctuary
Welcome Center, a dirt path veers east
about 0.5 miles down to the Kanab
Creek, a shallow, clear creek that's ex-
cellent for dogs and kids. A mile further,
just beyond the horse corral on the left,
is **Angel's Landing**. This small natural
amphitheater borders a grassy field
and makes a perfect picnic spot. To get
to Angel Canyon, look for the signs for
Best Friends Animal Sanctuary,
5 miles northwest of Kanab on Hwy 89;
the road loops 5 miles and reconnects
with Hwy 89.

Quail Park Lodge
MOTEL $$

(☑ 435-215-1447; www.quailparklodge.com; 125 N
300 W St; r/ste $155/203; ❄ @ 🐕 ♿ 🐾) With
Schwinn cruiser bicycles and a postage-
stamp-sized pool, retro pervades all 13
rooms at this refurbished 1963 motel with
surprisingly plush rooms. Mod cons include
free phone calls, microwaves, minifridges
and complimentary gourmet coffee.

🍴 Eating & Drinking

Escobar's
MEXICAN $

(mains $7-12; ⊘ 11am-9:30pm Sun-Fri) Sometimes
it feels like all of Kanab is stuffed into this
busy, family-run restaurant with swift service
and big portions. Start with the complimentary homemade chips and salsa and move on
to a green chili burrito and a chilled beer.

Fusion House
ASIAN $

(☑ 435-644-8868; www.fusionhousekanab.com;
18 E Center St; mains $9-15; ⊘ 10:30am-9pm Mon-
Sat, noon-9pm Sun; 🐕 🐾) Casual Asian fusion –
Japanese-style pork *katsu* curry, coconut
shrimp, udon noodle soups, and fried rice
with spinach and pine nuts – served in a
diner-like setting on Kanab's main drag.

Honey's Marketplace
MARKET

(260 E 300 S; ⊘ 7am-10pm) Full grocery store.

★ Rocking V Cafe
AMERICAN $$

(www.rockingvcafe.com; 97 W Center St; lunch $8-
18, dinner $15-34; ⊘ 11:30am-10pm; 🐾) Fresh
ingredients star in dishes such as hand-cut
buffalo tenderloin and chargrilled zucchini
with curried quinoa. Local artwork decorat-
ing the 1892 brick storefront is as creative as
the food. Off-season hours vary.

☆ Entertainment

Old Barn Playhouse
THEATER

FREE During the summer, the Parry Lodge
shows free classic Western films every night
at 8pm in the Old Barn Playhouse behind
the lodge. Seating ranges from overstuffed
to folding wood, and the popcorn and ice
cream are cheap. Movies open with two
short films about the Western film industry
and Kanab history, so come at about 8:30pm
if you just want to catch the feature.

Crescent Moon Theater
THEATER

(☑ 435-644-2350; www.crescentmoontheater.
com; 150 S 100 East St; ⊘ May-Sep) Cowboy po-
etry, bluegrass music and comedic plays are
just some of what is staged here. Monday is
Western-movie night.

🛍 Shopping

Willow Canyon Outdoor Co OUTDOOR EQUIPMENT
(263 S 100 East St; ⊗7:30am-8pm, off-season hours vary) It's easy to spend hours sipping espresso and perusing the eclectic books here. Before you leave, outfit yourself with field guides, camping gear, United States Geological Survey maps and hiking clothes.

Denny's Wigwam GIFTS
(78 E Center St; ⊗8:30am-9:30pm Mon-Sat, 9am-9:30pm Sun) For all kinds of cowboy gear, as well as Native American pottery, jewelry and rugs. Dress up in old-fashioned duds and get your photo taken, or pick up anything from a John Wayne mug and toilet paper to rhinestone flip-flops – this is the place for touristy shopping.

ℹ Information

A good online resource is www.visitsouthern utah.com.

BLM Kanab Field Office (☑435-644-4600; 318 N 100 East St; ⊗8am-4pm Mon-Fri) Provides information and, November 16 through March 14, issues permits for hiking the Wave in Paria Canyon-Vermilion Cliffs Wilderness Area.

Kanab Visitor Center (☑435-644-4680; 745 E Hwy 89, Kanab; ⊗7:30am-5:30pm) Park headquarters in the Southwestern section.

Kane County Hospital (☑435-644-5811; 355 N Main St; ⊗24hr) The closest medical facility to GSENM.

Kane County Office of Tourism (☑435-644-5033, 800-733-5263; www.visitsouthernutah.com; 78 S 100 East St; ⊗8:30am-6pm Mon-Fri, to 4pm Sat) The main source for area information; great old Western movie posters and artifacts on display.

Post office (39 S Main St; ⊗9am-4pm Mon-Fri, to 2pm Sat)

ℹ Getting There & Around

There is no public transportation to or around Kanab.

AIR

The closest airline hubs are Las Vegas (four hours southwest) and Salt Lake City (five hours north). Flagstaff, 200 miles and almost four hours south, offers limited airline service.

CAR

Kanab is about a 2½-hour drive northwest of the North Rim. The only car rental in town is **Xpress Rent-a-Car** (☑435-644-3408; www.xpress rentalcarofkanab.com; 1530 S Alt 89).

Ramsey Towing and Service Garage (☑435-644-2468; 115 S 100 East St) offers a full-service garage with 24-hour towing service.

Along Highway 89 From Kanab to Page

☑435 / ELEV 3100FT TO 6600FT

The interior of the oval formed by Hwys 89 and 89A, and the surrounding area, is comprised of the Paria Canyon-Vermilion Cliffs Wilderness (including Vermilion Cliffs National Monument), the southern section of the 2970-sq-mile Grand Staircase-Escalante National Monument, the southeast corner of Glen Canyon National Recreation Area, the Navajo Indian Reservation and the northern tip of the Kaibab National Forest.

For the traveler, however, these are arbitrary distinctions. Whenever you peer out your car window, it's all simply desert. Dry, windy, seemingly endless desert. This is a lonely, desperate kind of wilderness that lures photographers and hikers with its brilliant red and chalky-white buttes, slot canyons and multihued rock formations. While dirt roads may tempt drivers into exploring, the roads are sandy and unpredictable; with a little bit of rain, they can become impassable within minutes and slot canyons can fill with torrents of water that wash away or kill anything or anyone in its path. Do not depend on GPS navigation beyond Hwys 89 and 89A, as it tracks roads that are, at best, rough 4WD trails and tragically miscalculates driving times.

Between the tourist hubs of Kanab and Page, there's mile after mile after mile of emptiness. Highway 89A, the southern stretch of the oval, winds up from Lees Ferry and Marble Canyon several thousand feet and about 45 miles to Hwy 67 at Jacob Lake, 44 miles north of the North Rim, and then loops back down and north to Kanab. From Kanab, Hwy 89 passes several scenic drives, hiking trails, and two visitor centers on the 74-mile stretch to Page.

◉ Sights & Activities

Big Water Visitor Center (p161) has a small dinosaur museum 16 miles northwest of Page, with displays on the extensive paleontology research in the area. Check out the tray of what looks like black stones – they're 200-million-year-old sharks' teeth, all found in the area.

Paria Townsite FILM LOCATION

The town of Paria was originally settled in 1865, but Indian raids forced it to move upstream in 1870, and by 1910 floods forced settlers to leave the area altogether. In 1963 Hollywood chose the site to build a Western movie set, and it was used for films and TV shows until 1991. Flooding in 2003 forced local volunteers and the Bureau of Land Management (BLM) to dismantle and move the set to drier ground.

Paria Outpost ADVENTURE TOUR

(☑ 928-691-1047; www.paria.com; Mile 21, Hwy 89 half-day tour $125) Friendly, flexible and knowledgeable, and offers guided horseback rides in Grand Staircase-Escalante National Monument, as well as 4WD tours and guided hikes.

Johnson Canyon DRIVING TOUR

Heading into GSENM, the paved scenic drive into Johnson Canyon is popular. More movies were filmed here, and 6 miles along you can see in the distance the Western set where the long-time TV classic *Bonanza* was filmed (on private land). Turn north off Hwy 89, 9 miles east of Kanab.

Houserock Road DRIVING TOUR

While there isn't much in particular to see along the way, this beautiful drive passes through piñons and junipers, hugs the brilliant red sandstone cliffs of the Vermilion Cliffs National Monument and offers an excellent opportunity to get off the main drag.

Wire Pass to Buckskin Gulch Trail HIKING

A perfect jaunt for anyone looking to experience Utah's slot canyons without a tour or a commitment to a wilderness expedition, this easily accessible hike requires a bit of scrambling and includes several stretches where the slot canyon is only about 30ft wide and walls tower more than 50ft high. After 1.7 miles the trail reaches **Buckskin Gulch**.

THE WAVE & CLASSIC HIKES IN THE PARIA CANYON-VERMILION CLIFFS WILDERNESS

Many travelers come to the region just for the chance to see the otherworldly sandstone rock formation known as the Wave, accessible only to a lucky few who win one of the permits available each day. But two other classic canyon hikes also attract photographers and outdoor enthusiasts from around the world.

North Coyote Butte (the Wave) Only 20 people per day are allowed to hike 3.5 miles to North Coyote Butte, a trail-free expanse of slickrock that ends at a smooth, orange-and-white-striped rock, shaped into a perfect wave and big enough to climb over. Of these 20 permits, 10 are issued online in advance, and another 10 via a walk-in lottery that happens daily at 9am at the Kanab Visitor Center (p159). Your chances are much better with the latter option, though the competition is stiff in April, May, September and October, when 150 people may be trying for one of 10 daily permits. Visit www.thewave.info for details.

Paria Canyon Serious canyoneers can tackle the five-day trek along unforgettable 38-mile Paria Canyon from White House Campground to Lees Ferry. With numerous stretches of knee-deep muddy water, this hike winds in and out of a slot canyon, past sandstone cliffs, petroglyphs and a handful of campsites.

Buckskin Gulch The world-famous 20.3-mile hike (best accessed from Wire Pass to Buckskin Gulch trailhead and White House Campground, both off Hwy 89 between Kanab and Page) is the longest and deepest slot canyon in the United States. Be prepared to wade, possibly swim, through sections and to squeeze through 15 miles of canyon with nothing more than glimpses of the sky above. Sandstone walls soar upward of 200ft, and there are long stretches not much wider than your shoulders. The hike takes anywhere from three to seven days, depending on conditions and pace. The BLM Kanab Field Office (p159) has the latest information and can help you plan.

Overnight permits are required for Paria Canyon and Buckskin Gulch. Absolutely do not attempt any of these hikes without checking trail conditions and the weather forecast at the Paria Contact Station. Call ☑ 435-688-3246 for details and access www.blm.gov/az for permits.

Cottonwood Road
DRIVING TOUR

This washboard dirt road heads through the magnificent rocky desert landscape of **Grand Staircase-Escalante National Monument** and **Kodachrome Basin State Park**. The entrance, 3 miles west of the Paria Contact Station, heads north 49 miles to Cannonville, just outside **Bryce Canyon National Park**, and beyond.

Toad Stools
HIKING

This wander gives passersby a taste of the harsh Utah desert and cool rocks. The thin sand trail meanders through the scrubbrush, desert boulders and hoodoos about 1 mile to the first toadstool, a sandstone rock in the form of, you guessed it, a toadstool. The unmarked trailhead sits at a small parking area 1.4 miles east of the Paria Contact Station.

🛏 Sleeping & Eating

State Line Campground
CAMPGROUND

(House Rock Valley Rd; 🚻) **FREE** There are bathrooms, but no water, at this lovely desert spot. It's 40 miles east of Kanab and 10 miles south of Hwy 89.

Paria Outpost & Outfitters
B&B $

(☎928-691-1047; www.paria.com; Mile 21, Hwy 89; r incl breakfast $65; 🚻🐾) Paria has spartan B&B rooms at its kicked-back lodge and campground. Sign up for a half-day 4WD tour ($125 with lunch) to area slot canyons or set up a trailhead shuttle with them.

Paria Canyon Guest Ranch
CABINS $

(☎928-660-2674; www.pariacampground.com; Hwy 89; camping/dm $10/20, full hookups $35, cabin $50; 🚻🐾) Offering horseback rides along the Paria River, this friendly, lowkey ranch caters to folks looking for some action with their desert silence. It has one cabin (with a double and trundle bed) and a bunkhouse hostel that sleeps 14, and you can pitch your tent anywhere on its 30 acres.

ℹ Information

Paria Contact Station (☎435-644-1200; www.blm.gov; Mile 21, Hwy 89; ⊘8:30am-4pm Mar 15-Nov 15) This seasonal information center can provide important weather and road updates and is the last place to fill up on water before you begin your backcountry exploits. It's 44 miles east of Kanab.

Big Water Visitor Center (☎435-675-3200; 100 Upper Revolution Way, Big Water; ⊘9am-5.30pm Apr-Oct, 8am-4.30pm Tue-Sat Nov-Mar) Near Lake Powell.

ℹ Getting There & Around

The only way to get to and around the region is by car, and you'll need a 4WD for most roads beyond the highway. Paria Outpost offers a hikers' shuttle service for the area.

Page & Glen Canyon National Recreation Area

In 1972, Glen Canyon Dam, Lake Powell, Lees Ferry and more than a million acres of surrounding desert were established as Glen Canyon National Recreation Area (GCNRA). The main attraction here is the 186-mile-long Lake Powell, with 1960 miles of empty shoreline set amid striking red-rock formations, sharply cut canyons and dramatic desert scenery. The windy outpost of Lees Ferry, best known as the jumping-off point for Grand Canyon raft trips, lies 15 miles below the dam but is an hour's drive from Page.

Page, a small town that services Lake Powell and the Colorado River, sits 142 miles north of Flagstaff and 124 miles northeast of the North Rim. The N Lake Powell Blvd loops off Hwy 89 and forms Page's main strip. Given its spectacular setting, Page is a fairly charmless town: mostly chain hotels, gas stations converted into tour outfitters and BBQ joints.

The town of Lees Ferry was named after polygamist John D Lee, who started the Lonely Dell Ranch and a primitive ferry service here in 1873. Today, Lees Ferry is best known as the jumping-off point for rafting trips, and it isn't much more than a boat launch, a couple of hiking trails, a campground and some historic buildings.

⊙ Sights

For one of the best views of the Colorado River – snaking its way through the canyon to Glen Canyon Dam – head to the overview just behind the Denny's in Page. A 940ft round-trip walk down stairs and over sandstone leads to a sheltered overlook.

Glen Canyon Dam
DAM

(☎928-608-6072; www.glencanyonnha.org; Colorado River & Hwy 89, Page; tour adult/child 7-16yr $5/2.50; ⊘tours 8.30am-4pm mid-May–mid-Sep, tour hours vary rest of year) At 710ft tall, Glen Canyon Dam is the nation's second-highest concrete arch dam – Hoover Dam is only 16ft taller. Construction lasted from 1956 through 1964. From April through October, 45-minute guided tours depart from the Carl

Hayden Visitor Center (p165) and descend deep inside the dam in elevators. Exhibits tell the story of the dam's construction, complete with all kinds of astounding technical facts. Three different videos spotlight various aspects of the region.

Historic Lees Ferry & Lonely Dell Ranch
HISTORIC SITE

(www.nps.gov/glca/planyourvisit/lees-ferry.htm; Glen Canyon National Recreation Area) Lees Ferry was the site of the region's original ferry crossing, and of Charles Spencer's 1910 effort to extract gold from the surrounding hills. Today it's the launching area for rafting trips down the Colorado through the Grand Canyon. Nearby, Lonely Dell Ranch provided for families who worked at the crossing in the 1880s and '90s. Their log cabins and a pioneer cemetery remain, as well an an idyllic orchard where visitors are welcome to pick (and eat) the fruit.

Navajo Bridge Interpretive Center
MUSEUM

(928-355-2319; www.nps.gov/glca; Hwy 89A; 9am-5pm late Apr–Oct) The spectacular Navajo Bridge spans the Colorado River at Marble Canyon along Hwy 89A, about 14 miles past the Hwy 89/89A fork. Actually, there are two bridges: a modern one for motorists that opened in 1995, and a historical one from 1929. The Navajo Bridge Interpretive Center on the west bank has good background information. Look up – California condors are often spotted overhead – and look down, too, to possibly catch a view of rafting groups who've recently left nearby Lees Ferry on the start of a river journey through the Grand Canyon.

Rainbow Bridge National Monument
PARK

(928-608-6200, tours 928-645-2433; www.nps.gov/rabr) Rainbow Bridge is the largest natural bridge in the world, at 290ft high and 275ft wide. A sacred Navajo site, it resembles the graceful arc of a rainbow. Most visitors arrive by boat (www.lakepowell.com), with a 2-mile round-trip hike. The natural monument is located on the south shore of Lake Powell, about 50 miles by water from Wahweap Marina.

John Wesley Powell Museum
MUSEUM

(928-645-9496; www.powellmuseum.org; 64 N Lake Powell Blvd; adult/child 5-15yr $3/1; 9am-4:30pm Mon-Fri 9am-2pm Sat Apr-Oct; hours vary in winter) In 1869, one-armed John Wesley Powell led the first Colorado River expedition through the Grand Canyon. This small museum displays memorabilia of early river runners, including a model of Powell's boat, with photos and illustrations of his excursions. Also houses the regional visitor center.

Activities
Boating & Cruises
Most marinas rent kayaks, 18ft runabouts and 14ft fishing boats, as well as water skis and other 'toys.' Distances on Lake Powell are long. Organized trips are available through Lake Powell Resorts & Marinas, with a helpful tour desk at Lake Powell Resort.

Houseboating is also hugely popular and, with its many coves and beaches to explore, Lake Powell is perfect for kayaking. Expect wind in the spring and monsoon rains in late July and August.

DON'T MISS

ANTELOPE CANYON

Many visitors plan trips to Page just to experience the oft-photographed Antelope Canyon, a surreal landscape you'll have to see to believe. It's divided into two sections, Upper and Lower. The Navajo names for both sides hint at what to expect: the Upper Canyon is *Tsé bighánílíní* ('the place where water runs through rocks') and the Lower Canyon is known as *Hasdestwazi* ('spiral rock arches').

The Upper Canyon is more accessible and appropriate for small children, while the Lower Canyon involves steep staircases and is considered more beautiful.

Managed by the Lake Powell Navajo Tribal Park, the canyon is only accessible by tour through one of several local outfitters, such as Ken's Tours (928-606-2168; www.lowerantelope.com; guided tour adult/child $28/20) or Roger Ekis' Antelope Canyon Tours (928-645-9102; www.antelopecanyon.com; 22 S Lake Powell Blvd; adult/child 5-12yr from $37/27). Reservations are recommended if you'd like to secure a particular tour time; otherwise, walk-ins are served on a first-come, first-served basis. For the best lighting for photographs, try to get in a tour between 8am and 10.30am, or one in the later afternoon.

Fishing

The calm waters of the Colorado River, deep in a canyon between the dam and Lees Ferry, offer excellent and world-renowned nymph fly-fishing. Call **Lees Ferry Anglers** (928-355-2228; www.leesferry.com) for current conditions and to arrange a guided trip. To fish the Arizona portion of Lake Powell and the Colorado River, you must have an Arizona fishing license. Fishing the Utah portion of the lake requires a Utah fishing license. Children under 14 years old do not need a license. All marinas sell licenses, and several offer boat rental.

Guided fly fishing trips (for one/two/three people $350/450/550) can accommodate up to three passengers per boat. Non-fishing guests pay $20 each. The rates are the same for guided spin-fishing on the river. If you don't need a guide, you can just rent a boat for $200 per day. Equipment is available for purchase in Lees Ferry Anglers' shop.

Hiking

If you only have time for one activity in the region, make sure it's the 1.5-mile round-trip hike to the overlook at **Horseshoe Bend**, where the river wraps around a monolithic outcropping to form a perfect U. Calling the view dramatic is an understatement – the overlook sits on sheer cliffs that drop 1000ft to the river below. Though it's short, the sandy, shadeless trail and moderate incline can be difficult for children and older travelers, especially if they're not wearing proper footwear. Toddlers should be secured safely in a backpack, as there are no guardrails at the viewpoint. The trailhead is south of Page off Hwy 89, just past Mile 545.

Hanging Garden is a 1-mile round-trip scramble across red rock that leads to an oasis above the Colorado River and Lake Powell. Spot the trailhead sign on Hwy 89 just past the dam on the way into Page. Rangers offer a free guided one-hour hike every evening at 6.30pm.

Swimming

The best place to enjoy Lake Powell's cold, clear water (short of jumping off your boat) is at the **Chains**. Look for the tiny hiking-trail sign just east of the dam and turn left; from the parking lot, a short walk leads to flat, smooth sandstone that juts directly into the water.

A good option for kids is the boat launch at **Antelope Point Marina**, about 8 miles east of town on Hwy 89, where you can wade into the water from the small, rocky areas.

Nine miles northwest of Page, across the Utah border, the area around **Lone Rock** offers endless shoreline access, though there's no shade. Its worth it to drive out here for the photo opportunity alone.

Tours

Colorado River Discovery   BOAT TOUR
(888-522-6644; www.raftthecanyon.com; 130 6th Ave, Page; half-day adult/child $92/82, full-day $112/102, raft & slot canyon tour $199/159; Mar-Nov) Offers smooth water float trips down the Colorado from Glen Canyon Dam. Boats stop at petroglyphs, where you can also splash and cool off in the frigid water, and guides explain the natural and human history along the way. Despite the fact that several boats, each holding about 20 people, depart at the same time, the ride is peaceful, bucolic and a lot of fun. It's a beautiful trip through the deep, sheer red-rock sides of Glen Canyon.

Lake Powell Resorts & Marinas   BOAT TOUR
(800-528-6154; www.lakepowell.com) Popular trips include the Rainbow Bridge cruise (adult/child $125/90, seven hours), the Canyons Adventure cruise (adult/child $70/45, three hours) and the Canyon Princess Dinner Cruise (adult/child $80/35, two hours, Tuesday and Saturday only). It also does half-day trips to Navajo Tapestry, and 1½-hour rides to Antelope Canyon.

Slot Canyon Hummer Adventures   DRIVING TOUR
(928-645-2266; www.hummeradventures.net; 22 N Lake Powell Blvd, Page; 1hr tour adult/child $90/65) Runs 4WD tours to several slot canyons on Navajo land. With only six people to a car, and no crowds vying for the perfect angle to shoot a photo, it's an excellent alternative to Antelope Canyon's mayhem.

Sleeping

You can camp anywhere along the Lake Powell shoreline for free as long as you have a portable toilet or toilet facilities on your boat. Six designated primitive campsites, accessible by boat only, sit on the Colorado River between the dam and Lees Ferry. Bullfrog and Hite Marinas offer primitive camping, and there are developed campgrounds at Wahweap (where you can also use the resort's two pools), Bullfrog and Halls Crossing Marinas (call 800-528-6154 for reservations). You'll also find standard chain motels along Lake Powell Blvd in Page.

Lone Rock Beach CAMPGROUND $
(Utah Hwy 89, Glen Canyon National Recreation Area; per vehicle $12; 🐾) A strikingly beautiful natural setting on the edge of Lake Powell is the home of this sprawling first-come, first-served campground. It's a popular spot with families and college revelers alike in high season – escape to the dunes or the far edges of the lot if you're looking for quiet. It's in Utah, just north of the state line, 2 miles south of Big Water.

Lu Lu's Sleep Ezze Motel MOTEL $
(📋 928-608-0273, 800-553-6211; www.lulussleep ezzemotel.com; cnr 8th Ave & Elm St; r $103-128; ✳@🅰🄿) Eight bright and tidy rooms share a small patio with two large tables, rattan umbrellas, two barbecues and pebble land-scaping. It's located on a residential street that runs parallel to Lake Powell Ave, part of Page's so-called 'historic little motels district.'

Best Western View of Lake Powell Hotel HOTEL $$
(📋 928-645-8868; www.book.bestwestern.com; 716 Rimview Dr; r $155-330; ✳🅰🄿) Possibly the nicest Best Western you've been to. Perched on the edge of a hill overlooking Glen Canyon Dam, this smartly updated chain has surprisingly modern guest rooms, a swimming pool with a spectacular view, and a complimentary breakfast buffet with a yogurt bar and make-it-yourself waffles.

Debbie's Hide a Way MOTEL $$
(📋 928-645-1224; www.debbieshideaway.com; 117 8th Ave; ste $129-199; ✳@🅰) Suites are dated but comfortable, and the owners are extremely helpful if you're trying to plan adventures in the area.

Lake Powell Resort RESORT $$$
(📋 888-896-3829; www.lakepowell.com; 100 Lakeshore Dr; r/ste from $199/344, child under 18yr free; ✳🅰🄿🐾) This bustling resort on the shores of Lake Powell offers beautiful views and a lovely little pool perched in the rocks above the lake, but it is impersonal and frenetic. Rates for lake-view rooms with tiny patios

are well worth the extra money. In the lobby you can book boat tours. Wi-fi is available in the lobby and lounge only.

🍴 Eating & Drinking

Most restaurants stretch along Dam Plaza, a back-to-back strip mall in the Safeway parking lot at the corner of Lake Powell Blvd and Navajo Dr. For a picnic with a lake view, pick up groceries (and coffee – there's a Starbucks kiosk inside) at Safeway and drive to the Wahweap picnic area, just past Lake Powell Resort on the road to the marina. Fast food options and a supermarket inside Wal-Mart are located on Rte 89 on the way into town from the turn-off for Horseshoe Bend.

★ River's End Café CAFE $
(📋 928-645-9175; www.raftthecanyon.com/rivers-end-cafe; 130 6th Ave; mains $7-12; ☺8am-3pm) 🍃 Tucked away inside Colorado River Discovery's headquarters, this espresso bar and cafe may be the best place in town for breakfast or a light lunch: have cappuccino and an egg-white omelet in the morning, or a Thai chicken wrap and cranberry feta salad later in the day. River's End also does takeaway bistro bags ($10.50) for hikers and rafters.

Big John's Texas BBQ BARBECUE $
(📋 928-645-3300; www.bigjohnstexasbbq.com; 153 S Lake Powell Blvd; mains $7-15; ☺11am-late; 🖐) Cheerfully occupying a partially open-air space that was once a gas station, this BBQ joint is a friendly place to feast on pulled-pork sandwiches and ribs. Pull up a seat at one of the casual picnic tables, and look for live folk-and-bluegrass music several evenings of the week.

Slackers BURGERS $
(www.slackersqualitygrub.com; 635 Elm St; mains $6-12; ☺10.30am-9pm Mon-Sat Apr-Sep, hours vary slightly in off-season; 🖐) A chalkboard menu includes excellent burgers, sandwiches, salads and kids' meals. Count on long lunch lines, or call to order in advance. Picnic tables offer shaded outdoor strip-mall seating.

HOUSEBOATING ON LAKE POWELL

Lake Powell is famous for its houseboating, and it's a huge attraction for families and college students alike. Though the lake hosts hundreds of houseboats daily, you can explore Lake Powell's secluded inlets, bays, coves and beaches for several days without seeing many folk at all. Contact the recommended Antelope Point Marina, which generally has more elegant boats and more personalized service, or Aramark for details and reservations.

Canyon Crepes Café
CREPERIE $

(📞928-614-453C; www.canyoncrepescafe.com; 669 Elm St, Ste 3; mains $8-9; ⏱7am-4pm Mon-Sat; 🛜📷) Creative sweet and savory crepes, plus soups, salads and free wi-fi, in a convenient location near many of Page's tour outfitters. It's just off the breezeway in the shopping complex across from Safeway.

Bonkers
AMERICAN $$

(📞928-645-2706; www.bonkerspageaz.com; 810 N Navajo Dr; mains $9-23; ⏱4pm-close Mar-Oct) Impressive murals of local landscapes cover the walls inside this unfortunately named restaurant – open for dinner only – that serves good steaks, seafood and pasta dishes.

Latitude 37
AMERICAN $$

(www.lakepowell.com; Lake Powell Resort, 100 Lake Shore Dr; mains $12-25; ⏱11am-9pm Fri-Sun, 4-9pm Mon-Thu Jun-Oct) Dine with a view at Lake Powell Resort's new floating restaurant, located a 10-minute walk from the hotel near Wahweap Marina. While it remains to be seen whether the Southwest-inspired menu of brisket nachos and burgers is worth the trip, there's no doubt that the vistas of Castle Rock and Navajo Mountain are lovely at sunset over a glass of wine.

Rainbow Room
BAR

(📞928-645-2433; www.lakepowell.com; Lake Powell Resort, 100 Lake Shore Dr; ⏱6-10am & 5-9pm) Perched above Lake Powell, picture windows frame dramatic red-rock formations against blue water. Eat elsewhere and come to the bar here for a beautiful sunset drink.

☆ Entertainment

From May through August, movies are screened at Memorial Park, but the schedule varies from year to year.

ℹ Information

The Glen Canyon National Recreation Area entrance fee, good for up to seven days, is $15 per vehicle or $7 per individual entering on foot or bicycle.

EMERGENCY

For the NPS 24-Hour Dispatch Center, call 📞800-582-4351 or 📞928-608-6300.

On the water, use Marine Band Channel 16.

Police Station (📞928-645-2462; 808 Coppermine Rd)

MARINAS

All the marinas except Antelope Point have rangers stations (call National Park Service Information at 📞928-608-6200 to connect to any of them), and Wahweap and Bullfrog rent boats. Check the Glen Canyon National Recreation Area newspaper for additional services at each marina. **Aramark** (📞888-896-3829; www.lakepowell.com) runs all the marinas except for Antelope Point, which is on Navajo land.

Antelope Point (📞928-645-5900; www.antelopepointlakepowell.com; 537 Marina Pkwy) Peaceful Navajo-owned marina, 8 miles northeast of Page.

Bullfrog (📞435-684-3000) Connects to Halls Crossing Marina by 30-minute ferry. It's on Lake Powell's west shore. 290 miles from Page.

Dangling Rope Smallest marina, accessible only by boat. Forty lake-miles from Page.

Halls Crossing (📞435-684-7000) Connects to Bullfrog Marina by 30-minute ferry. On Lake Powell's east shore, 238 miles from Page.

Hite May be closed due to low water levels. At Lake Powell's north end, 148 lake-miles from Page.

Wahweap (📞928-645-2433; www.nps.gov/glca) Frenetic place popular with shops, food, gas, lodging and campgrounds. Offers boat and water sport rentals, as well as tours. It's located 6 miles northwest of Page.

MEDICAL SERVICES

Page Hospital (📞928-645-2424; 501 N Navajo Dr) Has 24-hour emergency services.

Pharmacy (📞928-645-5714; 650 Elm St; ⏱9am-8pm Mon-Fri, 9am-6pm Sat, 10am-4pm Sun) Inside the Safeway

POST

Post office (📞928-645-2571; 44 6th Ave; ⏱7.30am-4pm Mon-Fri)

TOURIST INFORMATION

Bullfrog Visitor Center (📞435-684-7423; Hwy 276, north of Bullfrog Marina; ⏱9am-1pm Thu, 2-6pm Sun) On the lake's north shore, this is a drive of more than 200 miles from Page. Opening hours may vary based on personnel availability.

Carl Hayden Visitor Center (📞928-608-6404; www.nps.gov/glca; Hwy 89; ⏱8am-6pm mid-May–mid-Sep, shorter hours rest of year) A well-stocked bookstore and the best source of regional information in Page. It's at Glen Canyon Dam on Hwy 89, 2 miles north of Page.

Glen Canyon Natural History Association (📞928-608-6072; www.glencanyonnha.org; Hwy 89, Marble Canyon, AZ; ⏱8am-5pm, hours vary in winter) An excellent resource for the entire region, with maps and guides to Glen Canyon Dam, Grand Staircase-Escalante National Monument, Lake Powell and Vermilion Cliffs National Monument.

WEBSITES

Glen Canyon National Recreation Area (www.nps.gov/glca) Official website.

Lake Powell Resorts & Marinas (www.lake-powell.com) Marina lodging, boat rentals and boat tours for GCNRA.

Page/Lake Powell Tourism Bureau (www.pagelakepowelltourism.com)

Wayne's Words (www.wayneswords.com) Information on fishing in Lake Powell.

Getting There & Away

AIR

Flights between Page Municipal Airport and Phoenix are offered by two airlines.

Great Lakes Airlines (☑ 800-554-5111, 928-645-1355; www.flygreatlakes.com)

Scenic Airlines (☑ 800-634-6801; www.scenic.com)

CAR

Page sits 122 miles northwest of the North Rim. Car rental is available through **Avis** (☑ 928-645-2024, 800-331-1212; www.avis.com)

Getting Around

Powell Shuttle (☑ 928-693-0007) Provides on-demand shuttle transportation in the region. Rates and schedules vary; call for information.

Vermilion Cliffs & Marble Canyon

From Glen Canyon Dam, the Colorado River cuts through red rocks toward Navajo Bridge and the spectacular landscape around Marble Canyon, considered part of the sprawling **Vermilion Cliffs National Monument**.

Though most attractions that bring travelers to **Marble Canyon**, Arizona are managed within the nearby Glen Canyon National Recreation Area – including world-class fly-fishing spots and Lees Ferry, the jumping-off point for rafting trips through the Grand Canyon – the lodges and restaurants listed here, tucked into the base of the towering cliffs, provide places to eat and sleep nearby. There are some interesting hikes in the washes.

WORTH A TRIP

HOPI & NAVAJO RESERVATIONS

Many folk zoom past the Hopi and Navajo Reservations, registering them as nothing more than vast desert expanses and a few lonely souvenir huts standing windblown along the road between the North and South Rims. But for those with the time and a willingness to explore the unpolished reality of the American West, a side tour to this desolate area east of the Grand Canyon can be a highlight. Scenic rim drives offer breathtaking beauty, and you can explore the interior on guided hikes or horseback rides.

The surreal red-rock formations of **Monument Valley**, featured in hundreds of movies, advertisements, calendars and magazines, emerge magically from the flat and drab landscape 154 miles from Desert View and 246 miles from the North Rim.

Lying 208 miles east of Desert View on the New Mexico border, **Canyon de Chelly**, a many-figured canyon dotted with Ancestral Puebloan ruins and etched with pictographs, strikes even the most jaded traveler as hauntingly memorable. Navajo families winter on the rims and move to traditional hogans (one-room structures traditionally built of earth, logs, stone and other materials, with the entrance facing east) on farms on the canyon floor in spring and summer.

The private and isolated Hopi communities of **First**, **Second** and **Third Mesas**, about two hours from Grand Canyon's Desert View, consist of 12 traditional villages perched atop 7200ft mesas. At the end of First Mesa is the tiny village of **Walpi**, the most dramatic of the Hopi enclaves; Hopi guides offer 45-minute walking tours. The **Hopi Cultural Center**, on Second Mesa, has a small museum, and artisans sell woven baskets, kachina dolls and other crafts from roadside booths. On Third Mesa, **Old Oraibi** rivals Taos, New Mexico, and Acoma, New Mexico, as the oldest continuously inhabited village on the continent. Kachina dances are often open to the public, and tribe members sometimes personally invite visitors to other ceremonies. An invitation is an honor; be sure to respect local customs.

The Hopi strictly prohibit alcohol, as well as any form of recording, including sketching. Each of these spots has one or two motels, and there are a handful of chain motels in Kayenta, 24 miles south of Monument Valley.

They're located along Hwy 89A, a scenic road that winds 85 miles from Navajo Bridge to the North Rim of the Grand Canyon. To make the most of the beautiful drive, head up to the canyon in the evening, when twilight settles over striking rock formations and the cool desert evening stretches across the flat expanse. Open the windows, listen to the silence and wind your way up to the high meadows of the Kaibab Plateau.

◉ Sights & Activities

The calm waters of the Colorado between the dam and Lees Ferry draw fly-fishers from around the world. It's primarily a nymphing river, with opportunities for dry **fly-fishing** at certain times. Strenuous scrambles into the canyon aside, the only access is by boat. **Lees Ferry Anglers** (928-355-2261; www.leesferry.com; Cliff Dwellers Lodge, Alt 89, Marble Canyon) and **Marble Canyon Outfitters** (928-645-2781; www.leesferryflyfishing.com; inside Marble Canyon Lodge, Alt 89), both located along Hwy 89, offer guide services.

Whether you're staying the night or just passing through, there are some interesting day hikes and activities around Marble Canyon, including **Cathedral Wash**, a short canyon hike off Lees Ferry Rd, and **Soap Creek**, a trail accessible by the rock structures next to Cliff Dwellers Lodge. Stop into the lodge for a free information packet about these and other hikes in the region.

Condor Release Site at
Vermilion Cliffs   BIRD-WATCHING
(www.peregrinefund.org; Hwy 89A & House Rock Rd) Here is your best shot at catching a glimpse of these massive birds in and around the North Rim; it's well worth a detour. Coming from Vermilion Cliffs or Navajo Bridge, the site is located on Hwy 89A, on the way to Jacob Lake. Turn right at House Rock Rd. The release site is located 2 miles north.

🛏 Sleeping & Eating

Things around here are pretty quiet, especially in winter. Simple windswept motels dot Alt 89 in the shadow of the Vermilion Cliffs just west of Navajo Bridge, offering spectacular surrounds with panoramic views of the desert flatness to the south.

Lees Ferry Campground   CAMPGROUND $
(www.nps.gov/glca; Lees Ferry, Glen Canyon National Recreation Area; tent & RV sites $16) Flanked by red rocks, this a stunningly pretty campground. On a small hill, it has 54 riverview

sites along with drinking water and toilets, but no hookups.

Cliff Dwellers Lodge & Restaurant   MOTEL $
(928-355-2261, 800-962-9755; www.cliffdwellerslodge.com; Hwy 89, Marble Canyon; r $80-100; 6am-9pm; 🐾) This roadside lodge, charmingly set at the base of enormous cliffs, 10 miles west of Navajo Bridge, is ground zero for fly-fishing enthusiasts, and a popular stop for its excellent restaurant with breezy porch seating. Opt for a room with knotty pine walls and a recently remodeled bathroom. The owners run Lees Ferry Anglers: ask about local hikes.

Lees Ferry Lodge   MOTEL $
(928-355-2231; www.vermilioncliffs.com; Hwy 89A; r $65-75, apt $90-125; P ❄ 🐾) This handsome stone building has cozy rooms, decorated thematically – the cowboy room, for example, has animal skins and horseshoes on the wall, horse-print bed covers and a wood-burning stove. There's a pleasant roadside courtyard with spectacular views, and a popular diner-style restaurant on-site.

Marble Canyon Lodge   MOTEL $
(928-355-2225; www.marblecanyoncompany.com; Hwy 89, Marble Canyon; s/d/apt $75/80/140; 🐾) The closest accommodations to Navajo Bridge (and nearby Lees Ferry) are at this friendly lodge, with 60 rooms, eight suites and apartments for up to six people. There's also a mini-market and it's one of the only places around that offers wi-fi. It's located 0.4 miles west of Navajo Bridge

🛍 Shopping

Lees Ferry Anglers sells rods, reels, lines, flies and equipment for fly-fishing in the area and beyond, and giving anglers the lowdown on what's biting where. It's also one of the only places around to pick up snacks, drinks and postcards.

ℹ Information

A post office, laundromat and pay showers are next to the gas station just west of Navajo Bridge. Don't be surprised if you can't get a cell phone signal here – there's a wi-fi hotspot by Marble Canyon Lodge, but it wasn't working when we visited.

ℹ Getting There & Around

Marble Canyon and Lees Ferry are a 1½-hour drive northeast from the North Rim and an hour's drive southwest of Page. There is no public transportation to either.

HAGEPHOTO / GETTY IMAGES ©

1. Toroweap (p143)
Toroweap's stunning landscape is unlike anywhere else on the North Rim.

2. Thunder River Trail (p179)
This trail takes its name from Thunder River, one of the world's shortest rivers.

3. Bright Angel Point (p137)
A short walk leads to an overlook with sweeping views of Bright Angel Canyon.

4. Grand Canyon Lodge (p148)
Take in magnificent views from the lodge's rimside dining room and sun porches.

3

WHIT RICHARDSON / GETTY IMAGES ©

Colorado River

Best Hikes

➡ Tapeats Creek to Thunder Spring (p179)

➡ Deer Creek (p179)

➡ Matkatamiba (p179)

➡ Elves Chasm (p178)

➡ Beaver Falls (p180)

Best Rafting Companies

➡ Arizona Raft Adventures (p174)

➡ OARS (p174)

➡ Canyon Explorations/ Expeditions (p175)

➡ Outdoors Unlimited (p175)

➡ Hatch River Expeditions (p175)

Why Go?

As one park ranger recently said, 'rafting the Colorado is absolute bliss punctuated by moments of pure terror.' Indeed, a journey down the river is a once-in-a-lifetime experience – a virtual all-access pass to the Grand Canyon, in all its wildness, peace and ancient, mighty glory. There's the rush of running world-class rapids with spectacular canyon walls towering above, and the solitude of floating down sections of smooth water. Rafters have the exclusive privilege of hiking to beautiful side canyons, hidden waterfalls, petroglyphs and ruins. As you fall asleep on a sandy beach, under the stars, you'll feel connected to the people who lived here long before – and inspired by the tales of intrepid explorers who ran the river when it was still uncharted. Here at the bottom of the Grand Canyon, the depth and beauty of the gorge will take your breath away.

Road Distances (miles)

	Colorado River (Silver Suspension Bridge)	South Rim Entrance	North Rim Entrance	Lees Ferry	Phantom Ranch
South Rim Entrance	15				
North Rim Entrance	25	205			
Lees Ferry	90	140	65		
Phantom Ranch	1	15	25	85	
Whitmore Wash	180	300	155	155	175

Note: Distances are approximate

Entrance & Exit Points

Though boats must ply the full course, rafters may join, leave or rejoin a river excursion at several points

➤ Put in at Lees Ferry (river Mile 0), 15 miles below Glen Canyon Dam.

➤ Rafters can take out at Phantom Ranch (Mile 87.5) and hike up to the South Rim on the Bright Angel Trail.

➤ Rafters can also take out at Whitmore Wash (Mile 187.5), fly to the rim via helicopter and transfer to a plane bound for Las Vegas.

➤ The last takeout points are at Diamond Creek (Mile 226), or Pearce Ferry (Mile 279.5) or South Cove (Mile 296.5), both on Lake Mead.

DON'T MISS

Despite their thrills, walloping river rapids aren't the only attraction on this ride. One of the great rewards of floating the river is the opportunity to hike to places that are difficult to access from the rim – such as the Ancient Puebloan granaries at **Nankoweap** (p178), where you'll also discover gorgeous views of the river and inner gorge. Side canyons reveal cool, verdant grottos such as **Elves Chasm** (p178) and swirling rock formations such as **North Canyon** (p177). Set aside your pride and strap your personal floation device (PFD) to your bum to bump down the warm, turquoise waters of the **Little Colorado** (p180), a tributary sourced from mineral springs.

Be sure to stop for a cold lemonade and scribble a postcard at **Phantom Ranch** (p177), your one brush with civilization. And don't miss the otherworldly blue-green waters of **Havasu Creek** (p180).

When You Arrive

➤ Arrangements for river trips are usually made well in advance. By the time you arrive, you'll already have received plenty of information from your outfitter about the kind of trip you'll be taking, what to expect and what to pack.

➤ Generally speaking, travelers access the Colorado River through a commercial rafting trip that runs between three and 18 days, and runs part of the river from Lees Ferry to Diamond Creek.

➤ Boat options include large motorized rafts, oared rafts, paddle rafts and dories.

➤ Self-guided raft trips, or private river trips, are possible only with a permit that's available through a special weighted lottery

PLANNING TIP

Plan as far ahead as possible: many commercial trips book out a year in advance. Spring and fall trips mean pleasantly milder temperatures, but bring warm and waterproof gear; read the recommended packing list. Many outfitters supply travelers with large waterproof bags.

Fast Facts

➤ River miles: 277
➤ Major rapids: 160
➤ River drop: 1900ft
➤ Phantom Ranch elevation: 2400ft

Private Trip Permits

Apply for a permit through the **Grand Canyon River Permits Office** (☎800-959-9164, 928-638-7843; https://npspermits.us; application fee $25). Successful applicants are charged an automatic, nonrefundable $400 deposit to reserve a spot.

Resources

➤ **National Park Service** (www.nps.gov/grca/planyourvisit/whitewater-rafting.htm)

➤ **Grand Canyon River podcasts** (www.nps.gov/grca/learn/photosmultimedia/podcasts)

➤ **Grand Canyon River Outfitters Association** (www.gcroa.org)

➤ **Hualapai River Runners** (www.grandcanyonwest.com) One-day motorized trips on the Colorado.

Colorado River

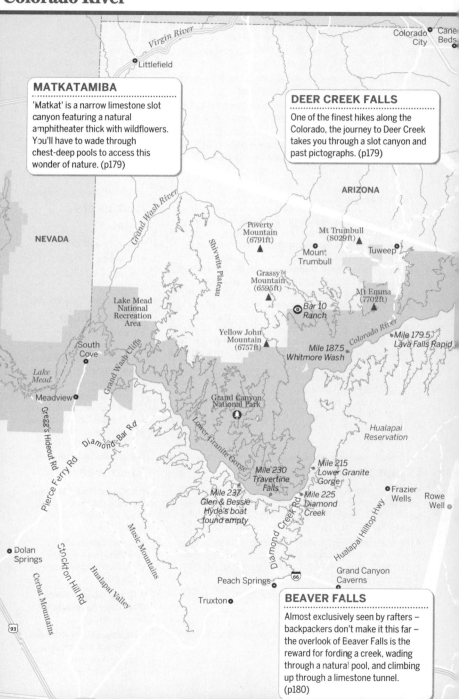

MATKATAMIBA

'Matkat' is a narrow limestone slot canyon featuring a natural amphitheater thick with wildflowers. You'll have to wade through chest-deep pools to access this wonder of nature. (p179)

DEER CREEK FALLS

One of the finest hikes along the Colorado, the journey to Deer Creek takes you through a slot canyon and past pictographs. (p179)

Virgin River

Littlefield

Colorado City

Cane Beds

ARIZONA

Grand Wash River

Shivwits Plateau

NEVADA

Poverty Mountain (6791ft) ▲

Mt Trumbull (8029ft) ▲

Mount Trumbull ▲

Tuweep

Grassy Mountain (6595ft) ▲

Mt Emma (7702ft) ▲

Lake Mead National Recreation Area

⊙ Bar 10 Ranch

Yellow John Mountain (6757ft) ▲

Mile 187.5 Whitmore Wash

Colorado River

Mile 179.5 Lava Falls Rapid

South Cove

Lake Mead

Grand Wash Cliffs

Meadview

Grand Canyon National Park

Hualapai Reservation

Gregg's Hideout Rd

Pierce Ferry Rd

Diamond Bar Rd

Lower Granite Gorge

Mile 230 Travertine Falls

Mile 215 Lower Granite Gorge

Mile 237 Glen & Bessie Hyde's boat found empty

Mile 225 Diamond Creek

Frazier Wells

Rowe Well

Diamond Creek Rd

Hualapai Hilltop Hwy

Music Mountains

Stockton Hill Rd

Dolan Springs

Hualapai Valley

Cerbat Mountains

Peach Springs

66

Grand Canyon Caverns

Truxton

93

BEAVER FALLS

Almost exclusively seen by rafters – backpackers don't make it this far – the overlook of Beaver Falls is the reward for fording a creek, wading through a natural pool, and climbing up through a limestone tunnel. (p180)

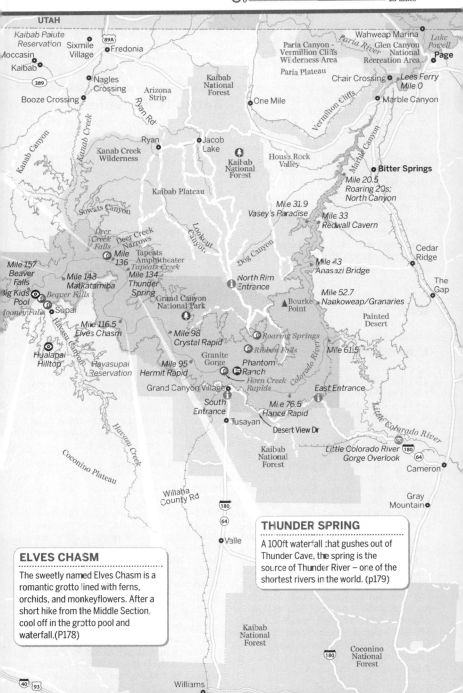

UTAH

Kaibab Paiute
Reservation   Sixmile
Moccaine   Village
Kaibab
(389)
Nagles
Crossing
Booze Crossing

Fredonia
(89A)

Wahweap Marina
Paria River
Glen Canyon
National
Recreation Area

Lake
Powell

Page

Paria Canyon -
Vermillion Cliffs
Wilderness Area

Chair Crossing

Lees Ferry
Mile 0

Arizona
Strip

Ryan Rd

Kaibab
National
Forest

One Mile

Paria Plateau

Vermillion Cliffs

Marble Canyon

Ryan

Jacob
Lake

House Rock
Valley

Marble Canyon

Kanab Creek
Wilderness

Kaibab
National
Forest

Bitter Springs

Kaibab Plateau

Sowats Canyon

Kanab Canyon

Kanab Creek

Lookout Canyon

Dog Canyon

Mile 20.5
Roaring 20s;
North Canyon

Mile 31.9
Vasey's Paradise

Mile 33
Redwall Cavern

Cedar
Ridge

Deer
Creek
Falls

Deer Creek
Narrows

Mile
136

Tapeats
Amphitheater

Tapeats Creek

Mile 43
Anasazi Bridge

The
Gap

Mile 157
Beaver
Falls

Mile 143
Matkatamiba

Mile 134
Thunder
Spring

North Rim
Entrance

Bourke
Point

Mile 52.7
Nankoweap/Granaries

Big Kids
Pool

Beaver Falls

Mooney Falls   Supai

Grand Canyon
National Park

Painted
Desert

Mile 116.5
Elves Chasm

Mile 98
Crystal Rapid

Roaring Springs

Mile 61.5

Havasu Canyon

Hualapai
Hilltop

Havasupai
Reservation

Granite
Gorge

Ribbon Falls

Hermit Rapid

Mile 95

Phantom
Ranch

Colorado River

East Entrance

Horn Creek
Rapids

Grand Canyon Village

Coconino Plateau

Havasu Creek

South
Entrance

Mile 76.5
Hance Rapid

Desert View Dr

Little Colorado River

Tusayan

Kaibab
National
Forest

Little Colorado River
Gorge Overlook

Cameron

(180)
(64)

Gray
Mountain

Willaha
County Rd

(180)

(64)

Valle

ELVES CHASM

The sweetly named Elves Chasm is a
romantic grotto lined with ferns,
orchids, and monkeyflowers. After a
short hike from the Middle Section,
cool off in the grotto pool and
waterfall.(P178)

THUNDER SPRING

A 100ft waterfall that gushes out of
Thunder Cave, the spring is the
source of Thunder River – one of the
shortest rivers in the world. (p179)

Kaibab
National
Forest

Coconino
National
Forest

(40)(93)

Williams

N 0 ———— 50 km
0 ———— 25 miles

PLANNING

The Grand Canyon stretch of the Colorado sees 22,000 annual visitors and is run year-round, though access to some sections is limited under certain conditions. Most commercial trips operate between April and October, with June, July and August being the peak months. Park regulations stipulate that individuals may take only one recreational river trip per calendar year, whether private or commercial.

While summer draws the most traffic, it also brings more afternoon thunderstorms and searing, triple-digit temperatures. The only way to stay cool is to engage in water fights with fellow rafters and take quick dips in the face-numbing water – controlled releases from Glen Canyon Dam keep water temperatures between 48°F and 55°F (9°C and 14°C) year-round. Monsoon rains in July and August can also spawn flash floods and increased sediment that turns the water a murky reddish-brown.

RAFTING

Commercial Trips

Given two or three weeks, you can run all 277 river miles through the canyon between Lake Powell and Lake Mead. If that's more vacation than you've got, you can raft one of three shorter sections (each 100 miles or less) in four to nine days, or raft a combination of two shorter sections. Choosing to run the river via motorboat rather than raft shortens the trip by several days.

Most rafters join a commercial outing with one of many accredited outfitters, who offer trips lasting from three to 21 days. Due to their popularity, tours often sell out a year in advance. However, a small percentage of cancellations do occur, so it's sometimes possible to get in on a trip at the last minute.

For those short on time, there are half- and full-day rafting trips, though not necessarily on sections within the Grand Canyon. Operating out of Diamond Creek, about four hours from the South Rim, **Hualapai River Runners** (☑ 928-769-2636, tourism office 928-769-2219; www.grandcanyonwest.com; adult/child $350/328; ☉ mid-Mar–Oct) offers daylong, motorized raft trips in the canyon's west end. Don't want a white-knuckle white-water experience? Wilderness River Adventures (p177) runs half-day float trips on the silky-smooth 16-mile stretch of the Colorado that flows between Glen Canyon Dam and Lees Ferry. Xanterra (p174) offers full-day trips from the South Rim that bus rafters to Page, where they connect with the float trip.

Rafting Companies

By far the most popular means of getting out on to the water is to join a tour run by one of the commercial rafting companies. There are many operators offering rafting trips, and all provide the boat, all rafting and camping gear, cooking equipment and food. Your multitalented guides wear yet another hat as chefs and prepare all meals. Oar-powered rafting trips cost $200 to $325 per day, while trips via motorboat cost $225 to $375 per day. The minimum age ranges from eight to 12, depending on the outfitter and type of trip. The trips are very popular, so make reservations six to 12 months in advance. If you feel overwhelmed with options, contact the Flagstaff-based booking agency **Rivers & Oceans** (☑ 928-526-4575, 800-473-4576; www.riversandoceans.com; ☉ 9am-6pm); it works with all of the companies running trips on the Colorado and doesn't charge a booking fee.

Pre- and post-trip accommodations as well as transportation to or from the trip's start/end point may not be included in the river-trip price. Many companies offer special-interest trips for those interested in subjects as diverse as geology, botany, classical music, art and wine.

Arizona Raft Adventures   RAFTING
(☑ 800-786-7238, 928-526-8200; www.azraft.com; 6-day Upper Canyon hybrid/paddle trips $2050/2150, 10-day Full Canyon motor trips $3000) 🍃 This multigenerational family-run outfit offers paddle, oar, hybrid (with opportunities for both paddling and floating) and motor trips. Music fans can join one of the folk and bluegrass trips, with professional pickers and banjo players providing background music.

OARS   RAFTING
(☑ 800-346-6277, 209-736-4677; www.oars.com; 6-to-7-day Upper Canyon oar trip $2607-2787, 14-to-18-day Full Canyon dory trips $5406-5905) 🍃 One of the best outfitters working in the canyon, OARS boasts the best guide-to-guest ratio in the business (1:4). With oar, paddle and dory

trips, and the option of carbon-offsetting your trip, OARS offers extra elegance than the standard – it claims you'll eat better with them than you do at home – and partners with local artisans.

Canyon Explorations/ Expeditions
KAYAKING, RAFTING

(☎928-774-4559, 800-654-0723; www.canyonexplorations.com; 7-day Upper Canyon trips $2300, 14-day Full Canyon trips $3800) ☞ Canyon offers two styles of trip: Hybrid (involving five oar boats, one paddle boat, and two inflatable kayaks) and All Paddle (with three paddle boats and four gear rafts). It also offers a 15-day journey with the accompaniment of a string quartet from the Seattle Symphony. During the trip, the classical musicians perform in side canyons, on the beach and in camp.

Outdoors Unlimited
RAFTING

(☎928-526-4511, 800-637-7238; www.outdoorsunlimited.com; 5-day Upper Canyon oar trips $1820, 13-day Full Canyon oar trips $3645) In business for more than four decades, Outdoors Unlimited specializes in all-paddle expeditions. As with most outfitters, some spring and fall trips stretch one or two days longer to allow more hikes and exploration along the way. To beat the crowds, ask about April and September departures.

Hatch River Expeditions
RAFTING

(☎800-856-8966; www.hatchriverexpeditions.com; 4-day Upper Canyon motor trips $1326, 7-day Full Canyon trips $2688) ☞ Repeat travelers rave about the good food and knowledgeable guides at Hatch River Expeditions, a company that's been around since 1929. For those

PIONEERS OF THE COLORADO

Today, a rafting trip down the Colorado River through Grand Canyon National Park is considered a once-in-a-lifetime experience. Excellent commercial outfitters take care of all the details, but as with any adventure sport there's risk involved – which is exactly what makes it so intriguing to consider what a similar trip might have been like for the river's earliest pioneers.

The geologist and ethnographer John Wesley Powell was one of the river's first explorers, leading a small group nearly 1000 miles down the river in the summer of 1869, when Powell was just 35 years old. It's not an exaggeration to say the trip was almost disastrous – the rapids were too powerful for the group's small boats. Powell was better prepared when he returned for another river trip, this one sponsored by the Smithsonian Institution, in 1871. He wrote extensively on his observations, and his work served as the early basis for knowledge about the Grand Canyon, an area that few people had seen in the late 19th century. Perhaps most eloquent were his thoughts about the ever-changing nature of the canyon's immense landscape, which, he said, couldn't be comprehended in a single glance. According to Powell, one had to experience it by wending through its maze of passageways and gullies.

Decades later, Nathaniel Galloway – today considered the father of modern whitewater rafting technique – changed the course of river running forever with the invention of his flat-bottomed upturned boat. Shallow and easier to maneuver, Galloway's boats were rowed backwards. In 1909, a financier named Julius Stone took advantage of Galloway's invention to organize the first rafting trip 'for pleasure' down the Colorado, starting in Wyoming and ending up three months later in California.

Around the same time, enterprising brothers Ellsworth and Emery Kolb were the first to film their own 101-day excursion down the river. They screened the film daily in their studio to the rapt attention of tourists.

Of course, there was tragedy, too, for the river's early runners: honeymooners Glen and Bessie Hyde vanished on the Colorado River in 1928. Bessie reportedly wanted to be the first woman to ride the river the entire way through the Grand Canyon, but she never made it: their boat was found floating upright and fully stocked the following winter, and the adventurers were never heard from again.

The ebullient Georgie White Clark took the title of first woman to row a boat through the Grand Canyon in the 1950s. And in 1955, encouraging others to share in the adventure, she began escorting tourists on 'share the expense' trips down the Colorado – making her the first professional woman outfitter, and the forerunner for the many rafting companies that run the river today.

seeking a faster trip down the river, it's a good option. In addition to partnering with Leave No Trace, Hatch is affiliated with organizations such as the Whale Foundation, Girl Scouts of America and the American Cancer Society.

Arizona River Runners   RAFTING
(☑ 602-867-4866, 800-477-7238; www.raftarizona. com; 6-day Upper Canyon oar trip $1984, 8-day Full Canyon motor trip $2745) Operating since 1970, offering oar-powered and motorized trips. Arizona River Runners specializes in family trips as well as 'Hiker's Special' trips that take place over six to 12 days in the cooler temperatures of April. The company also caters to travelers with special needs, offering departures for people with disabilities.

Canyoneers   RAFTING
(☑ 928-526-0924, 800-525-0924; www.canyoneers.com; 6-day Upper Canyon oar trips $2060, 7-day Full Canyon motor trips $2525-2625) In operation since 1938, the family-run Canyoneers is the oldest commercial river-running outfitter in the Grand Canyon. Choose between two options: motorized trips on pontoon rafts (convenient if you only have a few days and want to see more of the canyon) or human-powered rowing trips in inflatable rafts. Some oar-powered trips travel with the *Sandra*, a historic 'cataract boat' originally used in the '40s.

Grand Canyon Expeditions   RAFTING
(☑ 435-644-2691, 800-544-2691; www.gcex.com; 8-day rafting trip $2750, 14-day dory trip $3899) Travelers rave about the gourmet meals on the river provided by Grand Canyon Expeditions, offering oar, motor and dory trips. A popular option is the eight-day all-inclusive expedition; the outfitter also offers special trips focused on history, geology, photography, ecology and archaeology. Transportation to and from Las Vegas is included (but optional) in all trips.

Colorado River & Trail Expeditions RAFTING
(☑ 801-261-1789, 800-253-7328; www.crateinc. com; 5-day Upper Canyon paddle or rowing trips $1975, 5-day motor trip $1485) ✏ Offering a range of motorized and oar-powered trips, this outfit also includes transportation to or from Las Vegas. It's a proud partner with several environmental organizations, including Leave No Trace and the Utah Society for Environmental Education.

Grand Canyon Whitewater   RAFTING
(☑ 928-645-8866, 800-343-3121; www.grandcanyonwhitewater.com; 6-day Upper Canyon oar trips $1915, 8-day Full Canyon motor trips $2655) ✏ The environmentally friendly Grand Canyon Whitewater offers seven trip options, including oar-powered and motorized, that run from four to 14 days. The company contributes to the Grand Canyon Fund, which supports nonprofit groups working toward conservation in the canyon.

PRIVATE TRIPS

The Colorado River Management Plan (CRMP) serves to protect the river and to preserve a high-quality experience for visitors, carefully regulating the number of rafts on the Colorado. There are two kinds of rafting trips on the river: the more common commercial trip, run by one of many professional river outfitters in conjunction with the National Parks Service (NPS), and the less common private or non-commercial trip.

The private trip, is only available through a weighted lottery, and is usually arranged at least a year in advance. Even before you can begin working out the necessary details, from supplies to waste management to emergency options, you need to score a permit and will be required to have at least one member of your party with the technical rafting experience to run the Colorado. The application fee is $25. If accepted, you'll be awarded a launch date and must pay a deposit ($400 for standard trips, $200 for smaller trips). Ninety days before the launch date, each person on the trip will pay an addition $100. All fees are non-refundable. Visit www.nps.gov/grca/planyourvisit/weightedlottery.htm for more information on the lottery, and be sure to click over to the FAQs page.

There are no developed campsites or facilities anywhere along the Colorado. Because this is a wilderness area, where the Leave No Trace ethic applies, visitors are required to make the least impact possible by removing any waste generated and by sticking to established trails to minimize erosion. Groups on the river are self-sufficient, packing in all food and gear and packing out all waste. Rafters camp on pristine, sandy beaches, most of which are fringed with invasive (but lovely) tamarisk stands providing wisps of shade. Usually, only one group will camp on any given beach, affording everyone heaps of privacy.

Western River Expeditions RAFTING

(☑ 801-942-6669, 866-904-1160; www.western river.com; 6-/7-day Upper & Middle Canyon motor trips $2669-2962, 3-day Lower Canyon trips $1280-$1396) If you're starting or ending in Vegas, these three-day river trips are as convenient as it gets: the itinerary starts at the Las Vegas Marriott and includes flights, including a helicopter ride that takes you down to the rafts.

Wilderness River Adventures RAFTING

(☑ 800-992-8022, 928-645-3296; www.riverad ventures.com; 6-day Full Canyon motor trips $2500, 12-day Full Canyon oar trips $3775) 🛶 Wilderness River Adventures' hybrid trips give rafters the chance to be active and relaxed, combining hands-on paddling with floating. The company partners with Green Thread, an environmental organization operating in national parks. Check the website: you can save hundreds of dollars on the quoted rates by choosing the 'Pay Now' option online.

Tour West RAFTING

(☑ 801-225-0755, 800-453-9107; www.twriver. com; 3-day Lower Canyon motor trips $1455, 12-day oar trips $3750) Tour West, running the river since 1969, considers its greatest asset to be its well-informed guides. Trips include transportation to Las Vegas at the end of the trip as well as accommodations on the first night. Oar trips take out at Whitmore Wash; helicopter-to-rim and charter flights to Marble Canyon are also included.

🛈 Information

The Colorado River runs 277 miles from Lees Ferry to Lake Mead, with more than 160 sets of rapids keeping things exciting. Unlike most rivers, where the rapids are rated in difficulty as Class I through V on the American white-water rating system, Colorado River rapids are rated from Class 1 through 10 (a Class 10 on the Colorado being about equal to the standard Class V; that is, a King Kong rapid). The biggest single drop (from the top to the base of the rapids) is 37ft, and nearly 20 rapids drop 15ft or more.

The Colorado is a serious river and demands respect. If you do everything your guide tells you and take responsibility for your own safety and that of others, you should have an exciting but safe trip. Be aware that the temperature of the river remains cold year-round, and hypothermia can set in quickly. Always check with your guides whether a place is far enough removed from the swift current to be safe for a dip.

Along the length of the river, the side canyons and tributaries feeding into the Colorado provide a wealth of hidden places to explore. Many of the canyon's waterfalls, slot canyons and inviting pools are difficult to reach unless you start from the river, and most can't be seen from the rim. Visits to these remote spots can be the most rewarding part of a river trek.

RAFTING ROUTES

Upper Section: Lees Ferry to Phantom Ranch

MILE 0 TO MILE 87.5

Beginning at Lees Ferry, where it cuts through the top sedimentary layer of the Moenkopi shale, the upper section of the Colorado River then passes through Marble Canyon and Granite Gorge. The walls of **Marble Canyon** rise higher and higher, quickly exposing layers of rock beneath. Once you hit Mile 20.5, you've entered the **Roaring 20s**, a series of rapids (rated up to 8) that begin with North Canyon Rapid.

At Mile 31.9 you'll see, springing forth from the wall on the right, **Vasey's Paradise**, a lush garden nourished from the water escaping the Redwall Limestone. Shortly thereafter, the wide, low mouth of the enormous **Redwall Cavern** (Mile 33) appears ahead.

Around Mile 50, the beautiful dark-green, burgundy and purple layers of Bright Angel Shale appear, as do the doorways of **Ancient Puebloan granaries** (Mile 52.7) dating to AD 1100, sitting high above the water. The canyon reaches its confluence with the **Little Colorado River** at Mile 61.5.

This stretch features 28 rapids, 17 of which are rated 5 or higher. Nine rapids drop 15ft or more, including **Hance Rapid** (Mile 76.5), which boasts one of the river's largest single drops, a whopping 30ft. Near Mile 77 the appearance of pink Zoroaster granite intrusions into black Vishnu schist marks the start of **Granite Gorge**.

Side Hikes

Short hikes on the Upper Section end up in amazing little places.

🥾 North Canyon

Duration 1½ hours round-trip

Distance 2 miles round-trip

Difficulty Moderate

Start/Finish Mile 20.5, river right

Summary Hike up to a sculptural pool carved by water.

There isn't much elevation gain to this short hike, but it does entail a scramble up a wash to reach the pool. The erosion pattern above the pool has carved its sinuous curves with a design not unlike a three-dimensional topographic map or Georgia O'Keeffe painting.

🏃 Nankoweap to Granaries

Duration 1½ hours round-trip

Distance 1.5 miles round-trip

Difficulty Moderate

Start/Finish Mile 52.7, river right

Summary Steep hike which rewards the effort with an Ancestral Puebloan site and a killer view.

Though short, this steep hike takes you about 700ft above the river to the **Ancient Puebloan Granaries** built into the cliff face. The stacked-stone walls with their square openings can be seen from the river. From up on the ledge, those who aren't awed by the well-preserved archaeological site will be struck by the beautiful views downriver.

Middle Section: Phantom Ranch to Whitmore Wash

MILE 87.5 TO MILE 187.5

Rafters hike in from the South Rim to the boat beach near Phantom Ranch to raft **Middle Granite Gorge**, where Tapeats sandstone meets the Vishnu schist.

This section claims the Colorado's biggest white water, where 'Adrenaline Alley' begins with **Horn Creek Rapid** (Mile 90), and burly **Hermit Rapid** (Mile 95). It also offers the most technically challenging rapids: **Crystal Rapid** (Mile 98) and the grand-daddy **Lava Falls Rapid** (Mile 179.5), with its gut-in-throat drop of 37ft. From Lava Falls Rapid, the next 80 miles downstream are a geologic marvel. Columnar basalt lines the canyon walls for thousands of vertical feet.

To leave Whitmore Wash, rafters take a helicopter to the **Bar 10 Ranch** (www.bar10.com), a rustic Old West–style retreat located 80 miles (along a dirt road) from St George, Utah.

The middle section boasts 38 rapids, 23 of which are rated 5 or higher (Crystal and Lava Falls rapids are both rated 10s). Eight rapids drop between 15ft and 18ft. Operators run this stretch between May and July. Between July and September trips continue to **Diamond Creek** (Mile 226). Oar-powered rafts take seven to nine days; motorboats four to five.

Side Hikes

On the Middle Section you can float in a mossy pool or hike the world's shortest river.

🏃 Elves Chasm

Duration 20 minutes round-trip

Distance 1 mile round-trip

Difficulty Easy

Start/Finish Mile 116.5, river left

Summary Quick scramble to a pretty grotto.

Ferns, orchids and scarlet monkeyflowers drape the walls of this grotto, where a waterfall tumbles over intricate travertine formations. It takes five minutes to scramble up Royal Arch Creek from the river. Dive into the grotto's pool and swim to the base of the waterfall. Clamber up through the cave to an opening above a moss-draped rocky chute, then jump back into the pool below.

BOATS & RAFTS

➡ Most commonly used boats are 18ft neoprene rafts seating three to five passengers, with a guide rowing wooden oars. High center of gravity provides greater stability while giving the guide more power down big rapids.

➡ Dories – 17ft rigid, flat-bottomed boats – comfortably seat up to four passengers and a guide rowing a set of long wooden oars. Dory trips take one or two days longer than rafting trips.

➡ Motorized rafts are, typically, inflatable pontoons lashed together to create a 33ft craft. They seat eight to 16 passengers and two or three guides.

➡ Hard-shell kayaks are most often used on private trips, while some commercial operators provide inflatable kayaks on request.

🥾 Tapeats Creek to Thunder Spring

Duration 4½ hours round-trip

Distance 5 miles round-trip

Difficulty Moderate–difficult

Start/Finish Mile 133.7, river right

Summary Hike to one of the world's shortest rivers, then connect with the Deer Creek Trail.

Thunder Spring, the roaring 100ft waterfall that gushes out of the Muav limestone at Thunder Cave, is the source of Thunder River, one of the world's shortest rivers. Over its half-mile course it plunges more than 1200ft to the confluence with Tapeats Creek.

Just before Mile 134, follow the **Thunder River Trail** upstream along cottonwood-shaded **Tapeats Creek**, crossing it twice. You'll reach the first crossing, a thigh-deep ford of rushing water, in about 45 minutes. The second crossing, an hour later, is via a fallen log.

Leaving Tapeats Creek, you'll slowly zigzag up an open slope for 30 minutes to expanding views of **Tapeats Amphitheater** and **Thunder Spring** (3400ft) – you'll hear the roar before seeing the waterfall. Enjoy a picnic in the shade at the base of the fall before retracing your steps (1400ft elevation change).

You can make this a seven-hour near-loop hike by continuing on the Thunder River Trail beyond the waterfall, traversing Surprise Valley and descending the Deer Creek Trail to the Colorado.

🥾 Deer Creek

Duration 5 hours return-trip

Distance 6 miles return-trip

Difficulty Moderate–difficult

Start/Finish Mile 136.3, river right

Summary One of the inner gorge's finest hikes, with lush waterfalls and pictographs in a curvy slot canyon.

Downstream from Granite Narrows below Mile 136, **Deer Creek Falls** tumbles into the Colorado. From this welcoming trailhead you head 500ft up a steep, bushy slope to a stunning overlook. From here the trail leads into **Deer Creek Narrows**, an impressive

slot canyon where the walls bear remarkable pictographs. The narrows end in an inviting cascade. Above, lush vegetation lines the trail as it meanders along the cottonwood-shaded creek.

The trail crosses the creek and ascends open, rocky slopes to **Deer Creek Spring**, the trail's second waterfall. From here retrace your steps back to the river. Despite having to scramble up and down steep slopes over loose rocks and follow narrow, exposed trails, this hike is one of the inner canyon's best.

🥾 Matkatamiba

Duration 20 minutes round-trip

Distance 0.8 mile round-trip

Difficulty Moderate

Start/Finish Mile 148, river left

Summary Pull yourself through the narrows to get to the amphitheater at Matkatamiba.

Matkatamiba, named for a Havasupai family and nicknamed Matkat, is a very narrow Redwall limestone slot canyon that meets the Colorado at Mile 148. So, wet or dry? You must quickly decide how to spend the next 10 minutes heading up to Matkat's acoustically perfect natural **amphitheater**, lined by ferns and wildflowers. On the tricky wet route, you head upstream through the creek – wading when possible, and crawling on all fours and using handholds to pull yourself over slippery boulders.

RUNNING THE LITTLE COLORADO

In drier seasons, the Little Colorado flows down from a mineral spring, which gives the water its tropical warmth and turquoise hue. If the water is clear, the confluence with the big Colorado creates a lovely juxtaposition of colors. While a lucky few on rafting trips get the chance to see the mini-rapids up close, any visitor to the park can view the Little Colorado River Gorge from an overlook that's located in a section of the park informally known as Grand Canyon East, on the rim-hugging road between the South Rim and Cameron, AZ – travelers driving from the South Rim to North Rim pass right by the turn-off, about 12 miles west of Cameron between Miles 285 and 286. As it's part of Navajo Nation, you'll see several traditional Native American vendors selling crafts and jewelry near the scenic overlook. There's no price to enter, but tribespeople do encourage and accept donations.

But hang on, you get wet on the dry route too, since the first 25ft of both routes start by wading through a chest-deep pool, clambering over a boulder as wide as the creek, then wading through yet another pool. Here the dry route leaves the creek and ascends 100ft of steep rock to an exposed trail that overlooks the narrow chasm. At a sculpted curve where the amphitheater emerges, the two routes merge. The wet route is too dangerous to descend, so return via the dry route.

🏃 Beaver Falls

Duration 4 hours round-trip

Distance 8 miles round-trip

Difficulty Easy–moderate

Start/Finish Mile 157, river left

Summary Explore the blue-green waters of Havasu Canyon from the riverside.

The blue-green spring-fed waters of Havasu Creek plunge over a series of four breathtaking waterfalls to the Colorado. Beaver Falls, which tumbles over travertine formations with one prominent fall, is the cascade nearest to the river. Most backpackers hike in only as far as Mooney Falls, so **Beaver Falls** – 2 miles further – is almost the exclusive domain of rafters.

The slot canyon near Mile 157 doesn't hint at what lies further up **Havasu Canyon**. A few minutes from the Colorado, the rock walls part to reveal wild grapevines, lush ground cover and tall cottonwoods along the level creekside trail. On this gentle hike, you'll spend about 20 minutes in water as you ford Havasu Creek, cross deep pools and wade upstream through knee-deep

water. Once through the first and biggest water obstacle – the lovely, chest-deep **Big Kids Pool** – you'll emerge and climb a log staircase through a Muav limestone tunnel. The trail continues upstream to the base of a cliff near the confluence with Beaver Creek. Scramble up the cliff to reach an **overlook** of Beaver Falls. Retrace your steps, relaxing and swimming in the several pools.

Lower Section: Whitmore Wash to South Cove

MILE 187.5 TO BEYOND MILE 277

Rafters join the river at Whitmore Wash via helicopter from the North Rim. **Lower Granite Gorge**, the third and last of the canyon's sister granite gorges, starts at Mile 215, marked by the appearance of metamorphic and igneous rock. Though it features more flat water than other stretches, this section still boasts great white water, including 11 rapids, seven of which are rated 5 or higher. The two biggest drops are 16ft and 25ft. Oar-powered rafts take four to five days, motorboats three to four days.

In July and August the trip wraps up at **Diamond Creek** (Mile 226). Trips in May and June, however, continue downstream and can catch a glimpse of the water shimmering over the limestone deposits that make **Travertine Falls** (Mile 230) a petrified waterfall.

You might also muse over the unsolved mystery of Glen and Bessie Hyde's disappearance in 1928 at **Mile 237**, where their flat-bottomed boat was found peacefully floating with everything in it but the Hydes. Eventually, the trip continues beyond the canyon's terminus at **Grand Wash Cliffs** to end at South Cove on Lake Mead.

Understand the Grand Canyon

Grand Canyon Today

Grand Canyon National Park is a point of pride for the US, and continues to be one of the country's most popular national parks for both Americans and foreign visitors. The park is also the center of a thriving local economy. But it takes a little planning to keep this destination a classic: limiting helicopter traffic, minimizing trash, controlling crowds on the busy South Rim, and fostering Native American culture, to name just a few.

Best on Film

Koyaanisqatsi (1982) In this non-narrative, nonverbal film, the Grand Canyon appears in a time-lapse – clouds passing overhead, constantly changing light and color.
Thelma & Louise (1991) This women-on-the-run story ends at the Grand Canyon, though the final scene was actually shot near Moab, Utah.
Into the Wild (2007) Seeker and wanderer Chris McCandless runs the Colorado River rapids in this true-life tale.

Best in Print

Hiking Grand Canyon National Park (Ben Adkison; Falcon, 2011) Indispensable hiking guide to the canyon, with detailed descriptions and hiking tips.
Over the Edge: Death in the Grand Canyon (Michael P Ghiglieri & Thomas M Myers; Puma Press, 2001) Morbidly fascinating and informative survey of death in the canyon.
Beyond the Hundredth Meridian: John Wesley Powell and the Second Opening of the West (Wallace Stegner; Penguin, 1992) An illuminating look at John Wesley Powell's explorations of the Grand Canyon and his influence on US water policy.

Tourist Boom

A 2015 report from the National Park Service estimated that Grand Canyon National Park welcomed 4.7 million visitors in 2014 – and those visitors spent $509 million in Tusayan and other communities around the park, approximately 30% of it on lodging and another 20% on food and drink. These are significant numbers: the spending supported nearly 8000 jobs in the region and benefited the local economy to the tune of $711 million. Not bad for an attraction that only costs $30 per carload to enter.

Flyovers & Water Pollution

With annual visitor numbers to the Grand Canyon nearing five million, helicopter and plane tours do brisk business. For years, environmentalists and the NPS lobbied for the Federal Aviation Administration (FAA) to limit scenic flyovers in order to preserve a sense of serenity for other canyon visitors. In 1988 the FAA implemented flyover restrictions that limited helicopter and airplane traffic to specific corridors away from the most frequently used parts of the canyon. Scenic flyovers are also limited to certain hours of the day, and no flights are allowed below the rim except at Grand Canyon West, on the Hualapai Reservation. As a result, you probably won't notice the distant sounds of most scenic flights.

In mid-2015, the US Geological Survey released an alarming new report claiming that the levels of mercury and selenium in the Grand Canyon's section of the Colorado River – a 240-mile stretch of the waterway – were high enough to be considered a risk to fish and other wildlife. It's potentially dangerous for humans too. Scientists believe that the coal-powered Navajo Generating Station is one of the major culprits; further tests are scheduled.

Say No to Plastic

Like several other national parks in recent years, the Grand Canyon banned the sale of plastic water bottles and containers within the park in 2012. Though it's left big-name beverages brands bristling, the effort has cut down on the park's waste stream, of which plastic bottles previously accounted for 20%. The effort is part of Grand Canyon National Park's role as a Climate Friendly Park, with a goal of cutting greenhouse gas emissions by 30% by the year 2020. Bring your own water bottle and fill it up at one of the park's designated filling stations.

Native American Identity

A new initiative is set to pump up Native American cultural presence at Desert View Watchtower, one of the national park's main attractions. In July 2015, Art-Place America announced that the American Indian Alaska Native Tourism Association was the chosen recipient of a $500,000 grant that would be used to transform Desert View into an intertribal cultural heritage center – and to preserve the historic monument's famous murals. In conjunction with the annual Desert View Cultural Demonstration Series, now in its second year, the architectural monument will serve as a hub for the Grand Canyon's traditionally associated tribes, featuring artisan exhibitions, lectures, and special events.

Grand Canyon Skywalk & the Proposed Escalade

Opened in 2007, the Grand Canyon Skywalk generated a fair amount of controversy for its location, which is considered sacred, and the threat of overdevelopment around the site at Grand Canyon West, on the Hualapai Reservation. The Skywalk, an incongruously oddball glass semicircle hanging over a sheer cliff over the canyon, has proven to be an extremely popular attraction despite its relative remoteness. Bringing in much-needed revenue to the tribe, it has helped fund the paving of one of the reservation's main roads.

Following the commercial success of the Skywalk, Navajo leaders and Arizona developers have proposed the construction of the Grand Canyon Escalade, a 1.4-mile tramway that would carry visitors from the rim to the Grand Canyon's floor. Plans, which have not yet been approved, also include a restaurant and amphitheater – and the proposal has been met with heated controversy.

THE GRAND CANYON IS:

1 MILE DEEP

13 MILES ACROSS AT ITS WIDEST

277 RIVER MILES LONG

LOCATED IN COCONINO COUNTRY, ARIZONA

if 100 people visited where would they go?

82 would go to the South Rim
17 would go to the North Rim
1 would go to the Colorado River

seasonal visitation
(% of visitors)

39 — Jun-Aug
24 — Sep-Nov
13 — Dec-Feb
24 — March-May

population per sq mile

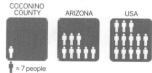

COCONINO COUNTY   ARIZONA   USA

= 7 people

History

The Grand Canyon's rich history dates back more than 10,000 years, when Paleo-Indian hunters first passed through, followed by Native American groups that migrated here in response to climate change. Later, the fate of modern Native Americans in the Grand Canyon would be determined not by the rhythms of nature, but by European encroachment and, ultimately, the US government. First protected as a game reserve and national monument, the Grand Canyon eventually became the country's 17th national park.

Ancient Cultures of the Grand Canyon

The Archaic Periods

Split-twig figurines depicting common prey like bighorn sheep, pronghorn antelope and deer can be viewed at the Tusayan Ruins & Museum on the South Rim. Radiocarbon dating tells us that these figurines are estimated to be 3200 to 5000 years old, dating to the Late Archaic period.

By 9000 years ago, Archaic cultures entered the Grand Canyon region from the Basin and Range Province to the northwest and replaced paleo culture. The Archaic cultures span the period 7000 BC to 1000 BC.

The Early Archaic period, characterized by seasonal habitation, *atlatl* (spear-throwers), woven sandals and groundstone tools, saw an increase in population on the plateaus despite the drier climate and the loss of large Pleistocene game.

About 6000 years ago, a drought that would last on and off for almost 2000 years defined the Middle Archaic period. Conditions became even tougher, and many peoples migrated to more amenable lands. Those who stayed moved between canyons and plateaus, sometimes camping in the caves and leaving evidence of their culture.

As the drought waned, about 4000 years ago (2000 BC), people returned to the region, and the 1000-year Late Archaic period began. Late Archaic evidence at the Grand Canyon includes dozens of elaborate split-twig animal figurines found in Stantons Cave, 50ft above the Colorado River in the Redwall limestone of Marble Canyon. Many are pierced by small twigs or cactus thorns, thought to represent arrows, and some were found in shrine-like arrangements. Archaeologists believe that nomadic groups used the caves for religious rituals, perhaps as a place to offer gifts to the gods in hopes of luring prey.

TIMELINE	8000 BC	7000 BC–1000 BC	1000 BC–AD 1300
	Paleo-Indian hunters migrate through the Grand Canyon region in pursuit of Pleistocene megafauna, such as mammoth and giant sloth, which had begun to disappear.	Archaic cultures occupy the canyon, leaving behind evidence of their existence in split-twig figurines and chipped-stone tools that were probably used for hunting.	Basketmaker and ancient Puebloan cultures develop farming communities in and around the canyon, establishing complex trail systems that allowed for outside contact and trade.

Ancestral Puebloans

Puebloan culture blurs with the Basketmaker culture (the canyon's earliest corn-growing people, named for the intricate coiled and watertight baskets they made), and the gradual shift from one period to the other is a result of complicated migrations and developments. Puebloan culture, as defined and explained by archaeologists, includes corn-growing cultures that inhabited the southern Colorado Plateau and the Four Corners Region. The word pueblo means 'town' and refers to the above-ground adobe or stone structures in which these people lived. Religious ceremonies took place in kivas (circular below-ground buildings reminiscent of pit houses).

Ancestral Puebloan culture is a general term that includes several distinct traditions based on pottery style, geographic location, architecture and social structure; among them are the Chacoan, Mesa Verde, Kayenta, Virgin River, Little Colorado River, Cohonina and Sinagua cultures. By about 700 AD, Basketmaker culture had been completely replaced by Puebloan culture.

Anasazi, the term traditionally used to describe the early Puebloan culture, translates roughly as 'Enemy Ancestors.' Because Hopi and Zuni find this term offensive, contemporary scholars refer to the Anasazi as 'ancestral Puebloans' or 'prehistoric Puebloans.'

HISTORY ANCIENT CULTURES OF THE GRAND CANYON

Agriculture & Abandonment

From 700 AD to 1000 AD, various strains of early Puebloan culture lived in and around the canyon. On the South Rim, the Cohonina inhabited the canyon west of Desert View (including Havasu Canyon and the Coconino Plateau) and mingled with the Kayenta, living seasonally in the uplands and along the river. Pottery shards found in Chuar Canyon, which were unearthed during a flash flood, suggest that, despite difficult conditions, a farming community thrived in the canyon 1200 years ago.

Paleoclimate research indicates that about 1000 years ago precipitation increased slightly. For the next 150 years, the Grand Canyon experienced a heyday of farming. Taking advantage of the subtle shift in climate, various bands of ancestral Puebloans spread out, strengthened and flourished. While the canyon was by no means lush, the high water table, increased precipitation and wide alluvial terraces made it more agriculturally productive than it would be today.

ANCIENT TRAILS

Ancestral Puebloan occupants of the Grand Canyon established an intricate trail system throughout the gorge and side canyons, allowing access all over the canyon and to the river. Spurs in all directions linked canyon communities and facilitated trade with cultures throughout the Southwest. Remnants of these paths can still be seen today: some were modified by prospectors, early tourist entrepreneurs and the National Park Service (NPS) and are still in use. One of the most striking of these ancestral Puebloan trails is a stick footbridge across a gap in the cliffs called the Anasazi Bridge, which can be seen on the north side of the river, upstream from President Harding Rapid.

1150–1300	1250	1540	1776
Puebloan tribes abandon their settlements across the Southwest for unknown reasons that might include severe drought, hostile invasions or a combination of both.	The Cerbat/Pai, ancestors of today's Hualapai and Havasupai, migrate from the Mojave Desert to the South Rim, while Southern Paiute migrate from southern Utah to the northern canyon.	Spanish explorer García López de Cárdenas and his party of 12 are led to the South Rim of the Grand Canyon by Hopi guides.	In searching for a path from Santa Fe to present-day Yuma, missionary Francisco Tomás Gárces encounters the Grand Canyon and is the first to call the river the Colorado.

Then relatively suddenly, between 1150 and 1200, Puebloans abandoned the Grand Canyon. Other centers of Puebloan culture, like Chaco Canyon in northwest New Mexico and Mesa Verde in Southern Colorado, were also abandoned during this period, and scientists cannot agree on exactly why such elaborate and thriving communities would so suddenly leave their homes. Analyses of tree rings, stalagmites and lake pollen suggest that a severe drought descended upon the region in about 1150.

After just a few years of drought, corn reserves dwindled and canyon people were faced with malnutrition and starvation. Though there was no single mass exodus from the canyon, Puebloan peoples drifted away. Cohonina migrated towards Flagstaff; Sinagua drifted to and blended with Hopi mesas to the east. The Kayenta villagers stayed a bit longer than their contemporaries to construct fortlike buildings along the South Rim. According to archaeologists, these defensive structures suggest that hostile invasions from migrating tribes further weakened the already vulnerable Puebloan communities and contributed to their withdrawal from the canyon.

Whatever the reason – drought, invasion or a combination of the two – by 1300 the Grand Canyon became merely an echo of the once-thriving agrarian Pueblo culture. Though the evidence suggests that they would return periodically, Puebloans never returned permanently.

The Tusayan Ruin, on the eastern side of the South Rim, may have been the last Puebloan community in the Grand Canyon region. Archaeological records show that it was not built until 1185 and was inhabited by a community of about 30 people for a mere 25 years.

Removal of Native Americans

As the farming cultures of the Pueblo people exited the canyon, other cultures moved in. The Cerbat/Pai, ancestors of today's Hualapai and Havasupai, arrived from the Mojave Desert to inhabit the western side of the canyon south of the river. It's not clear when they took up permanent residence – some scholars believe that they came to the region about 100 years after the ancestral Puebloans left, while others believe that it was their arrival that contributed to the Puebloans' departure.

From the early 19th century, US military forces pushed west across the continent, protecting settlers and wresting land from Native Americans, who had little use for European concepts of land ownership. With the 1848 Treaty of Guadalupe and the discovery of gold at Sutter's Mill in California, Americans crossed the continent in unprecedented numbers. It wasn't long before they intruded into and permanently transformed the lives and homes of Native Americans who had lived in and around the Grand Canyon for centuries.

Hualapai

After the murder of Hualapai chief Wauba Yuman in 1866, the result of ongoing conflict over land and the rights for outsiders to cross into native territory, Hualapai chief Sherum engaged American troops in a

1803	1821	1848	1850–51
The Louisiana Purchase makes the young US the northeastern neighbor of New Spain, sharing a border at the crestline of the Rocky Mountains and along the Rio Grande.	After over a decade of the Mexican War of Independence, Spain signs the Treaty of Córdoba, securing independence for the Mexican Empire (formerly known as New Spain).	The Treaty of Guadalupe Hidalgo ends the Mexican-American War and the US annexes Mexico's northern territory and Texas, a total of 914,166 sq miles that include Arizona.	The Territory of New Mexico is formed, which includes the Grand Canyon; military surveyors begin exploring and mapping the country's vast new territories.

three-year war. The US Army destroyed their homes, crops and food supplies until the Hualapai surrendered in 1869. They were forced onto a reservation on the lower Colorado and, deprived of rations and unused to the heat of the lower elevations, many died from starvation or illness. The Hualapai escaped the reservation, only to be confined again when President Chester Arthur set aside the current 1-million-acre reservation on the southern side of the Grand Canyon.

Puebloan Ruin Sites

Phantom Ranch

Tusayan Ruins & Museum

Walnut Canyon National Monument

Wupatki National Monument

Havasupai

Though the Havasupai escaped the brutality of the Indian Wars, they too were eventually forced to give up their lands and were confined to a reservation as European Americans settled in the Grand Canyon region. In 1880 President Rutherford Hayes established an area 5 miles wide and 12 miles long as the Havasupai Reservation, which eventually was expanded to its present-day boundaries. A few years later, the Bureau of Indian Affairs established schools for the Hualapai and Havasupai children to teach them the ways of the white man. Their canyon home was increasingly disturbed by Anglo explorers, prospectors and intrepid tourists as the 19th century drew to a close and the Grand Canyon became a destination for European Americans.

Paiute

Native Americans on the North Rim did not fare any better. US westward expansion brought disease to the Paiute, settlers stole the Paiute's best lands, and by the late 1860s conflict with Anglo pioneers had become common. In the early 20th century only about 100 Kaibab Paiute lived north of the canyon in Moccasin Spring. They were moved onto a reservation in 1907. Today the Kaibab Reservation surrounds Pipe Springs National Monument, in the desert about 80 miles north of the North Rim.

Spanish Explorers & Missionaries

Europeans saw the canyon for the first time in September of 1540. Spanish explorer Francisco Vásquez de Coronado believed that seven cities of gold lay in the northern interior of New Spain, and though several efforts had proved fruitless (he instead found Native American pueblos of stone and mud), he continued to traverse the region in search of gold. Native Americans told him about a great river that would reach riches at the Gulf of California, so he sent García López de Cárdenas and his party of 12 to investigate.

It is not clear where Cárdenas and his men stood when they first saw the Grand Canyon, but based on his written record historians believe it was somewhere between Moran Point and Desert View, on the South Rim. Though Hopi guides knew of relatively easy paths into the canyon,

1856–58	1858–59	1865	1866
Edward Fitzgerald Beale leads a survey mission across the desert with a caravan of camels, establishing the road that later became Route 66 (now the I-40).	First Lieutenant Joseph Christmas Ives and his expedition become the first European Americans to reach the river within the canyon; he declares the region 'altogether valueless.'	The Civil War ends; hundreds of Navajo die on the Long Walk to Fort Sumner after being forced from their traditional lands into an internment camp in eastern New Mexico.	Hualapai chief Wauba Yuman is murdered, precipitating a three-year war against the US military in which an estimated one-third of the Hualapai population are killed.

they didn't share them, and Cárdenas' men managed to descend only about one-third of the way before turning back. The canyon was too much of an obstacle, and the rewards were too little.

Finding no gold or riches of any sort, Spanish explorers left the canyon country to the Native Americans – who were not, however, left in peace. The Catholic church of Spain, more interested in converting the natives to Christianity than finding gold, spent the next several hundred years building missions in the Southwest and severely punishing resistors.

Despite the unwelcoming conditions, Spanish missionaries traversed the inhospitable terrain of Northern Arizona in search of both converts and routes to Santa Fe. Inevitably, some stumbled upon the canyon. In 1776, about 200 years after Cárdenas tried to reach the river, Francisco Tomás Gárces reached the canyon in an effort to find a path to Santa Fe from what is now Yuma, Arizona. A kind and gentle man who is widely regarded to be the second European visitor to the canyon, Gárces named the river 'Rio Colorado,' meaning 'Red River.' He spent several days with the hospitable Havasupai. Because they had been sheltered in their canyon home, the Havasupai had not yet developed a fear and hatred of Spanish missionaries, and they showered him with feasts and celebration. He marveled at their intricate system of irrigation and treated them with courtesy and respect. He continued east into Hopi country, but they refused to give him shelter or food. Later that year, Silvestre Vélez de Escalante, Francisco Atanasio Domínguez and Captain Bernardo Miera y Pacheco came upon the canyon while trying to find a route from Monterey, California, to Santa Fe.

Birth of the Southwest

In the mid-19th century several events occurred over the course of a few years that would transform the American Southwest within a half-century. With the Treaty of Guadalupe Hidalgo in 1848, the Mexican-American War ended, and the US acquired Mexico's northern territory, which would eventually become Arizona, California, Nevada, Utah, Colorado and New Mexico. This, along with the territories acquired with the Louisiana Purchase only 40 years earlier, more than doubled the size of the US and forced the federal government to grapple with the problem of running a Jeffersonian system of representative government while also maintaining a national identity despite great geographical and cultural distances. That same year, gold was discovered at Sutter's Mill in California. In 1850 the territory of New Mexico, including Arizona and the Grand Canyon, was created.

Forty-niners rushing toward gold in California, and pioneers hoping to build homes in the new West, needed wagon roads. Moreover, if the

1868	1869	1869	1870–90
The Navajo Reservation is established on 5500 sq miles in the heart of their ancient lands, eventually growing into the largest reservation in the country.	The transcontinental railroad is completed, connecting the existing eastern railroad from Council Bluffs, Iowa, to Oakland, California, and increasing the population of the West.	Geologist, naturalist and Civil War veteran John Wesley Powell and his crew of nine become the first people to successfully run the Colorado River.	Ranchers and settlers arrive in the Grand Canyon region; by 1890, the non–Native American population of the Arizona Territory reaches more than 88,000.

US was to retain control over the vast wilderness they had just acquired, it needed to know exactly what it was. And so the government sent military men to identify and map its new territory in the 1850s. Edward Fitzgerald Beale took a caravan of camels across the desert in the late 1850s, creating the road that would eventually become Route 66 (now replaced by the I-40).

In 1858 First Lieutenant Joseph Christmas Ives was appointed to explore the still-mysterious 'big canyon' region. Directed to find an inland waterway, Ives set off on the steamboat *The Explorer* on December 31, 1858, from the Gulf of Mexico. He traveled upriver for two months but crashed into a boulder in Black Canyon (near today's Hoover Dam) before ever making it into the canyon. He abandoned his river efforts and set off on Beale's road, along with artists Heinrich Baldwin Mollhausen and Baron Friedrich W Von Egloffstein, a geologist, various Native American guides, soldiers, packers, trail builders and about 150 mules. After about a month, they scrambled down a side canyon north of Peach Springs and became what historians believe to be the first European Americans known to reach the river within the canyon. Mollhausen and von Egloffstein are credited with creating the first visual representations of the Grand Canyon.

Frustrated with the difficulty of the terrain and the lack of water, Ives cut south to Beale's road west of Havasu Falls, and eventually returned east to organize the expedition's maps, landscape etchings and lithographs into a cohesive report on the 'big canyon.' While acknowledging its sublime beauty (perhaps the first to do so), Ives reported that the region was valueless, and that he expected that few (if any) explorers would find cause to venture into it again. Within 130 years of this statement,

MYSTERY IN THE CANYON

Of the many early tourists who tried to raft the river but never finished, honeymooners Glen and Bessie Hyde would become the most famous. They set out in 1928, without life jackets, to be the first man and woman pair to run the Colorado through the canyon. They ran the 424 miles from Green River, Utah, to Bright Angel Creek (including the rapids at Cataract Canyon) in 26 days and hiked up to Bright Angel Lodge for a rest, publicity photographs and interviews. Though witnesses say Glen seemed excited to continue, and loved the media attention, Bessie hinted at being less than thrilled to return to the river. As Emory Kolb and his daughter Edith walked them to the trailhead, Bessie noticed Edith's shoes and, looking at her own hiking boots, commented rather sadly, 'I wonder if I shall ever wear pretty shoes again.' As fate would have it, she never would. The honeymooners never emerged from the canyon, and their disappearance remains one of the park's greatest mysteries.

1876	1880	1883	1884
The Fred Harvey Company, aka the 'civilizer of the West,' is founded. Its owner plans to make the Grand Canyon a major tourist attraction by opening refined hotels with gourmet restaurants.	President Rutherford Hayes establishes the Havasupai Reservation on a mere 518 acres along Havasu Creek; the Havasupai accept this without opposition, for fear of expulsion from their ancestral land.	President Chester Arthur establishes the Hualapai Reservation on 1 million acres of land, part of which comprises ancestral lands of the Hualapai Nation.	Prospector John Hance, having given up on mining yields, takes the first tourists into the canyon on his mining trails and charges them $1 for dinner and lodging.

Thomas Moran's painting *The Grand Chasm of the Colorado,* purchased by Congress in 1874 for $10,000, hung in the National Capitol building and was influential in securing national park status for the Grand Canyon.

almost five million people were visiting the Grand Canyon National Park per annum, but the idea of nature as a destination in itself, as something to be preserved as an American treasure, did not become a popular notion until the late 19th century. Until that point Americans were interested in nature only in as much as it could be exploited for material gain.

John Wesley Powell

Fascinated by the reports of initial surveys of the Grand Canyon, John Wesley Powell cobbled together a makeshift team of volunteers and private funding to finance an expedition to the Colorado River. The work of this one-armed Civil War veteran and professor of geology would set the stage for the canyon's transformation from a hurdle to a destination.

In May of 1869, Powell and his crew of nine launched four wooden boats, laden with thousands of pounds of scientific equipment and supplies, from Green River, Wyoming. They floated peacefully until one of the boats, the *No Name,* smashed into rocks at rapids that Powell named Disaster Falls. Despite this and the loss of supplies, they continued down the Green River, joined the Colorado River on July 17 and floated through Glen Canyon without further mishap. The waters of the Colorado in the 'big canyon,' however, were not so kind. They portaged their heavy boats around rapids and ran others, baked under the hot sun, repaired leaks and sustained themselves on meager rations of flour, coffee and dried apples. Powell took notes on the geology and natural history, and they spent time scrambling over cliffs, taking measurements and examining rocks, canyons and streams in what Powell called their 'granite prison.'

On August 27 they came to a particularly wild rapid that Powell named Separation Rapid. Here, three men – Bill Dunn and brothers Seneca and Oramel Howland, who were exhausted, fed up with their wilderness conditions and convinced that they would never make it through alive – abandoned Powell and hiked north out of the canyon in hopes of finding civilization. Instead, it is believed that they were attacked and killed by Shivwits Paiute men who mistook them for prospectors who had murdered a Paiute woman. The Powell expedition made it through the wild water, as well as through several other rough rapids, and emerged three days later close to what is now Lake Mead. After 14 weeks on the river, Powell and his crew became the first known people to travel the length of the Colorado River through what Powell named the Grand Canyon.

Powell returned to the Colorado River in 1871 for a second expedition, this time with photographer EO Beaman, who produced about 350

1890	1890s	1893	1896
William Wallace Bass sets up a dude ranch on the South Rim and takes tourists into Havasu Canyon, befriending the Havasupai and facilitating cross-cultural exchange with the relatively isolated tribe.	A stagecoach line runs from Flagstaff to the South Rim, ferrying hardy tourists over bumpy, dusty roads on a journey that lasted one to two days.	President Benjamin Harrison proclaims the Grand Canyon a National Forest Preserve, a designation that offers some environmental protection but still allows mining and logging.	On the site where today's Bright Angel Lodge sits, the Bright Angel Hotel was originally established by James Thurber (not *that* James Thurber), who ran a stagecoach line from Flagstaff.

Hiking along the Colorado River (p170)

images of the Grand Canyon, and artist Frederick Samuel Dellenbaugh. In 1873 Thomas Moran, the landscape painter who would become the artist most associated with the Grand Canyon, and photographer John Hiller visited the rim country with Powell. Powell's 1875 report, entitled 'The Exploration of the Colorado River of the West,' as well as newspaper and magazine articles – and in particular the visual representations by Moran and Hiller that accompanied these written accounts – planted the seeds for the canyon as a tourist destination. For the first time, the general public saw spectacular images of the Grand Canyon, sparking their desire to see its grandeur for themselves. Within a quarter of a century, through the combined forces of the prospectors-turned-tourist-guides, the railroad and the Fred Harvey Company, the Grand Canyon would become an iconic American treasure.

1901	1902	1904	1905
The Atchison, Topeka and Santa Fe Railway completes a spur line to the South Rim and begins running from Williams directly to the Grand Canyon.	A survey crew caught in North Rim winter weather determined that Bright Angel Canyon was the best route to the river; this became the North Kaibab Trail.	Brothers Ellsworth and Emory Kolb set up their photography studio in a permanent building on the South Rim, directly adjacent to the Bright Angel Trailhead.	The Fred Harvey Company, in partnership with the Atchison, Topeka and Santa Fe Railway, opens El Tovar on the South Rim, designed by Mary Colter.

Tourists Arrive
Railroad to the Canyon

With the arrival of the Atlantic and Pacific Railroad to Flagstaff and Williams in the early 1880s, tourists trickled to the canyon's South Rim. In 1883 a total of 67 hardy tourists made the 20-mile trek from Peach Springs (the nearest train line to the Grand Canyon) to Diamond Creek. From there, they descended another 2 miles along Diamond Creek Wash to the Colorado River. In 1884 JH Farlee eked out the Grand Canyon's first wagon trail to Diamond Creek and built the canyon's first hotel at the end of the line.

When the railroad to the South Rim was completed in 1901, tourism at the canyon accelerated. Instead of paying $20 and enduring a teeth-rattling 12-hour stagecoach ride, visitors could pay $3.95 and reach the rim from Williams in three hours.

In 1902 brothers Ellsworth and Emery Kolb came to the canyon, and within a few years they set up a photography studio on the rim. Tourists could ride a mule into the canyon in the morning and have a photo of their journey by the next day. Fred Harvey, who joined the Santa Fe Railroad in 1876 to provide hotels and services to its passengers, earned a reputation for luxurious trackside accommodation, fine dining and impeccable service. In 1905, only four years after the train's arrival at the rim, his Fred Harvey Company built El Tovar, an elegant hotel, and established Hopi House. Fred Harvey hired Hopi to live there, demonstrate their crafts, wear native costumes and perform dances for the tourists.

Now that the Native Americans had been confined to reservations and the wilderness had been tamed, European Americans began to see an innocence and authenticity in Native American culture and in the natural landscape that was lacking in industrialized life. No longer a threat, Native Americans and their crafts and lifestyle became a subject for the tourist gaze.

The Grand Canyon, with its proximity to the Native Americans of the Southwest and its spectacular wilderness scenery that could be enjoyed from the comfort of rimside hotels, offered Americans a safe opportunity to return to a romanticized past. Furthermore, the magnificent landscape of the American West, unique in its geologic features, gave a young country looking for a history and a unifying sense of nationality something to claim. The American West gave the country a unique identity, and tourists flocked to the Grand Canyon.

Arnold Berke's *Mary Colter: Architect of the Southwest* is a beautifully illustrated and well-written examination of the life and work of Mary Colter.

1906	1907	1907	1908
Grand Canyon Game Preserve is set aside on the North Rim; it limits livestock grazing but also results in the hunting and eventual disappearance of indigenous wolves and mountain lions.	Tourists cross the Colorado River in a cage strung on a cable built by David Rust, who ran a tourist camp at the bottom of the canyon.	Kaibab Paiute are moved to a reservation encompassing fewer than 200 sq miles that do not border Grand Canyon National Park and comprise a fraction of their ancestral lands.	President Teddy Roosevelt creates Grand Canyon National Monument, one of the acts for which he became known as a pioneering conservationist in the US.

Tourism on the North Rim

Because of its isolation, tourism on the North Rim developed more slow-ly, and even today it only receives 10% of the park's visitors. The Arizona Strip, the remote desert country north of the rim, was originally settled in the mid-19th century by Mormons, who were trying to escape increasingly strict laws against polygamy.

Most visitors to the Kaibab Plateau went for sport hunting. In June 1906, Teddy Roosevelt created Grand Canyon Game Preserve. The United States Forest Service prohibited deer hunting in the preserve and set about eliminating all of the animal's predators. James T 'Uncle Jim' Owens, in his capacity as the reserve's first game warden, guided hunting trips and oversaw the killing of hundreds upon hundreds of badgers, coyotes, wolverines, cougars and grizzly bears.

MARY COLTER'S GRAND VISION

Mary Colter's buildings blend so seamlessly into the landscape that, were it not for the tourists strolling around them, you could conceivably not even notice the structures. Indeed, Colter's buildings add to the beauty of Grand Canyon National Park because they succeed so magnificently in adding nothing at all.

In 1883, at the age of 14, Mary Colter (1869–1958) graduated from high school in St Paul, Minnesota. She studied art in San Francisco and spent her entire career designing hotels, shops, restaurants and train stations for the Fred Harvey Company and the Santa Fe Railway. Beginning in the late 1870s, these two companies worked as a team to transform the American West into a tourist destination.

Colter's work follows the sensibility of the Arts and Crafts Movement. In keeping with the nationalist spirit of the late 19th century, and reacting against industrialized society, the Arts and Crafts aesthetic (or Craftsman style) looked toward American models, rather than European traditions, for inspiration. The movement revered handcrafted objects, clean and simple lines and the incorporation of indigenous materials. For an excellent example of well-preserved, classic Arts and Crafts design, stop by the Riordan Mansion in Flagstaff.

Colter spent a great deal of time researching all her buildings, exploring ancient Hopi villages, studying Native American culture and taking careful notes. The Colter buildings in Grand Canyon National Park use local materials such as Kaibab limestone and pine, and incorporate stone, wood, iron, glass and brick. They embrace Native American crafts like woven textile and geometric design, and echo Indian architecture with kiva fireplaces and vigas (rafters) on the ceiling.

The conundrum of preserving expanses of Western land as sacred American wilderness while at the same time developing them for tourists was solved in part by Colter's brilliant designs. Her buildings, known as 'National Park Service rustic,' stand in harmony with their natural environment and served as models and inspiration for subsequent tourist services in national parks throughout the country.

1919	1922	1926	1928
The Grand Canyon finally earns a national park designation, becoming the US' 17th national park; during this year, the Grand Canyon receives 44,000 visitors.	The Fred Harvey Company builds Phantom Ranch, designed by Mary Colter, along the Colorado River at the confluence of Bright Angel Creek and Phantom Creek.	Automobiles overtake the railroad as the most popular form of transportation to the canyon, an upward trend that continues to this day.	Construction of the Kaibab Suspension Bridge (Black Bridge), a rigid suspension span, replaces the old swinging bridge and completes the cross-canyon Kaibab Trail.

As the NPS developed Grand Canyon National Park, Havasupai who had been living around the South Rim and Indian Garden area for generations were compelled to move off the land. The last Havasupai living at Indian Garden were forced out by the NPS in 1928.

Following the arrival of the first car to the North Rim in 1909, the forest service began advertising scenic attractions on the Kaibab Plateau. In 1913 the forest service built the 56-mile Grand Canyon Hwy to the Bright Angel Ranger Station, at Harvey Meadow. Aldus Jensen and his wife ran a small tourist service with tent accommodation. They led guests along the Rust Trail to the river, where they would connect with Fred Harvey wranglers. In 1917 Wylie's Way Camp opened near the fire tower at Bright Angel Point, and Jensen closed down his services. A step above tents, Wylie's Way Camp could accommodate up to 25 guests and offered tent cabins; guided tours to Cape Royal, Point Sublime and other destinations; mule trips; and a central dining room.

Visitors arriving at the North Rim from the north had to take the 135-mile stagecoach from Marysvale, Utah, to Kanab and then travel the 80 miles or so to the rim by whatever means they could find. Alternatively, beginning in 1907, they could hike into the canyon from the South Rim, cross the Colorado River in a cage strung on a cable, and hike up to the North Rim on the North Kaibab Trail (constructed in 1903). On the canyon's bottom, visitors stayed in a tourist camp at the mouth of Bright Angel Creek, the predecessor to Colter's 1922 Phantom Ranch.

Also in 1922, Gronway and Chauncey Parry began automobile tours to the North Rim, and Will S Rust opened a tourist camp north of the park. In 1919 a rough dirt road from Kanab to the North Rim was completed, and by 1925 more than 7000 visitors arrived at Bright Angel Point. In 1928 Union Pacific architect GS Underwood designed the original Grand Canyon Lodge, and a suspension bridge was built across the river to connect the South and North Kaibab Trails. Though a fire on September 1, 1932, destroyed the main lodge on the North Rim, it was rebuilt in 1937, and the guest cabins, still used today, were left unharmed.

Evolution of a Park

In 1908, President Theodore Roosevelt created the Grand Canyon National Monument, and in 1919 President Woodrow Wilson made Grand Canyon the 17th national park in the US. Over 44,000 people visited the park that year. By 1956 more than one million people would visit the Grand Canyon annually.

The Great Depression slowed the frenzy of park development, and from 1933 to 1942, the Civilian Corps Conservation, the Public Works Administration and the Works Progress Administration did everything from touching up buildings to creating trails and cleaning ditches. Fewer tourists visited during this period, giving rangers breathing room to develop interpretive programs – the predecessors of today's ranger talks.

The dearth of visitors from the Depression through to the end of WWII resulted in a quieter, more relaxed Grand Canyon National Park.

1932	1936	1937	1952
A fire destroys most of the original Grand Canyon Lodge, built just a few years earlier. A new (and smaller) lodge, the one we know today, goes up in the same location in 1936.	Hoover Dam (formerly known as Boulder Dam), a feat of engineering, is built on the Colorado River west of the canyon, creating Lake Mead.	After a fire destroys the main lodge, Grand Canyon Lodge on the North Rim is rebuilt according to the original aesthetic, with ponderosa-pine logs and Kaibab limestone.	Georgie White becomes the first woman to raft the full length of the Grand Canyon, then goes on to become the first woman to offer commercial rafting trips in the region.

However, as soon as the war ended, Americans – in love with their cars and eager to explore and celebrate their country – inundated the national parks. The flood prompted another flurry of construction, and from 1953 to 1968 the park built more trails, enhanced existing trails, improved roads and built Maswik, Kachina and Thunderbird Lodges. Steel and concrete buildings joined the classic rustic style of El Tovar and Mary Colter's architecture.

In 1975, President Gerald Ford signed the Grand Canyon National Park Enlargement Act, doubling the size of the park by integrating it with Grand Canyon National Monument and Marble Canyon National Monument. This same act returned land to the Havasupai. The following year, the park received three million visitors. In 1979, Grand Canyon National Park was designated a Unesco World Heritage site.

Over at the West Rim, the Hualapai Nation opened Grand Canyon Skywalk in 2007. This horseshoe-shaped glass platform, cantilevered 4000ft above the canyon floor, brought with it a flood of tourism and controversy over the sustainability of more development in this fragile environment. Fortunately for the tribe, the Skywalk is a wildly popular attraction despite its relative isolation, bringing much-needed revenue to the Hualapai. As in the national park and Havasu Canyon, the constant challenge of balancing tourism with environmental stewardship continues.

Proposed construction of two gigantic dams on the Colorado in the mid-'60s was famously quashed by public protest after the Sierra Club published full-page ads in major newspapers asking, 'Should we also flood the Sistine Chapel so tourists can get nearer the ceiling?'

HISTORY EVOLUTION OF A PARK

1956	1963	1979	2007
Two airplanes on eastward flights from Los Angeles collide mid-air over the canyon, resulting in the establishment of a national air-traffic control system.	Controversial Glen Canyon Dam is built on the Colorado River east of the canyon, flooding and thus destroying Glen Canyon to create what is now Lake Powell.	Grand Canyon National Park is designated a Unesco World Heritage site, recognized not only for its extraordinary beauty but also for its geologic and ecological significance.	The Hualapai Nation opens the controversial glass Skywalk at Grand Canyon West, bringing droves of tourist traffic to the relatively remote West Rim.

Grand Geology

While neither the longest nor the deepest canyon in the world, the Grand Canyon is certainly one of the most awe-inspiring. For geologists, the canyon showcases a remarkably well-preserved, two-billion-year-old slice of geologic history. In these exposed layers, half of the earth's life span is revealed, serving as a window into our planet's past. And for nongeologists? One look down from the canyon's edge, and you might develop a sudden interest in the field.

The Story in the Rocks

Vishnu Schist & Zoroaster Granite

The comprehensive, authoritative (and rather technical) *Grand Canyon Geology*, edited by Stanley Beus and Michael Morales, is an informative read for those interested in geology.

The story begins in the canyon's innermost recesses, where the Colorado River continues to carve a deep channel into progressively older rock. The bottommost layer, Vishnu schist, is dark and fine-grained, with vertical or diagonal bands that contrast with the canyon's horizontal upper layers. Down around Phantom Ranch, look for intruding bands of pinkish Zoroaster granite, in gorgeous contrast. Together, these are among the oldest exposed rocks on the earth's surface.

The schist offers evidence that two billion years ago the canyon region lay beneath an ancient sea. For tens of millions of years, silt and clay eroded into the water from adjacent landmasses, settling to the seafloor. These sediments, along with occasional dustings of lava and ash, accumulated to a thickness of 5 miles and were later buried beneath another 10 miles of additional sediment. By 1.7 billion years ago these layers had buckled and uplifted into a mighty mountain range that rose above the water. In the process, intense heat and pressure transformed the sedimentary layers into metamorphic schist and gneiss.

Stromatolites

At the time, 1.7 billion years ago, the region lay near the equator, but the uplifted landmass soon began a northward migration while undergoing a long spell of erosion. So much of the uplifted material eroded away that it left a significant gap (known as the Great Unconformity) in the geologic record – from 1.7 billion to 1.2 billion years ago. Lost with hardly a trace was the mountain range itself, which finally wore down into a low coastal plain. Gradually the landmass sank back into the sea, providing a platform for marine algae, which secreted the Bass limestone that now sits atop the Vishnu schist. Marine fossils in the Bass limestone include such primitive life forms as cabbage-like stromatolites.

The Precambrian Era & the Great Unconformity

In the late Precambrian era (1.2 billion to 570 million years ago) the region alternated between marine and coastal environments as the ocean repeatedly advanced and retreated, each time leaving distinctive layers of sediment and structural features. Pockmarks from raindrops, cracks in drying mud and ripple marks in sand have all been preserved in one form or another, alongside countless other clues. Much of this evidence was lost as the forces of erosion scraped the land back down to Vishnu schist. The resulting gap in the geologic record is called the Great Uncon-formity, where older rocks abut against much newer rocks with no in-tervening layers. Fortunately, pockets of ancient rock that once perched atop the Vishnu schist still remain and lie exposed along the North and South Kaibab Trails, among other places.

The Paleozoic Era

The Precambrian era came to an end about 570 million years ago. The subsequent Paleozoic era (570 to 245 million years ago) spawned nearly all of the rock formations visitors see today. The Paleozoic also ushered in the dramatic transition from primitive organisms to an explosion of complex life forms that spread into every available aquatic and terrestri-al niche – the beginning of life as we know it. The canyon walls contain an abundant fossil record of these ancient animals, including shells such as cephalopods and brachiopods, trilobites, and the tracks of reptiles and amphibians.

The Paleozoic record is particularly well preserved in the layers cut by the Colorado, as the region has been little altered by geologic events such as earthquakes faulting or volcanic activity. Every advance and retreat of the ancient ocean laid down a characteristic layer that documents whether it was a time of deep oceans, shallow bays, active coastline, mudflats or elevated landscape. Geologists have learned to read these strata and to estimate climatic conditions during each episode.

The science of stratigraphy (the reading of rock layers) stemmed from work at the canyon in the 19th and early 20th centuries, at a time when American geology was in its infancy and considered vastly inferior by European geologists.

The Mesozoic Period & the Kaibab Uplift

Considering the detailed Paleozoic record, it's puzzling that evidence of the following Mesozoic period (245 to 70 million years ago) is entirely ab-sent at the canyon, even though its elaborate layers are well represented just miles away on the Colorado Plateau and in nearby Zion, Bryce and Arches National Parks. Towering over the landscape just south of the South Rim, Red Butte is a dramatic reminder of how many thousands of feet of Mesozoic sediments once covered the canyon 70 million years ago. So what happened to all of this rock, which vanished before the river even started shaping the canyon? About 70 million years ago the same events that gave rise to the Rocky Mountains created a buckle in the earth known as the Kaibab Uplift, a broad dome that rose several thousand feet above the surrounding region. Higher and more exposed, the upper layers of this dome eroded quickly and completely.

Evidence from the past 70 million years is equally scarce at the canyon, as the movement of materials has been away from the canyon rather than into it. Volcanism has added a few layers of rock in parts of the west canyon, where lava flows created temporary dams across the canyon or simply flowed over the rim in spectacular lava waterfalls, the latter now

On the South Rim, rangers lead daily fossil walks; these easy walks examine marine fossils along a half-mile stretch along the rim. Better yet, they offer the opportunity to ask questions and chat with the canyon's experts.

GRAND GEOLOGY THE STORY IN THE ROCKS

TRAIL OF TIME

As you walk the Rim Trail on the South Rim, you'll notice the Trail of Time exhibit, which debuted in 2010. Each one million years is represented by 1m (3.3ft) along the way, marked by bronze signs embedded in the trail. Alongside the trail are beautiful, polished examples of stone from geologic layers deep within the canyon that correspond with the time period on the trail. Interpretive signs and viewing spots dot the gentle trail, which you can follow for about two miles from Yavapai Geology Museum & Observation Station back to the Bright Angel Lodge area.

Even on the shortest walk along the edge of the South Rim, you'll spot many rocks that are relatively easy to identify. A few to look for include quartz, calcite, clay, gypsum, dolomite, hematite, feldspar and augite.

frozen in time in places such as Lava Falls. The stretching of the earth's crust also tilted the region to the southwest, shifting drainage patterns accordingly.

But the story that interests visitors most, namely how the canyon has changed in the past five million years, is perhaps the most ambiguous chapter of all. Geologists have several competing theories but few clues. One intriguing characteristic is that the canyon's eastern end is much older than the western portion, suggesting that two separate rivers carved the canyon. This fits into the oft-repeated 'stream piracy' theory that the Kaibab Uplift initially served as a barrier between two major river drainage systems. The theory assumes that the western drainage system eroded quickly into the soft sediments and carved eastward into the uplift, eventually breaking through the barrier and 'capturing' the flow of the ancient Colorado River, which then shifted course down this newly opened route.

Alternate theories assume other river routes or different timing of the erosion, placing it either before or after the uplift. Until more evidence is uncovered, visitors will have to simply marvel at the canyon and formulate their own theories about how this mighty river cut through a giant bulge in earth's crust millions of years ago.

A ROCK PRIMER

Rocks are divided into three large classes – sedimentary, igneous and metamorphic – each of which are well represented in the Grand Canyon.

Sedimentary

Sedimentary rock originates as accumulations of sediments and particles that cement together over time. Borne by water or the wind, the sediments generally settle in horizontal layers that preserve many features, suggesting how they formed. Three types of sedimentary rock are present in the canyon:

Limestone Comprises little more than calcium carbonate, a strong cement that softens and easily erodes when wet.

Sandstone Consists of sand particles that stack poorly, leaving lots of room for the calcium carbonate cement to penetrate, making this a very hard and durable rock.

Mudstone (including shale) At the opposite end of the spectrum from limestone, mudstone consists of flaky particles that stack so closely together there's little room for the binding cement, thus it is often very soft and breakable.

Igneous

Igneous rock originates as molten magma, which cools either deep underground or after erupting to the surface as lava or volcanic ash. Volcanic rocks are common west of Toroweap Valley, where they form such prominent features as Vulcans Throne and Lava Falls. Granite that cooled deep inside the earth lies exposed along the inner gorge – in fact, canyon explorer John Wesley Powell originally named the river corridor Granite Gorge.

Metamorphic

Metamorphic rock starts out as either sedimentary or igneous, then transforms into other kinds of rock following exposure to intense heat or pressure, especially where the earth's crust buckles and folds into mountain ranges. Metamorphic rock usually remains hidden deep underground. Two types of metamorphic rock are common in the canyon:

Schist Deriving from shale, sandstone or volcanic rock, schist lines the inner gorge and is distinguished by narrow, wavy bands of shiny mica flakes.

Gneiss Forming light-colored intrusions within the schist, gneiss is characterized by its coarse texture and the presence of quartz (crystalline and colorless or translucent) and feldspar.

Reading the Formations

After the initial awe has worn off, many visitors are eager to learn how to identify the formations that so neatly layer the canyon. The distinctive sequence of color and texture is worth learning, as you'll see it over and over again on each rim, from each viewpoint and along each trail.

Kaibab Limestone

Starting at the top, a layer of creamy white Kaibab limestone caps the rim on both sides of the canyon. This formation is about 300ft thick and erodes to form blocky cliffs. Limestone surfaces are pitted and pock-marked, and rainwater quickly seeps into the rock to form sinkholes and underground passages. Fossils include brachiopods, sponges and corals.

Toroweap Formation

The Toroweap Formation is the vegetated slope between the cliffs of Kaibab limestone above and the massive Coconino cliffs below. Similar in composition to the Kaibab, the Toroweap is a pale yellow to gray crumbly limestone that also contains marine fossils.

Coconino Sandstone

It's quickly evident how sandstone erodes differently from limestone when you descend past Coconino sandstone along the Bright Angel Trail, one of the few places a trail can negotiate these sheer 350ft cliffs. Inspect the rock face closely to spot fine crosshatches, evidence of windblown ripples that once crisscrossed huge sand dunes. Even more fascinating is the wealth of fossilized millipede, spider, scorpion and lizard tracks found in this formation.

Hermit Shale

Below the mighty Coconino sandstone cliffs lies a slope of crumbly red Hermit shale. This fine-grained shale formed under shallow tidal conditions and contains fossilized mud cracks, ripple marks and the footprints of reptiles and amphibians. Today it supports a distinctive band of shrubs and trees including oak, hop tree and serviceberry. Hermit shale is so soft that in the western canyon it has eroded completely, leaving a broad terrace of Esplanade sandstone.

Supai Group

Just below the Hermit shale are the red cliffs and ledges of the Supai Group, similar in composition and color but differing in hardness. This is a set of shale, limestone and sandstone layers, and each dominates different portions of the canyon. All formed under similar swampy coastal conditions, where shallow waters mingled with sand dunes. Deposited some 300 million years ago when amphibians first evolved, these formations preserve early footprints of these new animals. Supai cliffs can be stained red by iron oxides or black from iron or manganese.

Redwall Limestone

After the Supai Group comes the famous Redwall limestone, one of the canyon's most prominent features. Viewed from the rim, the Redwall is a huge red cliff that towers 500ft to 800ft over the broad Tonto Platform. The Redwall also forms a dividing line between forest habitats above and desert habitats below. The rock is actually light-gray limestone that has been stained red by iron oxides washed down from layers above. This formation is pitted with many caves and alcoves and contains abundant marine fossils, including trilobites, snails, clams and fish.

The steep Hermit Trail offers excellent opportunities to see various types of fossils. Near the trailhead, the Kaibab limestone holds marine fossils. About a mile down the trail, fossilized reptile tracks appear in Coconino sandstone, and not quite 2 miles down you can find fossils of ferns.

To identify what geologic layers you're gaping at as you hike the Bright Angel Trail, pocket the fabulous laminated *Field Guide to Geology Along the Bright Angel Trail* by Dave Thayer. Containing basic explanations and illustrations about canyon geology, it's a handy little reference guide that weighs next to nothing.

The Yavapai Geology Museum & Observation Station on the South Rim, aside from having fantastic canyon views, features kid-friendly interactive exhibits explaining the geology of the canyon from various angles, and binoculars to check out the main exhibit. Rangers give daily geology talks here; for current info check *The Guide,* the NPS-produced guide that all visitors receive upon entry to the park.

Muav Limestone

Muav limestone is a small slope of varying thickness that marks the junction of Redwall sandstone and the Tonto Platform. This marine formation contains few fossils but features many eroded cavities and passages.

Bright Angel Shale

Perched just above the dark inner gorge, the broad, gently sloping Tonto Platform is the only break in a long jumble of cliffs and ledges. The platform is not a formation at all but rather the absence of one, where soft greenish Bright Angel shale has been largely stripped away to reveal the hard Tapeats sandstone beneath. These slopes of grayish-green shale can be seen on the South Kaibab Trail; however, seen from the river its intact layers of green and purple are remarkably colorful.

Tapeats Sandstone

The last and oldest Paleozoic sedimentary layer is the Tapeats sandstone, below which lies the huge gap (the Great Unconformity) that separates the sedimentary layers of the canyon from the ancient Vishnu schist of the inner gorge. Collectively referred to as the Tonto Group, Tapeats, Bright Angel and Muav all formed along the same ocean shoreline. Tapeats originated with coarse cobbles along an ancient beach, Bright Angel shale comprises fine mud deposits that collected just offshore from the beach, and Muav limestone consists of calcium carbonate that fused in deep water.

A Pioneering Geologist

The first geologist to visit the Grand Canyon was a trailblazer in his field. John Strong Newberry, born in Connecticut in 1822, wasn't just a geologist, either: he was also a physician and a writer, and the driving force behind the construction of one of the finest museums of his time.

After studying both paleontology and medicine in Paris, Newberry returned to the US, where he joined several exploratory expeditions in the western US, specifically in the uncharted regions around present-day Arizona, New Mexico, California, Utah and Colorado. One of these expeditions, in 1859, yielded a surprising result: Newberry and his colleagues found the remains of the 12-ton dinosaur known as Dystrophaeus. Around the same time, Newberry became the first geologist to visit the Grand Canyon. His hand-colored map, *Rio Colorado of the West*, is considered one of the earliest visual representations of the region. One of Newberry's students, Grove Karl Gilbert, visited the Grand Canyon in 1871 and 1872 and named several natural features, including the Colorado Plateau.

Around the same time as his Grand Canyon expedition, Newberry was offered a professorship at Columbian University (now Columbia University). In 1866, he became chair of the geology department. Donating a number of rocks and fossils from his personal collection, Newberry founded a museum at the university featuring 100,000 specimens: one of the best mineral museums in the world at the time. Today, Newberry is widely hailed as one of the grandfathers of American geology.

Forces at Work

What's truly remarkable about the Grand Canyon is not how big it is, but how small it is. In terms of sheer volume, much more material has been removed from the Grand Wash Trough just below the canyon or other stretches where the river meanders across vast floodplains. But the canyon's narrow scale continues to concentrate erosive forces in dramatic fashion.

Obviously foremost among the erosive forces is water, which chisels virtually every inch of the landscape. Its differing effect on various rock types is readily apparent in the canyon's stair-step profile – the softer rock formations crumbling into gentle slopes at the foot of sheer hard cliffs.

On a subtle level, water may simply seep deeply into the rock. The water gradually weakens the rock matrix, causing large or small bits of rock to break free in the form of landslides.

A weathering effect known as frost riving occurs when water works down into cracks and freezes. Freezing water exerts a tremendous outward force (20,000lb per square inch), which wedges into these crevices, prying loose blocks of rock from the canyon cliffs.

Streams have gradually eroded defined side canyons cn both rims, cutting back ever deeper into their headwalls. This effect is especially pronounced on the higher-altitude North Rim, as it catches more runoff from passing storm systems. This rim angles to the south, pouring its runoff into the canyon. As the South Rim likewise slopes to the south, its waters flow away from the canyon.

As parallel side canyons cut back toward their headwalls, they create the canyon's distinctive temples and amphitheaters. Neighboring streams erode either side of a long promontory or finger of rock, then carve the base of the promontory, leaving the tip stranded in open space. Over time these isolated islands of elevated rock weather into rugged spires called temples, while the headwalls of the side canyons become amphitheaters.

Water is not always as patient and imperceptible. Late-summer thunderstorms cause flash floods that resculpt the landscape in minutes. A tiny trickling brook carrying grains of sand can quickly explode into a torrent that tosses house-sized boulders with ease.

Although the Colorado cut through the soft sedimentary layers at lightning speed. the river has now reached extremely hard Vishnu schist, and erosion has slowed dramatically. As the river approaches sea level, downward erosion will cease altogether, even as the canyon continues to widen. This lateral (sideways) erosion proceeds 10 times faster than downward cutting. Thus, far in the future, the Grand Canyon may be referred to as the Grand Valley.

Memorize the catchphrase 'Know The Canyon's History, Study Rocks Made By Time,' in which the capital letters represent the formations frcm rim to canyon floor (eg K for Kaibab limestone). Know (Kaibab limestone) The (Toroweap Formation) Canyon's (Coconino Sandstone) History (Hermit Shale) Study (Supai Formation) Rocks (Redwall Limestone) Made (Muav Limestone) By (Bright Angel Shale) Time (Tapeats Sandstone).

GRAND GEOLOGY FORCES AT WORK

ED FREEMAN / GETTY IMAGES ©

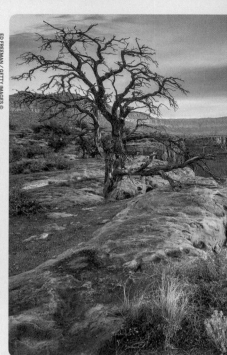

1. Mather Point (p81) offers a view of Vishnu Temple **2.** Toroweap (p143) **3.** Havasu Falls (p110) **4.** Bright Angel Trail (p60)

THOMAS JANISCH / GETTY IMAGES ©

Geologic Wonders

The entire national park is a geologic spectacle, but a few landmarks stand out from the rest. Even if you don't get the chance to see all of the following natural wonders in person, you may recognize them: they're prominently featured on postcards.

Bright Angel Canyon

An excellent example of how creeks follow fault lines across the landscape. Accessible from the South Rim, it's located partway down the Bright Angel Trail (p60) on the path to Phantom Ranch.

Havasu Creek

Stupendous travertine formations and beautiful waterfalls. A tributary leading into the Colorado River, Havasu Creek (p180) runs through Havasu Canyon and the village of Supai.

Toroweap Overlook

The canyon's most dramatic viewpoint (p143). It's located 3000ft above the Colorado River in a remote section of the North Rim, approximately 55 miles west of the North Rim headquarters.

Vishnu Temple

One of the canyon's most prominent temples (p140), it's visible from the South Kaibab Trail and lookout points such as Mather Point on the South Rim.

Wildlife of the Grand Canyon

Wildlife in the park ranges from secretive bighorn sheep and prehistoric condors to scampering lizards and nosy ringtail cats, all scattered across a vast region. For some species the Grand Canyon presents an insurmountable obstacle, while for others it's a life-sustaining corridor through a forbidding desert. If you remain patient and alert, you'll spot some of these canyon denizens, but while you wait for an appearance, it doesn't hurt to learn about their background and habitat. For more information about the mammals, birds and reptiles and amphibians living in the Grand Canyon, see p211.

Whether you enjoy the aerial acrobatics of swifts and swallows atop rimside cliffs or the bright songs of warblers among riverside thickets, there's no question that the canyon's 373 bird species are among the region's premier highlights.

Animals

Grand Canyon National Park is home to 373 bird species, 89 mammal species, 56 reptile and amphibian species, and 17 fish species.

Insects

Summer visitors will likely hear desert cicadas, whose ceaseless rasping and clicking is produced by vibrating membranes stretched over resonating sound chambers. Finding one of these inch-long insects is another matter altogether, as they're masters of camouflage – one reason they're able to screech all day and avoid predators.

Also notable are inch-long, shiny metallic-blue carpenter bees, which tunnel through dead wood in dry forested areas. Unlike colonial hive-making bees, carpenter bees lead solitary lives and spend much of their time chasing away interlopers who might move into their tunnels.

The canyon's many butterfly species are highlighted by the distinctive orange-and-black monarch butterfly, which flutters through the park in large numbers in late summer, en route to Mexican wintering grounds. This large, showy butterfly avoids predators because as a larva it feeds on milkweed plants that contain noxious alkaloids – animals that try to eat monarchs suffer a severe reaction to these plant compounds.

Fish

The Colorado River was once the watery home to a thriving variety of fish. But only the strong survived: it's an aquatic habitat characterized by floods and freezes, heavy silt, and hot summertime temperatures, not to mention major alterations to the environment by the construction of the Glen Canyon Dam upstream.

As a result, the river has just eight fish species considered native to the Grand Canyon, and only five are still found in the park. Many are endemic, found only here in the river basin. The Grand Canyon's resident fish include the large humpback chub and razorback suckers, both considered endangered species.

Efforts are underway to restore some of the park's native fish. At the time of writing, park biologists were working to remove non-native trout from Bright Angel Creek and Shinumo Creek to make room for a reintroduction of native fish, which is considered an important step toward sustaining ecological integrity in the park.

Plants

The park supports a fantastic mix of plant communities and is home to more than 1400 species from four of North America's major biological provinces – the Rocky Mountains and the Mojave, Sonoran and Great Basin Deserts. Each province contributes unique species to the mix. Plants of the Rocky Mountain province are found on both rims, especially the North Rim, where Engelmann spruce and quaking aspen form distinctive moist forests. Plants of the desert provinces occupy the inner canyon, where the climate is much hotter and drier. Mojave plants are found from downriver up to Hundred and Fifty Mile Canyon, Sonoran plants (including ocotillo and mesquite) dominate the central canyon, while Great Basin plants (such as rabbitbrush and sagebrush) take over from lower Marble Canyon to Lees Ferry.

Trees

Pine, Spruce & Aspen

Due to their prominence and longevity, trees serve as excellent indicators of different life zones and local environmental conditions. The stately ponderosa pine, for example, defines the distinctive belt between 6000ft and 8000ft. In many places along the North Rim and on the highest points of the South Rim, this species forms nearly pure stands that cover many acres. To identify this species, look for large spiny cones, long needles in clusters of three, and yellowish bark that smells like butterscotch.

At higher elevations ponderosa pines mingle with two other species that characterize the Rocky Mountain boreal forest. Engelmann spruce has a curious bluish tinge to its needles and inch-long cylindrical cones with paper-thin scales. To confirm its identity, grasp a branch and feel for sharp spiny-tipped needles that prick your hand. Young Engelmann spruces are a favorite choice for Christmas trees because they flaunt such perfect shapes. Quaking aspen is immediately recognizable for its smooth, white bark and circular leaves. Every gust of wind sets these leaves quivering on their flattened stems, an adaptation for shaking off late snowfalls that would otherwise damage fragile leaves.

Aspen groves comprise genetically identical trunks sprouting from a common root system that may grow to more than a hundred acres in size. By budding repeatedly from these root systems, aspens have what has been called 'theoretical immortality' – some aspen roots are thought to be more than a million years old.

WILDLIFE OF THE GRAND CANYON PLANTS

Of the six rattlesnake species found in the canyon, the most common is the Grand Canyon pink rattlesnake, a subspecies of the Western Diamondback that evolved to blend in with the warm tints of the canyon's geologic layers.

If you spend a night below the rim – at Indian Garden or in Havasu Canyon, for example – you may be treated to an incredible chorus of frogs and toads croaking en masse, the barbaric yawps echoing off canyon walls like some Godzilla-sized canyon creature.

WILDLIFE SPOTTING

California condors In front of Bright Angel Lodge at the South Rim, look for California condors hanging out on ledges below. From any viewpoint on either rim, you will often see them wheeling around on thermals.

Elk and mule deer It's not uncommon to encounter roaming elk and mule deer in wooded areas on both rims, even in the middle of the day. Show up in the early morning around El Tovar, on the South Rim, or around dusk.

Bighorn sheep More elusive, but we've encountered one grazing placidly in a drainage off of the heavily trafficked Bright Angel Trail. You'll have a better chance of spotting them from a river vantage point.

Mountain lion If you are lucky enough to sight a mountain lion, buy yourself a lottery ticket immediately.

THIRSTY ELK

It might be difficult, or even impossible, to spot a bear in the park – but it's not the case when it comes to elk. The largest members of the deer family have made their presence known quite visibly, as in a famous 2014 incident when hikers ran into several elk helping themselves to water at one of the national park's water bottle filling stations on the South Kaibab Trail, using their snouts to push up the levers that open the taps. Though no one was hurt, the elk reportedly behaved aggressively to the hikers, and the incident led park officials to 'elk-proof' some of the park's water stations.

There are two varieties of elk in the park today, including the Rocky Mountain Elk, a group introduced to the Grand Canyon from Yellowstone from 1913 to 1928. Males are lighter in color than females and can reach up to 700lb. Females give birth to calves in the late spring and early summer. Both are considered the most dangerous animals in the park: don't approach them for any reason, even if you're eager to fill your water bottle.

Piñon-Juniper Woodlands

Habitats at the lower edge of the ponderosa pine belt are increasingly arid, but two trees do particularly well along this desert fringe. Piñon pines are well known for their highly nutritious and flavorful seeds, sold as 'pine nuts' in grocery stores. These same seeds have been a staple for Native Americans wherever the trees grow, and many animals feast on the seeds when they ripen in the fall. Piñons have stout rounded cones and short paired needles. Together with Utah junipers, piñon pines form a distinctive community that covers millions of acres in the Southwest. Such 'PJ woodlands' dominate broad swaths of the South Rim and canyon walls down to 4000ft. Blue, berrylike cones and diminutive scalelike needles distinguish junipers from other trees. Birds feed extensively on juniper 'berries', prompting the seeds to sprout by removing their fleshy coverings.

Oaks

Consorting with piñons, junipers and ponderosas is the beautiful little Gambel oak, whose dark-green leaves turn shades of yellow and red in autumn and add a classy palette of color to an already stunning landscape. Often occurring in dense thickets, oaks produce copious quantities of nutritious, tasty acorns long favored by Native Americans and used to make breads, pancakes, soups and ground meal.

Removal of invasive tamarisk is an ongoing task in the riparian areas in and around the Grand Canyon. You can often find excellent short-term volunteer opportunities through Grand Canyon Trust Volunteers (www. grandcanyon trust.org/ volunteer), which works in conjunction with the National Park Service to remove tamarisk and other non-native plants.

Cottonwood

Rivers and watercourses in this harsh desert landscape are lined with thin ribbons of water-loving plants that can't survive elsewhere. Towering prominently above all others is the showy Fremont cottonwood, whose large, vaguely heart-shaped leaves rustle wildly in any wind. Hikers in the canyon's scorching depths find welcome respite in the shade of this tree. In spring, cottonwoods produce vast quantities of cottony seed packets that fill the air and collect in every crack and crevice.

Tamarisk

Since construction of upstream dams, aggressive weedy tamarisk has replaced ancestral communities of willows and other native plants. Though this delicately leaved plant from Eurasia sports a handsome coat of soft pink flowers through summer, its charms end there, for this plant robs water from the soil and completely overwhelms native plant communities. Producing a billion seeds per plant and spreading quickly, this species now dominates virtually every water source in the Southwest deserts.

Shrubs

Acacia & Mesquite

Despite the prevalence of tamarisk along stream banks, a few native plants manage to hold on. Easily recognized are catclaw acacia and honey mesquite, thorny members of the pea family that produce seeds in elongated, brown peapods. Each species features delicate leaflets arranged in featherlike sprays. Mesquite was a staple among Southwest Indians, providing food, fuel, building materials and medicines. Charcoal from this bush is prized today for the unique flavor it lends to barbecues.

Fendlerbush

Many shrub species cloak the canyon walls above the Tonto Platform. Here the steep slopes offer a variety of shaded niches, seeps and springs where shrubs form thickets. In spring and early summer, these sweet-scented thickets fairly hum with bees, butterflies and birds at work among the abundant blossoms. While blooming, the white-flowered fendlerbush is a powerful magnet for such butterflies as admirals and painted ladies. This 9ft-high shrub sports curious flowers with four widely separated, spoon-shaped petals.

Big Sagebrush

Abundant on both rims is the distinctive big sagebrush, a plant that dominates millions of acres of dry desert habitat from northern Arizona to Canada. Tolerant of cold and rain to a degree not found in other desert species, sagebrush ranges from valley floors to high desert peaks across the West. Three-lobed leaves and an aromatic scent make identification of this species a cinch.

Wildflowers

The park's dazzling variety of wildflowers put on an extravagant show – and because habitats range from arid desert to snowy heights there are always flowers blooming somewhere from early spring on. Even in midsummer, pockets of water foster lush wildflower gardens in shaded recesses within the canyon, while sudden thunderstorms trigger brief floral displays.

Raising eyebrows whenever encountered by hikers, the oddly inflated desert trumpet presents its loose arrangement of tiny yellow flowers any time between March and October. Just below the flowers, the stem balloons out like a long slender lozenge. Old stems maintain this shape and are just as curious as the living plant. Sometimes wasps drill into the plant and fill its hollow stems with captured insects as food for developing larvae.

A ponderosa pine will turn anyone into a tree-hugger. Look for one with gold-colored bark, and commune with it for a moment. Don't be shy, really get your nose up against that sweet tree and take a deep breath – the scent is redolent of vanilla, maple syrup, butterscotch, or...?

WILDLIFE OF THE GRAND CANYON PLANTS

Amateur naturalists should track down *A Field Guide to the Grand Canyon* by Stephen Whitney (also available in e-book version) or *A Naturalist's Guide to Canyon Country* by David Williams, both of which cover the region's common plants and animals.

HANGING GARDENS

Even though much of the Grand Canyon region appears arid, there is in fact water locked up inside the layers of porous sandstone – the byproduct of countless torrential rainstorms, which pour down onto the surface and percolate deep into the stone. Over time this water flows laterally and emerges from cliff faces as various seeps and springs. Flowing waters erode soft sandstone, causing the rock to collapse and form cool, shady overhangs. The constant water supply then fosters a rich community of algae on vertical surfaces and, below that, lush gardens of delicate flowering plants and ferns known as hanging gardens. These gardens of lacy and delicate maidenhair ferns, columbines, orchids, monkeyflowers and primroses are a welcome sight to parched desert travelers. Botanists also treasure these alcoves, as many of the plants are unique to the Colorado Plateau, occurring nowhere else but in these hanging gardens.

BEAR SIGHTINGS

It's extremely rare to spot a black bear in the Grand Canyon, though not an impossibility. From time to time, one of the national park's surveillance cameras records one, and it's usually reported in the local news. Indeed, there's a small population of black bears in and around the canyon, mostly in the quiet forested areas on the North Rim.

Black bears need easy and frequent access to water, and when drought conditions plague the region, more bears venture into the park to find new water sources. It's at these times that park visitors should be particularly mindful of the potential presence of bears. Don't leave food out, pack up your trash, and, if you're traveling with pets, be careful about their food too. If you do spot a bear, don't approach him – and definitely do not feed him.

And as for the grizzly bear, a longtime member of the endangered animals list, you won't see one. But there is talk of reintroducing the species to the Grand Canyon, and other protected areas in the West, to promote wildlife diversity.

One of the more conspicuous desert flowers, especially along roadsides, is the abundant peachy-pink globe mallow. Shooting forth as many as 100 stems from a single root system, it can tint the desert with its distinctive color. At least 10 mallow species live within the park.

Seeps, springs and stream banks are fantastic places to search for some of the most dramatic flower displays. The brilliant flash of crimson monkeyflowers amid lush greenery comes as something of a shock for hikers who've trudged across miles of searing baked rock. Apparently, someone once saw enough of a monkey likeness to name this wildflower, but you're more likely to notice the 'lips' that extend above and below the flower.

Columbines are also common at these seeps and springs, though some species range upward into moist forested areas of the park. The gorgeous golden columbine is most common in wet, shaded recesses of the inner canyon. Red columbine is a rare find in a wide range of forests and shaded canyons, while the blue-and-white Colorado columbine is a resident of Rocky Mountain spruce-fir forests along the North Rim. The long spurs of columbine flowers hold pockets of nectar that attract large numbers of butterflies and hummingbirds.

Though this hardly seems the place to find orchids, the beautiful giant helleborine is, in fact, common at seeps and springs within the canyon. The distinctly orchid-like flowers are a medley of green and yellow petals with purple veins. Though it goes without saying that you should never pick flowers in a national park, it's especially important that these precious orchids be admired and left undisturbed.

Cacti

Botany enthusiasts will appreciate *A Field Guide to the Plants of Arizona*, by Anne Epple, while those interested in how regional plants can be used will enjoy *Wild Plants and Native People of the Four Corners*, by William Dunmire and Gail Tierney.

Although they could be classified with wildflowers, the park's two dozen cacti are a group of plants unique unto themselves. Foremost among the cacti are the 11 members of the prickly pear group, familiar for their paddle-shaped pads that resemble beaver tails. In fact, one of the most common species is called beavertail cacti, while a rarer species is known as pancake pear. Both the pads and fruit are commonly eaten after proper preparation. Be aware that the spines (glochids) detach easily on contact and are highly irritating.

Often dubbed the classic beautiful cacti, stunning claret cup hedgehog cacti shine like iridescent jewels in the dusty desert landscape, where they are the first to bloom in spring. Their deep scarlet flowers burst forth from as many as 50 stems per clump, blooming simultaneously for a period of several days.

Life Zones

Boreal Forest

On the highest peaks of the North Rim perches boreal forest, an offshoot of the Rocky Mountains and home to many of the same plants and animals. Unlike other canyon habitats, this is a land of cool, moist forests and lush meadows. Snowfall may exceed 150in and persist for six to seven months of the year, conditions that favor trees such as the Engelmann spruce, Douglas fir and quaking aspen and animals such as red squirrels, blue grouse and broad-tailed hummingbirds.

Ponderosa Pine Forest

Broad, flat plateaus on both rims are dominated by ponderosa pine forest. This species forms nearly pure stands of stately, fragrant trees at around 7000ft, where temperatures are moderate and rainfall averages about 20in a year. Characteristic species populating these forests include the unique Abert's and Kaibab squirrels, as well as a variety of bird species, ranging from American robins to northern flickers.

Piñon-Juniper Woodlands

Sharing the rim with ponderosa pines and cloaking the canyon walls down to about 4000ft are piñon-juniper woodlands. These forests of piñon pines and Utah junipers signal desertlike conditions, where snow scarcely ever falls and annual rainfall hardly exceeds 10in. Shrubs such as cliff rose, sagebrush and Mormon tea thrive here. Animals include rock squirrels, cliff chipmunks, and scrub and piñon jays.

Desert Scrub Community

Between the canyon's inner gorge and the cliffs above is a broad apron known as the Tonto Platform. Here, in a zone of blazing summer heat and little rain at 3000ft to 4000ft, clings the desert scrub community. Dominating the platform is low-growing blackbrush, along with a handful of other

The last wild condor to soar over the Grand Canyon was spotted in 1924 – until the US Fish & Wildlife Service released six endangered California condors in northern Arizona in 1996, the happy result of a captive breeding program.

CONDORS

When critically endangered California condors were released at the nearby Vermilion Cliffs in 1996, the canyon experience was forever and profoundly altered. As was the case when wolves were reintroduced to Yellowstone National Park, visitors seem fascinated by the condors. With 9ft wingspans and bare, featherless heads, these birds are an unforgettable sight.

It's a miracle condors are around at all, seeing as their world population declined to less than two dozen birds in the 1980s. Many assumed these gigantic prehistoric holdovers were on the brink of extinction. Following a concerted captive breeding effort, however, there are now more than 70 condors flying around the park and nearby areas.

Fortunately for park visitors, condors have a strong affinity for large crowds of people. This is an evolutionary trait, as condors are carrion feeders, and crowds of large mammals such as humans are more likely to produce potential food. As a result, condors often hang around popular rim viewpoints such as Grand Canyon Lodge on the North Rim and Grand Canyon Village on the South Rim.

Condor populations are far from secure, however, even in the park, where they seem to have plenty of food and room to roam. The true test will be whether the species can continue to reproduce successfully. Pairs laid their first egg in 2001 and a total of 13 chicks have been born in the wild since reintroduction began. The canyon birds are all still young and inexperienced, so biologists hope that as the birds mature, more pairs will form and try to breed. Given that condors live about 50 years, there's plenty of time for these birds to settle down in their new home.

How can you tell a California condor from a common turkey vulture? Condors have a wingspan of about 9ft, while those of turkey vultures are about 6ft. Turkey vultures tend to rock slightly in the wind and flap more often than condors, who soar more smoothly.

THE MEXICAN WOLF

In 1998 an endemic Southwestern predator took its first tentative steps back to the wild. Eleven captive-bred Mexican wolves, a subspecies of the gray wolf, were released in east-central Arizona in a project aimed at reintroducing 100 wolves into a 7000-sq-mile area over 10 years. The current population stands at about 50.

The Mexican wolf traditionally ranged in 'sky islands' (high-elevation areas) as far south as central Mexico and as far north as southern Colorado. They are the smallest, most genetically distinct subspecies of gray wolf in North America. But government campaigns to eradicate predators resulted in the wild US population of Mexican wolves going extinct by the 1950s. In 1976 they were declared an endangered species, a designation that remains in place today.

Gray wolves have been reintroduced successfully in the northern Rockies, where the landscape actually rebounded as a result. Aspen groves became healthier as they were no longer overgrazed by elk and mule deer. Of course, wary local residents and ranchers who lose livestock oppose the addition of Mexican wolves to the ecosystem. As with any top-tier predator, on-the-ground issues of reintroduction are quite complex.

The US Fish and Wildlife Service, in collaboration with state and Native American agencies, oversees the reintroduction program and is currently investigating further action to create a wild, healthy, sustainable population of Mexican wolves. One idea is to reintroduce the wolves in a range near the North Rim of the Grand Canyon, where human population, cattle ranching and road density are low but where mule deer and elk are plentiful. But at the moment, the continued existence of the wild Mexican wolf remains tenuous.

hardy species such as prickly-pear cacti. Visitors will spot few birds and only the occasional black-tailed jackrabbit or white-tailed antelope squirrel.

Riparian Zone

Lining every waterway in the area is a separate and distinct habitat known as the riparian zone. The presence of precious water draws many plants and animals to this zone. Crimson monkeyflowers and maidenhair ferns mark the scattered seeps and springs, while stream banks near the river are choked by tamarisk, an aggressive introduced plant. Red-spotted toads and beavers share these waters with ducks and other birds that come to drink.

Life Through the Seasons

The canyon encompasses such a wide variety of climatic extremes that the seasons are as complex as the landscape. While one rim celebrates spring, the other rim may still languish in the grip of winter, and in the depths of winter the canyon floor can experience hotter temperatures than in summer elsewhere in the country.

April ushers in the first long spells of fair weather, interrupted by lingering wet winter storms. Even as golden eagles and peregrine falcons nest along the river, the North Rim may remain under many feet of snow. Migrant birds arrive in numbers through May. Along the South Rim and within the canyon itself, wrens, phoebes and warblers fill the air with song and activity. Mammals likewise take advantage of the short season between winter cold and summer heat.

By June temperatures begin to soar, and animal activity slows to a trickle. Daytime temperatures in excess of 100°F (38°C) are the norm through August. Torrential afternoon thunderstorms alleviate the agony for a few hours each day. June through August is usually the best time to observe wildflowers along the North Rim.

Clear, cool days make autumn the ideal time for visits to the park, though wildflowers have gone to seed and many birds have already made the journey south. Remaining behind are the resident animals – mammals fattening up for hibernation and a handful of birds that feast on the plentiful seeds. Other animals remain active through winter, especially on the canyon floor, where temperatures remain moderate and snow rarely falls.

Want to know how things are looking in the canyon today? Visit Yavapai Point on the South Rim vicariously via the webcam at www.explorethecanyon.com/grand-canyon-webcam. The image is refreshed every half hour.

STEVECOLLENDER / GETTY IMAGES ©

Bald eagle flying above the Grand Canyon

Wildlife of the Grand Canyon

The Grand Canyon isn't all about geology: the park is also the home to a rich and varied wildlife population, from birds and mammals to amphibians and reptiles.

IRINAK / SHUTTERSTOCK ©

1. Hummingbird 2. Junco 3. Golden eagle 4. Great horned owl

2

STEVEN LOVE / GETTY IMAGES ©

Birds of the Grand Canyon

Look up: many of the Grand Canyon's most interesting residents are flying overhead or perched on tree branches.

Small birds

A harbinger of spring the broad-tailed hummingbird zips energetically about the park from May through August, common in wildflower-filled forest glades on both rims. The sparrow-sized junco, conspicuous for its black hood, hops about the forest floor in search of seeds and insects. White-throated swifts swoop and dive over towering cliff faces at rim viewpoints. The stirring song of the canyon wren is, for many visitors, the most evocative sound in the park — so haunting that it's hard to believe that the tiny reddish rock-dweller could produce such music. Intrepid hikers may also spot a black-throated sparrow (at the sparsely vegetated Tonto Platform) or an American dipper (beside streams deep inside the canyon).

Birds of Prey

Of the six owl species occurring regularly in the park, none is as familiar as the common and highly vocal great horned owl, which regularly fills the echoing canyons with its booming hoots. This is among the largest and most fearsome of all the region's raptors, and when one moves into the neighborhood, other owls and hawks hurry on to more favorable hunting grounds or run the risk of being hunted down as prey themselves.

Commanding vast hunting territories of some 50 sq miles, powerful golden eagles may be observed as they travel widely in search of jackrabbits and other prey.

Given their endangered status in recent decades, peregrine falcons are surprisingly common throughout the park. Look for the falcon's long, slender wings and dark 'moustache.'

4

S.B. NACE / GETTY IMAGES ©

Mammals of the Grand Canyon

A total of 89 mammal species live in Grand Canyon National Park, from the solitary mountain lion to the amusing nocturnal ringtail. While some of the following species inhabit only certain sections of the park, you're likely to spot one of the following during a quiet hike on either rim.

1. Mule Deer
Rim forests and meadows are the favored haunts of mule deer, which commonly graze at dusk in groups of a dozen or more, moving seasonally to find water and avoid deep snows.

2. Ringtail
One of the area's most intriguing creatures is the nocturnal ringtail, which looks like a wide-eyed housecat with a raccoon's tail.

3. Mountain Lion
The canyon rates among the best places in North America to spot this elusive cat, reaching up to 8ft in length and weighing as much as 160lb. They gravitate to forests along the North Rim in pursuit of their favorite food, mule deer.

4. Bighorn Sheep
Like solemn statues, bighorn sheep often stand motionless on inaccessible cliff faces or ridgelines and are readily identified by their distinctive curled horns. Bring binoculars.

5. Fox
The coyote's much smaller cousin, the gray fox, often emerges at night, when you might spy one crossing a trail or road.

6. Chipmunk
The South Rim is the exclusive domain of the gray cliff chipmunk, an extremely vocal species that can bark an estimated 5800 times in half an hour, twitching its tail with each call.

7. Coyotes
Wild members of the dog family include the ubiquitous coyote. You stand a good chance of seeing coyotes in the daytime, especially around meadows, where they hunt for rodents.

8. Squirrel
Living on opposite rims, Abert's and Kaibab squirrels were a single population only 20,000 years ago, then the forested climate warmed and dried, and the canyon was transformed into desert habitat.

9. Bat
You'll spot plenty of these, especially close to the Colorado River, but don't get too close: the NPS reported that several local bats tested positive for rabies in 2014.

Amphibians & Reptiles

Frogs & Toads

The bleating choruses of common canyon tree frogs float up from boulder-strewn canyon streams each night. Gray-brown and speckled like stone, these tiny frogs dwell in damp crevices by day, emerging at night beside rocky pools. Occupying similar habitats: the aptly named red-spotted toad.

Lizards

Perhaps the most abundant and widespread reptile in the park is the eastern fence lizard, a creature 5in to 6in long which you'll likely see perched atop rocks and logs or scampering across trails.

As delicate in appearance as a fragile alabaster vase, the banded gecko has thin, practically translucent velvety skin. Emerging at night to hunt small insects, this lizard is not readily found unless you're hiking the desert slopes at night with a flashlight.

The strangest reptile in the park is the rarely seen Gila monster, which looks like a 2ft-long, orange-and-black sequined sausage. Mostly placid, it's capable of quick lunges and powerful bites with its massive black-rimmed jaws. Though encounters are rare, this lizard is best left alone.

Snakes

Home to some 20 snake species, including six resident species of rattlesnake, the park is a great place to learn about these misunderstood animals. The southwestern speckled and the northern black-tailed rattlesnake are the rarest, while the other four are subspecies of the western diamondback rattlesnake family: the Great Basin, the Mojave, the Hopi and, the most common of all, the Grand Canyon pink rattlesnake.

JARED HOBBS / GETTY IMAGES ©

1. Great Basin rattlesnake **2.** Gila monster **3.** Black-tailed rattlesnake

Environmental Issues & Conservation

Sprawling across 1875 sq miles, Grand Canyon National Park protects a sizable portion of the Colorado Plateau, as well as 277 free-flowing miles of the Colorado River. The fact that millions of people visit this fragile desert landscape each year means that tourism and development have a lasting impact. Even an action as simple as walking off the trail is detrimental when multiplied many times over by a steady stream of visitors, most of whom drive to the park in private vehicles.

Combining powerful advocacy with a passion for the landscape, the Glen Canyon Institute (www.glencanyon.org) is dedicated to restoring a healthy Colorado River system, while Grand Canyon Trust (www.grandcanyontrust.org) aims to 'Keep the Canyon Grand.'

Damming Consequences

Locked in by Glen Canyon Dam at its eastern end and Hoover Dam to the west, the once mighty Colorado River has undergone profound changes, with significant impacts on the many plants and animals that depend on the river and its natural cycles.

The handful of native fish that once thrived in the warm, sediment-laden waters of the Colorado have been particularly hard hit. Upstream from the canyon, Glen Canyon Dam now captures nearly all of the 380,000 tons of sediment that once flowed annually through the canyon. The dam instead releases clear cold water in a steady year-round flow that hardly resembles the ancestral seasonal flood cycle. Under this managed regime, unique fish such as the Colorado squawfish, razorback sucker and prehistoric-looking humpback chub have been almost entirely displaced by introduced trout, carp and catfish that flourish in the current conditions.

Another change has been the gradual loss of riverside beaches, as the river no longer deposits sediments in backwater stretches. Beaches have also become overgrown, since the river no longer floods away seedlings that take root on open sand; many former sandbanks are now densely vegetated with thickets of highly invasive tamarisk. Additionally, algal

CRYPTOBIOTIC CRUSTS

One of the Grand Canyon's most fascinating features is also one of its least visible and most fragile. Living cryptobiotic crusts cover and protect desert soils, literally gluing sand particles together so they don't blow away. Cyanobacteria, among earth's oldest life forms, start the process by extending mucous-covered filaments that wind through the dry soil. Over time, these filaments and the sand particles adhering to them form a thin crust that is colonized by microscopic algae, lichens, fungi and mosses. This crust absorbs tremendous amounts of rainwater, reducing runoff and minimizing erosion.

Unfortunately, this thin crust is quickly fragmented under the impact of heavy-soled boots, not to mention bicycle, motorcycle and car tires. Once broken, the crust takes 50 to 250 years to repair itself. In its absence, the wind and rains erode desert soils, and much of the water that would otherwise nourish desert plants is lost.

Visitors to the canyon and other sites in the Southwest bear the responsibility to protect cryptobiotic crusts by staying on established trails. Literally look before you leap – intact crusts form a glaze atop the soil, while fragmented crusts bear sharp edges.

growth has skyrocketed due to sunlight penetrating clear water that was once murky; the algae then supports a food chain benefiting non-native rainbow trout. Algae also soak up phosphorus, a critical nutrient that otherwise fuels aquatic diversity.

Efforts to alleviate this damage include a series of experimental, high-volume releases of water from the Glen Canyon Dam that have helped re-build beaches and stabilize humpback chub populations. Even better news for these native fish is that several populations of juvenile humpback chub have been translocated successfully to Shinumo Creek and Havasu Creek which bodes well for their reintroduction to their natural habitat.

Controversial Development

At the time of writing, Navajo leaders were in talks with developers based in Scottsdale, Arizona, to build a 1.4-mile tramway that would carry tourists deep into the canyon to the place known as the Confluence – where the Little Colorado feeds into the Colorado River. Plans include building an elevated walkway, a restaurant and an amphitheater. The impact of the infrastructure on a place considered sacred to many tribal groups, not to mention new traffic of a projected 4000 tourists a day, has caused furious opposition and an ongoing battle between the park's superintendent, local politicians and developers, and the Grand Canyon Trust. Initial estimates say that construction will cost around $1 billion, and that annual revenue would hit between $20 million and $65 million.

Water Conservation

Water remains a critical issue because it's gathered from wells and seeps on the Coconino Plateau, and nearby developments threaten to strain the limits of the supply. Because water use in the region is expected to double over the next 50 years, there's growing uncertainty about whether the area's natural seeps and springs will start drying up as the aquifer is drawn down.

The Grand Canyon Trust works to protect the springs and seeps. The organization is also involved in the reintroduction of beavers, whose dams help to restore creeks and ponds, into the canyon.

Air Pollution

It's a grim reminder of modern life that a pall of air pollution frequently hovers over the canyon, in both summer and winter. Unfortunately, the haze comes from sources as far away as Los Angeles, and not much can be done locally to remedy incoming pollution.

Inside the park, the South Rim has been developing an effective public transit system, and a growing network of pedestrian and bicycle trails on both rims, as a way of reducing traffic congestion and air pollution.

Uranium Mining

The park is threatened by a modern-day gold rush taking place right on its borders. More than 1100 uranium mining claims have been staked within 5 miles of the park since 2003, and there is considerable evidence that mining activity on this scale could severely and adversely impact the precious water supply and air quality.

There are a number of abandoned government-run uranium-mining operations in the Navajo Nation that were never properly closed. The Environmental Protection Agency is assessing these mines and the health of the Navajo people living near them. Exposure to uranium increases the risk of lung and bone cancer.

In 2012, the US Secretary of the Interior issued a 20-year ban on new uranium mining claims to protect a million acres of public land adjacent to the Grand Canyon – a major win for conservationists.

One of the lesser-known conservation projects at the Grand Canyon is happening on the remote North Rim, where the Grand Canyon Trust is working to restore springs, remove unnecessary fences, and support sustainable wildlife grazing on 1328 sq miles of ranch land.

Wildfires are a perpetual problem in this arid landscape. But fire, as you'll learn in many park ranger programs, is also used intentionally to maintain forest health. During an active fire, the best source of up-to-date information is the national park's Twitter feed, www.twitter.com/GrandCanyonNPS.

ENVIRONMENTAL ISSUES & CONSERVATION CONTROVERSIAL DEVELOPMENT

Native Americans of the Grand Canyon

Human habitation of the Grand Canyon region dates back at least 4000 years – according to carbon dating of split-twig animal figurines – and continues to the present day. Tribes whose reservations now border Grand Canyon National Park and who reside on the land surrounding the park include the Hualapai, Havasupai, Navajo, Hopi and Paiute peoples. It would be a mistake to generalize about Native American cultures in the region: each has its own traditions, sacred lands and specific (sometimes complicated) relationships to other tribes.

The Havasupai (Havsuw' Baaja)

Wade deeper into the background of the Havasupai with the ethnography *I Am the Grand Canyon: The Story of the Havasupai People,* by Stephen Hirst, told largely in their own words.

Well known for their beadwork and basketry, the Havasupai (whose name translates as 'people of the blue-green waters') share the Yuman language with the Hualapai. Both tribes are together referred to as Northeastern Pai. Their legends tell them that mankind originated on a mountain near the Colorado River. They left their Mojave relatives behind and headed to Meriwitica, near Spencer Canyon (a tributary of Grand Canyon). The Hualapai stayed near Meriwitica, but one story explains that a frog, enticed by the stream and lush vegetation, led the Havasupai east to Havasu Canyon. Archaeological records indicate that the Northeastern Pai arrived at the Grand Canyon around AD 1150, and the Havasupai have occupied Havasu Canyon since about that time.

Today, over 30,000 tourists visit Havasu Canyon every year, and the Havasupai's lives and economic survival are integrally related to the tourist industry that has developed in and around Grand Canyon National Park. They, along with the Hualapai, do not participate in the gaming industry. In Supai, the village at the bottom of the canyon, the Havasupai run a lodge and campground, as well as a small village store, serving the tourist industry.

The village's isolation probably magnifies the tension created by the outside influence of mainstream American culture on the younger generation of Havasupai. The traditional structure of Havasupai society, based on respect for tribal elders and the tribal council, remains in place despite such outside pressures – but as with much of life for many Native Americans, this continues to be a struggle.

The Hualapai (Hwal' bay)

The Hualapai trace their origins to Kathat Kanave, an old man who sometimes took the form of a coyote and lived in Mada Widita Canyon (also known as Meriwitica), on the canyon's westernmost edge. He taught the Pai (literally 'the People') how to live in the canyon, explaining what herbs cured which ailments and how and what to plant. The Hualapai and Havasupai developed complex systems of irrigation and spent summers farming within the canyon, at places like Havasu Canyon and Indian Garden. During the winter, they hunted on the plateau. Through trade with other tribes, they acquired peaches, figs, wheat, melons, cattle and horses.

Nowadays the Hualapai Reservation, bordering a large section of the Grand Canyon's South Rim, stretches as far south as Route 66. The Hualapai (meaning 'people of the pine trees') counts itself among the few tribes in the Southwest that do not generate revenue from gambling; instead, they've tried their hand at tourism, most successfully through motorized rafting tours on this section of the Colorado River, and through tourism on the scenic West Rim (known as Grand Canyon West). If you plan to travel off Route 66 on the Hualapai Reservation, you must purchase a permit in tiny Peach Springs.

Like the Havasupai, the Hualapai are renowned for their basketry.

At the bottom of Havasu Canyon, two Supai sandstone rock spires stand over the village of Supai. Known as Wii Gl'iiva, the spires – one male, one female – are believed to be guardian spirits watching over the Havasupai.

The Navajo (Diné)

The Navajo people comprise one of the largest tribes in North America; about one of every seven Native Americans are Navajo. Bordering the eastern edge of the national park, the 27,000-sq-mile Navajo Reservation is the biggest in the US. If you enter the park through the East Entrance, you'll pass through the Navajo Reservation; the tiny outpost of Cameron, also on the reservation, marks the intersection of Hwys 89 and 64, which leads to the East Entrance.

The Navajo Nation (also known as the Diné) has historically been adaptable to the ways of other tribes and cultures, which perhaps has contributed to the nation's strength and size. But the Navajo people have certainly not been exempted from the poverty and historical struggle of all Native American tribes.

RESERVATION ETIQUETTE

Visitors are usually welcome on Native American reservations, as long as they behave in an appropriately courteous and respectful manner. Tribal rules are often clearly posted at the entrance to each reservation, but here are some general guidelines.

➡ Most reservations ban the sale or use of alcohol.

➡ As a rule of thumb: don't bargain. You can't know the larger effects you might have caused just to save a few dollars.

➡ Ceremonials and powwows are either open to the public or exclusively for tribal members. Ceremonials are religious events, and applauding, chatting, asking questions or trying to talk to the performers is rude. Photography and other forms of recording are rarely permitted. While powwows also hold spiritual significance, they are usually more informal.

➡ Modest dress is customary. Especially when watching ceremonials, you should dress conservatively; tank tops and short shorts are inappropriate.

➡ Many tribes ban all forms of recording, be it photography, videotaping, audiotaping or drawing. Others permit these activities in certain areas only if you pay the appropriate fee (usually $5 to $10). If you wish to photograph a person, do so only after obtaining his or her permission. A posing tip is usually expected. Photographers who disregard these rules can expect tribal police officers to confiscate their cameras and then escort them off the reservation.

➡ Don't trespass on private property unless invited. Don't climb on ruins or remove any kind of artifact from a reservation. Kivas (ceremonial chambers) are always off-limits to visitors. Off-road travel is not allowed without a permit.

➡ Activities such as backpacking, camping, fishing and hunting require tribal permits. On Native American lands, state fishing or hunting licenses are not valid.

➡ It is considered polite to listen without comment, particularly when an elder is speaking. Be prepared for long silences in the middle of conversations; such silences often indicate that a topic is under serious consideration.

ETHICAL TOURISM

To varying degrees, the region's local tribes rely on tourism coming through the Grand Canyon National Park. You'll be contributing to the tribes' economies if you take tribal-run tours, stay at camp sites or lodges on the reservations or purchase handicrafts and art directly from tribal members.

When visiting reservations, keep in mind that they are sovereign nations within the US and that tribal laws may apply (though federal laws supersede them). In addition to obeying stated rules and respecting tribal codes of etiquette, it's wise to take a cue from the tribespeople and consider the environment: be careful with water; leave no trace.

The Navajo are renowned not only for their jewelry, pottery and sand paintings, but most famously for their weaving. Sought-after Navajo rugs, which can take months to complete, can be found for sale throughout the region, from Sedona to the South Rim. Most of the processes are still done by hand: carding the wool, spinning the thread, dying the threads with natural concoctions, and hand-weaving the designs themselves.

Between Cameron and the East Entrance of the park, Navajo stalls along the side of the highway sell jewelry and handicrafts. Some are preceded by hand-painted signs announcing, 'Friendly Indians Ahead!' These are great opportunities to buy locally, and often directly, from the artisans.

The Hopi

East of the Grand Canyon lies the 2410-sq-mile Hopi Reservation, which is completely surrounded by the Navajo Reservation. The Hopi are Arizona's oldest tribe and are probably best known for their unusual, often haunting kachina dolls.

On the Hopi Reservation, Old Oraibi is one of the oldest continuously inhabited villages in the US and site of the tribe's most sacred traditions. There is no official census data for the village, nor contemporary photographs, as photos and drawings are not allowed here.

According to Hopi religion, kachinas (*katsinam* in Hopi) are several hundred sacred spirits that live in the San Francisco Peaks north of Flagstaff. At prescribed intervals during the year, they come to the Hopi Reservation and dance in a precise and ritualized fashion. These dances maintain harmony among all living things and are especially important for rainfall and fertility. Kachina dolls, elaborate in design and color and traditionally carved from the dried root of the cottonwood tree, represent these sacred spirits.

While some kachina dolls are considered too sacred for public display or trade, Hopi artisans carve kachina dolls specifically to be sold to the general public. You can buy these, as well as pottery, basketwork and jewelry, at Hopi House in Grand Canyon Village; at the Watchtower at Desert View; at the Cameron Trading Post; and in the trading companies of Flagstaff.

The Paiute (Nuwuvi)

The Southern Paiute people occupy land north of the Colorado River in what is known as the Arizona Strip, and have traditionally used the canyon for hundreds of years. After contact and conflict with Navajo and Ute slavers, Spanish explorers, Mormon settlers and the US government, the Southern Paiute now live in scattered settlements and reservations in California, Utah, Nevada and Arizona.

One branch of this tribe, the Kaibab Paiute, occupies a reservation in northern Arizona, just west of Fredonia and south of Kanab, Utah. The tribe is largely involved in both agriculture and tourism and runs a visitor center and campground at Pipe Spring National Monument.

Survival Guide

Clothing & Equipment

Arriving outfitted with the proper clothing and equipment will keep you comfortable and safe on your adventures. Much of what is appropriate to bring depends, of course, on the season you're visiting and what activities you plan to pursue.

Plan carefully, particularly if you are going to explore the backcountry for the first time. Many first-time visitors are surprised by the weather, especially the extreme heat of summer and the high-country cold of the North Rim. Summer temperatures on the canyon bottom regularly soar beyond 100°F (38°C), and unlike the canyon rims, where higher elevations mean cooler temperatures, the interior remains stifling throughout the night. In the winter, it's not unusual to find mild and sunny skies on the South Rim, and a blinding blizzard 10 miles as the crow flies on the North Rim. Hike prepared for dramatic shifts in weather regardless of the season.

When selecting clothing and equipment, a guiding principle should be the balance of safety and comfort with weight considerations.

Think carefully about when, where and how long you are hiking. Plan, and pack, accordingly.

CLOTHING

Modern outdoor garments made from synthetic fabrics (which are breathable and actively wick moisture away from your skin) are better for hiking than anything made of cotton, but in cooler temperatures wool shirts, socks and sweaters are preferred.

Layering

To cope with changing temperatures and exertion, layering your clothing is a good way to regulate your body temperature.

➡ Upper body: start with a base layer made of synthetic thermal fabric or merino wool; second layer is a long-sleeved shirt; third layer can be a fleece sweater or jacket that wicks away moisture. Outer shell consists of a waterproof and breathable jacket.

➡ Lower body: shorts will be most comfortable in mid-summer, although some prefer long pants – light, quick-drying fabric is best. Waterproof overpants form the outer layer.

Footwear & Socks

➡ Some hikers prefer the greater agility that lightweight boots allow, while others insist on heavier designs that give firm ankle support and protect feet in rough terrain. Hiking boots should have a flexible (preferably polyurethane) midsole and an insole that supports the arch and heel.

Nonslip soles (such as Vibram) provide the best grip.

➡ When considering what type and style of footwear to bring, weigh the advantages of heavier hiking boots with the burden of the added weight; a couple extra pounds on your feet can make a noticeable difference when tackling switchbacks out of the canyon.

➡ Ideally, purchase shoes in-person rather than online so you can try on several options to see what works best with your feet.

➡ Try on hiking boots, preferably in the afternoon or evening, to accommodate for foot swell. Try boots on with whatever socks you plan on wearing; they should still offer plenty of toe room.

➡ Most hikers carry a pair of river sandals to wear around camp. River sandals are also useful when fording waterways.

➡ Merino wool socks that draw moisture away from your feet are a must; synthetic options can also work.

➡ Do not wait for the day before to purchase footwear, as you'll want at least a week or so to break it in.

Waterproof Shells

Grand Canyon hikers should always carry a windproof, waterproof rain jacket and pants and headwear. Gore-Tex or similar breathable fabrics work best.

NAVIGATION

Maps & Compasses

You should always carry a good map of the area you are hiking in, and know how to read it. Before setting off on your trek, ensure that you understand the contours and the map symbols, plus the main ridge and river systems in the area. Also familiarize yourself with the true north–south directions and the general direction in which you are heading. On the trail, try to identify major landmarks such as mountain ranges and gorges, and locate them on your map. This will give you a better understanding of the region's geography.

Buy a compass and learn how to use it. The attraction of magnetic north varies in different parts of the world, so compasses need to be balanced accordingly. Compass manufacturers have divided the world into five zones. Make sure your compass is balanced for your destination zone. There are also 'universal' compasses on the market that can be used anywhere in the world.

This is a very basic introduction to using a compass and will only be of assistance if you are proficient in map reading. For simplicity, it doesn't take magnetic variation into account. Before using a compass we recommend you obtain further instruction.

Reading a Compass

Hold the compass flat in the palm of your hand. Rotate the bezel so the red end of the needle points to the N on the bezel. The bearing is read from the dash under the bezel.

Orienting the Map

To orient the map so that it aligns with the ground, place the compass flat on the map. Rotate the map until the needle is parallel with the map's north–south grid lines and the red end is pointing to north on the map. You can now identify features around you by aligning them with labeled features on the map.

Taking a Bearing from the Map

Draw a line on the map between your starting point and your destination. Place the edge of the compass on this line with the direction-of-travel arrow pointing toward your destination. Rotate the bezel until the meridian lines are parallel with the north–south grid lines on the map and the N points to north on the map. Read the bearing from the dash.

Following a Bearing

Rotate the bezel so that the intended bearing is in line with the dash. Place the compass flat in the palm of your hand and rotate the base plate until the red end points to N on the bezel. The direction-of-travel arrow will now point in the direction you need to walk.

Determining Your Bearing

Rotate the bezel so the red end points to the N. Place the compass flat in the palm of your hand and rotate the base plate until the direction of travel arrow points in the direction in which you have been trekking. Read your bearing from the dash.

GPS

The Global Positioning System (GPS) is a network of more than 20 earth-orbiting satellites that continually beam encoded signals back to earth. Small computer-driven devices (GPS receivers) can decode these signals to give users an extremely accurate reading of their location – to within 100ft, anywhere on the planet in almost any weather.

The cheapest hand-held GPS receivers now cost less than US$100 (although these may not have a built-in averaging system that minimizes signal errors). Other important factors to consider when buying a GPS receiver are its weight and battery life.

ROUTE FINDING

If backpacking beyond Grand Canyon's maintained and National Park Service–patrolled corridor trails (Kaibab and Bright Angel) and campgrounds (Bright Angel, Cottonwood and Indian Garden), it is essential that you invest in a waterproof topographic map (see www.grandcanyon.org). Even with a detailed map, however, some basic route-finding techniques can be helpful.

➡ Be aware of whether the trail should be climbing or descending.

➡ Check the north-point arrow on the map and determine the general direction of the trail.

➡ Time your progress over a known distance and calculate the speed at which you travel in the given terrain. From then on, you can determine with reasonable accuracy how far you have traveled.

➡ Watch the path – look for boot prints and other signs of previous passage.

CLOTHING & EQUIPMENT CHECKLIST

Though it's tempting to simply toss everything into the car at the last minute, taking time to think things through as you pack can save you a lot of headaches down the road. Organizing clothes and gear into packing cubes (available in various sizes, shapes and weights most predominantly by Eagle Creek) minimizes the frustration of digging for things while on the trail.

If hiking during the summer heat, consider hats and shirts with 25 to 50 Ultraviolet Protection Factor (UPF) ratings that provide sun protection beyond a standard shirt.

Clothing

☐ broad-brimmed hat in summer (one that ties under the chin is required for mule trips)
☐ hiking boots or sturdy trail-running shoes, plus river sandals or flip-flops
☐ shorts and lightweight trousers or skirt
☐ sweater or fleece plus thermal underwear (synthetic or merino wool)
☐ T-shirt and long-sleeved shirt with collar (for sun protection)
☐ warm hat, scarf and gloves in winter
☐ waterproof pants and jacket

Equipment

☐ backpack with a rain cover
☐ first-aid kit
☐ cramp-ons (for winter hiking)
☐ DEET insect repellent
☐ survival bag or blanket, sunglasses, sunscreen and lip balm
☐ high-energy food and snacks
☐ LED flashlight or headlamp with new batteries
☐ map, compass and guidebook with a map case or clip-seal plastic bags
☐ pocket knife and watch
☐ safety mirror and whistle to attract attention in emergencies
☐ toilet paper and trowel
☐ trekking poles and paracord or similar utility rope
☐ water bottle and reservoir (like a Camelbak); water-purification tablets, iodine or filter

Overnight Hikes

☐ biodegradable soap; toiletries and towel
☐ cooking, eating and drinking utensils, including a stove and fuel and dehydrated food
☐ matches and lighter
☐ sewing/repair kit
☐ sleeping bag and/or liner, plus sleeping mat
☐ lightweight tent, tarp or rainfly

Optional Items

☐ binoculars
☐ camera and/or cell phone plus a portable power supply (such as a solar charger)
☐ gaiters
☐ GPS receiver and/or altimeter
☐ mosquito net
☐ swimsuit (for creeks – currents in the Colorado River can be deadly)
☐ tenacious tape (for patching jackets, tents etc)

Remember that a GPS receiver is of little use to trekkers unless used with an accurate topographical map. The receiver simply gives your position, which you must then locate on the local map. More expensive receivers, however, can include topographical maps among other capabilities.

GPS receivers will only work properly in the open. The signals from a crucial satellite may be blocked (or bounce off rock or water) directly below high cliffs, near large bodies of water or in dense tree cover and give inaccurate readings.

GPS receivers are more vulnerable to breakdowns (including dead batteries) than the humble magnetic compass – so don't rely on them entirely.

EQUIPMENT

Making sure you have the basic equipment will contribute greatly to a safe and comfortable journey.

Backpacking equipment is continually getting lighter, better designed and more comfortable. Be sure when selecting both day and overnight packs that your backpack can accommodate your gear.

Backpacks & Daypacks

➡ Look for a comfortable backpack that effectively distributes the weight between shoulders, spine and hips. Take plenty of time to try on backpacks and find one that fits to your body and is comfortable. Of all gear, this is one thing that is best purchased in-person.

➡ Carefully consider the length of your trip before selecting a backpack.

➡ Internal-frame backpacks fit snugly against your back, keeping the weight close to your center of gravity. Look for one with good ventilation.

➡ Even if the manufacturer claims your pack is waterproof, use a super lightweight rain cover.

➡ For day hikes or side trips from camp, use daypacks that double as hydration systems (like Camelbaks); if using a reservoir system, you'll still want to bring a water bottle as a back up.

Tents

➡ A three-season tent will suffice for most backpacking expeditions. Winter overnight trips will necessitate a four-season tent for protection from the elements.

➡ The floor and the outer shell, or rain fly, should have taped or sealed seams and covered zips to stop leaks.

➡ Consider the tent's weight.

Sleeping Bags & Pads

➡ Three-season sleeping bags will serve the needs of most campers. Down fillings are warmer than synthetic for the same weight and bulk but, unlike synthetic fillings, do not retain warmth when wet.

➡ Mummy bags are the best shape for weight and warmth. Third-party European Norm (EN) temperature ratings (30°F, for instance) show the coldest temperatures at which a typical person should feel comfortable in the bag.

➡ An inner liner helps keep your sleeping bag clean, as well as adding an insulating layer. Silk liners are lightest.

➡ During summer, the canyon floor is usually sweltering enough to forego a sleeping bag; backcountry campers might consider bringing just a sleeping-bag liner or a sheet. Some even soak a sheet in the river for the evaporative cooling effect.

➡ Cooler seasons, especially on the North Rim, call for both sleeping bag and sleeping pad for insulation from the cold

ground. Inflatable sleeping pads work best; foam mats are a low-cost but less comfortable alternative.

Stoves & Fuel

The type of fuel you'll use most often will help determine what kind of camp stove is best for you. The following types of fuel can be found in the US, and local outdoors stores can help you choose an appropriate camp stove if you aren't traveling with your own.

White gas Inexpensive, efficient and readily available throughout the country, reliable in all temperatures and clean-burning. More volatile than other types of fuel.

Butane, propane and isobutane These clean-burning fuels come in nonrecyclable canisters and tend to be more expensive. Best for camping in warmer conditions, as their performance markedly decreases in below-freezing temperatures.

Denatured alcohol Renewable; the most sustainable alternative. Burns slowly and quietly.

BUYING & RENTING LOCALLY

It can be a boon to buy or rent locally, as you can take advantage of local expertise on what works best in the region. Canyon Village Marketplace, the South Rim's full-sized grocery, sells and rents camping equipment, and several places offer water-purification tablets, flashlights and thermal blankets. The bookstore in Visitor Center Plaza offers the best selection of trail guides and maps. Outdoor stores in Flagstaff sell and rent camping equipment.

On the North Rim, the North Rim General Store also sells a limited selection of camping gear, including fuel, sleeping bags and pads. Willow Canyon Outdoor Co in Kanab sells outdoor gear, books and maps.

Directory A–Z

Accommodations

Accommodations in the park range from historic lodges to rustic cabins and standard motel rooms. Reservations are accepted 13 months in advance. Be sure to book early, particularly if you are traveling from May through August or if you have a specific lodging in mind (for example, Phantom Ranch or a rim-side cabin on the North Rim). You can cancel up to 48 hours in advance with no penalty.

All but two park lodges are on the South Rim. The North Rim offers one lodge and one campground. Below the rim, there are three maintained corridor campgrounds and several backcountry campsites, but the only lodge is Phantom Ranch.

If you're looking for a room with character, your best bets are Sedona and Flagstaff; Kanab and Williams also offer some interesting options, but choices are more limited, and you'll find short-term house rental throughout the region. Tusayan, the closest town to the park, caters to canyon tourists but offers little more than a short strip of tired chain motels and uninspired eateries.

Rates listed are high season (May through August). During holidays, special events and weekends, prices will be higher. While some hotels maintain the same rates year-round, it's more common to find room rates drop drastically in the winter (except in Las Vegas, when they drop in the summer).

B&Bs

In the South Rim region, Williams, Sedona and Flagstaff have several B&Bs. B&B hosts tend to be knowledgeable about the area and offer great advice on things to see and do in their hometowns and at the canyon. Most don't welcome children.

Camping

➡ Camping is allowed anywhere in Kaibab National Forest, which borders both rims.
➡ Don't camp within a quarter-mile of the highway or any surface water, within a half-mile of any developed campground, or in meadows.
➡ Showers and laundry facilities are available (p232).
➡ Fires are not permitted, and campers are expected to leave no trace.
➡ Women who are camping solo should avoid isolated campsites.
➡ The National Forest Service (NFS) offers several tent-only campgrounds around Sedona, Flagstaff and Williams; prices are minimal, and you'll find fire rings and bathrooms.

Hostels

Hostels in the Grand Canyon region are few and far between, but they all promise a quality experience. Look for the two lovely sister hostels in Flagstaff and the Grand Canyon Hotel in Williams, which offers hostel-style accommodations in addition to private rooms.

Hotels & Motels

This being Route 66 territory, a handful of roadside motels have charm emanating from the walls. Most, however, are of the tiny, run-down variety; chain hotels provide a consistent level of quality, and there are some great historic hotels and independent options outside both rims.

The majority of hotels and motels have air-conditioning, wi-fi (sometimes for a small fee), telephones, TVs and complimentary parking.

Lodges

Inside the park, lodges are basically the park's hotels, where the rooms are comfortable enough but very basic. The only exceptions are the South Rim's El Tovar and Bright Angel Lodge cabins, the North Rim's Grand Canyon Lodge, and Phantom Ranch, on the canyon bottom.

Resorts

In Sedona and Las Vegas, full-service resorts offer luxury accommodation and amenities, beautiful surrounds, excellent restaurants and first-class service. Many offer on-site spas, activities and elegant pools.

Price Ranges

The following price ranges refer to a double room with bathroom in high season. Unless otherwise stated tax is included in the price.

Resorts and lodges, particularly in and around Las Vegas and Sedona, often charge a mandatory resort fee. Expect to pay from $15 to $30 per day on top of quoted daily rate. and always ask in advance.

$ less than $100

$$ $100 to $200

$$$ more than $200

Courses

Several organizations offer year-round classes on a variety of subjects, from one-day photography classes to extended learning vacations. While most require advance reservations, both rims offer regularly scheduled ranger talks open on a drop-in basis.

Grand Canyon Field Institute (☑866-471-4435, 928-638-2485; www.grandcanyon.org/fieldinstitute) Run by the Grand Canyon Association (official nonprofit partner of the park), the field institute offers more than 100 classes annually. Subjects include natural history, wilderness studies, backcountry medicine and photography. Most instructors have advanced degrees in their field of study and have led canyon trips for several years.

Canyon Field Schools (www.nps.gov/grca/learn/kidsyouth/camp.htm) National Park Service (NPS) backpacking and rafting classes for middle- and high-school students. Classes generally range from four to eight days, and cost between $100 and $230.

Museum of Northern Arizona (☑928-774-5213; www.mnaventures.org) Organizes an array of customized, small-group educational tours led by scientists, writers and artists through its MNA Ventures program. Options include hiking, backpacking, river rafting, horseback riding, van tours and hotel-based trips throughout the Southwest.

Northern Arizona University's Grand Canyon Semester (☑928-523-3334; https://nau.edu/honors/gcs) Three-month interdisciplinary semester (comparable to a semester abroad), examining the region's geology, history, ecology, geography and politics, among other topics. While most participants are college-age students, the course is open to anyone.

Discount Cards

American Automobile Association (AAA) members can get hotel, rental-car and National Park Pass discounts by showing their cards – always ask about AAA discounts.

Park Passes

All passes are available at the park entrance stations; the only pass available in advance online is the standard **America the Beautiful Pass** (http://store.usgs.gov/pass). It takes up to two weeks to receive and there's an additional cost for shipping.

➜ **Grand Canyon Annual Pass** ($60) Unlimited visits to passholder and accompanying guests arriving in a noncommercial vehicle, or family members arriving by train, shuttle, bike or foot.

➜ **America the Beautiful Pass** ($80) Access for passholder and up to three adults, and also includes all National Park Service (NPS), US Forest Service (USFS) and Bureau of Land Management (BLM) sites. Children under 16 free.

Climate

South Rim

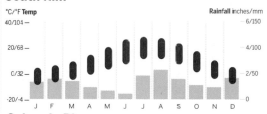

Colorado River

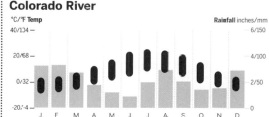

➡ **America the Beautiful Annual Pass for Military** (free) Access to NPS, USFS, and BLM sites for active military personnel and dependents.

➡ **America the Beautiful Access Pass** (free) Lifetime pass for US citizens or permanent residents with permanent disability; medical proof required.

➡ **Frequent Hiker Membership** ($25) Hikers who pay the up-front fee do not have to pay the $10 permit processing fee for one year after the membership is purchased; saves some money if you plan on multiple backcountry excursions.

Senior Cards

Travelers aged 50 and older can receive rate cuts and benefits in many places. Inquire about discounts at hotels, museums and restaurants before you make reservations or purchase tickets.

➡ **American Association of Retired Persons** (AARP; www.aarp.org) Members receive 10% discount at South Rim Lodges, 15% discount on Grand Canyon Railway, and varying discounts at area lodges, restaurants and attractions.

➡ **America the Beautiful Senior Pass** ($10) Lifetime pass to federal lands for US citizens or permanent residents 62 or older; includes access to cardholder and up to three adults.

Food

Picnicking is a great way to save money and enjoy some quiet moments. If you're visiting the park for more than a day, it's worth investing in a small cooler. On the South Rim, you can buy ice at Market Plaza and Desert View; on the North Rim, there's free ice at the ice machine behind the Visitor Center and bags for purchase at the North Rim General Store. Most South Rim lodges provide small in-room refrigerators, but only a couple cabins on the North Rim have refrigerators.

While the South Rim has a full-size grocery store, the North Rim General Store offers only a small but thorough selection of groceries, including diapers, alcohol and firewood. The closest full grocery store is in Kanab, a 1½-hour drive north.

Eating Price Ranges

The following price ranges are for a main dinner meal, not including tip.

$ less than $15

$$ $15 to $25

$$$ more than $25

Insurance

The US is an expensive country in which to get sick, crash your car or be robbed, so protect yourself. To insure yourself from theft from your car, consult your homeowner's (or renter's) insurance policy before leaving home.

Worldwide travel insurance is available at www.lonelyplanet.com/bookings. You can buy, extend and claim online any time – even if you're already on the road.

Internet Access

➡ Most accommodations and coffee shops offer wi-fi. It's usually free though sometimes there's a small fee.

➡ On the North Rim, you'll find wi-fi at the campground's general store; on the South Rim, there's 24-hour wi-fi in hotel lobbies and a public computer terminal in Yavapai Lodge's lobby.

➡ The only park accommodation with a public computer terminal is the South Rim's Yavapai Lodge.

Maps

Do not hike beyond the three maintained corridor trails without purchasing an appropriately detailed topographical map.

NPS (www.nps.gov/grca/planyourvisit/maps.htm) For

Electricity

120V/60Hz

120V/60Hz

LAST-MINUTE ACCOMMODATIONS

Because of the flexible cancellation policy, it's not unusual to secure last-minute rooms even during summer peak season. Advanced reservations are taken Monday through Friday, from 7am to 6pm Pacific time. There's no waiting list, so keep trying If all else fails, you can camp for free just about anywhere in Kaibab National Forest on either rim.

South Rim & Phantom Ranch (at the Canyon Bottom)

➡ For reservations up to 48 hours in advance, call ☎888-297-2757; for Yavapai, call ☎877-404-4611.

➡ For same-day or day-before accommodation, reach individual lodges through the South Rim Switchboard (☎928-638-2631); for Yavapai, call ☎928-638-6421.

➡ If you don't find a room on the South Rim, check motels in Tusayan (7 miles from the canyon rim), or the roadside motel in Valle, about 28 miles further south.

➡ In Cameron, 32 miles east of the East Entrance along Hwy 64 (but otherwise in the middle of nowhere), is the pleasant Cameron Trading Post & Motel which often has vacancies.

➡ Safest bets are further away in Williams (59 miles south of the rim) and Flagstaff (80 miles south), both of which offer pedestrian-friendly historic downtowns.

North Rim

➡ For reservations up to 48 hours in advance, call ☎877-386-4383.

➡ For same-day or day-before accommodation, call ☎928-638-2611.

➡ The closest accommodation outside Grand Canyon Lodge on the North Rim is Kaibab Lodge (18 miles north of the rim) or Jacob Lake Lodge (44 miles north).

➡ DeMotte Campground, across from Kaibab Lodge, is arguably the nicest campground in the region and there's also a campground in Jacob Lake.

➡ If everything is booked, head to Kanab, a pleasant town about 80 miles north of the rim, where you'll find several motels with rates from $70 to $160.

---

downloadable PDFs of official NPS maps of the region, scenic drives, corridor hiking trails and South Rim shuttles.

Grand Canyon Association (www.grandcanyon.org) For backcountry maps, visit the online shop for individual trail guides ($4.50) and waterproof National Geographic Trails Illustrated maps.

Media

➡ **Newspapers** *Arizona Daily Sun* (www.azdailysun. com), *Salt Lake Tribune* (www.sltrib.com), *Deseret News* (www.deseretnews. com), *Las Vegas Review Journal* (www.lvrj.com) and *Las Vegas Sun* (www. lasvegassun.com).

➡ **TV** Local NPR stations include KNAD (91.7 in Page),

KNAG (90.3 at the Grand Canyon) and KNAJ (88.7 in Flagstaff).

➡ **Twitter** The NPS runs an Official Twitter Feed (https://twitter.com/ grandcanyonnps) and a Grand Canyon Weather Feed (https://twitter.com/ grandcanyonwx).

Opening Hours

Grand Canyon's North Rim is closed from mid-October through mid-May. You can backcountry camp with a backcountry permit, but note that the 44-mile road from Jacob Lake to the rim is not plowed – snow can hit as early as October or as late as May.

Generally speaking, business hours are from 9am to 5pm. Expect shorter hours

in and around the park from September through April; around the North Rim, sights, shops and restaurants offer drastically shorter hours or close altogether from November through February.

Banks 10am to 5pm Monday to Friday

Bars 5pm to 2am

Restaurants breakfast 7am to 10:30am lunch 11am to 2:30pm, dinner 5 to 9pm

Shops 9:30am to 5:30pm

Public Holidays

Public holidays do not affect park opening hours.

New Year's Day January 1

Martin Luther King, Jr, Day 3rd Monday in January

Presidents Day 3rd Monday in February

INTERNATIONAL VISITORS

Entering the Region

➜ **US Department of State** (www.travel.state.gov) Up-to-date visa and immigration information.

➜ **US Department of Homeland Security** (www.dhs.gov) Clear details on requirements for travel to the US; follow links How Do I?/For Travelers/Visit the US.

➜ **Visa Waiver Program** (VWP; www.dhs.gov/visa-waiver-program-requirements) Though most foreign visitors to the US need a visa, the VWP allows citizens of 38 countries to enter the US for stays of 90 days or less without first obtaining a visa. Go to the website for a list of participating countries and detailed information.

➜ **Electronic System for Travel** (ESTA; https://esta.cbp.dhs.gov/esta) Visitors eligible for the VWP must apply for entry approval via ESTA; while it is recommended travelers apply at least 72 hours before travel, you may apply any time before boarding your flight and in most cases the process takes no more than half an hour.

➜ Your passport should be valid for at least another six months after you leave the US.

➜ The USA recognizes foreign drivers' licenses and does not require an International Driving Permit (IDP); some car-rental agencies, however, do require an IDP so be sure to ask in advance.

Embassies & Consulates

For contact information on embassies not listed here, go to https://embassy-finder.com.

Australia (Los Angeles; ☑310-229-2300; http://losangeles.consulate.gov.au)

Canada (Phoenix; ☑602-508-3572; www.canadainternational.gc.ca)

France (Los Angeles; ☑310-235-3200; www.consulfrance-losangeles.org)

Germany (Los Angeles; ☑323-930-2703; www.germany.info/losangeles)

Japan (Los Angeles; ☑213-617-6700; www.la.us.emb-japan.go.jp)

New Zealand (Los Angeles; ☑310-566-6555; www.nzembassy.com/usa-los-angeles)

UK (Los Angeles; ☑310-789-0031; http://ukinusa.fco.gov.uk/la)

Money

➜ You'll find 24-hour ATMs at most banks, shopping malls, grocery and convenience stores. Bank surcharges often apply in addition to fees charged by your own bank.

➜ Most ATMs are affiliated with international networks and offer reasonable exchange rates.

Easter Late March or early April

Memorial Day Last Monday in May

Independence Day July 4

Labor Day 1st Monday in September

Columbus Day 2nd Monday in October

Veterans Day November 11

Thanksgiving Day 4th Thursday in November

Christmas Day December 25

Showers & Laundry

Camper Services Building (Market Plaza, Grand Canyon Village; ☉8am-6pm) Near Mather Campground on the South Rim. Provides daytime coin laundry and pay showers.

North Rim Campground (Map p149; ☑928-638-7814, 877-444-6777; www.recreation. gov; tent sites $18, RV sites $18-25; ☉mid-May–mid-Oct by reservation, first-come, first-served Oct 16-31; ⏹) Has pay shower and laundry facilities on the access road leading to the campground.

Tourist Information

Grand Canyon National Park (www.nps.gov/grca) Best source for all things Grand Canyon.

Grand Canyon Association (www.grandcanyon.org) Official nonprofit partner of Grand Canyon National Park, with travel

➨ Hotels, restaurants and shops generally accept cash and credit cards.

➨ It's customary to tip restaurant waitstaff 15% to 20% of the pretax bill, and tip bartenders $1 per drink. Tips make up a significant part of food-service workers' income.

➨ Large banks in Flagstaff, Las Vegas and Phoenix offer currency exchange; in the park, the South Rim's Chase Bank offers currency exchange for Chase Bank customers only.

Post

The **US Postal Service** (www.usps.com) is inexpensive and reliable. Standard letters up to 1oz (about 28g) cost $0.49 within the US; postcards and letters to destinations outside the USA cost a universal $1.20.

Telephone

CELL PHONES

You'll need a multiband GSM phone to make calls in the US. Installing a US prepaid re-chargeable SIM card is usually cheaper than using your own network. They're available at major telecommunications or electronics stores in Flagstaff and Las Vegas. If your phone doesn't work in the US, these stores, as well as superstores, also sell inexpensive prepaid phones.

DIALLING CODES

➨ US phone numbers begin with a three-digit area code, followed by a seven-digit local number.

➨ When dialing a number within the same area code, simply dial the seven-digit number; for long-distance calls, dial the entire 10-digit number preceded by ☑1.

➨ For direct international calls, dial ☑011 plus the country code plus the area code plus the local number.

➨ If you're calling from abroad, the US country code is ☑1.

Time

➨ Arizona is on Mountain Standard Time (MST) but does not observe Daylight Saving Time (DST).

➨ The Navajo Reservation does observe Mountain Daylight Savings Time during the summer, putting it one hour ahead of Arizona and on the same time as Utah and New Mexico.

➨ DST starts on the second Sunday in March (clocks are set ahead one hour) and ends on the second Sunday in November (clocks are set back one hour).

---

information, trail guides and online shop.

US Forest Service (www.fs.fed.us) Cabins, camping and hiking in national forests, including the Kaibab that surrounds the Grand Canyon.

Flagstaff Visitor Center (www.flagstaffarizona.org) Accommodation, events, regional activities.

Sedona Visitor Center (http://visitsedona.com) Planning tips for red rock country and Oak Creek Canyon.

Las Vegas Visitor Center (www.lasvegas.com) Show tickets, maps and more.

Travelers with Disabilities

Around the Southwest, public buildings are required to be wheelchair accessible and to have appropriate restroom facilities. Public transportation must be accessible to all, and most chain hotels have rooms or suites for travelers with disabilities. Telephone companies provide relay operators for those with hearing impairments. Many banks provide ATM instructions in braille.

Park shuttles (South Rim only) can accommodate wheelchairs up to 30 inches wide and 48 inches long, but cannot accommodate scooters. The only wheelchair rental at the park is at **Bright Angel Bicycles** (Map p76; ☑928-814-8704, 928-638-3055; www.bikegrandcanyon.com; Visitor Center Plaza, Grand Canyon Village;

24hr rental adult/child 16yr & under $40/30, 5hr rental $30/20, wheelchair $10, single/double stroller up to 8hrs $18/27; ☺Apr-Nov; 🚲Village, 🚲Kaibab/Rim) on the South Rim, which also rents adult tricycles; on the North Rim, there is one complimentary wheelchair available on a first-come first-served basis at the Visitor Center.

Grand Canyon National Park Accessibility (www.nps.gov/grca/planyourvisit/accessibility.htm) Maps and details on accessibility at park lodging, campgrounds, trails and sights; available as a downloadable PDF, or at park visitor centers.

Scenic Drive Accessibility Permit Allows entrance for visitors with mobility issues to park roads otherwise closed to private vehicles (for example, the South Rim's Hermit Drive) and temporary parking permit; available at entrance gates, park visitor centers and park hotel lobbies.

Volunteering

There are loads of opportunities to volunteer at and around Grand Canyon National Park, for one-day projects or longer-term endeavors. Volunteers can work on trail maintenance, restore grasslands, pull invasive plants from the inner gorge, train to be an interpretive ranger or work with youth organizations.

Grand Canyon Association (GCA; www.grandcanyon.org) Partners with NPS to offer multiple week-long volunteer projects on both the North and South Rims; participants must be GCA members at $50 level or above. A $100 participation fee covers accommodation and meals.

American Conservation Experience (www.usaconservation.org) Restoration and conservation work in and around the park for men and women aged 18 to 35. In exchange for 40 hours' work a week, volunteers are housed (often in on-site campgrounds) and fed.

Grand Canyon Trust Volunteers (www.grandcanyontrust.org) The volunteer arm of the nonprofit Grand Canyon Trust offers opportunities to participate in its Grand Canyon Volunteers projects. These range from assisting graduate students with research at Northern Arizona University in Flagstaff to week-long tamarisk-removal trips in the backcountry.

National Park Service (www.volunteer.gov/gov) Lists available volunteer positions in the park, including year-round openings for revegetation volunteers. Duties include seed collection, plant propagation and non-native plant removal. Limited free camping may be available.

Student Conservation Association (www.thesca.org) Opportunities for high school and college-aged students interested in hands-on conservation work.

Work

Work at the park tends to be low-paying service jobs; on the North Rim especially, where jobs are available from mid-May through mid-October only, jobs are mostly filled by young people. North Rim employment offers shared accommodations and three meals for $12 per day, or RV hookup in the pet-friendly and wooded staff RV park for $6 per day.

Planning ahead is essential, whether you are applying for NPS or park concessionaire jobs – applications for summer jobs are typically due during December and January. Non-US citizens must apply for a work visa from the US embassy in their home country before leaving. Visas vary, depending on how long you're staying and the kind of work you plan to do.

Cool Works (www.coolworks.com) Central resource for non-NPS jobs and volunteer opportunities in and around the Grand Canyon, as well as throughout the USA.

Grand Canyon National Park (www.nps.gov/grca) Follow links to Get Involved/Work With Us for current information on NPS employment.

South Rim (www.grandcanyonlodges) Online application for employment at South Rim restaurants, shops and hotels.

North Rim (www.grandcanyonlodgenorth.com) Information on employment at the North Rim's Grand Canyon Lodge.

Transportation

GETTING THERE & AWAY

If you're headed to the South Rim, the easiest way to arrive is to fly to Phoenix (223 miles). For the North Rim, fly into Las Vegas (277 miles). From these points, travelers can rent cars or make connections by bus or shuttle. Greyhound buses stop in Flagstaff, and regular shuttle services serve the South Rim from Sedona, Williams, Flagstaff and the airports in Phoenix and Las Vegas. A daily shuttle (with two daily departures mid-May to mid-October) runs from rim to rim (four to five hours). Apart from this shuttle, the only way to reach the North Rim is by car.

Flights, cars and tours can be booked online at lonely planet.com/bookings.

Air

Airports

The main air hubs to the park are Las Vegas, Nevada; Phoenix, Arizona; Salt Lake City, Utah; and Albuquerque, New Mexico.

McCarran International Airport (LAS; Map p122; ☑702-261-5211; www.mccarran.com; 5757 Wayne Newton Blvd; ☎) Las Vegas is served by McCarran International Airport, just a few miles from the southern end of the Strip, and a few smaller general aviation facilities around the city. McCarran ranks among the USA's 10 busiest airports. Many domestic airlines use Terminal 1; international, charter and some domestic flights depart from Terminal 3. Free trams link outlying gates. There are ATMs, a full-service bank, a post office, first-aid and police stations, free wi-fi and slot machines with reputedly bad odds.

Sky Harbor International Airport (☑602-273-3300; http://skyharbor.com; 3400 E Sky Harbor Blvd; ☎) Located in Phoenix, this busy airport is 220 miles from the South Rim of the Grand Canyon and 335 miles from the North Rim.

Salt Lake City International Airport (SLC; www.slcairport. com; 776 N Terminal Dr; ☎) Serving Salt Lake City and northern Utah, it's also a good choice if you're headed to the North Rim of the Grand Canyon and the Arizona Strip.

Albuquerque International Sunport (ABQ; ☑505-244-7700; www.cabq.gov/airport; ☎) Serving Albuquerque and all of New Mexico, this is a small and friendly airport that's easy to navigate.

Airlines

DOMESTIC & CANADIAN

Air Canada (www.aircanada. com)

Alaska Airlines (www.alaskaair. com)

American Airlines (www. aa.com)

CLIMATE CHANGE & TRAVEL

Every form of transportation that relies on carbon-based fuel generates CO_2, the main cause of human-induced climate change. Modern travel is dependent on airplanes, which might use less fuel per mile per person than most cars but travel much greater distances. The altitude at which aircraft emit gases (including CO_2) and particles also contributes to their climate change impact. Many websites offer 'carbon calculators' that allow people to estimate the carbon emissions generated by their journey and, for those who wish to do so, to offset the impact of the greenhouse gases emitted with contributions to portfolios of climate-friendly initiatives throughout the world. Lonely Planet offsets the carbon footprint of all staff and author travel.

Delta (www.delta.com)

Frontier Airlines (www.frontier airlines.com)

JetBlue (www.jetblue.com)

Southwest Airlines (www.southwest.com)

United Airlines (www.united.com)

US Airways (www.usairways.com)

FROM THE UK, IRELAND & EUROPE

Aer Lingus (www.aerlingus.com)

Air France (www.airfrance.com)

British Airways (www.british airways.com)

Virgin Atlantic (www.virgin-atlantic.com)

FROM AUSTRALIA & NEW ZEALAND

Air New Zealand (www.air newzealand.com)

Qantas (www.qantas.com.au)

Land

Bus

Arizona Shuttle (☑800-563-1980, 928-225-2290; www.arizonashuttle.com) Offers three daily shuttles between Flagstaff and the Grand Canyon's South Rim (per person $30) and between Williams, AZ, and the Grand Canyon (per person $22). Save $2 reserving the shuttle online.

Grand Canyon Shuttle Service (Flagstaff Shuttle & Charter; ☑888-215-3105; www.grand canyonshuttles.com) Runs on-demand shuttles between Flagstaff, Sedona, Williams, and the South Rim of Grand Canyon National Park. Also runs rim-to-rim shuttles. Call for prices and availability. Also called Flagstaff Shuttle & Charter.

Greyhound (☑800-231-2222, 928-774-4573; www.greyhound.com) Runs Flagstaff to Albuquerque ($65, six hours), Las Vegas (from $48, 5½ hours), Los Angeles (from $80, 13 hours) and Phoenix (from $24, three hours). Save money by booking

RV RENTAL

Recreational vehicles are a great way to travel the Grand Canyon region, where campgrounds are plentiful. If you need to rent a vehicle anyway, renting an RV can save money on accommodations. RV rental rates vary by vehicle size, model and mileage; expect to pay at least $100 per day.

Apollo (☑800-370-1262; www.apollorv.com) With a branch in Las Vegas, Apollo rents everything from cozy campervans for two, to family-size motor homes.

Cruise America (☑800-672-8042; www.cruiseamerica.com) Rents nationwide and has offices in Phoenix, Flagstaff and Las Vegas. Has an online Renters Assistance Guide, with RV operating tips.

online and traveling at non-peak times.

Trans-Canyon Shuttle (☑877-638-2820, 928-638-2820; www.trans-canyonshuttle.com; one way rim to rim $85, one-way South Rim to Marble Canyon $70; ☑mid-May–mid-Oct) The shuttle leaves Grand Canyon Lodge at 7am and 2.30pm. It departs the South Rim (Bright Angel Lodge) at 8am and 1:30pm. Cash only. Reserve well in advance, if possible.

Car & Motorcycle

From Las Vegas, it's an easy drive to either rim. To get to the North Rim, head north on I-15 into Utah. Just past St George, take Hwy 9 east to Hurricane. You can either continue on Hwy 9 through Zion National Park, then connect with Hwy 89 down through Kanab to Fredonia, or take Hwy 59/389 southeast to Fredonia and connect with Alt 89. Alt 89 heads southeast to Jacob Lake, where Hwy 67 leads 30 miles to the park entrance station. The most direct route to the South Rim is Hwy 93 south to I-40, then east to Williams, where you'll turn north on Hwy 64 to Valle, then follow Hwy 180 into the park.

From Phoenix, take I-17 north to Flagstaff and continue on Hwy 180 north to the South Rim. Another option is to take Hwy 60 northwest to Hwy 89 through Prescott, then connect with Alt 89, which winds northeast through forested mountains to Sedona. From there it's a short jaunt north through Oak Creek Canyon to Flagstaff. It is a beautiful drive, but traffic can be brutal in summer, particularly around Sedona. If you're continuing to the North Rim from Flagstaff, take Hwy 89 north. (At Cameron, Hwy 64 leads 32 miles west to the South Rim's East Entrance.) About 60 miles north of Cameron, Alt 89 turns east through Lees Ferry and Marble Canyon to Jacob Lake.

AUTOMOBILE ASSOCIATIONS

American Automobile Association (AAA; ☑877-428-2277, emergency roadside assistance 800-222-4357; www.aaa.com; annual membership from $52) Along with maps and trip-planning information, AAA members also receive discounts on car rentals, air tickets, hotels and attractions, plus emergency roadside service and towing. It has reciprocal agreements with international automobile associations such as CAA in Canada; be sure to bring your membership card from your country of origin.

Better World Club (☑866-238-1137; www.betterworldclub.com) This ecofriendly association supports environmental causes in addition to offering emergency roadside assistance for drivers and cyclists, discounts on vehicle rentals (including hybrids and biodiesels) and auto insurance.

DRIVER'S LICENSE

If you're a foreign visitor, you will need your vehicle's registration papers, liability insurance and an International Driving Permit (IDP) in addition to your domestic license. Contact your local automobile association for details about required documentation. An international driver's license, obtained in your home country, is only necessary if your country of origin is a non-English-speaking one.

RENTAL

Most car-rental agencies require renters to be at least 25 years old, and some have an upper age limit as well. When shopping around always check with the agency itself. It's illegal to drive without automobile insurance, so consult your policy from your home country before leaving.

A number of major car-rental agencies operate out of the airports in Las Vegas and Phoenix. You can also rent cars in Flagstaff, though rates are higher than in Phoenix or Las Vegas. Note that car rentals are no longer available in Tusayan, though they were in the past.

INSURANCE

Liability insurance covers people and property that you might hit. For damage to the rental vehicle a collision damage waiver is available

for about $15 per day. Collision coverage on your vehicle at home may also cover damage to rental cars; check your policy before leaving home.

Some credit cards offer reimbursement coverage for collision damage if you rent the car with that credit card, although most do not cover rentals of more than 15 days or exotic models, vans and 4WD vehicles.

Most rental companies stipulate that damage a car sustains while driven on unpaved roads is not covered by the insurance they offer. Check with the agent when you make your reservation.

ROAD RULES

Throughout the US cars drive on the right side of the road. Apart from that, road rules differ slightly from state to state, but all require the use of safety belts as well as the proper use of child safety seats for children under the age of five.

➔ Speed limits vary; on rural interstates the speed limit is 75mph, but this drops down to 65mph in urban areas (55mph in Arizona).

➔ Pay attention to livestock- or deer-crossing signs – tangle with a deer, cow or elk and you'll total your car in addition to killing the critter.

➔ You can incur stiff fines, jail time and other penalties if caught driving under the influence of alcohol. The legal limit for blood alcohol level is 0.08% in Arizona and most other states.

Train

Operated by **Amtrak** (☑800-872-7245; www.amtrak.com; 233 N Grand Canyon Blvd), the *Southwest Chief* makes a daily run between Chicago and Los Angeles, with stops at Flagstaff and Williams. In Williams you can connect with the historic Grand Canyon Railway, with original 1923 Pullman cars chugging the scenic 65 miles to the South Rim.

GETTING AROUND

On the South Rim, the most hassle-free way to get around is to drive into the park, park your car and use the convenient shuttles and your own pedestrian power. On the North Rim, unless you're taking the Trans-Canyon Shuttle, you'll have to drive in yourself, as there are few services on this rim (none during winter).

Bicycle

Inside the Park

Because roads on the South Rim are so heavily trafficked, a great alternative is to get around by bicycle. As much of the park-wide Greenway Trail is completed, pedaling through the park has become an ever more refreshing way to get around. Bikes are allowed on all roads but none of the trails (except the Greenway Trail) on the South Rim. Rent 'comfort cruiser' bikes at **Bright Angel Bicycles** (Map p76; ☑928-814-8704, 928-638-3055; www. bikegrandcanyon.com; Visitor Center Plaza, Grand Canyon Village; 24hr rental adult/child 16yr & under $40/30, 5hr rental $30/20; wheelchair $10, single/double stroller up to 8hr $18/27; ☺Apr-Nov; ☐Village, ☐Kaibab/Rim).

On the North Rim, you can fashion a terrific extended ride out to Point Imperial and on to Cape Royal, about 45 miles

ROAD DISTANCES (M)

ROUTE	MILES
Albuquerque to South Rim	400
Las Vegas to South Rim	277
Las Vegas to North Rim	268
Phoenix to South Rim	223
Salt Lake City to North Rim	392
Los Angeles to South Rim	490

each way from Grand Canyon Lodge. The park's 35mph speed limit ensures slow traffic, and the pine-fringed road offers a good riding surface.

For a short, sweet North Rim ride that's well suited to families, take the Bridle Trail, which leads from the North Kaibab Trailhead to the campground (0.5 miles) and lodge (1.5 miles). Mountain bikes are allowed on blacktop roads only, except for the 17-mile dirt road to Point Sublime, and the Bridle Trail from the campground to the lodge.

Beyond the Park

Check out Sarah Alley's detailed book *The Mountain Biker's Guide to Arizona* for more information on self-guided biking around the Grand Canyon.

Outside the South Rim, great mountain-biking trails in Kaibab National Forest include a 16-mile trail from the Tusayan Trailhead to the Grandview Lookout Tower. Stop at the **Tusayan Ranger Station** (☑928-638-2443; www.fs.usda.gov/kaibab) for trail maps and directions.

Beyond the North Rim, outside the park, there's plenty of good single-track for mountain bikers in Kaibab National Forest, teeming with old-growth ponderosa pines, steep-sided canyons, aspen groves and velvety meadows. The 18-mile Rainbow Rim Trail winds along the rim through aspen and ponderosa, passing five viewpoints with gorgeous panoramas. Pick up a map and information at the Kaibab Plateau Visitor Center in Jacob Lake.

RIDING THE RAILS

On September 17, 1901, the first Grand Canyon Railway train departed Williams to carry its pioneering passengers to the South Rim – and so began the modern era of the canyon as tourist destination. Instead of the hurdle of a long and arduous stagecoach ride, tourists could now travel to the canyon in relative comfort. By 1968, car travel had made the train obsolete. Only three passengers were on that year's final trip to the rim.

In 1989, Max and Thelma Biegert bought and lovingly restored the train, resuming passenger service after a 21-year absence. The Biegerts sold the company in 2007 to Xanterra Parks & Resorts, the concessionaire at the South Rim.

Today, diesel locomotives make the daily journey to Grand Canyon Village. On a few select days each year, the railway runs a steam locomotive with engines powered by waste vegetable oil. A 1952 parlor car doubles as a cafe, selling coffee, candy, box lunches, sunscreen, water and film.

Even if you're not a train buff, or if you generally shrink from traveling en masse, the train can be a lot of fun if you get into the spirit. A banjo player or other musician wanders the aisles, joking with passengers and strumming such folk classics as 'I've Been Working on the Railroad.' A mock horseback chase and train robbery enliven the return trip.

The train departs the 1908 Grand Canyon Railway Depot in Williams at 9:30am, following a 9am Wild West shoot-out by the tracks (a slapstick performance to put you in the mood). You'll arrive at Grand Canyon Depot at 11:45am. The return train pulls out at 3:30pm, arriving back in Williams at 5:45pm. Most people approach it as a day trip, but you can purchase a one-way ticket or spend a few days in the park and return on a later train. Packages are available through the Grand Canyon Railway Hotel in Williams, and lodgings at the rim. For reservations and details, contact **Grand Canyon Railway** (☑reservations 800-843-8724; www.thetrain.com; Railway Depot, 233 N Grand Canyon Blvd; round-trip adult/child from $65/25; ☑).

Passengers can choose from the following classes of service. Prices quoted are for round-trip journeys:

Pullman Class (adult/child $65/29) The standard seats on the train are in these refurbished 1923 Harriman-style coach cars.

Coach Class (adult/child $75/45) Features 1950s-style cars with large windows and room for roving musicians and marauders.

First Class (adult/child $149/115) Has air-conditioning, spacious reclining seats, and snacks and beverages on offer in both directions.

Observation Dome ($179) With upper-level seating in a glass-enclosed dome, featuring snacks, beverages and a champagne toast on the return trip; not open to children under 16.

Luxury Dome & Luxury Parlor ($216) Incredibly comfortable cushioned window seats and an open-air rear platform; not open to children under 16.

SAFE CYCLING

On the South Rim, cycling is permitted on the Greenway Trail, as well as on all paved and unpaved roads. Cyclists must adhere to traffic regulations and should use caution along the heavily trafficked roads, especially during the busy summer season. On Hermit Rd, cyclists are required to pull off the road to allow vehicles to pass. Always wear a helmet and bright colors to improve your visibility to drivers.

Cycling around the North Rim is a whole other animal. Single-track trails and forest roads abound in the Kaibab National Forest for mountain bikers. Because the area is so remote compared with the developed South Rim, cyclists should wear helmets and come supplied with water, food and first aid.

Car & Motorcycle

RV traffic is commonplace in this region, so you won't have any problems finding pull-through campsites and dump stations.

There's a **service station** (☉8am-5pm, 24hr pay at the pump, mid-May–mid-Oct) on the access road to North Rim Campground, where basic repairs can be completed. On the South Rim, **Desert View service station** (Desert View, East Entrance; ☉9am-5pm Mar-Oct; open 24hr for credit-card service) sits next to the East Entrance. There's also a gas station in Tusayan, about 7 miles from Grand Canyon Village and just outside the South Entrance. The **garage** (☏928-638-2631; Grand Canyon Village; ☉8am-noon & 1-5pm) in Grand Canyon Village also offers limited service and repairs, plus 24-hour emergency towing.

Road Conditions & Hazards

Check road conditions within the park by calling the automated information line at ☏928-638-7888. For conditions in Kaibab National Forest (South Rim), call the **Tusayan Ranger Station** (☏928-638-2443; www.fs.usda. gov/kaibab); for conditions in Kaibab National Forest (North Rim), call the **Kaibab**

Plateau Visitor Center (☏928-643-7298; cnr Hwys 89A & 67; ☉8am-4pm mid-May–mid-Oct).

Ranging between 6500ft and 7500ft in elevation, roads in Flagstaff and environs may experience snow and ice from October through April. At elevations approaching 9000ft, roads along the North Rim are even more susceptible to weather. The drive up from deserts north and east of the park climbs about 4000ft, and conditions change rapidly – you may start out in sunny, dry weather in Kanab or Lees Ferry and wind up battling rain, hail or snow in Jacob Lake. The forest service's dirt roads, particularly those in Kaibab National Forest, may be impassable after even light rain. Always check with a ranger before heading out.

You'll need a high-clearance 4WD vehicle to tackle both the 17-mile road to Point Sublime (a minimum two-hour round-trip) and the 60-mile dirt road to Toroweap. Absolutely do not attempt these drives without first telling someone where you're going, and take plenty of water.

If driving to Grand Canyon West on the Hualapai Reservation, be aware that 9 of the 21 miles of Diamond Bar Rd are regularly graded but unpaved road. In wet weather, a 4WD vehicle is advisable. Be sure to start out with a full tank of gas and a good supply of water. Also on the Hualapai Reservation, Diamond Creek Rd is best traveled by 4WD with a plentiful supply of water. Even in the best of circumstances, this rough road leading directly to the Colorado River necessitates at least two creek crossings.

The main hazard to look out for is wildlife in and around the parks, or livestock in rural areas surrounding the park.

Shuttle

Free shuttle buses operate every 10 to 15 minutes along three connecting routes on the South Rim. Except for an early-morning shuttle to the North Kaibab Trailhead, the only way to explore the North Rim is by car, bicycle or foot.

Hermits Rest Route Accesses the 8-mile stretch of rim road west of Grand Canyon Village. This road is closed to private vehicles from March through November; the only way to see the overlooks then is via shuttle, bicycle or on foot.

Village Route You can drive to most facilities in the village, but it's easier to park your car and take one of the shuttles.

Kaibab/Rim Route Stops at Pipe Creek Vista, South Kaibab Trailhead and Yaki Point, the last of which is closed to private vehicles year-round.

Tusayan Route Runs between the South Rim's visitor center and Tusayan from May to September.

Taxi

Taking a **taxi** (☏928-638-2822, ext 6563, 928-638-2631) anywhere within the park is an expensive option. Even a short drive from Grand Canyon Village to a trailhead could cost $50, depending on how far you're going. It's best to use taxi services only if you have no other option.

Health & Safety

Educating yourself on the Grand Canyon's unique environment and hazards will go a long way toward making your visit a safe and healthy one.

BEFORE YOU GO

Even strolling the scenic viewpoints around the Grand Canyon will be easier and more enjoyable if you're somewhat physically fit, especially if you plan on doing any hiking.

When possible, visitors from lower elevations and cooler climes should allow several days to acclimatize before undertaking any strenuous activity at the Grand Canyon.

Insurance

Review the terms of your health-insurance policy before going on a trip; some policies don't cover injuries sustained as a result of dangerous activities, which can include rock climbing or mountaineering. Double-check that emergency medical care, and emergency evacuation to your home country (if you're not from the US), is covered by your policy.

Medical Checklist

Your first-aid kit should include the following:

➡ adhesive tape
➡ bandages and safety pins
➡ elasticized support bandage for knees, ankles etc
➡ gauze swabs
➡ nonadhesive dressings
➡ paper stitches
➡ small pair of scissors
➡ sterile alcohol wipes
➡ thermometer (note mercury thermometers are prohibited by airlines)
➡ tweezers

Medications & Miscellany

In addition to regular medications you need, consider including some of these over-the-counter meds:

➡ antidiarrhea and antinausea drugs
➡ antifungal cream or powder
➡ antihistamines
➡ antiseptic
➡ calamine lotion, sting-relief spray or aloe vera
➡ cold and influenza tablets, throat lozenges and nasal decongestant
➡ eye drops
➡ insect repellent
➡ multivitamins – especially for longer hikes, when dietary vitamin intake may be inadequate
➡ painkillers (such as aspirin, acetaminophen or ibuprofen)
➡ rehydration mixture – particularly important when traveling with children
➡ sunscreen and lip balm
➡ water-purification tablets, iodine or Steripen

IN THE PARK

For the casual park visitor, health and safety usually requires little effort apart from keeping sufficiently hydrated and not goofing off on the rim. However, for those heading below the rim, preparation and responsibility for one's own safety are key to a safe adventure. Many emergencies below the rim occur because visitors overestimate their abilities and come underprepared to deal with the consequences.

Always lock your car and put valuables in the trunk, particularly if you park at a trailhead. Physical assault is rare in the park, but use caution when hiking alone.

Medical Assistance

In an emergency on either rim, dial 🕿911; from your lodge or cabin, dial 🕿9-911.

South Rim

At Grand Canyon Village, the **North County Community Health Center** (🕿928-

638-2551; www.northcountry healthcare.org; 1 Clinic Rd; ⊘8am-6pm mid-Oct–mid-May) offers walk-in medical care. The nearest pharmacy is 60 miles south at the **Safeway** (pharmacy ☎928-635-0500; 637 W Route 66; ⊘5am-10pm) in Williams. The nearest hospitals to the South Rim are 80 miles south in Flagstaff, including the top-notch **Flagstaff Medical Center** (☎928-779-3366; www.flagstaff medicalcenter.com; 1200 N Beaver St; ⊘emergency 24hr).

North Rim

Rangers provide emergency medical care within the park; the nearest hospital, **Kane County Hospital** (☎435-644-5811; 355 N Main St; ⊘24hr), is 80 miles north in Kanab, Utah. Also in Kanab is the nearest pharmacy, **Zion Pharmacy** (☎435-644-2693; 14 E Center St; ⊘9am-6pm Mon-Fri, to noon Sat).

Page Hospital (☎928-645-2424; 501 N Navajo Dr) is 114 miles from the North Rim in Page, Arizona. Page also has a pharmacy at the local **Safeway** (☎928-645-5714; 650 Elm St; ⊘9am-8pm Mon-Fri, 9am-6pm Sat, 10am-4pm Sun).

Common Ailments

Blisters

To avoid blisters, make sure your walking boots or shoes are well worn in before you hit the trail. Boots should fit comfortably with enough room to move your toes. Socks should fit properly and be specialized for walkers; be sure there are no seams across the widest part of your foot. Wet and muddy socks can cause blisters, so pack a spare pair. If you feel a blister coming on, treat it sooner rather then later by applying a bit of moleskin or duct tape.

Fatigue

More injuries happen toward the end of the day than earlier, when you're fresher. Although tiredness can simply be a nuisance on an easy hike, it can be life-threatening on narrow exposed ridges or in bad weather. Never set out on a hike that is beyond your capabilities on the day. If you feel below par, have a day off.

Don't push yourself too hard – take rests every hour or two and build in a good half-hour lunch break. Toward the end of the day, take the pace down and increase your concentration. Drink plenty of water and eat properly throughout the day – nuts, dried fruit and chocolate are all good energy-rich snacks.

Giardiasis

This parasitic infection of the small intestine, commonly called giardia, may cause nausea, bloating, cramps and diarrhea, and can last for weeks. Giardia is easily diagnosed by a stool test and readily treated with antibiotics.

To protect yourself from giardia, avoid drinking directly from lakes, ponds, streams and rivers, which may be contaminated by animal or human feces. Giardia can also be transmitted from person to person if proper hand washing is not performed.

Knee Strain

Many hikers feel the burn on long, steep descents. Although you can't eliminate strain on the knee joints when dropping steeply, you can reduce it by taking shorter steps that leave your legs slightly bent and ensuring that your heel hits the ground before the rest of your foot. Some walkers find that compression bandages

help, and trekking poles are very effective in taking some of the weight off the knees.

Travelers' Diarrhea

Serious diarrhea caused by contaminated water is an increasing problem in heavily used backcountry areas. Fluid replacement is the mainstay of management. A rehydrating solution is necessary for severe diarrhea, to replace minerals and salts. Commercially available oral rehydration salts (ORS) are very useful.

Environmental Hazards

Altitude

As the South Rim is more than 7000ft above sea level and the North Rim 8801ft at its highest point, altitude sickness is fairly common. It's characterized by shortness of breath, fatigue and headaches. Taking a day or two to acclimatize before attempting any long hikes may help decrease the likelihood of getting altitude sickness; any symptoms should be taken seriously.

Bites & Stings

SCORPIONS

Commonly found in Arizona, the bark scorpion is the only dangerous species of scorpion in the US. To prevent scorpion stings, inspect and shake out clothing, shoes and sleeping bags before use. If stung, immediately apply ice or cold packs, immobilize the affected body part and go to the nearest emergency room.

PREHYDRATION

Since your body can only absorb about a quart of water per hour, it's highly beneficial to prehydrate before embarking on a long hike. To get a head start on hydration, drink plenty of water the day and evening before your hike, and avoid diuretics such as caffeine and alcohol.

SNAKES

Several species of rattlesnake are found in the Grand Canyon. Most snakebites can be prevented by respecting the snake's space – if you do encounter one, move away slowly – and by wearing boots when hiking. Those bitten will experience rapid swelling, severe pain and possibly temporary paralysis. Death is rare, but children are at higher risk.

To treat snakebite, place a light constricting bandage over the bite, keep the wounded part below the level of the heart and move it as little as possible. Attempting to suck out the venom is not considered an effective strategy. Stay calm and get to a medical facility for antivenin treatment as soon as possible.

TICKS

Wear long sleeves and pants to protect from ticks. Always check your body for ticks after walking through high grass or thickly forested areas. If ticks are found unattached, they can simply be brushed off. If a tick is found attached, press down around the tick's head with tweezers, grab the head and gently pull upward – do not twist it. (If no tweezers are available, use your fingers, but protect them from contamination with a piece of tissue or paper). Don't douse an attached tick with oil, alcohol or petroleum jelly.

Lyme disease, transmitted by ticks, is uncommon in Arizona, but you should consult a doctor if you get sick in the weeks after your trip.

Climate
HYPOTHERMIA

This life-threatening condition occurs when prolonged exposure to cold thwarts the body's ability to maintain its core temperature. Hypothermia is a real danger for winter hikers. Remember to dress in layers and wear a windproof outer jacket. If possible, bring a thermos containing a hot (nonalcoholic) beverage.

Hypothermia doesn't just occur in cold weather – dehydration and certain medications can predispose people to hypothermia, especially when they're wet, and even in relatively warm weather. Symptoms include uncontrolled shivering, poor muscle control and a careless attitude. Treat symptoms by putting on dry clothing, giving warm fluids and warming the victim through direct body contact with another person.

DEHYDRATION & HEAT EXHAUSTION

The canyon is a dry, hot place, and even if you're just walking along the rim, lack of water can cause dehydration, which can lead to heat exhaustion. To prevent dehydration, take time to acclimatize to high temperatures, wear a wide-brimmed hat and make sure to drink plenty of fluids. Hikers should drink a gallon of water per day. It's also wise to carry water in your car in case it breaks down.

Take note if you haven't had to pee as often as usual, or if your urine is dark yellow or amber-colored. These are indicators of dehydration, which can rapidly spiral into more dire health concerns. Loss of appetite and thirst may be early symptoms of heat exhaustion, so even if you don't feel thirsty, drink water often and have a salty snack while you're at it. Add a little electrolyte replacement powder to your water. Err on the side of caution and bring more water and food than you think you'll need – even if it turns out you don't need it, it could save someone else's life.

Characterized by fatigue, nausea, headaches, cramps and cool, clammy skin, heat exhaustion should be treated by drinking water, eating high-energy foods, resting in the shade and cooling the skin with a wet cloth.

Heat exhaustion can lead to heatstroke if not addressed promptly.

HEATSTROKE

Long, continuous exposure to high temperatures can lead to heatstroke, a serious, sometimes fatal condition that occurs when the body's heat-regulating mechanism breaks down and one's body temperature rises to dangerous levels.

Symptoms of heatstroke include flushed, dry skin, a weak and rapid pulse, poor judgment, inability to focus and delirium. Move the victim to shade, remove clothing, cover them with a wet sheet or towel and fan them continually. Hospitalization is essential for heatstroke.

HYPONATREMIA

While drinking plenty of water is crucial, it's also important to supplement water intake with salty snacks and electrolyte drinks to avoid hyponatremia (a dangerously low sodium level in the blood). In the dry heat of the canyon, sweat can evaporate off of your skin so quickly that you may not notice how much you've perspired. Salt lost through sweating must be replaced in order to keep a balanced sodium level in the blood.

Symptoms of hyponatremia are similar to early signs of heat exhaustion: nausea, vomiting and an altered mental state. Give the victim salty foods and seek immediate help if their mental alertness diminishes.

SUNBURN

In the desert and at high altitude you can sunburn in less than an hour, even through cloud cover. Use lots of sunscreen (with a high SPF), especially on skin not typically exposed to sun, and wear long sleeves. Be sure to apply sunscreen to young children, particularly babies, and wear wide-brimmed hats.

Weather & Flash Floods

Even if the sky overhead is clear, distant rainstorms can send walls of water, debris and mud roaring through side canyons without warning. Such flash floods have killed people caught in creeks and dry riverbeds. Never camp in dry washes, and be sure to check weather reports for the entire region before venturing into the canyon. This is crucial if you're planning on hiking through any slot canyons. Flash floods are most common during summer storms in July, August and September.

Don't underestimate the summer heat – temperatures routinely soar past 100°F (38°C) in the canyon. In winter months, snow and ice can make trails slick and dangerous. Ask a ranger about conditions before heading out.

Wildlife

For their own safety and yours, it's illegal to approach or feed any wildlife. In the canyon, always shake out shoes and sleeping bags to dislodge hiding scorpions. Also keep an ear out for rattlesnakes, whose rattle is a warning signal.

Safe Hiking

It's easy to become complacent when hiking in the Grand Canyon, given the clearly marked trails and ease of descent. But hiking here can be serious business. On average, there are 400 medical emergencies each year on canyon trails, and more than 250 hikers need to be rescued at their own hefty expense. Several have died.

Time and again, hikers who have been rescued from the canyon say that their biggest mistake was underestimating how hot the canyon can be. The best way of ensuring a rewarding hike is proper planning. Learn about the trails, honestly assess your limitations and respect them.

Falls

Almost every year people fall to their death at the Grand Canyon. Stay on the trails, refrain from stepping over guardrails, and do not allow children to run along the rim. There isn't as much railing as you may expect. Carry toddlers in baby backpacks and wear sturdy shoes or boots.

SAFETY TIPS FOR HIKING SMART

Nuts and bolts for safe hiking in the Grand Canyon:

➡ Make 'down = 2x' up formula your hiking mantra. Generally speaking, it takes twice as long to wheeze back up the canyon as it does to breeze down. So if you'd like to hike for six hours, turn around after two. Most first-time canyon hikers slog uphill at about 1mph.

➡ Stay on marked trails, both for safety and erosion control. Nowhere is this more important than in the Grand Canyon, where hazards include stupefying drop-offs. It's also extremely difficult for rescuers to find a hiker who has wandered off-trail.

➡ Don't hike alone. Most of those who get in trouble in the canyon are solo hikers, for whom the risks are multiplied. Backcountry hikes are safer (and more enjoyable) with a companion.

➡ Given the altitude and extreme aridity, go slow to avoid overexertion. Ideally, you should be able to speak easily while hiking, regardless of the grade. Be sure to take a five- to 10-minute break every hour to recharge, in the shade if possible.

➡ Pay close attention to your intake of food and fluids to prevent dehydration and hyponatremia (low blood sodium level). One good strategy is to have a salty snack and a long drink of water every 20 to 30 minutes. In summer months each hiker should drink about a gallon of water per day. Eat before you're hungry and drink before you're thirsty.

➡ In addition to sturdy, comfortable, broken-in boots and medium-weight socks, bring moleskin for blisters and make sure your toenails are trimmed. On long hikes, soak your feet in streams to reduce inflammation and safeguard against blisters (just be sure to dry them thoroughly before replacing your socks). After hiking, elevate your feet.

➡ Don't be overly ambitious. Particularly for novice hikers, it's a good idea to spend the first day or two gauging your ability and response to the climate and terrain. If you're planning long hikes, test your desert legs on a more level hike or a short round-trip of 2 to 4 miles, then work your way up to more difficult trails.

➡ Hike during the cooler early-morning and late-afternoon hours, especially in summer. Splash water on your face and head at streams and water sources, and soak your shirt or bandana to produce an evaporative cooling effect.

Getting Lost

The park comprises 1904 sq miles of desert terrain, making it too easy to lose your way in its labyrinth of side canyons and sheer cliffs. It is imperative that you plan any hike carefully and appropriately. Whether backcountry hiking or driving in remote areas, always carry an adequate map and supply of drinking water.

Leave a detailed itinerary with a friend, listing routes and dates, as well as identifying details of your car. Cell phones won't get a signal inside the canyon. For backcountry hikes, bring a topo map, know how to read it and never stray from trails under any circumstances.

If you do get lost, search-and-rescue operations may take days to find you. Stay calm and stay put, making your location as visible as possible by spreading out colorful clothing or equipment in an exposed place. Use a signal mirror (an old CD is a good lightweight substitute) and ration food and water. Do not attempt to blaze a shortcut to the river; people have died from falls, exposure or dehydration after stranding themselves on steep, dead-end ledges or ridges.

Lightning

Being below the rim does not protect you from lightning strikes. If a thunderstorm catches you on an exposed ridge or summit, look for a concave rock formation to shelter in, but avoid touching the rock itself. Never seek shelter under objects that are isolated or higher than their surroundings.

In open areas where there is no shelter, find a depression in the ground and take up a crouched-squatting position with your feet together; do not lie on the ground. Avoid contact with metallic objects such as pack frames or hiking poles.

Should anyone be struck by lightning, immediately begin first-aid measures such as checking their airway, breathing and pulse, and starting burn treatment. Get the patient to a doctor as quickly as possible.

Rescue & Evacuation

Hikers should take responsibility for their own safety and aim to prevent emergency situations, but even the most safety-conscious hiker may have a serious accident requiring urgent medical attention. In case of accidents, self-rescue should be your first consideration, as search-and-rescue operations into the canyon are very expensive and require emergency personnel to put their own safety at risk.

If a person in your group is injured, leave someone with them while others seek help. If there are only two of you, leave the injured person with as much warm clothing, food and water as it's sensible to spare, plus a whistle and flashlight. Mark their position with something conspicuous.

Rockfall

Always be alert to the danger of rockfall, especially after heavy rains. If you accidentally loosen a rock, loudly warn other hikers below. Bighorn sheep sometimes dislodge rocks, so animal-watchers should be especially vigilant.

Traumatic Injuries

If the victim is unconscious, immediately check if they are breathing. Clear their airway if it's blocked, and check for a pulse – feel the side of the neck rather than the wrist. Check for wounds and broken bones. Control any bleeding by applying firm pressure to the wound.

FRACTURES

Indications of a fracture are pain (tenderness of the affected area), swelling and discoloration, loss of function or deformity of a limb. Unless you know what you're doing, don't try to straighten an obviously displaced broken bone. To protect from further injury, immobilize a nondisplaced fracture (where the broken bones are in alignment) by splinting it, usually in the position found, which will probably be the most comfortable position. If you do have to splint a broken bone, remember to check regularly that the splint is not cutting off the circulation to the hand or foot.

Compound fractures (or open fractures, in which the bone protrudes from the skin) require urgent treatment, as there is a risk of infection. Fractures of the thigh bone also require urgent treatment as they involve massive blood loss and pain. Seek help and treat the patient for shock. Dislocations, where the bone has come out of the joint, are very painful and should be set as soon as possible.

Broken ribs are painful but usually heal by themselves and do not need splinting. If breathing difficulties occur, or the person coughs up blood, medical attention should be sought urgently, as this may indicate a punctured lung.

SPRAINS

Ankle and knee sprains are common injuries among hikers, particularly when crossing rugged terrain. To help prevent ankle sprains, wear boots that have adequate ankle support. If you suffer a sprain, immobilize the joint with a firm bandage, and if possible, immerse the foot in cold water. Relieve pain and swelling by resting and icing the joint, and keeping it elevated as much as possible for the first 24 hours. Take over-the-counter painkillers to ease discomfort. If the sprain is mild, you may be able to continue your hike after a couple of days.

Behind the Scenes

SEND US YOUR FEEDBACK

We love to hear from travelers – your comments keep us on our toes and help make our books better. Our well-traveled team reads every word on what you loved or loathed about this book. Although we cannot reply individually to your submissions, we always guarantee that your feedback goes straight to the appropriate authors, in time for the next edition. Each person who sends us information is thanked in the next edition – the most useful submissions are rewarded with a selection of digital PDF chapters.

Visit **lonelyplanet.com/contact** to submit your updates and suggestions or to ask for help. Our award-winning website also features inspirational travel stories, news and discussions.

Note: We may edit, reproduce and incorporate your comments in Lonely Planet products such as guidebooks, websites and digital products, so let us know if you don't want your comments reproduced or your name acknowledged. For a copy of our privacy policy visit lonelyplanet.com/privacy.

AUTHOR THANKS

Jennifer Rasin Denniston

Thank you to Alex and Bridget, the South Rim backcountry office, Grand Canyon rangers, and to Brian Mildenstein for his help with outdoor gear and clothes. Especially thanks to my husband, Rhawn, who shares my love for the road and indulges my passion for research trips, and to Anna and Harper. Finally, thanks to my extended family for our North Rim trip a couple years ago – it was awfully nice to share one of my favorite places with you all.

Bridget Gleeson

Thanks to my diligent co-author Jennifer Rasin Denniston for sharing her regional knowledge and helping me to navigate the North Rim. A special thanks to the National Park Service Rangers in Grand Canyon National Park and Glen Canyon National Recreation Area — whether at formal lectures at Grand Canyon Lodge or guided hikes around Lake Powell, your enthusiasm and expertise added so much to my experience.

ACKNOWLEDGMENTS

Climate map data adapted from Peel MC, Finlayson BL & McMahon TA (2007) 'Updated World Map of the Köppen-Geiger Climate Classification', Hydrology and Earth System Sciences, 11, 163344.

Cover photograph: The Grand Canyon and the Colorado River Maurizio Rellini/4Corners

THIS BOOK

This 4th edition of Lonely
Planet's *Grand Canyon
National Park* guidebook was
researched and written by
Jennifer Denniston and Bridget
Gleeson. The previous two
editions were written by Sarah
Chandler, Jennifer Denniston,
David Lukas and Wendy Yan-
agihara. This guidebook was
produced by the following:

Destination Editor
Alexander Howard

Product Editors Kate
Mathews, Luna Soo

Senior Cartographer
Alison Lyall

Book Designer Katherine
Marsh

Cartographer Anthony
Phelan

Assisting Editors Kate
Evans, Trent Holden, Gabby
Innes, Helen Koehne

Cover Researcher Marika
Mercer

Thanks to Ryan Evans, Andi
Jones, Bella Li, Jenna Myers,
Karyn Noble, Susan Paterson,
Kirsten Rawlings, Diana Saeng-
kham, David Smallwood, Ross
Taylor, Angela Tinson, Lauren
Wellicome, Tony Wheeler,
Clifton Wilkinson

Index